WITHDRAWN

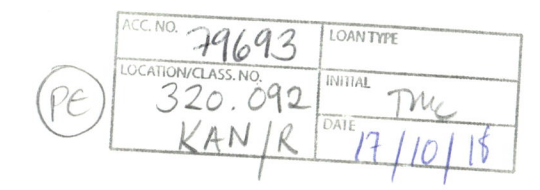

ACC. NO. 79693
LOCATION/CLASS. NO. 320.092 KAN/R
PE
LOAN TYPE
INITIAL TMc
DATE 17/10/18

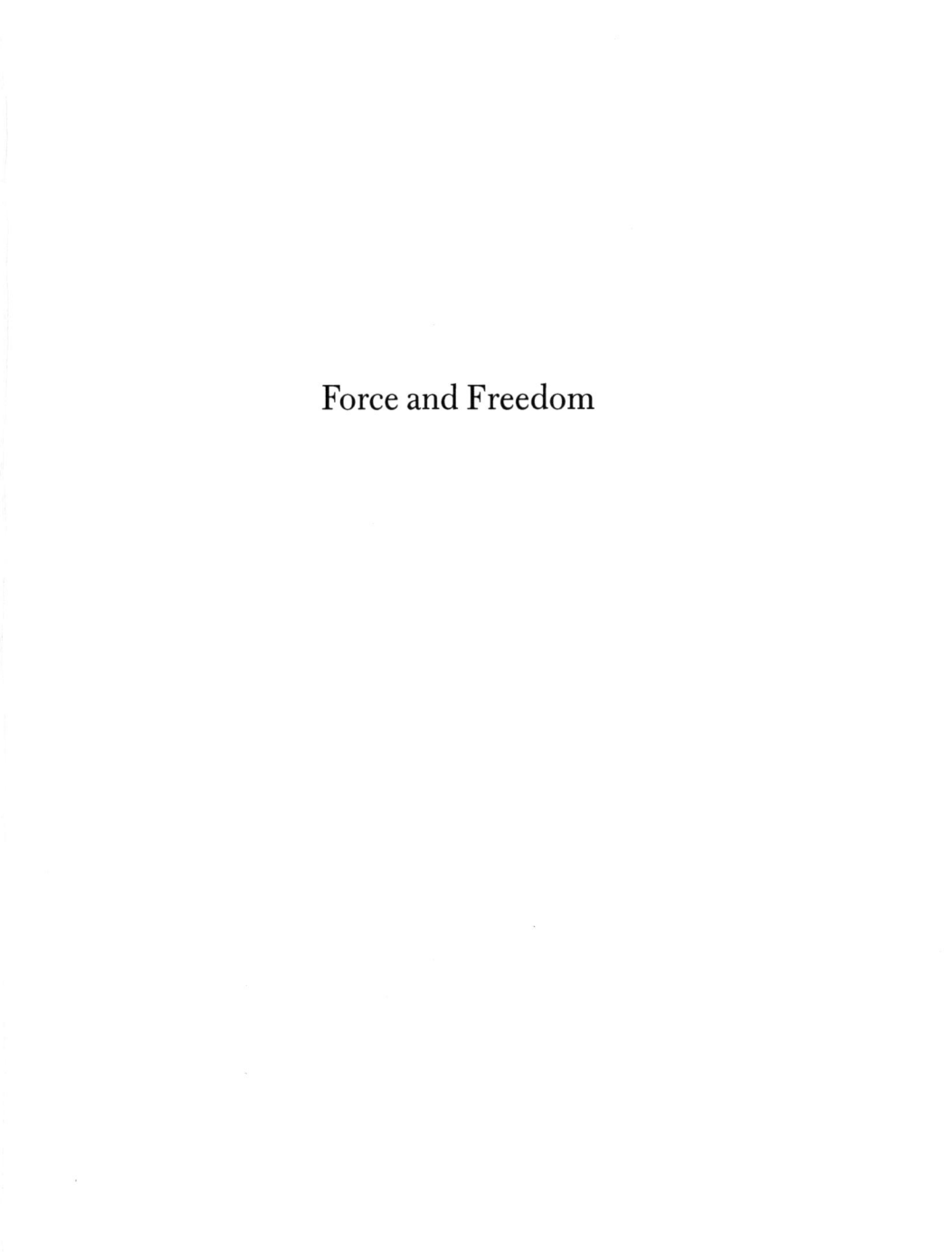

Force and Freedom

Force and Freedom

Kant's Legal and Political Philosophy

Arthur Ripstein

Harvard University Press
Cambridge, Massachusetts · London, England
2009

Copyright © 2009 by the President and Fellows of Harvard College
All rights reserved
Printed in the United States of America

Library of Congress Cataloging-in-Publication Data

Ripstein, Arthur.
Force and freedom : Kant's legal and political philosophy / Arthur Ripstein.
p.   cm.
Includes bibliographical references and index.
ISBN 978-0-674-03506-5 (alk. paper)
1. Kant, Immanuel, 1724–1804—Political and social views.   2. Law—Philosophy.
I. Title.

JC181.K4R57 2009
320.092—dc22   2009000225

To Noah, Aviva, Karen

∾

Fellow Kantians

Contents

	Preface	ix
1.	Kant on Law and Justice: An Overview	1
2.	The Innate Right of Humanity	30
3.	Private Right I: Acquired Rights	57
4.	Private Right II: Property	86
5.	Private Right III: Contract and Consent	107
6.	Three Defects in the State of Nature	145
7.	Public Right I: Giving Laws to Ourselves	182
8.	Public Right II: Roads to Freedom	232
9.	Public Right III: Redistribution and Equality of Opportunity	267
10.	Public Right IV: Punishment	300
11.	Public Right V: Revolution and the Right of Human Beings as Such	325
	Appendix: "A Postulate Incapable of Further Proof"	355
	Index	389

Preface

KANT'S INFLUENCE on contemporary political philosophy is indisputable. The idea that citizens are "free and equal" figures prominently in liberal thought, as do the value of autonomy and the demand that people be treated as ends rather than as mere means. Yet Kant himself lies outside the primary canon of political philosophy, his influence largely indirect. Despite his insistence on a sharp distinction between questions of right and questions of ethics, the main path of influence has been through the moral philosophy that he develops in the *Groundwork of the Metaphysics of Morals*.

My aim in this book is to develop and defend Kant's own statement of his political philosophy, particularly as he articulates it in the *Doctrine of Right*, the first part of the *Metaphysics of Morals*. I intend it as a work of political philosophy, which engages with Kant's ideas, in part through a consideration of them in light of trends in political philosophy in the two centuries since he wrote. Most of those trends have been hostile to Kant's central ideas: the claim that it is possible to construct a system of equal freedom has been the target of many attacks, as has his focus on coercion as the distinctive feature of legal systems; his further identification of a system of equal freedom with a system of reciprocal limits on coercion forms a sort of double-sided target. His fundamental distinction between private and public law is also widely rejected as indefensible. More generally, even Kant's admirers often doubt the possibility of articulating the requirements of justice without recourse to views about human inclinations and vulnerabilities. It is now thought that these ideas cannot even be given a coherent statement. In their place, most political philosophers suppose that formal ideas must give way to substantive ones, and that institutions have no choice but to focus on competing interests, however exactly those interests might be specified, and whatever restrictions might be placed on the balancing of especially important ones. My development of Kant's view will show that his ideas can be coherently stated, and that they are both conceptually powerful and normatively appealing. Kant is most resolute in his development of these ideas in the *Doctrine of Right*, so I have not relied on his mass of unpublished notes, drafts, and lecture transcripts where these are not fully consistent with his final statement of his position.

The *Doctrine of Right* is not an easy work to read. Many readers have accepted Schopenhauer's harsh assessment of it as a work written by a great thinker who was past his prime. Some of Kant's core arguments and distinctions are stated in the vocabulary of the Transcendental Idealism he developed in the *Critique of Pure Reason,* others in the traditional language of Roman private law. And sometimes the two technical vocabularies are interwoven, as when Kant identifies the categories of relation, substance, causality, and community with the Roman categories *facto, pacto, lege*. Insofar as it is possible to do so, I have tried to keep Kant's technical apparatus in the background, and sought to fill out what he characterizes as the "easy inference" from the highly structured apparatus of Private Right to the seemingly more fluid arguments of Public Right. I have reserved to an appendix the question of the relation between the Universal Principle of Right and the Categorical Imperative as developed in the *Groundwork of the Metaphysics of Morals*.

My focus on Kant's central preoccupations and attempt to engage them with more recent ideas will seem to some to take Kant outside of his historical context. I make no apology for doing so. States claim authority—the entitlement to tell people what to do—and coercive power—the right to force them to do as they are told. How can these powers be consistent with each human being's entitlement to be his or her own master? Kant saw two centuries ago that the question is compelling because everyone has a right to be free, and that any adequate answer must itself rest on freedom.

I have spent many years on this book, and benefited from comments and discussion with many people. Tom Hill first suggested to me that I write about the *Rechtslehre,* and Chris Korsgaard gave me encouragement early on. My editor at Harvard University Press, Lindsay Waters, was supportive from the start. The Social Sciences and Humanities Research Council of Canada provided me with research funding.

The University of Toronto provided the perfect place in which to write this book. I think it is unlikely that anywhere else on Earth could so many people be interested in engaging with Kant's political and legal ideas. A large group of colleagues, in both law and philosophy, joined me for six and a half years of weekly meetings as we worked our way through Kant's text at what used to be called a glacial pace. I am grateful to the regulars—Yehuda Adar, Peter Benson, Alan Brudner, Simone Chambers, Bruce Chapman, Abraham Drassinower, Anver Emon, Mohammad Fadel, Khalid Ghanayim, Bob Gibbs, Willi Goetschel, Marcio Grandchamp, Alon Harel, Louis-Philippe Hodgson, Karen Knop, Sophia Moreau, Hamish Stewart, Sergio Tenenbaum, Mohammed Wattad, Ernest Weinrib, Jacob Weinrib, and Lorraine Weinrib, and to many visitors to the "Kant Lunch," and to our caterer, Patrick Zappia, who provided further incentives to attend. I am grateful to former dean Ron Daniels and current dean Mayo Moran for supporting the lunches. While writing the book, I also benefited from discussions with Michael Blake, Sharon Byrd, Paul Franks, Joachim Hruschka, Gregory Keating, Christopher Morris, Scott Shapiro, Seana Shiffrin, Gopal Sreenivasan, Hannes Unberath, Arnold Weinrib, and Marcus Willaschek.

I benefited as well from interactions with students in multiple courses on the *Rechtslehre,* the *Groundwork,* and the *Critique of Pure Reason.* I thank Donald Ainslie, chair of the philosophy department, for first enabling and later compelling me to teach the *First Critique.* I learned much from the graduate students whose dissertations I supervised during this period—Lisa Austin, Martín Hevia, Sari Kisilevlsky, Paul Miller, Jonathan Peterson, and Helga Varden.

Earlier versions of arguments contained in this book were presented to audiences in Canada, Germany, Israel, and the United States, and were improved by their comments and discussion. David Dyzenhaus convinced my colleagues in the law and philosophy discussion group to turn to my manuscript as soon as we had finished reading the *Rechtslehre*. The philosophy department at Georgia State University sponsored a workshop on the manuscript in May 2008. I am grateful to Andy Altman and Andrew I. Cohen for their initiative in organizing the workshop, and to the wonderful team of participants they recruited. Each of them gave detailed comments on one or more chapters, and everyone read the entire manuscript and gave me comments that were both demanding and constructive: Thomas Hill, Jr. (Chapters 1 and 12), Lara Denis (chapter 2), Melissa Merritt (chapter 3), Andrew J. Cohen (chapter 4), Andrew I. Cohen (chapter 5), George Rainbolt (chapter 6), John Simmons (chapter 7), William Edmundson (chapter 8), Bernard Boxill (chapter 9), Andrew Altman (Chapter 10), Sebastian Rand (chapter 11). Larissa Katz arranged for me to discuss the property-related chapters with the Property Working Group at its July 2008 meeting at New York University Law School, where James Penner led the discussion. Malcolm Thorburn organized another workshop on it at Queen's University in October 2008, at which Stephen Smith, Dennis Klimchuk, and Evan Fox-Decent led discussions. Chris Korsgaard invited me to discuss several chapters at her Kant seminar. A number of people sent me detailed comments on the entire manuscript: Katrin Flikschuh, Paul Hurley, Martin Stone, Malcolm Thorburn, Catherine Valcke, Helga Varden, and Garrath Williams. Two readers for Harvard University Press also provided helpful suggestions.

In addition to all this help, I am grateful in the highest degree to Ernest Weinrib and Jacob Weinrib for their input. Ernie's groundbreaking work on private right in Kant provides the starting point for my approach to Kant's work, and we spent countless hours poring over every detail of Kant's argument. Jacob was my student, research assistant, and interlocutor in later parts of the project, and his comments and reflections were extraordinarily helpful (as was the fact that he had committed the *Rechtslehre* to memory).

My wife, Karen Weisman, was a constant source of support and encouragement, both personal and intellectual. Aviva and Noah were always willing to take time off from their busy lives as children to discuss the book's central issues, and showed both sensibility and understanding about the fact that I was working on this book for what must have seemed, from their perspective, to be a lifetime.

Several parts of this book rework material that has been published elsewhere. Chapter 1 includes material from "Kant on Law and Justice" in *A Companion to Kant's Ethics,* edited by Thomas Hill, Jr., used by permission of Blackwell Publishing. Chapters 2 and 3 incorporate sections of "Authority and Coercion," *Philosophy & Public Affairs* 32, 1 (2004): 2–35, and "Beyond the Harm Principle," *Philosophy & Public Affairs* 34, 3 (2006): 216–246, both used by permission of Wiley Blackwell. Chapter 10 incorporates material that appeared in "Hindering a Hindrance to Freedom," *Jahrbuch für Recht und Ethik* 16 (2008), by permission of Duncker & Humblot. Cambridge University Press granted permission to quote material from Immanuel Kant, *Practical Philosophy,* translated by Mary Gregor.

Force and Freedom

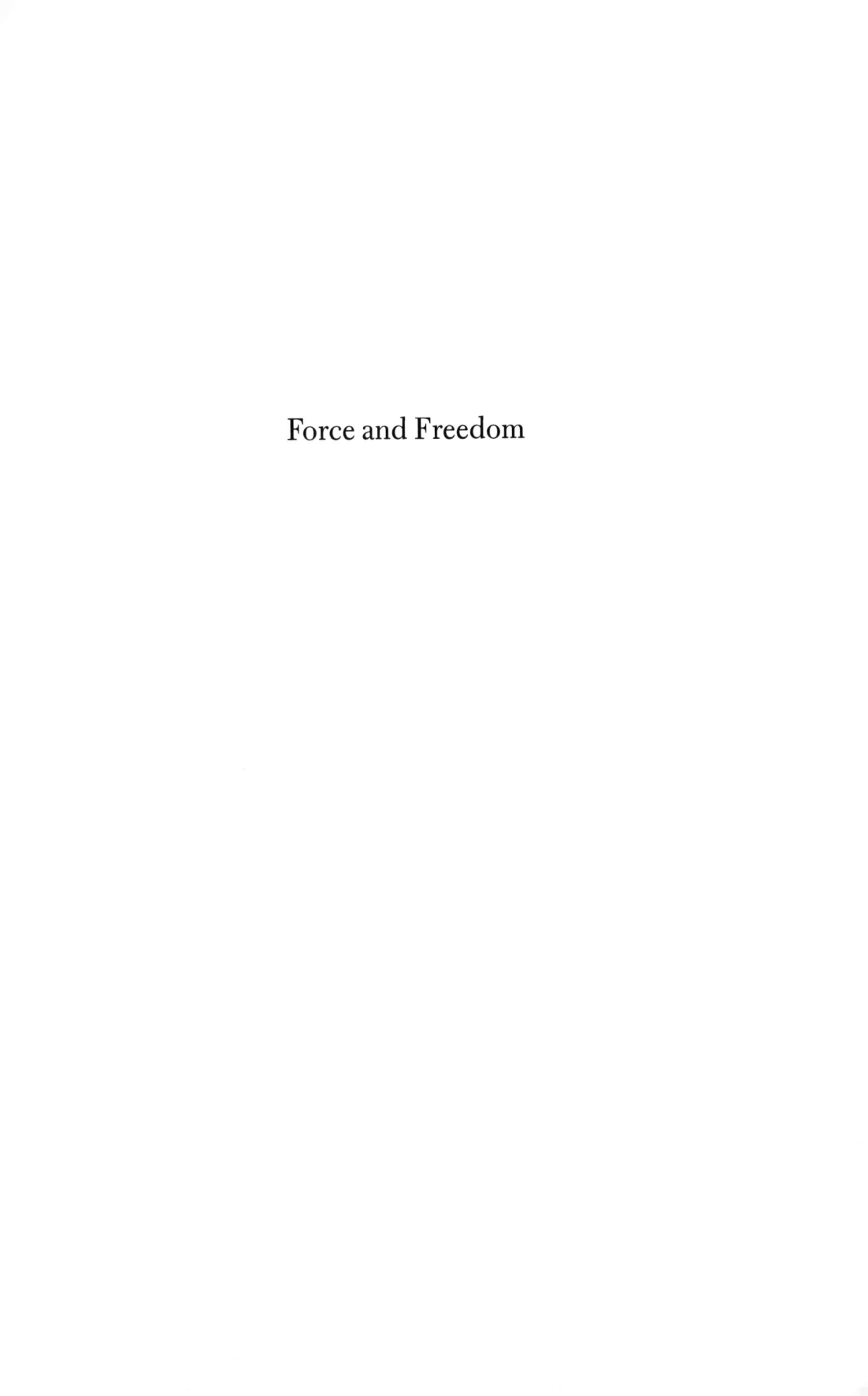

CHAPTER 1

Kant on Law and Justice:
An Overview

POLITICAL PHILOSOPHY is often thought of as an application of general moral principles to the factual circumstances that make political institutions necessary. For example, John Stuart Mill seeks to justify liberal institutions by showing that they will produce the best overall consequences, given familiar facts about human nature and circumstances; for John Locke, institutions can only be justified by showing that they are the results of individuals exercising their natural prepolitical rights in response to the "inconvenience" of a state of nature.

Kant might be expected to adopt a parallel strategy, applying the Categorical Imperative to questions of political legitimacy, state power, punishment, or taxation, or perhaps viewing the state as a coordinating device that enables people to carry out their moral obligations more effectively. Alternatively, Kant might be expected to stand back from such questions, and recommend indifference to worldly matters of politics. Kant is often taken to understand morality exclusively in terms of the principles upon which a person acts. As such, it might be thought to depend contingently or not at all on the kind of society in which the agent found herself.

Such expectations quickly lead to disappointment: Stuart M. Brown's assessment is harsher than many, but representative both in its conception of Kant's project and in the criteria of its success:

For all Kant needs to do in order to complete his program in philosophy of law is to show how the Categorical Imperative may be used to test the moral status of the rules in a body of positive law. If the test is met, the law is what it ought to be. If the test is failed, the law is morally defective and ought to be changed. At this point in the argument, Kant's task seems almost certain of accomplishment. . . . But in fact, the argument is never advanced beyond this point. Instead of showing how the Categorical Imperative may be applied to test the rules of positive law, Kant introduces a number of different principles which range in degree of generality between the extremes of the Categorical Imperative and the rules of positive law. Many of these principles have no discernible logical relationship to the Categorical Imperative and no clear application to positive law.[1]

Brown summarizes his disappointments: "The difficulty with Kant is not that he lacks opinions on these matters or that he fails to affirm ideals to which we are strongly committed; the difficulty is that his opinions neither are nor can be justified and elucidated by using the principles to which his moral philosophy commits him. Because of this difficulty, Kant fails to accomplish the task he set himself and has no philosophy of law."[2]

Kant not only denies that political philosophy is an application of the Categorical Imperative to a specific situation; he also rejects the idea that political institutions are a response to unfortunate circumstances. He insists on a sharp divide between the *metaphysics* of morals he will provide and an *anthropology* of morals that focuses on human nature,[3] and argues that law and justice are morally required "no matter how well-disposed

---

1. Stuart M. Brown, Jr., "Has Kant a Philosophy of Law?" *Philosophical Review* 71 (1962): 36.

2. Ibid., 33.

3. Immanuel Kant, *The Doctrine of Right,* Part I of the *Metaphysics of Morals* in *Practical Philosophy,* trans. and ed. Mary Gregor (Cambridge: Cambridge University Press, 1996), 6:217. Because the work exists in so many different editions and translations, and even the Gregor translation in multiple editions and paginations, all references are to the Prussian Academy pagination appearing in the margins. References to the *Doctrine of Right* are by academy pagination only; others works included in the *Practical Philosophy* volume are by title and academy pagination.

and right-loving human beings might be."[4] He denies that need generates direct enforceable obligations of aid, dismissively treating it as no different from "mere wish."[5] He formulates many of his arguments in terms of coercion, which most recent philosophers assign a secondary role in law and politics.

Most striking of all from the perspective of contemporary readers, he denies that justice is concerned with the fair distribution of benefits and burdens. None of the principles he articulates are formulated in terms of them. The distinctiveness of his approach can be brought out by contrasting it with the broadly Kantian political philosophy developed in John Rawls's theory of justice. Rawls employs Kantian concepts to address a question about social cooperation that is posed in terms of the benefits it provides and the burdens it generates. Rawls describes his account of justice as "overcoming the dualisms"[6] inherent in Kant's views, and recasting them "within the canons of reasonable empiricism."[7] The moves from the metaphysical to the empirical, the abstract to the concrete, and the universal to the historical enable Rawls to provide a broadly Kantian perspective on a set of questions that have their roots less in Kant than in the empiricist and utilitarian tradition of Bentham and Mill.[8] For that tradition, the use of state power and the ability of some people to make rules that others must follow are ultimately to be assessed in terms of the benefits they provide and the burdens they create. Rawls rejects the utilitarian approach to the distribution of benefits and burdens on recognizably Kantian grounds, but in its place offers an alternative principle for thinking about the same basic questions: given the benefits that all can

---

4. 6:312. Mary Gregor translates Kant's *"rechtliebend"* as "law-abiding" and John Ladd as "righteous." Each is misleading in different ways. I am grateful to Helga Varden for suggesting "right-loving."

5. 6:230.

6. Rawls, "The Basic Structure as Subject," *American Philosophical Quarterly* 14, 2 (1977): 165.

7. Rawls, "Kantian Constructivism in Moral Theory," in his *Collected Papers* (Cambridge, Mass.: Harvard University Press, 1999), 304.

8. See, for example, the remarks about the importance of psychological assumptions in any normative theory in the concluding discussion of J. S. Mill in Rawls, *Lectures on the History of Political Philosophy*, ed. Samuel Freeman (Cambridge, Mass.: Harvard University Press, 2007), 313.

expect from social cooperation, and the burdens that it generates, what terms of cooperation are acceptable to persons considered as free and equal?[9]

Kantian answers to questions about benefits and burdens are not the same as Kantian answers to Kant's own questions.[10] The focus of this book is on defending Kant's answers, but in so doing I will provide an indirect defense of his questions, and thereby of the presuppositions of those questions. Kant's critics often accuse him of being driven by architectonic concerns, or committed to an outdated "foundationalist" methodology that prefers *a priori* answers to empirical ones. Although architectonic and methodological factors shape Kant's presentation of his arguments, his grounds for rejecting empirical and anthropological starting points in political philosophy rest on the simple but compelling *normative* idea that, as a matter of right, each person is entitled to be his or her own master, not in the sense of enjoying some form of special self-relation, but in the contrastive sense of not being subordinated to the choice of any *other* particular person. This starting point is explicit in Kant, but it also animates many of the familiar questions of political philosophy. The nature and justification of authority, the authorization to coerce, the significance of disagreement, political obedience, democracy, and the rule of law arguably acquire their interest against some version of the assumption that each person is entitled to be his or her own master. Any real or claimed entitlement of a person or group of persons to tell another what to do, or force him to do as he is told, is potentially in ten-

---

9. I believe that there is a more Kantian way of understanding the entire Rawlsian enterprise, focused on his conception of persons as free and equal, and on his emphasis on the coercive structure of society. If such a reading of Rawls is possible, it is certainly not the dominant one, and this is not the place to develop it.

10. Even contemporary "rights-based" accounts of justice frame their questions in terms of benefits in burdens in a way that Kant rejects. For example, after invoking Kant's idea that people are never to be treated as mere means in pursuit of the purposes of others, Robert Nozick proceeds to frame his account of rights in terms of benefits and burdens. His theory of property rests on the claim that appropriation does not disadvantage others, and his theory of the state rests on a theory of compensation which makes the negative experience of fear the basis of prohibition, and the disadvantage of being prohibited from doing as you wish as generating a basis of compensation. Each of these is measured in terms of its welfare effects. See Nozick, *Anarchy, State and Utopia* (New York: Basic Books, 1974), 32–33, 178–182, 71–87.

sion with the latter person's entitlement to be his own master. Again, normative questions about how to manage disagreement or the pluralism that is a feature of modern societies are pressing because all parties to the disagreement and diversity are each their own master, so none is entitled to force a particular resolution on others. The same point applies to questions about what it is for people to rule themselves through institutions, or to be ruled by laws rather than individual persons.

Kant's full explanation of what it is for each person to be his or her own master rather than the servant of another will take up most of this book. For now I merely want to indicate why this normative starting point leads Kant to reject anthropological and empirical factors in general, and benefits and burdens in particular. Both the empirical peculiarities of human inclinations and vulnerabilities and the consideration of where benefits or burdens fall can only be brought in insofar as they can be shown to be consistent with a condition in which every person is his or her own master as against each of the others. The systematic implications of that right have to be worked out first, before any "principle of politics" incorporating information based on experience can be introduced.[11] This sequenced way of framing the issues limits the ways in which benefits and burdens can be relevant to either the formulation or the application of any basic normative principle. Your right to be your own master entails that no other person is entitled to decide for you that the benefits you will receive from some arrangement are sufficient to force you to participate in it. You alone are entitled to decide whether a benefit to you is worth the burdens it brings. Nor can others justify authority over you, or use force against you, on the ground that the restrictions thereby placed on you will generate greater benefits for others. The same fundamental idea blocks the appeal to the sort of value pluralism according to which competing political values rather than interests must be "balanced" against one another. The authority of any person or institution's mandate to balance competing values must itself be reconciled with each person's right to be his or her own master. That does not mean that political authority or justified coercion is impossible, or even that institutions are never compe-

---

11. Kant, "On a Supposed Right to Lie from Philanthropy," in Gregor, *Practical Philosophy*, 8:429.

tent to balance competing values, only that the authority to make or enforce decisions needs to be established by showing it to be consistent with each person's right to freedom before competing interests or values can be considered.

My aim in this introductory chapter is to give a broad overview of Kant's position and the arguments he gives for it. The argumentation here will, of necessity, be sketchy. My main purpose is to lay out his conclusions, and, in so doing, preempt certain recurrent misunderstandings. Before doing so, I will identify some of those misunderstandings, each of which reflects some version of an "applied ethics" reading of Kant. Some arise because of Kant's mode of argumentation; others because Kant refuses to separate an action from its effects; still others because of the familiarity of other aspects of Kant's broader project in practical philosophy.

Mode of Argumentation. First, Kant approaches the question of the legitimate use of force through a sequence of arguments, rather than by attempting to reconcile each stage of the argument with the considered judgments of his readers. Not all of Kant's conclusions will accord with the judgments of contemporary readers, but some conflicts between his arguments and those judgments are only apparent. As the argument proceeds, new legal actors are introduced, so that, for example, although no private person has the right to tax or punish, the state has the power to do both. By identifying these arguments at the outset, I hope to preempt any impression that everything a legitimate state does must be a *direct* application of Kant's starting point in the idea of equal freedom (as Brown expects a direct application of the Categorical Imperative).

Kant's mode of argumentation reflects his attitude toward examples. He develops many examples in the course of his argument, but rejects the idea that examples can replace arguments, or that philosophy is charged primarily with accounting for examples. Instead, he remarks that "all examples (which only illustrate but cannot prove anything) are treacherous, so that they certainly require a metaphysics."[12] The metaphysics he speaks of is not a catalogue of claims about what is most real; it is a *practical*

12. 6:355.

metaphysics, an articulation of the limits that each person's claim to be his or her own master impose on the conduct of others.[13]

But to say that Kant does not regard examples as dispositive is not to say that his arguments lead to conclusions that cannot survive reflection. The direct implications that Kant draws from the Universal Principle of Right—each person's right to be his or her own master, to be presumed innocent, and to speak in his or her own name—sit well enough with considered judgments. Other, less direct implications are neither unfamiliar nor foreign. Kant understands ordinary moral thought as the exercise of practical reason, and as such, the broad structural features of familiar legal institutions will, unsurprisingly, be understandable in terms of the broad structure of practical thought. Even the less familiar aspects of Kant's arguments need to be understood in light of their relation to his austere starting point. Kant's view does conflict with what have become entrenched philosophical commonplaces, both about the anthropological nature of questions of justice and, more generally, about the appropriate concepts for practical thought. How much weight to attach to *those* disagreements depends at least in part on whether the familiar views turn out to be in tension with the equally well-rooted idea that no person is the master of another.

The Normative Status of Rules and Institutions. A second aspect of the applied ethics approach to political philosophy supposes that law and the state are instruments for approximating underlying factors that really matter. Bentham's utilitarianism provides a particularly stark example of this idea. He argues that the purpose of legal and political institutions, and indeed even the purpose of general rules in morality, is to approximate a moral result—the greatest happiness of the greatest number—which could in principle be specified without any reference to institu-

---

13. Against the "two worlds" reading of Kant's distinction between the realm of freedom and the realm of nature, in favor of the view that they constitute different standpoints, one theoretical and the other practical, see, for example, Henry Allison, *Kant's Transcendental Idealism* (New Haven: Yale University Press, 1983); Onora O'Neill, "Reason and Autonomy in *Grundlegung* III," in her *Constructions of Reason: Explorations of Kant's Practical Philosophy* (Cambridge: Cambridge University Press, 1989); Christine Korsgaard, "Morality as Freedom," in her *Creating the Kingdom of Ends* (Cambridge: Cambridge University Press, 1996).

tions or rules. Legal and political institutions interest Bentham because he believes that over the long run, in human circumstances as we know them, making rules and assigning rights to people is most likely to conduce to happiness overall. Many contemporary egalitarian theories have a similar structure: society should be arranged so as to bring about an equal distribution, or one that is sensitive to the choices people have made but not the circumstances in which they find themselves, or, in another version, to properly measure the costs that one person's choices impose on another.[14] On these views, rules are appropriate because reliable, but imperfect, tools for producing morally desirable outcomes. The only basis for setting up legal institutions is that they are likely to produce the right results, as identified by external criteria, more often than they get the wrong ones.

The alternative to consequentialist and egalitarian theories is sometimes thought to be some sort of deontological theory that identifies moral value in a way that makes no reference to the state. Such theories may speak of rights or rules in specifying their moral ideals, but they make no direct reference to institutions or law. Examples include desert-based theories of distributive justice that suppose that benefits and burdens should track moral merit or individual choices, desert-based theories of punishment, and Lockean "natural rights" theories that claim that persons have fully formed moral rights in a state of nature, and that the only legitimate purpose of legal institutions is to solve problems of self-preference or insufficient knowledge in the application of those rights to particulars. For both the utilitarian/egalitarian and the Lockean or deontologist, public legal rules are justified by the likelihood that they will bring about better results than could be achieved in their absence, where success is measured in terms of tracking the preinstitutional values. On these views, if people knew more, cared more about the moral considerations that apply independently of institutions, or were more fair-minded in their judgments about particulars, legal institutions would not be required at all.

---

14. G. A. Cohen gives a clear formulation of this idea: "My concern is *distributive justice*, by which I uneccentrically mean justice (and its lack) in the distribution of benefits and burdens to individuals." *If You're an Egalitarian, How Come You're So Rich?* (Cambridge, Mass.: Harvard University Press, 2000), 130.

If institutions are tools for the indirect pursuit of something that can be fully specified without reference to them, Kant's focus on coercion is also bound to seem misplaced. The question of what results the state should aim to produce is prior to any question about the most effective means of producing it. So, too, with Kant's focus on rules. If rules or institutions are supposed to produce results that matter apart from them, then their normative significance is limited to the cases in which they tend to produce those results.

Kant rejects the suggestion that legal norms or institutions are instruments for achieving results that can be specified apart from them. As we shall see in more detail in Chapters 7, 10, and 11, the utilitarian/egalitarian and the Lockean/deontologist are caught up in what Kant would characterize as an "antinomy." The source of their intractable differences is a shared premise about the nature of morality. Both the utilitarian and Lockean or desert-based theories presuppose the idea that the way people should behave in any particular situation is fully determinate, though perhaps unachievable or unknown. Thus they suppose that what morally matters to social life is a result that could be specified without reference to legal institutions and, at least in principle, that in a better world with better people, the morally desired result could be achieved without them. They disagree about what the desirable result is, but share the view that the question has a completely determinate answer in every case, and it is the job of legal and political institutions to arrange things so as to increase the likelihood of achieving it.

Kant's opposing idea is that each person's entitlement to be his or her own master is only consistent with the entitlements of others if public legal institutions are in place. Much of this book will take up the task of explaining this idea in detail. The important point for now is that for Kant, both institutions and the authorization to coerce are not merely causal conditions likely to bring about the realization of the right to freedom, or even prudent sacrifices for individuals to make if they are concerned to secure their freedom. Instead, the consistent exercise of the right to freedom by a plurality of persons cannot be conceived apart from a public legal order.

This noninstrumental conception of the right to freedom gives Kant his distinctive view about the significance of coercion. If legal institutions and political power are understood as tools for realizing moral results that are in principle achievable without them, the familiar claim that the use of state power faces a special burden of justification[15] invites an obvious line of objection: other factors, including both individual choices and natural contingencies, also make a significant difference to people's lives along almost any dimension. Why focus on the state, let alone on its coercive actions, rather than on individual actions?[16] As we shall see, Kant's noninstrumental account of the system of equal freedom provides a principled basis for making the legitimate use of force a self-contained issue.

Kant's rejection of the instrumental conception of legal rules and institutions does not commit him to the view that the normative principles he does develop are sufficient to resolve all issues of right. Kant's critics have often read him to be making such a claim in moral philosophy, and sometimes characterized his emphasis on moral rules as the product of a fear of going "off the rails."[17] It is not surprising that similar criticisms have been directed at his political philosophy.[18] The principles of right that Kant introduces are highly abstract, and require the exercise of judgment to apply them to particulars. Although some, such as Henry Sidgwick, have thought that any concept that did not classify particulars in a fully determinate way must be suspect,[19] Kant's view is that moral concepts are ab-

---

15. See, for example, Jürgen Habermas, *Between Facts and Norms: Contributions to a Discourse Theory of Law and Democracy* (Cambridge: MIT Press, 1999), 447–462; John Rawls, *Justice as Fairness: A Restatement* (Cambridge, Mass.: Harvard University Press, 2001), 40; Ronald Dworkin, *Law's Empire* (Cambridge, Mass.: Harvard University Press, 1986), chap. 4.

16. See, for example, G. A. Cohen, *Rescuing Justice and Equality* (Cambridge, Mass.: Harvard University Press, 2008); Liam Murphy, "Institutions and the Demands of Justice," *Philosophy & Public Affairs* 27, 4 (1998), 251–291.

17. See, for example, John McDowell, "Virtue and Reason," in his *Mind, Value, and Reality* (Cambridge, Mass.: Harvard University Press, 1998), 50–73. For discussion of why these criticisms fail to engage Kant's ethical philosophy, see Barbara Herman, *The Practice of Moral Judgment* (Cambridge, Mass.: Harvard University Press, 1993), and Onora O'Neill, *Towards Justice and Virtue* (Cambridge: Cambridge University Press, 1996), 77–89.

18. The standard site of this misreading is Hannah Arendt, *Lectures on Kant's Political Philosophy,* trans. Ronald Biener (Chicago: University of Chicago Press, 1982). For discussion, see Otfried Hoffe, *Kant's Cosmopolitan Theory of Law and Peace* (Cambridge: Cambridge University Press, 2006), chap. 3.

19. Sidgwick, *The Methods of Ethics* (Indianapolis: Hackett, 1981), 421.

stract because they are normative. As such, they require judgment to apply them to particular circumstances. As we shall see, Kant does not provide detailed formulae for the resolution of private disputes or the content of public legislation. His argument shows how those issues must be framed, consistent with each person's right to be his or her own master, and also why public institutions must be set up to resolve them.

The Categorical Imperative. The most direct version of the applied ethics reading looks, as Brown does, to Kant's moral philosophy. The moral philosophy has had a significant impact on post-Kantian political philosophy, through the work of Hermann Cohen[20] in the nineteenth century and John Rawls in the twentieth. The lesson that many have taken from Cohen and Rawls, whether rightly or wrongly, is that Kantians suppose that the autonomous life is the best one, and political institutions must be designed to promote autonomy.[21] This conception of the "Kantian" position places it squarely in the instrumentalist camp. Whatever its appeal, it is not Kant's view. The first task in this chapter will be to lay out the basic distinctions between right and ethics, deferring to later chapters the detailed arguments for them.

I. Right and Ethics: Why Kant Does Not "Apply" the Categorical Imperative

Kant draws a series of sharp divisions between right and ethics. Ethical conduct depends upon the maxim on which an action is done; rightful conduct depends only on the outer form of interaction between persons. The inner nature of ethical conduct means that the only incentive consis-

---

20. Hermann Cohen, *Kants Begründung der Ethik*, 2d ed. (Berlin: Bruno Cassirer, 1910). At 394, Cohen acknowledges the influence of Paul Johann Anselm Feuerbach, *Kritik des natürlichen Rechts als Propädeutik zu einer Wissenschaft der natürlichen Rechte* (Altona: Bei der Veringsgesellschaft, 1796).

21. See, for example, Jeffrie G. Murphy, *Kant: The Philosophy of Right* (New York: St. Martin's, 1970), and Patrick Riley, *Kant's Political Philosophy* (Totowa: Rowman & Littlefield, 1983), 98–99. For criticism of these and other assimilations, see Onora O'Neill, "Kant's Justice and Kantian Justice," in her *Bounds of Justice* (Cambridge: Cambridge University Press, 2000), 65–80.

tent with the autonomy at the heart of morality must be morality itself; rightful conduct can be induced by incentives provided by others. Other persons are entitled to enforce duties of right, but not duties of virtue. Each of these differences precludes any direct appeal to the Categorical Imperative. Yet the vocabulary that typically surrounds the Categorical Imperative in Kant's other works can be found at various pivotal points in the argument: right is only possible "under universal law"; you must never allow yourself to be "treated as a mere means," and the people must "give laws to themselves."

Each of these differences between right and ethics turns on Kant's representation of principles of right as governing persons represented as occupying space. The basic case for thinking about your right to your own person is your right to your own body; the basic case for thinking about property is property in land, that is, a right to exclude others from a particular location on the Earth's surface; the basic case for thinking about contract is the transfer of an object from one place to another; the basic case for thinking about a state involves its occupation of a particular region of the Earth's surface.

Space is more than a useful metaphor for Kant. Its normative significance arises from the ways in which separate persons who occupy space can come into conflict in the exercise of their freedom, depending on where they are doing their space-occupying activities and what others happen to be doing in the same location. This basic normative structure is different from the normative structure contained in the idea of a rational will being in conflict with itself on the basis of its principle of action. As we shall see in the appendix, Kant's own characterization of the relation between inner and outer freedom grows out of his more general philosophical understanding of the difference between monadic and relational properties. Those differences help explain why Kant characterizes the Universal Principle of Right as a "postulate incapable of further proof." But his normative arguments both for the Universal Principle of Right and for extending it as he does do not depend on those broader philosophical grounds. The normative arguments work out the implication of free persons whose movements of their bodies can come into conflict. They are of interest even to those who remain unconvinced by other aspects of Kant's broader critical project.

Before turning to those normative arguments, it is also worth contrasting the arguments of the *Doctrine of Right* with the interpretation of the Categorical Imperative according to which it provides a test for conduct based on general features of the human situation. On this interpretation, the question of whether a maxim could be a universal law depends on the likely effects of its widespread adoption. This "teleological" interpretation has motivated many of Kant's most prominent critics, including Hegel and Sidgwick, and has generally been rejected by Kant's defenders.[22] The teleological approach may indeed be what Brown expects to see applied in the *Doctrine of Right*, that is, a formula that could be "applied to test the rules of positive law," presumably by determining whether they could pass a test of generality. His disappointment reflects the fact that Kant attempts nothing of the sort. Any principle that depended on the effects of adopting this or that legal rule would have to be what Kant characterizes as a "material" principle, that is, one that depends on the ends that persons happen to (or are likely to) have. As we shall see in Chapter 7, a material interpretation of the Universal Principle of Right can only generate rules that are both material and conditional, and so inconsistent with a system of equal freedom in which each person is his or her own master and none is the master of another.

II. The Stages of Kant's Argument

The Universal Principle of Right says that "an action is *right* if it can coexist with everyone's freedom in accordance with a universal law, or if on its maxim the freedom of choice of each can coexist with everyone's freedom in accordance with universal law."[23] The universal principle generates each person's "one innate right" to "Freedom (independence from being constrained by another's choice), insofar as it can coexist with the freedom of every other in accordance with a universal law," which "is the only original right belonging to every human being by virtue of his humanity."[24] This innate right leads to private right, which governs the inter-

---

22. Korsgaard, *Creating the Kingdom of Ends*, 87–92.
23. 6:230.
24. 6:237.

actions of free persons, and then to public right, which requires the creation of a constitutional state. The idea of independence carries the justificatory burden of the entire argument, from the prohibition of personal injury, through the minutiae of property and contract law, on to the details of the constitutional separation of powers. Kant argues that these norms and institutions do more than enhance the prospects for independence: they provide the only possible way in which a plurality of persons can interact on terms of equal freedom. Kant's concern is not with how people should interact, as a matter of ethics, but with how they can be forced to interact, as a matter of right.[25]

The core idea of independence is an articulation of the distinction between persons and things. A person is a being capable of setting his or her own purposes, while a thing is something that can be used in pursuit of purposes. Kant follows Aristotle in distinguishing choice from mere wish on the grounds that to choose something, a person must take himself to have means available to achieve it.[26] You can wish that you could fly, but you cannot choose to fly unless you have or acquire means that enable you to do so. In this sense, having means with which to pursue purposes is conceptually prior to setting those purposes. In the first instance, your capacity to set your own purposes just is your own person: your ability to conceive of ends, and whatever bodily abilities you have with which to pursue them. You are independent if you are the one who decides which purposes you will pursue.

It may seem misleading to conceive of your own bodily powers as a means that you have, if this suggests that they are somehow external to your ability to set and pursue purposes, or that they only matter insofar as you are actively using them. Kant makes the different claim that you are independent if your body is subject to your choice rather than anyone else's, so that you, alone or in voluntary cooperation with others, are entitled to decide what purposes you will pursue. You are dependent on an-

---

25. The German word *recht* and its cognates have no exact English equivalent. It covers both law and the more general idea of a legitimate power. Recent translators have used the word "right," which has the merit of preserving some of this ambiguity in a way that neither "law" nor "justice" does. In Kant's usage, right refers to the domain of enforceable obligations.

26. 6:213; Aristotle, *Nicomachean Ethics*, 1111a 25.

other person's choice if that person gets to decide what purposes you will pursue. The person who uses your body or a part of it for a purpose you have not authorized makes you dependent on his or her choice; your person, in the form of your body, is used to accomplish somebody else's purpose, and so your independence is violated. This is true even if that person does not harm you, and indeed, even if he benefits you.

This recasting of the familiar Kantian distinction between means and ends provides a distinctive understanding of the ways in which one person can interfere with the independence of another, either by drawing that person into purposes that she has not chosen or by depriving her of her means. Literally forcing or fraudulently luring another person into helping you pursue your purposes generates familiar examples of the first type of interference, bodily injury a familiar example of the second. In doing either, a wrongdoer fails to respect another person's capacity to set her own purposes, treating her instead either as a means to be used in pursuit of his own purposes, or as a mere obstacle to be gotten around.

Interference with another person's freedom creates a form of dependence; *independence* requires that one person not be subject to another person's choice. Kant's account of independence contrasts with more robust conceptions of autonomy, which sometimes represent it as a feature of a particular agent. On this conception, if there were only one person in the world, it would make sense to ask whether and to what extent that person was autonomous. Kantian independence is not a feature of the individual person considered in isolation, but of relations between persons. Independence contrasts with dependence on another person, being subject to that person's choice. It is relational, and so cannot be predicated of a particular person considered in isolation. The difference is important from two directions. First, in principle a slave with a benevolent master and favorable circumstances could be autonomous in the contemporary technical sense. A slave could never be independent, because what he is permitted to do is always dependent on his master's choice or grace. Second, autonomy can be compromised by natural or self-inflicted factors no less than by the deeds of others; Kantian independence can only be compromised by the deeds of others. It is not a good to be promoted; it is a constraint on the conduct of others, imposed by the fact that each person is entitled to be his or her own master.

Independence is the basic principle of right. It guarantees equal freedom, and so requires that no person be subject to the choice of another. The idea of independence is similar to one that has been the target of many objections. The basic form of almost all of these focuses on the fact that *any* set of rules prohibits some acts that people would otherwise do, so that, for example, laws prohibiting personal injury and property damage put limits on the ability of people to do as they wish. Because different people have incompatible wants, to let one person do what he wants will typically require preventing others from doing what they want. Thus, it has been contended, freedom cannot even be articulated as a political value, because freedoms always come into conflict, and the only way to mediate those conflicts is by appealing to goods other than freedom. As I will explain in more detail in Chapter 2, such an objection has some force against freedom understood as the ability to do whatever you wish, but fails to engage Kant's conception of independence. Limits on independence generate a set of restrictions that are by their nature equally applicable to all. Their generality depends on the fact that they abstract from what Kant calls the "matter" of choice—the particular purposes being pursued—and focus instead on the capacity to set purposes without having them set by others. What you can accomplish depends on what others are doing—someone else can frustrate your plans by getting the last quart of milk in the store. If they do so, they don't interfere with your independence, because they impose no limits on your ability to use your powers to set and pursue your own purposes. They just change the world in ways that make your means useless for the particular purpose you would have set. Their entitlement to change the world in those ways just is their right to independence. In the same way, your ability to enter into cooperative activities with others depends upon their willingness to cooperate with you, and their entitlement to accept or decline your invitations is simply their right to independence.

Kant aims to show that independence, understood in this way, comprises a self-contained domain of reciprocal limits. The idea of a system of equal freedom both poses the problem and gives him the resources to provide a principled account of the most striking features of political life. Those who imagine that political powers can be used whenever doing so will bring about beneficial consequences see no need to draw a principled line around them. The Kantian commitment to freedom requires a principled account. Both the power to displace individual judgment, by having institutions and officials empowered to make decisions binding on everyone, and the power to enforce those decisions appear to be in tension with the idea that individuals are free to set their own purposes according to their own judgment. Kant aims to do no less than show that the existence of such powers are not only consistent with but in fact required by individual freedom.

Kant develops the idea of independence in three stages. He first articulates the relation of independence in its simplest form as a constraint on interactions between persons. He calls this "the innate right of humanity" in one's own person, because it does not require any act to establish it. Instead, people are entitled to independence simply because they are persons capable of setting their own purposes. This form of independence is incomplete, and needs to be extended to take account of the possibility that people could have entitlements to things other than their own bodily powers. Those entitlements fall under private right, and cover the traditional categories of Roman private law, relations of property, contract, and status, which govern rights to things, to performances by other persons, and, in special cases, rights *to* other persons. These categories provide a complete specification of independence between interacting persons, but can only be consistently enjoyed by all in a condition of public right with legislative, executive, and judicial branches. Each of these branches in turn has further powers grounded in its role in providing a rightful condition.

Innate Right

Kant formulates the innate right of humanity from two directions. First, each person has the right to independence from each of the others. None is born either a master or a servant. Each enjoys this right to juridical equality innately, prior to any affirmative act to establish it.[27] Your right to your own person guarantees that you are entitled to use your own powers as you see fit, consistent with the freedom of others to do the same. Innate

---

27. 6:237.

right also includes the right to be "beyond reproach,"[28] to have only your own deeds imputed to you, and to be assumed innocent unless you have committed a wrong.

From the other direction, innate right carries with it the imperative of rightful honor. Kant interprets the Roman jurist Ulpian's precept *honeste vive* ("living honorably") as the requirement not to allow yourself to be a mere means for others.[29] He also characterizes rightful honor as an "internal duty," something that might at first appear to have no place in a doctrine of external freedom. It is an internal duty because no other person can enforce it; it is a duty of right because it creates the boundary within which freedom can be exercised, and thereby governs the arrangements that a person can enter into as a matter of right. So your entitlement to make your own voluntary arrangements with others is limited to arrangements that are consistent with the Universal Principle of Right. As a result, you cannot give another person a right to treat you as a mere means by binding you in ways in which you cannot bind them. These limits on the ways in which you can exercise your freedom have important implication for the *Doctrine of Right* as a whole. At the level of private right, you cannot sell yourself into slavery; at the level of public right, the state lacks the power to make arrangements for you requiring you to advance another person's private purposes.

Innate right governs interactions between free persons, but does so in a way that is incomplete. Each of Kant's subsequent extensions of the idea of a right of humanity in one's own person is required because of the human capacity for choice. The extensions also show how the two striking inequalities of political life are consistent with the equal freedom required by innate right. *Private right*—the areas of law governing property, contract, and other legal relationships between private parties—explains how inequalities in material wealth, including holdings of property, contractual obligations, and employment and familial relationships, can be consistent with the equality of innate right. *Public right*—the areas of law governing the lawmaking powers of the state, including constitutional law, criminal law, and the public functions falling under the state's police

28. 6:238.
29. 6:236.

power- explains how differentiated offices are both consistent with and required by innate right.

Private Right

Innate right is an incomplete account of independence, because it regulates only a person's entitlement to his or her own person and reputation. This opens the possibility that there could be other means available that a person might use in setting and pursuing purposes. This possibility requires a further "postulate," an extension consistent with but not contained in innate right.[30] Kant argues that it would be inconsistent with right if usable things could not be rightfully used. The ability to use things for your purposes could be satisfied through a system of *usufruct,* in which things are borrowed from a common pool for particular uses. However, because of the way that Kant conceives of the relation between having means and setting ends, permissibly using things is not enough to extend your freedom; it would merely enable you to succeed at some particular purpose or other. Freedom requires that you be able to have usable things fully at your disposal, to use as you see fit, and so to decide which purposes to pursue with them, subject only to such constraints imposed by the entitlement of others to use whatever usable things *they* have. Any other arrangement would subject your ability to set your own ends to the choice of others, since they would be entitled to veto any particular use you wished to make of things other than your body. The innate equality of all persons entails that nobody could have standing to limit the freedom of another person, except to protect his or her own independence. Nobody else is deprived of *his* means simply because you have external things as *yours*. At most, your use of what is yours deprives him of things that he might *wish* for, but frustrating the wishes of others is not inconsistent with their freedom, because nobody is entitled to have others organize their pursuits around his or her wishes. So it must be possible to have external means as your own. All persons are symmetrically situated with respect to innate right; private right introduces the space for

---

30. 6:246. (Because of the recent discovery of a printing error in earlier German editions, the postulate appears *after* 6:250 in recent editions, but still has its academy pagination.)

an asymmetry, because it allows different people to have different claims. You and I can own different things, and we can stand in different contractual and status relations.

Kant presents private right through an analysis of the categories of Property, Contract, and Status, which form the backbone of all Western legal systems. They provide an exhaustive specification of the possible types of interaction consistent with freedom. Property concerns rights to things; contract, rights against persons; and status contains rights to persons "akin to" rights to things. Kant remarks that applying the person/thing dichotomy to itself generates four possibilities, but that the fourth, rights to things akin to rights to persons, is empty, because a thing could not owe a contractlike obligation.[31] The intuitive idea is that free persons can only interact in three basic ways. They can interact independently, each pursuing his or her separate purposes. This is the structure of innate right. Property has a corresponding structure, because as a proprietor, I possess property that is subject to my purposes and nobody else's. I can be wronged with respect to property in the same two ways that I can be wronged with respect to my person: by having my property used on behalf of another, or by being prevented from using my property on my own behalf. I have both possession and use of my property. If you use my horse without my permission, you use it on your behalf, not mine; if you damage it, you prevent me from using it on my own behalf. Contract covers the case in which parties interact interdependently and consensually. If I invite you into my home, you do not wrong me; if I agree to do something for you, my powers to do so are now at your disposal, and you are entitled to use them as specified in our agreement. If I fail to do what I have agreed to do, I wrong you, by depriving you of means that you were entitled to.

For Kant, a contract is not understood as a narrow special case of the more general moral obligation of promise keeping,[32] but as a specifically legal institution through which the parties vary their respective rights and

---

31. 6:358.

32. Most enforceable contracts involve promises because they concern future arrangements. On Kant's analysis, the consensual change of rights is fundamental to a contract, whether it is a present transfer or a future one expressed through a promise.

obligations.[33] Making an agreement is something that the two parties must do together; neither can vary his or her rights against the other unilaterally. The powers that can be created include the entitlement to transfer property, compel services, or undertake responsibility for the deeds of another.

Relations of status are the mirror image of contractual relations, because in relations of status one person has possession of but *not* the use of another person. Such relationships are possible when people interact interdependently but nonconsensually. The structure of this relationship parallels the situation when one person is in possession of another's property: if I am repairing your car, I am allowed to take it for a drive to see if it is working properly, but not to take it to visit friends. To do so would be to use what is yours in pursuit of my purposes rather than your own. Kant recognizes that there is a limited class of cases in which one person can be in possession of another, in a way that the latter is not in a position to consent to the ways in which his or her affairs are managed. Of the examples that Kant considers, the most familiar is the relationship between parents and children. Kant notes that parents bring children into the world "without the consent of the children and on their own initiative,"[34] and takes this to entail that parents have both a duty to act on behalf of their children and a right to "manage and develop"[35] them. In such circumstances, the only way their interaction can be rendered rightful is if the parents act on behalf of their children. Once again, the intuitive idea is familiar in a wide variety of contexts. Teachers are not allowed to take advantage of their students, because their asymmetrical relationship undermines the ability of the students to give genuine consent. Because teachers are precluded from acting for their own purposes, the relationship can only be rightful if they act on behalf of their students.

This analysis of the basic types of rightful interaction makes no use of any conception of harm. It is possible for one person to harm another without wronging her—as when I open a competing business that lures away your customers, or use my property so that you no longer have the

33. 6:271.
34. 6:280.
35. 6:281.

pleasant view you once did. It is also possible to wrong someone in each of the three ways without doing that person any harm. If I touch you without your consent while you sleep, or use your property without your consent while you are absent, I draw you into my purposes and wrong you, even if, as it turns out, you never learn of my action, and your body or property suffers no identifiable harm. If I breach a contract with you, I wrong you, even if, as it turns out, you had not yet done anything in reliance on it, and the expectation I deprived you of was purely prospective. The person in possession of another in a status relation who takes advantage of the relationship does wrong even if the ward of the relationship suffers no loss. This is not to say that Kant's analysis has no explanation of when or why harm is significant—it is significant when it wrongfully diminishes a person's powers, and so her freedom. But it is not significant merely because it diminishes either welfare or wealth.

The relations of right that Kant focuses on are initially introduced as ways in which free persons can interact consistent with each being independent of all the others. Kant devotes a separate discussion to the question of how a person can *come to have* a right to a particular thing, whether a piece of property or another person's performance, or to have another person act on his or her behalf. If recent political philosophers have considered property at all, they have tended to follow John Locke in assuming that the starting point for understanding property is an explanation of how acquisition of property differentiates the owner from all others in relation to a thing. Kant sees that this strategy cannot work. He rejects it as the "guardian spirit" theory of property, noting that property is a relation between persons, not a relation between a person and a thing.[36] Kant's theory of property explains the nature of that relationship, before explaining how persons can come to stand in that relationship with respect to a specific previously unowned thing. It also explains why property can be had "provisionally" in a "state of nature" without institutions of public law, but only conclusively in a civil condition.

---

36. 6:260.

From Private Right to Public Right

Early in his discussion of private right, Kant writes that "it is possible to have something external as one's own only in a rightful condition, under an authority giving laws publicly, that is, in a civil condition."[37] Kant characterizes the need for a rightful condition in a numbers of places and a number of seemingly distinct ways, appealing to each of assurance, indeterminacy, and a problem about unilateral judgments. The three arguments are each supposed to show that a system of private right without a public authority is morally incoherent, because the conceptual requirements of private right—the security of possession, clear boundaries between "mine and thine," and the acquisition of property—cannot be satisfied without a public authority entitled to make, apply, and enforce laws.

The first two types of argument have a long history in political philosophy: Hobbes speaks of assurance, Locke about problems of judgment, and Aquinas about the need for positive law to make normative concepts determinate. Yet Kant does not simply borrow from these traditional views: he develops each in a distinctive way. Assurance is characterized in these terms: "I am therefore not under an obligation to leave objects belonging to others untouched unless everyone provides me with an assurance that we will behave in accordance with the same principle with regard to what is mine."[38] The point about determinacy is also familiar: Kant characterizes the "indeterminacy, with respect to quality as well as quantity, of the external object that can be acquired" as the "hardest of all to solve," and notes that it can only be solved in a civil condition.[39] Later he notes that parts of natural right—including inheritance by bequest and the possibility of prescriptive acquisition by long possession—require positive legislation to make them determinate.

Kant subordinates these two familiar lines of argument to a broader argument, which is supposed to show that the acquisition of property

37. 6:255.
38. 6:256.
39. 6:266.

raises the basic issue of political authority, because it is an instance of one person's discretionary act changing the normative situation of others. By passing a law, a legislature purports to place citizens under an obligation that they would not be under had the law not been passed. The acquisition of unowned property shows that private right presupposes such public authority relations. One person, acting on his or her own initiative, unilaterally places others under a new obligation to stay off the property. Such a unilateral act could only be consistent with the freedom of others provided that it has a more general, omnilateral authorization. The omnilateral authorization is only possible in a rightful condition. Any other legal act, including that of resolving a private dispute or enforcing a binding resolution, requires legal authorization for just the same reasons.

Kant's detailed development of each of these arguments will be considered in Chapter 6. The key to his appeal to seemingly disparate grounds for entering a civil condition is that each of them is required to establish one of the branches of government under the separation of powers as he conceives it. The argument about unilateral judgment introduces the basic principle of public law, and provides an argument for a single legislative authority, capable of making laws from the standpoint of what he calls an "omnilateral will." The argument about assurance establishes the need for an executive branch, charged with enforcing law. The determinacy argument introduces the need for a judiciary, charged with applying the law to particular cases. Both executive and judicial powers are subject to law, because omnilateral law is the condition of acting together.

The functions of the three separate powers are distinct because only the legislature has the power to make law. It does so as the voice of the people, so that they rule themselves. The executive branch does not make general rules, but takes up means to give effect to them. The judiciary resolves particular disputes and calls upon the executive to "render to each what is his."[40] Together the divided powers preserve independence by putting people under common rules governing their interactions, and common procedures enforcing them so that no person is subject to the power or judgment of others.

40. 6:317.

Public Right

To the modern reader, Kant's list of public powers looks like a grab bag of eighteenth-century examples: the role of "supreme proprietor of the land," including the power to tax and overturn perpetuities in land ownership;[41] a separate duty to impose taxes in support of the poor; the right to distribute offices; the right to punish and grant clemency. Underlying this apparent miscellany is a principle that Kant articulates both in the *Doctrine of Right* and in the essay *Theory and Practice,* according to which the sovereign may not give a people laws that it could not give to itself, and its corollary that the people must give to itself laws that are the preconditions of its own continued lawgiving.[42]

This general way of framing the issue generates the catalogue of the powers that the state must have, as well as a set of limits on the ways in which those powers may be used. The broad range of powers included in the category of Police Power, as well as the general power to tax in support of those activities, depend upon the fundamental claims that each person has as a member of the public, rather than as a private citizen. As we shall see in Chapter 8, these powers include the maintenance of public roads and the guarantee of public spaces.

The requirement that the state support those who are unable to support themselves follows from the need for the people to be able to share a united will, as a precondition of their giving themselves laws together. As a matter of private right, nobody has a right to means that are not already his or her own, and, as Kant coldly remarks, "need or wish" is irrelevant. The duty to support the poor is not a way of coordinating efforts to discharge prior obligations to support those in need. There are no enforceable private obligations to do so. The only private obligation to support the needy is an obligation of charity, which does not dictate specific actions, but requires only that each person make the needs of (some) others one of her ends.[43] The state's duty to support the poor enters in a different way. A rightful condition makes property rights, especially the right to

---

41. 6:233.
42. *Theory and Practice,* 8:297. See also 6:329.
43. *Doctrine of Virtue,* 6:390.

exclude others, conclusive. In a state of nature, a person does others no wrong by taking from them; in a rightful condition, such forms of self-help are prohibited, and the person who takes what is needed to survive wrongs those from whom it is taken. Such a person is subject to the grace of those who have more. Kant's argument is that such a condition of dependency is inconsistent with the rightful honor of the dependent person. Citizens lack the rightful power to bind themselves to such a situation; as a result, enforceable private property is only rightful under a law that precludes that possibility.[44] The only way in which the right to exclude can be made the object of the general will is to guarantee public support for those unable to support themselves.

The state may not create classes or ranks of citizens, because, as Kant remarks, "talent and will" cannot be inherited. Kant is not making an empirical observation about who is likely to be most able at which jobs, but rather a normative claim about the basic entitlement to use whatever powers you have as you see fit. Hereditary classes or ranks of citizens would prevent people from using whatever abilities they had. Thus people concerned to protect their freedom—the sole concern that leads them to enter a rightful condition—could not consent to such a possibility, for they would be "throwing away their freedom."

Kant's use of "the idea of the original contract" contrasts with contractarian thought that has been prominent in more recent political philosophy. As a matter of private right, for Kant, only actual agreement matters. As a matter of public right, the state is under a positive obligation to take steps to secure, maintain, and improve a rightful condition. This positive obligation in turn generates a right on the part of officials to make and implement judgments about how best to do this. They cannot make arrangements for the people that those people could not make for themselves. Instead, the only factor relevant to determining whether citizens could give themselves a certain law is the question of whether it is consistent with their entitlement to exercise their freedom consistent with the entitlement of others to do so. The idea of people giving themselves laws constrains legislation in two directions. It carries with it a specification of properly public purposes—those of creating, sustaining, and improving a

---

44. 6:326.

rightful condition—which are the only purposes a state may rightfully pursue. How exactly they are best pursued—whether, for example, the best way of providing for the poor includes job training or public health insurance against debilitating illnesses—is a question for a principle of politics to decide. From the other direction, the idea of people giving laws to themselves also restricts a possible means that can be used in pursuing properly public purposes to those that are consistent with each person's innate right of humanity. Even if it could be shown that a hereditary bureaucracy would be more efficient than a system that left careers open to talents, Kant's argument shows that citizens concerned to stay in a rightful condition would have to forgo those benefits, because their power to give themselves laws is restricted to those things that are required by or implied in their interest in protecting their freedom. The principle of public right thus does not seek to generate a specific answer to every question of politics, only to show that having public bodies reach decisions which could have been different is consistent with each person's right to be his or her own master.

Kant's approach to punishment also focuses on the requirements of maintaining a rightful condition. Kant's approach is broadly retributive, in that he supposes the seriousness of the wrong provides the appropriate measure of punishment. This commitment to retributivism does not, however, reflect any belief that it is good for people to suffer in proportion to their inner wickedness, but rather a distinctive interpretation of the preconditions of the rule of law. The underlying idea is simple, even if its application is complex: whenever someone acts in a way contrary to right, others are entitled to constrain the wrongdoer's conduct. Such constraint is not an interference with freedom; it is the hindering of a hindrance to freedom. In the analytically simpler case of private damages, the person who pays compensation is required to "preserve undiminished" what the aggrieved party already had.[45] As we shall see in Chapter 10, punishment provides a further application of the same idea. Punishment upholds the supremacy of law by upholding the state's entitlement to direct conduct, both prospectively and retrospectively. Prospectively, it provides an incentive to conformity with law by announcing that the state will see to it

45. 6:271.

that wrongs have no legal effect. Retrospectively, it upholds the supremacy of law even in the face of its violation.

Kant also argues that the idea of the original contract precludes a right of revolution.[46] These notorious arguments are better known than other parts of the *Doctrine of Right*. As we shall see in Chapter 11, they turn on a simple and powerful idea: the revolutionary does not claim to be speaking for himself, but rather to be acting on behalf of "the people." Yet the idea that there is such a thing as a people only has application in a rightful condition. A rightful condition solves the problem of unilateral choice and action by creating institutions through which the people can act as a collective body. The most that the revolutionary can claim to do is speak unilaterally for some end or other. His unilateral claim, however, could never authorize the use of force. Thus, the revolutionary has no right, that is, no title to coerce.

Understood in this way, Kant's arguments against revolution do not, however, lead to the conclusion that some of the horrible regimes that the world has seen must not be resisted. To the contrary, the most egregious of these are not even candidates for a united will, because their founding principles, such as slavery or genocide, do not create a rightful condition in which all can be secure in their rights. They are, in Kant's technical sense, conditions of barbarism, that is, not defective versions of an ideal republican system of government, but rather defective versions of a state of nature. In a state of nature, everyone is authorized to use force to bring others into a rightful condition.

The Right of Nations and Cosmopolitan Right

The *Doctrine of Right* concludes with the claim that "universal and lasting peace" is not a part but "the entire final end of the doctrine of right." As a final end, it is internal to the doctrine of right, rather than outside it; the full realization of rightful relations is a condition in which every claim is defended through law rather than violence. The requirement that interaction be subordinated to law has led many readers to expect Kant to endorse some form of a world government, but he explicitly rejects that possibility.

---

46. 6:320.

Relations between states differ from relations between persons in two fundamental respects, each of which enters into Kant's unwillingness to generalize his argument for entering a state to an argument for a single world government. First, as a condition of public right, a state is only entitled to act for public purposes, rather than for the private purposes of its rulers or officials. Second, states do not have acquired rights to things outside their boundaries. Based on these contrasts, an association to guarantee peace requires neither a sovereign legislature nor the power of enforcement. States need only to agree to accept the decisions of a body like the court so as to settle their differences peacefully.

Although contemporary writers often regard Kant's emphasis on the state as a holdover from a very different historical period, his restriction of state powers and obligations in light of each state's borders reflects his underlying account of the basis for enforceable obligations. As we will see in Chapter 10, foreigners have only the right to visit, except when they have no place else to go.

III. Conclusion

Kant's legal and political philosophy starts with a simple but powerful conception of freedom as independence from another person's choice. The idea of freedom provides him with a systematic answer to the most basic questions of political philosophy. It explains how (and when) inequalities in wealth and power are consistent with the innate equality of all persons. It also shows that giving special powers to officials is consistent with equal freedom for all. It shows why some people must be given the power to tell everyone (including themselves) what to do by making laws, and why others must be empowered to force people to do as they are told. The answer is distinctively Kantian: political power is legitimate and enforceable because freedom requires it.

CHAPTER 2

The Innate Right of Humanity

THE UNIVERSAL PRINCIPLE OF RIGHT states that "an action is right if it can coexist with everyone's freedom in accordance with a universal law, or if on its maxim the freedom of choice of each can coexist with everyone's freedom in accordance with universal law."[1] An action is wrong if it hinders an action or "condition" that is itself rightful, that is, one that can coexist with everyone's freedom.

Kant also identifies a right as a "title to coerce." He goes on to argue that it follows from this, by "the principle of contradiction," that any act that hinders another person's use of freedom may in turn be hindered by others. This idea of hindrance, and the analogy with general dynamics through which Kant explicates it, have been the source of some confusion. I will examine Kant's direct arguments for the Universal Principle of Right, as well as the analogies he draws with dynamics, in the appendix. My task in this chapter will be to lay out his conception of equal freedom in normative terms.

My focus in outlining the broad idea of equal freedom will be on what Kant characterizes as the "innate right of humanity in your own person," which he also identifies as the right to be your own master—that is, the

1. 6:230.

30

right that no other person be your master. I will explain the social and interpersonal dimension of this conception of self-mastery, its relation to a system of equal freedom in accordance with universal law, and Kant's characterization of that system in terms of coercion.

By making the innate right to freedom the basis for any further rights, Kant imposes an extreme demand for unity on his account of political justice. The rights that each person has against others must be derived from it, as must the fundamental constitutional rights that protect political freedoms and freedom of religion. The same right to independence also limits state action to genuinely public purposes and the means that the state may use in achieving them. In particular, state power may not be used to subject one private person to the choice of another. All of this is to come. The basic case of a system of equal freedom under law must first be established.

Both the idea of right as a system of equal freedom and the related idea that a right is a title to coerce incorporate ideas that have fallen from favor in recent political philosophy, because they are widely thought to be subject to fatal objections. The idea of equal freedom is said to be unable to balance competing exercises of freedom against each other except by attending to the underlying interests that are at stake, and so to those interests, rather than freedom as such. The claim that a distinctive set of standards governs the use of force is said to overlook the fact that the concept of a norm is prior to the concept of a sanction for its violation.

I will introduce Kant's conception of innate right as a system of equal freedom by engaging these two objections. I will first introduce the idea of a system of equal freedom, and then show how it allows coercion to be understood as a hindrance to freedom.

I. Purposiveness and Its Restriction

The idea of a system of equal freedom for all has come in for a rough ride in recent times, to the point where it strikes many people as hopeless, because subject to a devastating objection. I will introduce the core ideas through a dialogue with this objection. In *A Theory of Justice*, John Rawls advocated a principle of "maximum equal liberty," but, in response to criticisms by H. L. A. Hart, conceded that his approach to justice lacked the theoretical resources to develop that idea.[2] Other attempts to formulate liberty-based principles have fallen victim to other, equally familiar criticisms. Remarking that libertarianism is a poorly named doctrine, G. A. Cohen has argued that any set of rules protects some liberties at the expense of others. Cohen gives the example of the way in which property rights restrict the freedom of nonowners to use land.[3] From another perspective, Ronald Dworkin has used the example of driving the wrong way on a one-way street to illustrate the difficulty with liberty-based accounts of justice.[4] Writing from yet another tradition, Charles Taylor has emphasized the differences between freedom of religion and the freedom to cross intersections unimpeded.[5] These critics of the principle of equal freedom differ in many ways, but are united in supposing that in a world in which one person's actions affect another, liberty is not a self-limiting principle, so societies and theories of justice that aspire to guide them must decide which liberties to favor, or how to weigh liberty against other values.

This objection was first put forward close to two centuries ago, by Samuel Taylor Coleridge. Like Cohen, he argues that property constitutes an external limit on freedom, which is imposed for purposes that have no relation to freedom as such and depend entirely on advantage. Coleridge's argument was repeated without a reference to him by Henry Sidgwick, and explicitly endorsed by Frederick Maitland, both of whom Hart referred to in introducing his own version of it.[6]

All of the standard objections to the idea of equal freedom conceive of

2. Hart, "Rawls on Liberty and Its Priority," in Norman Daniels, ed., *Reading Rawls* (New York: Basic Books, 1975).

3. Cohen, "Freedom, Justice, and Capitalism," *New Left Review* 1, 126 (1981): 9.

4. Dworkin, *Taking Rights Seriously* (Cambridge, Mass.: Harvard University Press, 1977), 271.

5. Taylor, "What's Wrong with Negative Liberty?" in *Philosophy and the Human Sciences*, Philosophical Papers, vol. 2 (Cambridge: Cambridge University Press, 1985).

6. See F. W. Maitland, "Mr. Herbert Spencer's Theory of Society III," *Mind* 8 (1883): 506–524. Maitland in turn attributes its general thrust to Samuel Taylor Coleridge. See Coleridge, "Section the First on the Principles of Political Knowledge" (1818), in Kathleen Coburn, ed., *The Collected Works of Samuel Taylor Coleridge*, vol. 4/1 (Princeton: Princeton University Press, 1969). Both Maitland and Coleridge argue that property requires a compromise of freedom in conditions of scarcity in which "not every man can get what he wants."

freedom as a person's ability to *achieve* his or her purposes unhindered by others. This understanding of freedom, described as "negative liberty" in Isaiah Berlin's essay "Two Concepts of Liberty," characterizes any intentional actions or regulations that prevent a person from achieving his or her purposes as hindrances to freedom.[7] Some critics have questioned the special significance of the actions of others in limiting freedom on this account—lack of resources or internal obstacles may frustrate your purposes at least as much as other people's deliberate actions. Other critics have wondered how different freedoms could be measured to determine whether people had equal amounts.[8] These difficulties aside, the deeper problem is that how different exercises of negative liberty interact with each other depends on the particular purposes the people are pursuing, or what Kant would call the "matter" of their choice. If our purposes come into conflict, so too must our negative freedom. Any purpose, whether my private purpose of crossing your yard or the state's public purpose of coordinating traffic flow, can come into conflict with some person's ability to get what he or she wants.

Kant conceives of equal freedom differently. It is not a matter of people having equal amounts of some benefit, however it is to be measured, but of the respective independence of persons from each other. Such independence cannot be defined, let alone secured, if it depends on the particular purposes that different people happen to have. One person cannot be independent of the *effects* of choices made by other people, except by limiting the freedom of those people. Instead, a system of equal freedom is one in which each person is free to use his or her own powers, individually or cooperatively, to set his or her own purposes, and no one is allowed to compel others to use their powers in a way designed to advance or accommodate any other person's purposes.

You are independent if you are the one who decides what ends you will use your means to pursue, as opposed to having someone else decide for you. At the level of innate right, your right to freedom protects your

---

7. Berlin, "Two Concepts of Liberty," in his *Four Essays on Liberty* (Oxford: Oxford University Press, 1969), 118–134.

8. Onora O'Neill, *Towards Justice and Virtue* (Cambridge: Cambridge University Press, 1996), 161–162.

purposiveness—your capacity to choose the ends you will use your means to pursue—against the choices of others, but not against either your own poor choices or the inadequacy of your means to your aspirations. You remain independent if nobody else gets to tell you what purposes to pursue with your means; each of us is independent if neither of us gets to tell the other what purposes to pursue.

This right to independence is not a special case of a more general interest in being able to set and pursue your purposes. Instead, it is a distinctive aspect of your status as a person in relation to other persons, entitled to set your own purposes, and not required to act as an instrument for the pursuit of anyone else's purposes. You are sovereign as against others not because you get to decide about the things that matter to you most, but because *nobody else* gets to tell you what purposes to pursue; you would be their subject if they did. Thus Kant's conception of the right to independence rests on neither of what is referred to in recent literature as "interest theory" or "will theory" of rights.[9] Underlying the other differences between these accounts is a shared conception of rights as institutional instruments that constrain the conduct of others in order to protect things that matter apart from them. Kant's account identifies a right with the restriction on the conduct of others "under universal law," that is, consistent with everyone having the same restrictions. Each person's entitlement to be independent of the choice of others constrains the conduct of others because of the importance of that independence, rather than in the service of something else, such as an interest in leading a successful, worthwhile, or fully autonomous life. Those things can be specified without reference to the conduct of others, and constraining the conduct of others is, at most, a useful way of securing them. If rights are understood in this instrumental way, they are always at least potentially *conditional* on their ability to secure the underlying values that they are supposed to protect. The Kantian right to independence, by contrast, is always an entitlement within a system of reciprocal limits on freedom, and so can only be violated by the conduct of others, and its only point is to prohibit that conduct. The protection of independence and the prohibi-

---

9. Joseph Raz, "On the Nature of Rights," *Mind* 93 (1984): 215–229; H. L. A. Hart, "Are There Any Natural Rights?" *Philosophical Review* 64 (1955): 175–191.

tion of one person deciding what purposes another will pursue stand in a relation of equivalence, rather than one of means to an end. As a result, the constraint a system of equal freedom places on conduct is *unconditional*. An unconditional constraint does not preclude the possibility of hindering the action of a person, or even of using lethal force to do so, because the unconditional right is not a right to a certain state of affairs, such as the agent staying alive. Instead, it is a right to act independently of the choice of others, consistent with the entitlement of others to do the same. The principle of mutual restriction under law applies unconditionally, because it is not a way of achieving some other end.

Your sovereignty, which Kant also characterizes as your quality of being your "own master *(sui juris),*" has as its starting point your right to your own person, which Kant characterizes as innate. As innate, this right contrasts with any further acquired rights you might have, because innate right does not require any affirmative act to establish it; as a right, it is a constraint on the conduct of others, rather than a way of protecting some nonrelational aspect of you. It is a precondition of any acquired rights because those capable of acquiring them through their actions already have the moral capacity to act in ways that have consequences for rights, that is, for the conduct of others. That any system of rights presupposes some basic moral capacities that do not depend on antecedent acts on the part of the person exercising them does not yet say what the rights in question are, or how many such rights there might be.

Kant writes that there is "only one innate right."

> *Freedom* (independence from being constrained by another's choice), insofar as it can coexist with the freedom of every other in accordance with a universal law, is the only original right belonging to every human being by virtue of his humanity.[10]

The innate right is the individualization of the Universal Principle of Right, applied to the case in which only persons are considered. The Universal Principle of Right demands that each person exercise his or her choice in ways that are consistent with the freedom of all others to exer-

---

10. 6:237.

cise their choice; the innate right to freedom is then each person's entitlement to exercise his or her freedom, restricted only by the rights of all others to do the same under universal law. No issues of right would arise for someone who succeeded in "shunning all society,"[11] and if there were only one person in the world, no issues of independence or rightful obligation would arise.[12]

Kant offers different formulations of innate right, each of which elaborates an aspect of the idea that one person must not be subject to the choice[13] of another, which Kant glosses in terms of one person being a mere means for another. This familiar Kantian theme is explained in terms of the classic distinction, from Roman law, between persons and things. A person is a being capable of setting its own purposes. A thing is something that can be used in the pursuit of whatever purposes the person who has it might have. The classic example of a person being treated as a mere thing is the slave, for a slave is entirely at the disposal of his or her master. The slave's problem is that he is subject to the master's choice: the master gets to decide what to do with the slave and what the slave will do. The slave does not set his own ends, but is merely a means for ends set by someone else. To call it "the" problem is not too strong: if the other problems a slave has—low welfare, limited options, and so on—were addressed by a benevolent master, the *relationship* of slavery would perhaps be less bad, but it would not thereby be any less wrong. The right to be your own master is neither a right to have things go well for you nor a right to have a wide range of options. Instead, it is explicitly contrastive and interpersonal: to be your own master is to have no *other* master. It is not a claim about your relation to yourself, only about your relation to others. The right to equal freedom, then, is just the right that no person be the master of another. The idea of being your own master is also equivalent to an idea of equality, since none has, simply by birth, either the right

11. 6:236.
12. Ibid.
13. Kant distinguishes between will *(Wille)* and choice *(Willkur)*. Choice is the ability to decide what purpose to pursue; will is pure practical reason, the capacity for self-determination in accordance with the representation of a rule (6:214). The classic discussion of this distinction is Lewis White Beck, "Kant's Two Conceptions of Will," *Annales de Philosophie Politique* 4 (1962): 119–137.

to command others or the duty to obey them. So the right to equality does not, on its own, require that people be treated in the same way in some respect, such as welfare or resources, but only that no person is the master of another. Another person is not entitled to decide for you even if he knows better than you what would make your life go well, or has a pressing need that only you can satisfy.

The same right to be your own master within a system of equal freedom also generates what Kant calls an "internal duty" of rightful honor, which "consists in asserting one's worth as a human being in relation to others, a duty expressed by the saying do not make yourself into a mere means for others but be at the same time an end for them."[14] Kant says that this duty can be "explained ... as obligation from the right of humanity in our own person."

Kant's characterization of this as an "internal duty" may seem out of place, given his earlier characterization of the Universal Principle of Right in terms of restrictions on each person's conduct in light of the freedom of *others*. But the duty of rightful honor is also relational: it is a duty because it is a limit on the exercise of a person's freedom that is imposed by the Universal Principle of Right. Just as the rights of others restrict your freedom, so that you cannot acquire a right to anything by acting in ways inconsistent with the innate right of another person, so, too, the humanity in your own person restricts the ways in which you can exercise your freedom by entering into arrangements with others. Your innate right prevents you from being bound by others more than you can in turn bind them; your duty of rightful honor prevents you from making yourself bound by others in those ways. Rightful honor does not warn you away from some juridical possibility that would somehow be demeaning or unworthy. You do not wrong yourself if you enter into a

---

14. Kant introduces the idea of rightful honor as a gloss on Roman jurist Ulpian's precept *"honeste vive"* (6:237). See Ulpian, *Rules*, Book 1, recorded in Justinian, *Digest*, Book I, 1.10. A more literal translation would be "living honorably." The Ulpian precepts appear to have been a standard reference point in discussion; they appear in Baumgarten's textbook from which Kant taught moral philosophy. Kant concedes that his reading of them involves putting content into them. Kant uses the Latin phrase *Lex iusti* ("What is right"), as well as the phrases "the law of outer freedom" and "the axiom of outer freedom," to mark this idea elsewhere in the *Doctrine of Right*.

binding arrangement inconsistent with the humanity in your own person. Instead, your duty of rightful honor says that no such arrangement can be binding, so no other person could be entitled to enforce a claim of right against you that presupposes that you have acted contrary to rightful honor.

Rightful honor does not demand that you behave selfishly, or refrain from helping another person with some particular project, or make another person's ends your own. To do any of these things is just to adopt some particular purpose, and so is an exercise of your freedom. In later chapters, we will see that rightful honor prevents you from giving up your capacity to set your own purposes, and so prevents others from asserting claims of right that assume that you did. In private right your rightful honor prevents you from entering into an enforceable contract of slavery, even if you were to believe the arrangement to be to your advantage. In public right, it prevents officials from making arrangements on your behalf that are inconsistent with your innate right. Rightful honor also provides the link from private right to public right by imposing a duty on each to leave the state of nature, which Kant characterizes as a condition in which everyone is subject to the choice of others.

Understood in this interpersonal way, the idea of independence contrasts with the idea of freedom as independence from empirical determination that some interpreters take to be central to Kant's *Groundwork*, insofar as the latter is often taken to depend only contingently on the existence or deeds of others.[15] It also contrasts with prominent contemporary views according to which natural and social obstacles pose equally serious impediments to freedom.[16] Finally, Kant's account of independence

---

15. If this reading of the *Groundwork* is the canonical statement of Kant's position—an issue on which I take no stand here—the existence of a *Doctrine of Right* is surprising and its content even more so. For one such expression of surprise, consider Robert Pippin's comment, "It would not be unreasonable to expect Kant at this point to suggest a certain sort of stoic indifference to the practical affairs of politics." See Pippin's "Dividing and Deriving in Kant's Rechtslehre," in Otfried Höffe, ed., *Immanuel Kant, Metaphysische Anfangsgründe der Rechtslehre* (Berlin: Akademie Verlag, 1999), 63–85.

16. For example, in *A Theory of Justice* Rawls speaks of freedom in terms of independence from natural contingencies and natural fortune. See Rawls, *A Theory of Justice* (Cambridge, Mass.: Harvard University Press, 1971), 73.

does not aspire to isolate people from the effects of other people's choices. Instead, my independence of your choice must be understood in terms of my right that you not choose for me. I remain independent if your choices have effects on me, as when you decline to cooperate with me on some project, or you pursue purposes of your own, and in so doing render things I had hoped to use unavailable. Any such idea of independence from all effects of the actions of others violates Kant's basic idea of equal freedom. To insulate one person from all effects of the choices of others would subordinate everyone else to that person's choice. This last contrast between independence of the choice of others and independence of the effects of their choices underlies Kant's conception of a number of familiar legal doctrines: you do me no wrong by offering a product similar to mine but at a better price, even though I lose customers. Nor do you wrong me by damaging something that I am accustomed to using but do not own; nor do you violate any right of mine by breaching a contract with someone other than me, or by taking down your fence so that my land is now exposed to wind. In each of these cases, I remain independent, that is, entitled to use my means as I see fit. These differences are central to Kant's argument.

Once freedom is understood in terms of people's respective independence, one person's freedom need not conflict with another's. Each person is free to use his or her own abilities to set and pursue his or her own purposes, consistent with the freedom of others to use their abilities to set their purposes. A system of equal freedom demands that nobody use his own person in a way that will deprive another of hers, or use another person's without her permission.

Each of these ideas requires filling out: the idea that your freedom is to be identified with your purposiveness; the idea that your right to your own person is tied up with your right to decide what to do with your body; and the idea that the separate or cooperative exercise of those powers can form a system of equal independence. Once the account of independence is in place, it also provides an account of wrongdoing as the violation of independence. It also generates the other "authorizations" that Kant says are included in innate right, both the right to speak your mind and the right to be "beyond reproach."

II. Freedom and Choice

The idea that you exercise your freedom by setting and pursuing purposes is familiar, common to Rawls's emphasis on the moral power to "set and pursue a conception of the good," and the distinction, common to Aristotle and Kant, between choice and wish. The ability to choose in this sense doesn't depend on the ability to stand outside the causal world, or even to abstract from your own purposes in making choices. Instead, it rests on the familiar observation that if you choose to do something, you must set about doing it, which requires that you take it to be within your power to pursue.

A different conception of choice sometimes appears in philosophy, according to which people simply have certain purposes and then select means to achieve them.[17] This conception is exactly backward. Even if your wishes are fixed by your biology and upbringing, you can only *do* something if you set out to do it, and you can only set out to do what you take yourself to have the power to do. You might be mistaken about what your powers can achieve, but your freedom to choose your own purposes just is your freedom to decide how to use the powers you have. Hobbes could set out to square the circle, even though he was mathematically doomed to fail, because he took himself to have the requisite means—a compass, a straightedge, and one of the best minds of the seventeenth century. Without the powers, you can wish for anything—to walk on the moon and be home in time for dinner—but it is not a choice you can make. Your wishes may all come true, but you only *do* things by exercising your powers.

You do not, and could not, have a right against others to purposiveness as such. Instead your right is that you, rather than any other person, be the one who determines which purposes you will pursue. In the first instance, your right to your person is your right to your body. Your body is the sum of your capacities to set and pursue your purposes; your right to

---

17. As economics textbooks frequently put it, preferences are "given." As a matter of the best empirical theory of human motivation, this may be true. If so, the distinction between choice and wish applies *within* a person's preference profile.

it is your right that no other person determine what purposes you will pursue, not that you exercise that capacity successfully.

This formulation of your right to your person as your right to your body neither presupposes nor conflicts with any more general metaphysical claims about the relation between your person and your body. At the level of theoretical metaphysics, your person might be kept track of in other ways- the narrative of your actions, the fluctuations of your bank account, or your own conscious thoughts. As far as your claim against others, and the claims of others against you, however, the starting point must be your person as your body. You are the one to whom various things happened, the one who engaged in various transactions, and every time you did something or something happened to you, your body did it, or it happened to your body. If somebody wrongs you, he typically interferes with one or more aspects of your person; all are wrongs against your person by being wrongs against its aspects. Your person is not just a set of means that are at your disposal, but if another person interferes with your body, he thereby interferes with your ability to set and pursue your own purposes by interfering with the means that you have with which to set them, namely your bodily powers or abilities. Some philosophers have thought that you can keep track of your conscious thoughts without keeping track of your body. Any such possibility is irrelevant to the ways in which you may treat others, or others may treat you, consistent with your respective purposiveness. Your thoughts make no difference to the capacity of others to set and pursue their own purposes unless you act on them. You exercise your purposiveness by choosing, rather than merely wishing.

There is thus a fundamental distinction between interfering with the *purposiveness* of another person and interfering with that person's *purposes*. I can interfere with your purposes in a variety of ways—I might occupy the space that you had hoped to stand in, make arrangements with the person you had hoped to spend time with, and so on. Actions that affect you in these ways leave your purposiveness intact, because you still have the ability to determine how to use what you already have, and you are still the one who gets to determine how it will be used. All I have done is change the world in which you act.

Innate right entitles each person to use his or her bodily powers as he or she sees fit, consistent with the ability of others to do the same with theirs. The consistency is achieved through the idea of noninterference and the correlative requirement that cooperative activity be voluntary. Each person is only entitled to use his or her means in ways that are consistent with the entitlement of others to use theirs under universal law. This consistency requirement precludes anyone from using another person's means without that person's permission. The qualification "under universal law" entails that you could not have a right to a certain state of affairs so that, for example, others were required to organize their activities in such a way as to guarantee that it continued to obtain. Any means that you have may be subject to generation and decay, and others are not required to use their means in ways that protect you from such possibilities. Instead, they are only required to use them in ways that do not themselves damage or destroy what is already yours.

III. Domination

The right to freedom as independence provides a model of interaction that reconciles the ability of separate persons to use their powers to pursue their own purposes. In so doing, it also provides a distinctive conception of the wrongs that interfere with this independence. Wrongdoing takes the form of domination. Both your right to independence and the violations of it can only be explicated by reference to the actions of others. Wrongs against your person are not outcomes that are bad for you which other people happen to cause. Unlike the familiar "harm principle" put forward by Mill, which focuses exclusively on outcomes that can be characterized without reference to the acts that bring them about, the right to freedom focuses exclusively on the acts of others. It is not that somebody does something that causes something bad to happen to you; it is that somebody does something to you.

The idea of freedom as nondomination has a distinguished history in political philosophy. Recent scholars have pointed out that Berlin's dichotomy between negative and positive liberty leaves out a prominent idea of liberty, sometimes referred to as the "republican" or neo-Roman conception of liberty, according to which liberty consists in independence from others. These scholars argue that this conception was central to the political thought of the civic republicans of the Renaissance, who were centrally concerned with the dangers of despotism. On this reading, the early modern republicans did not object to despotism because it interfered with their negative or positive liberty (to use anachronistic terms they would not have recognized). A despot who was benevolent, or even prudent, might allow people, especially potentially powerful ones, opportunity to do what they wanted or be true to themselves. The objection was to the fact that it was up to the despot to decide, to his having the power, quite apart from the possibility that he would use it badly. Unless someone has a power, there is no danger of it being used badly, but the core concern of the civic republicans was the despot's entitlement to use it, and the subjugation of his subjects that followed regardless of how it was used.[18] Berlin is aware of this difference when he writes, "It is perfectly conceivable that a liberal-minded despot would allow his subjects a large measure of personal freedom."[19]

Freedom as independence carries this same idea of independence further, to relations among citizens. It insists that everything that is wrong with being subject to the choice of a powerful ruler is also wrong with being subject to the choice of another private person. As a result, it can explain the nature of wrongdoing even when no harm ensues. One person is subject to another person's choice; I use your means to advance purposes you have not set for yourself. Most familiar crimes are examples of one person interfering with the freedom of another by interfering with either her exercise of her powers or her ability to exercise them. They are small-scale versions of despotism or abuse of office.

Your powers can be interfered with in two basic ways, by usurping them or by destroying them. I *usurp* your powers if I exercise them for my own purposes, or get you to exercise them for my purposes. If I use force or fraud to get you to do something for me that you would not otherwise

---

18. See generally Philip Pettit, *Republicanism: A Theory of Freedom and Government* (Oxford: Oxford University Press, 1997), and Quentin Skinner, *Liberty Before Liberalism* (Cambridge: Cambridge University Press, 1998). In "A Third Concept of Liberty," *Proceedings of the British Academy* 117 (2002): 239, Skinner points out that Berlin's idea of positive liberty is not an idea of self-mastery but of mastering yourself.

19. Berlin, "Two Concepts of Liberty," 129.

do, I wrong you, even if the cost I impose on you is small. I have used you, and in so doing made your choice subject to mine, and deprived you of the ability to decide what to do. If you chose to do the same thing and I got the same benefit from it, but I had no role in making you do it, I haven't wronged you; I just took advantage of the effects of something you were doing anyway.

I can use you in other ways as well. Suppose that you are opposed to the fluoridation of teeth on what you believe to be health-related grounds. You are mistaken about this, but committed to campaigning against fluoridation. As your dentist, I use the opportunity created by filling one of your (many) cavities to surreptitiously fluoridate your teeth, pleased to have advanced the cause of dental health, and privately taking delight in doing so on you, the vocal opponent of fluoridation. In this example, I don't harm you, and there is even a sense in which I benefit you. I still wrong you because I draw you into a purpose that you did not choose. You remain free to use your other powers to pursue other purposes. But part of being free to use your powers to set and pursue your *own* purposes is having a veto on the purposes you will pursue. You need more than the ability to pursue purposes you have set; you also need to be able to *decline* to pursue purposes unless you have set them.[20] When I usurp your powers, I violate your independence precisely because I deprive you of that veto. I am like the despot who uses his office for a private purpose.

The other way in which I can subject you to my choice is by injuring you or, in the limiting case, killing you, ending your purposiveness. If I break your arm, I wrong you because I interfere with your person. The wrong interferes with a specific aspect of your purposiveness: in this case, I destroy your ability to use your arm (for some period of time) and in so doing limit the ends that you are able to set and pursue for yourself. The wrong does not consist in the fact that you no longer *have* those powers; you are not wronged if a disease or a wild animal produces the same result. I subject you to my choice because I deprive you of them. I dominate you because I treat your powers as subject to my choice: I take it upon

---

20. This idea receives its classic legal articulation in Judge Benjamin N. Cardozo's remark that "every human being of adult years and sound mind has a right to determine what shall be done with his own body" (*Schloendorff v. Society of New York Hospital*, 211 NY 125 (1914)).

myself to decide whether you can keep them. If I usurp your powers, I decide what purposes you will pursue, and make you dependent on me in one way; if I destroy them, I may not set any particular purposes for you, but treat your means as though they were mine to dispose of.

This second category of wrongdoing enables the right to freedom to account for all of the core examples that make Mill's harm principle seem plausible. Bodily injury reduces your powers no matter how it comes about, but it only violates your independence if another person injures you. Any injury potentially reduces your ability to set and pursue your own purposes, but intentional injury does something more: if I set out to deprive you of powers you have, I subordinate your ability to use your powers to set and pursue your own purposes as you see fit to my pursuit of my purposes. I set myself up as your master by deciding that you will no longer have them. Intentional injury is despotism by another name. Harm merits prohibition when it is a manifestation of despotism, but not otherwise.

Use and injury exhaust the space of possible violations of independence. Other possible losses are excluded. Your entitlement to be your own master is only violated if another person makes you pursue an end you have not chosen, by using your powers without your authorization, or restricts your ability to use your powers, either by physically constraining you or by depriving you of the ability to use them. Your self-mastery is not compromised if others decline to accommodate you, because the idea of self-mastery is explicitly contrastive. The person who declines to exercise his own self-mastery in aid of your wishes or needs does not thereby become your master. Indeed, any other restrictions on the freedom of others would require them to use their powers for another person's purposes.

Many wrongs against persons combine use and injury. Touching a person without her consent uses her for a purpose she didn't authorize; if she is also injured in the process, it may limit her ability to use her powers, at least temporarily. But intentional touching is objectionable even if harmless or undetected, or the injury is small. Your person—your body— is yours to use for your own purposes, and if I take it upon myself to touch you without your permission, I use it for a purpose you haven't authorized. The problem is not that I interfere with your use of your person or powers, but that I violate your independence by using your powers for my purposes. The trespass against your person is primary, and any consequent injury secondary to it. If I cause you minor harm, such as the distraction of the few seconds of pain you experience when slapped, the small injury is serious because it aggravates an unauthorized touching. That is why an unauthorized caress or kiss can be a serious wrong, even if the victim is asleep or anesthetized.

Other people might do various things that annoy you in various ways. You might be happier if other people dressed in ways that you found tasteful or modest, or refrained from public displays of affection. However troubling you might subjectively find such conduct, your right to your own person does not entitle you to constrain it, because it does not stop you from using your body as you see fit. Again, you could not enjoy a right against others looking at you under a universal law, because embodied and motile persons can only avoid bumping into each other by looking where they are going, and so sometimes at each other.[21]

Defenders of Mill's harm principle have sought to explain the wrong in harmless trespasses against persons by pointing to their effects on third parties, arguing, for example, that people are particularly likely to be upset by or afraid of such forms of conduct[22] or, alternatively, that most trespasses against persons are harmful, and so it is better to have a general rule proscribing them.[23] The Kantian idea of an innate right of humanity

---

21. It does not follow from this that your right to your person does not include rights against assault, that is, rights against what the law calls "an apprehension of a battery." Nor does it preclude the possibility that your right against assault could be engaged by others stalking you or even leering at you without touching you, even though you could not have a right against their looking at you as they go about their own business. Another person may wrong you without actually touching you in those cases in which he induces the expectation of a battery in you. That person is not entitled to put you in a position of using your powers defensively, because in so doing, he is dictating how you will use your powers. The standard by which an assault is judged must be objective, so that neither the assailant nor the person complaining determines whether a particular case is in fact an assault.

22. Colin Bird, "Harm Versus Sovereignty: A Reply to Ripstein," *Philosophy & Public Affairs* 35 (2007): 182–185; John Gardner and Stephen Shute, "The Wrongness of Rape," in Jeremy Horder, ed., *Oxford Essays in Jurisprudence: Fourth Series* (Oxford: Oxford University Press, 1999), 193–218.

23. See, for example, Joel Feinberg, *Harmless Wrongdoing* (Oxford: Oxford University Press, 1990).

in your own person provides a simpler explanation: the person who touches you without your authorization uses you for a purpose that is his but not yours. The ground for prohibiting such conduct does not depend on any hypothesis about the likelihood that some third person will harm yet a fourth.

More generally, innate right's indifference to harm, considered as such, enables it to explain the familiar exceptions to the harm principle.[24] Self-inflicted injury involves no despotism—it is not something that one person has done to another. Ordinarily, injury that results from consensual undertakings will not involve despotism either. If consent is genuine, the person injured as a result of a voluntarily undertaken danger is not subject to another person's despotism. By consenting, you can turn an act that would otherwise be another person's despotism over you into an exercise of your own freedom. The right to engage in consensual interactions and the rights you acquire through consensual interactions are, strictly speaking, not parts of the innate right of humanity as such. Instead, they are acquired rights, which require affirmative acts to establish them. We will return to them in detail in Chapter 4.

The idea of independence also explains why other harms do not matter to right. Voluntary cooperation enables people to use their powers together to pursue purposes they share. It can be made to look as though potential cooperators are always subject to each other's choice: unless you agree to cooperate with me, I can't use my powers in the way I want to. But this is an example of our respective independence. Cooperation only contrasts with domination when it is voluntary on both sides. You get to decide whether to cooperate with me because you get to decide how your powers will be used. I can no more demand that you make your powers available to accommodate my preferred use of mine than you can make that demand of me. Each of us is sovereign over our powers, and the power to decide who to cooperate with is a basic expression of that sovereignty. That is why I wrong you when I use your powers for my purposes,

---

24. The ways in which these exceptions follow directly from innate right might lead some to suspect that the harm principle is just a façade for arguments that appeal to independence rather than harm.

even if it doesn't cost you anything: in appropriating your powers as my own, I force you to cooperate with me.

Each person's entitlement to decide how his or her powers will be used precludes prohibiting many of the setbacks people suffer as effects of other people's nondominating conduct. People always exercise their powers in a particular context, but that context is normally the result of other people's exercises of their own freedom. To protect me against the harms that I suffer as you go about your legitimate business, perhaps because you set a bad example for others, or deprive me of their custom, would be inconsistent with your freedom, because it would require you to use your powers in the way that most suited my wishes or vulnerabilities. You do not dominate me by failing to provide me with a suitable context in which to pursue my favored purposes. To the contrary, I would dominate you if I could call upon the law to force you to provide me with my preferred context for those purposes. That would just be requiring you to act on my behalf, to advance purposes I had set. That is, it would empower me to use force to turn you into my means. Refusing to provide me with a favorable context to exercise my powers is an exercise of your freedom, not a violation of mine, no matter how badly the refusal reflects on your character.[25]

Indifference to harm that is suffered as a result of one person's failure to provide another with a favorable context is just the generalization of the protections the right to freedom provides. That is the precise sense in which it articulates reciprocal limits on freedom: you would be wronged if I could prohibit you from doing something that doesn't wrong me. You can be prohibited from dominating me, but the basis for that prohibition is also the basis for prohibiting me from calling on the state to make you provide me with favorable background conditions to use my own powers.[26]

In the same way, if you defeat me in a fair contest, you do not deprive

---

25. If you can be required to perform acts for others, such as easy rescues, the rationale must have another source, since failing to rescue doesn't usurp or destroy a person's powers, it just fails to rescue her. I examine this issue in more detail in "Three Duties to Rescue," *Law and Philosophy* 19 (2000): 751–779.

26. Interests can be set back in ways that are more closely connected to freedom when, for example, parents or guardians fail to see to the development of the powers of their children. I examine these issues in the next chapter.

me of any of my powers. I merely failed at something that I was trying to do. That failure may disappoint me, but it doesn't deprive me of means that I already had, it only prevents me from acquiring further ones. My defeat may change the context in which I use those powers in the future: if you win the championship, others may no longer hire me to endorse their products. But I had no entitlement against you to a favorable context or to have those other people enter into cooperative arrangements with me.

This remains the case even if I use up my means, and so have less after the contest than before: I haven't been deprived of them, I have just used them in trying to acquire something I didn't get. The fact that this happened in the context of a contest with other people doesn't make this expenditure any different from any other case in which I might expend my means while trying unsuccessfully to get more. They are mine to use, and as long as nobody forces me to use them one way or another, I am free to use them as I see fit. Conversely, if I squander them, I can't say that anyone else deprived me of them. Reasonable people may disagree about what counts as a fair contest, or about the familiar example of economic competition for which the idea of fair contest is so often invoked. Nobody can coherently dispute the claim that a fair contest is one that nobody is entitled to win in advance. No matter how significant the impact on those who lose at fair contests, the loss does not amount to the despotism of the winner over the loser.

Cases of economic competition presuppose a further context not yet contained in the idea of innate right: rights to property, obligations under contracts, and institutions charged with enforcing acquired rights. Nonetheless, they illustrate an important structural feature of the difference between wronging a person and changing the context in which that person acts. If you lure my customers away by providing a better combination of product and price, I may be much worse off. You do not wrong me, because I still have my means at my disposal: my (unsold) stock, my premises, and my abilities as a salesman. I had no right that my customers continue to patronize me. I only had a right to offer them incentives to enter into commerce with me. You have the same formal right, and so you, too, may offer them incentives. They are free to respond to our respective incentives as they see fit. I cannot have a right to my customers, because if I did, such a right would limit their ability to use their means as they see fit, that is, by entering into transactions with whomever they please, on the terms they find most attractive.[27]

Independence can only be violated by the deeds of other persons, because it is an interest in independence of those deeds. Thus it cannot be treated as just another vulnerability, to be added to the harm principle's catalogue of protected interests. All of those interests can be set back by a variety of things other than the actions of others.

The sense in which I use you is particularly vivid if I willfully *decide* to use you, but the same point applies quite apart from my state of mind. My use of you is objectionable even if you are merely incidental to my purpose: I grab you and push you out of the way, or vent my frustration by hitting you. In either of these cases, you are an unwilling party to the transaction: I force you to participate in my pursuit of my petty purposes, either by forcing you to stand where I want you to, rather than where you were, or by volunteering you as my punching bag. Either way, subjecting your choice to mine is the means I use to get what I want; my act is objectionable because the means I use are properly subject to your choice, not mine. In so doing, I exercise despotism over you, and so treat you as subject to me. I can do the same carelessly or inadvertently. Not looking where I am going, I may injure you, or, absentmindedly, I sit on a chair, failing to notice that it is already occupied. In all of these cases, I act in ways inconsistent with our respective freedom under universal law, because I restrict your ability to use your person to set and pursue your own purposes.

IV. The Other "Authorizations"

The right to independence entitles each person to use his or her means to set and pursue his or her own purposes, consistent with the entitlement of others to do the same. Innate right also entitles you to tell others what you think or plan to do, without being held to account for saying so, and

---

27. It is conceivable that there might be grounds of public right to restrict economic competition in certain settings, since, as we shall see, the state has the right to "manage the economy," which entitles it to act on its best judgment about how to do so. If there are grounds for restricting competition, however, their basis cannot be traced to an individual right on the part of the person disadvantaged by the fact that people did not respond to the incentives he offered, because no person could ever have a right that others respond to his incentives or offers.

the right to be "beyond reproach," the right to have only your own deeds imputed to you. These authorizations are fundamental to public right, because they constrain the possible activities of the state in making law. The former provides the basis for rights of freedom of expression, limited only by the rights of others; the latter is the basis of both the right to sue in defamation for damage to your reputation and the right to place the burden of proof on a person who accuses you of having done wrong. These are both "already" included in innate right and "not really distinct from it" because each is an aspect of independence of the choice of others. The right to communicate your thoughts to others is just a special case of the right to use your powers as you see fit. Kant remarks that this extends even to deliberate falsehoods, because it is up to others to decide whether to believe what they are told. The only untruth "that we want to call a lie in a sense bearing on rights" is one that deprives another of some acquired right, such as a fraudulent claim that a contract has been concluded. The right to say what you think does not preclude liability for fraud, or injuring another person's reputation, or falsely shouting "fire" in a crowded theater when you know people will be trampled, because each of these deprives others of things to which they already had a right. To deprive you of property or get you to do something by lying to induce you to enter into an arrangement with me is not parallel to depriving you of property or getting you to do something with force.[28] Such cases contrast with those in which one person suggests that another do something, and the other follows the suggestion. In that case, the second person must be taken to act on his or her own initiative, because no person has a right that others use what is theirs in ways that most favor them. Using your power of speech is a special case of using your powers; saying things to others is ordinarily a matter of changing the context in which they act, rather than depriving them of what they already have.[29]

---

28. These cases are analyzed in detail in Chapter 5.

29. Kant's well-known essay "On the Supposed Right to Lie from Philanthropy" actually incorporates this analysis. Confronted with Constant's example of someone who comes to your door looking for a friend "just now bent on murder" (8:427), Kant contends that it is not permissible to lie, on the grounds that "truthfulness in statements that one cannot avoid is a human being's duty to everyone" (8:426), and then, surprisingly, remarks that the murderer "has no right to the truth." This latter claim follows from his claim that each person has a right to communicate thoughts to others, except where doing so directly infringes another person's

The right to be beyond reproach is another instance of the right to independence. No person can place you under a new obligation or restriction simply by alleging that you have done wrong. If he could, and thereby place the burden on you of clearing your name, he would be entitled to restrict your freedom entirely on his own initiative. Thus you would be subject to his choice. Your right to be "beyond reproach" just is the right that you never have to clear your own name; you are entitled to your own good name simply by virtue of your innate right of humanity.

V. Freedom and Coercion

We are now in a position to explain Kant's claim that right can be identified with the authorization to coerce. He writes that "right can also be represented as the possibility of a fully reciprocal use of coercion that is consistent with everyone's freedom in accordance with universal laws."[30]

This focus on coercion puts him at odds with the tradition that dominates political philosophy, at least in the English-speaking world, for which the primary normative question of political philosophy is what people ought to do, and the question of whether they should be forced to do those things is secondary.[31] A prominent version of this view receives a forceful statement by Mill in his discussion of justice in *Utilitarianism*. Mill there writes, "We do not call anything wrong unless we mean to imply that a person ought to be punished in some way or other for doing it; if not by law by the opinion of his fellow creatures; if not by opinion by the reproaches of his own conscience." For Mill, we only attach sanctions to a proper subset of the things that people should not do, and he argues that we should only do so based on the seriousness of the harm those acts

---

rights. No person has a right to be told the truth as such; a system of equal freedom is only possible if everyone has a right to what he or she already has, but not a right, absent some prior arrangement, to receive anything from anyone. Kant's conclusion is that lying in such cases violates the postulate of public right, and so, although it wrongs no one in particular, nonetheless does wrong in what Kant describes as "the highest degree" (6:307). For a careful discussion of these issues, see Jacob Weinrib, "The Juridical Significance of Kant's 'Supposed Right to Lie,'" *Kantian Review* 13 (2008): 141–170.

30. 6:321.

31. John Rawls's later work, with its emphasis on the coercive structure of society, is a clear exception to this tendency. See *Political Liberalism* (New York: Columbia University Press, 1993).

cause others and the costs and benefits of using threats to discourage them. So moral philosophy is concerned with the appropriate occasions of blame, and political philosophy is concerned with those moral demands a state can make and back with threats; the demands themselves are identified without reference to the concept of a threat. Mill goes on to add that "reasons of prudence, or the interests of other people, may militate against actually expecting it; but the person himself, it is clearly understood, would not be entitled to complain."[32] Mill himself develops this picture in detail in *On Liberty*, where he looks to the likely consequences and interests of other people that militate against threatening people for their own good.

For the tradition from which I have selected Mill as spokesman, coercion has two key features. The first of these is that coercion involves the shaping of behavior through the making and carrying out of threats. The second is that it is extrinsic to the wrong that it is supposed to address.[33] Let me explain these two features more carefully. The basic idea of the first is that coercion is to be identified with the deliberate setting back of a person's interests in order to shape his or her behavior. The second is perhaps more familiar. The basic idea is that a person's interests are set back in order to accomplish something, and that setting back those interests is an effective way of accomplishing that thing. The person who steals something gets locked up for a few years, so that he, and others like him, will not be tempted to steal.

If coercion is understood in terms of sanction, it must have a secondary place in political philosophy, and not figure in its basic principle, as Kant suggests. The idea that the making of threats is somehow constitutive of law or the state is vulnerable to a familiar line of objection, made prominent by H. L. A. Hart.[34] According to Hart, sanctions do not lie at the heart of any adequate conception of law. A noncoercive law is perfectly conceivable, because the concept of a rule, the violation of which

---

32. John Stuart Mill, "Utilitarianism," in J. M. Robson, ed., *Essays on Ethics, Religion and Society: Collected Works of John Stuart Mill*, vol. 10 (Toronto: University of Toronto Press, 1969), 245.

33. For another example, see Joseph Raz, *The Morality of Freedom* (Oxford: Oxford University Press, 1986), 148–149. Raz offers a detailed definition that focuses exclusively on coercion by threats, "since this is the form of coercion relevant to political theory."

34. See Hart, *The Concept of Law* (Oxford: Oxford University Press, 1962), 20–25.

invites sanction, is conceptually prior to the concept of a sanction for its violation, and so cannot be reduced to it. Instead, any adequate account of law must begin with the concept of a rule or norm, rather than trying to reduce it to the concept of a threat.

Kant does not conceive of coercion in terms of threats, but instead as the limitation of freedom. As we saw, freedom in turn is understood as independence from being constrained by the choice of another person. His examples of coercively enforceable obligations are drawn from the juridical categories of Roman private law, and he was presumably aware, as are all students of that legal system, that it existed without a centralized enforcement mechanism for private actions.[35] His initial, and indeed paradigmatic, example of coercion is the right of a creditor to demand payment from a debtor, a right to compel payment, not a right to punish nonpayment.

This way of setting up the idea of coercion differs from the sanction theory in two key respects: what coercion is, and what can make it legitimate. First, it supposes that although threats are coercive, actions that do not involve threats can also be coercive. An act is coercive if it subjects one person to the choice of another. One person can be subjected to the choice of another either directly, through acts, or indirectly, through threats of such acts. Kidnapping, for example, typically includes a threat addressed to the victim's family or business associates, but the wrong of kidnapping is constraining—coercing—another person, quite apart from the further wrong of extortion, that is, using the kidnapping to shape the conduct of third parties through threats. It is both artificial and misleading to suggest that only the family members or business associates are coerced, and no less so to suggest that kidnapping is only coercive if the victim is threatened directly. A more plausible view is that both victim and those who pay ransom are coerced, though in different ways, and that the direct use of force is the basic case of coercion.

Second, Kant's conception of coercion judges the legitimacy of any particular coercive act not in terms of its effects but against the background idea of a system of equal freedom. That is, unlike Bentham, he begins with the concept of a rule, but the rules in question govern the le-

---

35. See, for example, Barry Nicholas, *An Introduction to Roman Law* (Oxford: Oxford University Press, 1962), 27.

gitimate use of force in terms of reciprocal limits on freedom. Coercion is objectionable where it is a hindrance to a person's right to freedom, but legitimate when it takes the form of hindering a hindrance to freedom. To stop you from interfering with another person upholds the other's freedom. Using force to get the victim out of the kidnapper's clutches involves coercion against the kidnapper, because it touches or threatens to touch him in order to advance a purpose, the freeing of the victim, to which he has not agreed. The use of force is rightful because an incident of the victim's antecedent right to be free. The kidnapper hinders the victim's freedom; forcibly freeing the victim hinders that hindrance, and in so doing upholds the victim's freedom. In so doing, it *also* makes the kidnapper do what he should have done, that is, let the victim go, but its rationale is that it upholds the victim's right to be free, not that it enforces the kidnapper's obligation to release the victim. The use of force in this instance is an instance of the victim's right to independence, and so is a consistent application of a system of equal freedom.

If coercion is understood as justified if and only if it restricts a restriction on freedom, it does not need to be identified with a sanction. Aggression is coercive; defensive force is also coercive. The latter is not a further wrong that requires a special justification; it is just the protection of the defender's freedom. The person using defensive force is neither sanctioning the aggressor nor carrying out a threat that was supposed to deter aggression.

Kant's claim that it is legitimate to use force to hinder hindrances to freedom thus incorporates his more general idea of a system of equal freedom. He does not start with the idea that it is always wrong to restrict the choice of another person, and then struggle to show that doing so is sometimes outweighed on balance, in the way that Bentham, for example, thinks that causing pain is always bad but legitimate when outweighed by a greater good produced. Instead, the initial hindrance of freedom is wrongful because inconsistent with a system of equal freedom; the act that cancels it is not a second wrong that mysteriously makes a right, because the use of force is only wrongful if inconsistent with reciprocal limits on freedom. So force that restores freedom is just the restoration of the original right.

Examples like kidnapping and self-defense may seem too narrow to generate a full account of legitimate coercion as the protection of freedom, since both kidnappers and aggressive attackers *set out* to restrict others. But the same point applies to defensive force against accidental wrongdoing: you can protect your person against interferences by others, even if those others are merely careless in injuring you.

At the level of innate right, the entitlement to hinder hindrances of your freedom is always defensive. It may also operate prospectively; the expectation that others will defend themselves might lead someone considering aggression to refrain. The principle of right does not need to be the incentive to conduct; an act is right if consistent with the independence of others, regardless of the person's reasons for acting. In the next chapter, we will see that the introduction of acquired rights adds a further dimension to a system of equal freedom and a corresponding dimension to the possibility of reciprocal coercion.

Bentham and Austin are easy targets for Hart's criticism because they suppose that legal (or moral) rules are instruments created to serve a purpose. From that starting point, it is natural, if not inevitable, that they should also suppose that every creation has a creator, and so conclude that a rule must be an expression of a conditional intention expressed in order to produce a result. Kant rejects both their instrumentalist conception of rules and their concomitant attempt to reduce norms to intentions. He is thus in a position to conceive of coercion differently, simply as the restriction of freedom.

VI. Conclusion

The innate right of humanity is the basis of any further rights a person must have, because it is the entitlement that each person has to self-mastery, and so, as a result, also a right that limits the ways in which force may be used. So long as every person acts in conformity with the innate right of others, no coercion is used; the entitlement to coerce is simply the entitlement that others exercise their freedom consistent with your own. This same structure of equal freedom understood as restrictions on coercion governs further aspects of right, including both private right and public right. In private right, it structures the further rights that each person can acquire, and the restrictions on the capacity to acquire new rights. At the level of public right, it also restricts the means available to the state in achieving its public purposes, and imposes certain mandatory duties on it.

CHAPTER 3

Private Right I: Acquired Rights

AS A PRINCIPLE limiting the actions of separate persons, the Universal Principle of Right is silent on rights with regard to external objects of choice, that is, those things *other* than your own person that you can use in setting and pursuing your own purposes. Your right to your own person does not depend on any further rights you might have, whether to property, or to affirmative deeds, or to loyalty[1] on the part of others. Others would need to restrict their conduct in light of your right to independence even if no other things could be used to set and pursue purposes. Kant's point is not that these dimensions of private interaction are unrelated to your right to your own person. The normative basis of acquired rights depends on your right to your own person, but rights to external objects of choice are not reducible to your right to your own person.[2]

---

1. I use the term "loyalty" here as it is used in the law of fiduciary obligations, to characterize an affirmative obligation to act on behalf of another person.

2. In this respect, Kant's account contrasts in interesting ways with the otherwise very different theories of property found in Locke and Hegel. Both Locke and Hegel treat property as an extension of a person, and so treat initial acquisition as the normative basis for property. Kant's approach begins with an account of the rightfulness of *owning* property via the postulate, and treats acquisition as a secondary matter. Kant's differences from Locke parallel their differing approaches to perception: Locke treats sensory input as the basis and structure

Kant characterizes the principle of acquired rights as a "postulate." It serves to extend the Universal Principle of Right in light of the possibility that there might be powers subject to a person's choice—means through which a person can set and pursue purposes—that persons who occupy space do not have as part of their innate right of humanity, but must acquire through affirmative acts. The Universal Principle of Right would govern the legitimate exercise of freedom by persons even if they were incapable of setting and pursuing purposes with anything other than their own bodies. Whether and which things other than your person can be used to set and pursue purposes is, at least in part, contingent on the particular features of finite purposive beings. You can only have something subject to your choice if you are normally able to determine how it will be used. Purposive beings that were unable to manipulate or modify physical objects could not have property in them, because those objects would not be available to them as means. Such beings would still have a right to their own person. Once the possibility of rightful relations that can be created through affirmative acts is introduced—the possibility that there are things other than your own body through which you might set and pursue your own purposes—the Universal Principle of Right can only be consistently extended in a way that makes it an extension of freedom rather than a limitation on it. Any such extension must be organized around the concept of choice, so that the significance of what Kant calls "external objects of choice"—objects that can be owned as property, the deeds of others, and, in specific contexts, the person of others—can all be had in ways that makes one person's having of them as his own consistent with the free purposiveness of others.

Kant characterizes it as a "postulate" because it specifies what must be presupposed if moral concepts are to be applied to a new class of objects in space and time. Neither the concept of right alone nor any set of facts about those objects is sufficient to prove it. But if proof is unavailable, the postulate can still be defended, by considering how to extend concepts of right to the case in which there are objects of choice "which could ob-

---

of thought; Kant conceptualizes them as input into the structure of thought that is normatively and conceptually antecedent to it.

jectively be mine or yours."³ Kant's focus on what can be mine and yours in general captures the distinctive feature of acquired rights: unlike your own body, the object of an acquired right could, in principle, belong as a matter of right to somebody else. This structure applies to each of the three types of external objects of choice that Kant considers: property, contract, and status. You could have bought this pair of shoes, but as it turns out, I am their owner, because I am the one who bought them. If you had acquired them instead, then you would have property in them—the same power to exclude others that I have with respect to them. You and I may have a contract that requires me to cut your lawn every Wednesday, but you could have hired someone else to do the same thing, or I could have entered into an agreement with someone else to cut her lawn on Wednesdays instead. Had either of us done these things, we would not have a contract with each other, but we would have parallel sets of rights and obligations, in relation to other persons. As a matter of right, you could have married someone other than your spouse, and, provided that neither of you was already married to somebody else, it would have been a binding marriage just the same. In each case, Kant provides a systematic account of the structure of the rightful relationship—which type of right you have—and shows how the question of *who* has the right can only be answered by reference to the affirmative act required to acquire that type of right. Answering the question of who has the right is not the same as determining what type of right it is, that is, how it constrains the choice of other persons. Kant's strategy is to articulate the nature of acquired rights before turning to the manner in which they can be acquired.⁴

This "could be mine or yours" structure does not apply to the innate right of humanity in your own person. Your right to your own person—your right that your body be free from interference by others, and that you be the one who decides what to do with your body—could not, as a matter of right, belong to anyone other than you. As we saw in the last chapter, it follows from this understanding of your right to your own per-

---

3. 6:246. Gregor's translation of Kant's *"Mein und dein"* as "mine or yours" underscores the way in which a right to something that exists apart from me must also be a right to something that is only contingently connected to *me*.

4. 6:247–248.

son, first, that the right is innate, so that it does not require an affirmative act to establish it, and second, that it can pertain only to you. Acquired rights, by contrast, must be acquired: they must be established through an affirmative act, and nothing in the object of acquisition places any limits on who, in particular, might acquire them by performing the requisite act. So long as the object of the right is something that can be acquired rightfully, and it has not already been acquired by another, then the form of the right itself places no limits on who might acquire it.[5]

I. Acquired Rights and Novel Incompatibilities

The general principle of acquired rights is that a person can have a right to something apart from him in such a way that others do wrong by interfering with it. The introduction of external objects of choice creates new ways in which my choice and yours with respect to some object can be incompatible. The potential incompatibilities (and the constraints on conduct they generate) that are introduced by acquired rights function in addition to the constraints of innate right. Innate right requires that you and I do not interfere with each other's bodies, as delimited by the space that they currently occupy. Precisely because the object of an acquired right could in principle belong to someone else, any object of choice that is yours must be subject to your choice even when it is not either in your physical possession or subject to your factual control. So long as you are in physical possession of the object—you have your hand wrapped around an apple—I violate your innate right of humanity by interfering with your physical possession of it, simply because in so doing I interfere with your person.[6] The postulate extends the principle of right to the case in which I can wrong you with respect to an object even if I am *not*

---

5. The formulation in the text deliberately oversimplifies what are, from the standpoint of the issue under consideration here, minor complications raised by Kant's discussion of marriage. Kant excludes morganatic marriages and marriages between persons of the same sex, and his remarks elsewhere make it clear that he would also exclude marriages between parents and their children. Even if we keep only the last of these exclusions, the "could be mine or yours" is not perfectly general in the case of marriage. However, even subject to these restrictions, marriage right is general in a way that innate right is not.
6. 6:250.

interfering with your person, thus setting up a potential *further* incompatibility between my deeds and your rights. In the same way, the postulate extends the principle of right to the case in which I have transferred my future conduct to you through a contract. Without the postulate, I would owe you no affirmative obligations of right; it makes such obligations possible by setting up an incompatibility between my nonperformance and your right.

As we saw in our discussion of innate right, as a general matter, others wrong you if they interfere with your person, but they do no wrong by changing the context in which you use your means to set and pursue purposes. To have an acquired external object as your own, as a matter of right, is to have something other than your own person, which others may not use or change without wronging you.

Given that external objects of choice introduce these new potential types of incompatibility, it might seem natural to conclude that people cannot have them after all. The postulate is "incapable of further proof" inasmuch as it claims that norms, understood as laws of freedom, apply to external objects. Like the claim that the Universal Principle of Right is a postulate incapable of further proof, the characterization of the postulate in those terms turns on issues to be considered in the appendix. The impossibility of further proof does not mean that Kant gives no argument for the postulate, or reduces it to a stipulation. The normative argument is supposed to show that acquired rights are the only possible extension of the Universal Principle of Right to the situation in which there are external things that can be used by free persons in setting and pursuing ends. If people are factually capable of using things other than their bodies to set and pursue purposes, the terms of their use of them must be consistent with right:

> For an object of choice is something that I have the *physical* power to use. If it were nevertheless absolutely not within my *rightful* power to make use of it, that is, if the use of it could not coexist with the freedom of everyone in accordance with a universal law (would be wrong), then freedom would be depriving itself of the use of its choice with regard to an object of choice, by putting *usable* objects beyond any possibility of being used; in other words, it would annihilate them in a

practical respect and make them into *res nullius,* even though in the use of things choice was formally consistent with everyone's outer freedom in accordance with universal laws.[7]

The Universal Principle of Right does not presuppose the existence of "usable" things other than your own person that can be used for setting and pursuing purposes. If nothing other than each person's own bodily powers could be used to set and pursue purposes, free beings would remain in a condition only of innate right. Once the possibility of using usable things is introduced, however, the Universal Principle of Right must apply to the terms on which those things can be used. If persons can set and pursue purposes by using something other than their own bodies—if there are things that persons have the physical power to use—they must be entitled to do so, unless such an entitlement would restrict the freedom of others to use what is theirs to set and pursue their own purposes. Kant's argument shows, first, that the only way that a person could have an entitlement to an external object of choice is if that person had the entitlement formally, because having means subject to your choice is prior to using them for any particular purpose. Second, Kant argues that the exercise of acquired rights is consistent with the freedom of others, because it never deprives another person of something that person already has. So anything less than fully private rights of property, contract, and status would create a restriction on freedom that was illegitimate because based on something other than freedom. This argument focuses on having things as your own, rather than on acquiring them. Acquisition of property, in particular, raises further issues central to the argument for a rightful condition.

Consider first the formal nature of purposiveness and so of freedom. If Kant's argument depended on a premise about the benefits of having things subject to your choice, or about the need for having external objects to fully realize your purposiveness, it could not generate a constraint on the conduct of others. Others owe you no enforceable duty of right to see to it that you receive a benefit, or even that your purposive-

---

7. Ibid.

ness is realized.[8] Right abstracts from both wish and need; if your need for my assistance in order to survive cannot generate a right that I provide it, your need for my forbearance in order that you realize yourself cannot generate a right to that either. Also, if the basis of property rests on the advantages to the owner's range of choices, the Coleridge/Maitland/Sidgwick line of objection would apply, since expanding one person's range of choices potentially restricts the freedom of others. By focusing on the formality of choice, Kant avoids this line of objection; he does not ask how much property people should have, or how it should be distributed, but only whether it is consistent with the purposiveness of others for one person to have an object subject to his or her choice.

The formal consistency of having things with the freedom of others turns on the nature of choice. To be entitled to set and pursue your own purposes is to be entitled to use the means that you have to set and pursue whatever purposes you see fit, restricted only by the entitlement of others to do the same with their means. External objects of choice can only be integrated into a system of freedom for everyone[9] if they are integrated formally, as means subject to a person's choice for whatever uses that person wants to put them to, rather than depending on the particular purposes for which they are used. The only terms on which *"usable* objects" can be available for use must thus be as things that are subject to one person's choice, and so as constraints on the freedom of others. If people are physically capable of using external objects to set and pursue their purposes regardless of how they choose to use them, external objects can be incorporated into a formal system of equal freedom, in which each person's purposiveness is restricted only by the purposiveness of others. No other person is wronged by another's having an object subject to his or her choice. The freedom of others would only be compromised if one person's having a proprietary or contractual right deprived some other person of something he or she already had. From the standpoint of each person's right of humanity in his or her own person, the acquired rights

---

8. Something like this thought appears to underlie Hegel's claim that property is required for personality because a self must externalize itself in an object outside of it. See his *Philosophy of Right* (Oxford: Oxford University Press, 1967), 40 (§41).

9. Or, as Kant puts it, at 6:230, "in accordance with a universal law."

of others are just parts of the context within which they choose. So any restrictions on the possibility of a person having objects as her own would restrict one person's purposiveness for the sake of something other than freedom, and so interfere with each person's right to be *sui juris*, her own master. That is, they would limit freedom on the basis of something other than its own conditions.[10]

The same rightful power to use something for setting and pursuing purposes extends to the use of the thing when you are not in physical possession of it. This point is most obvious in relation to property: if something is subject to your choice, available for you to use for setting purposes with, you must be able to use it for *whatever* purposes you set, which is just to say that you must be able to put it down while using other means that you have. Your right must constrain others against interfering with your pan as you put it down while you mix the eggs for your omelet. This is not because making omelets is a fundamental exercise of freedom, or even because making complex plans is, but because your entitlement to use something cannot depend on the particular purpose you use it for.

The requirement that usable objects be available for use applies in the same way to contractual rights: if it is *physically* possible for one person to transfer property or perform a service for another, or for two people to do things together, then other people's powers are usable objects of choice. It would be an arbitrary restriction on freedom if a person could not make his person or powers available to others in cooperative activities. There are limits, both to the conditions under which consent is possible and to the interaction to which a person can consent, but it would be an arbitrary limit on independence if any third party were entitled to prohibit one person from doing something for another, or two persons from doing things together. The entitlement to do things for others cannot be limited to present performances, so people must be able to enter into binding bilateral arrangements. Just as I do you no wrong by cooperating with another person, (absent some prior arrangement between us), so, too, you and a third person do me no wrong by entering into a binding arrangement, because you do not thereby deprive me of anything I already had. The most such arrangements can do is change the context in which the

---

10. 6:231.

person not party to it acts. Thus if it is possible for people to do things for each other, it must be rightfully possible, and so it must be possible for one person to have a right to another's specific choice.

A parallel point applies to status relations: if one person is physically capable of making arrangements on behalf of another, consistent with their respective rights, it must be possible to do so rightfully, because they wrong no others simply in virtue of so doing. If others could prohibit such arrangements, they would thereby restrict the freedom of the parties to them. One person's power to act for another only arises in limited circumstances and restricted ways. Whether such circumstances will arise depends on particular features of the persons involved and on the ends they happen to have. If nobody ever wanted another person to manage part of his affairs while he attended to another part, or if people had such limited purposes that they could attend to all of their details at once, or if they were never children or asleep, perhaps nobody would ever enter into a relation of status. Those factors have no bearing on the rightfulness of the relation, however: free persons must be *entitled* to entrust their affairs to others, even if nobody ever does.

II. Three Kinds of Acquired Rights

Kant identifies three ways in which something can be "one's own," that is, where it can operate as a constraint on the conduct of others. He remarks that acquired rights can be distinguished in three ways: by their matter, their form, and their mode of acquisition.[11] In explaining Kant's view, I will focus primarily on their form, referring only in passing to their matter, and defer to later chapters questions of their mode of acquisition.[12] To those familiar with Lockean theories of property, this may seem surprising. Locke famously locates the basis of private property in an account of its acquisition. Kant works in a different direction. Rightful ac-

---

11. 6:259–260.
12. Kant notes that the basis of acquisition in unilateral, bilateral, or omnilateral choice (*facto, pacto, lege*) "is not, strictly speaking, a special member of the division of rights" (6:260). Part of the difficulty is that unilateral choice also requires an omnilateral authorization, and so the division does not follow the division from Roman law of *facto, pacto, lege,* or of property, contract, and status.

quisition always changes the rights of other persons, but in order to understand how those rights are changed, the nature of the rights must first be grasped.

To claim something is yours is to draw a contrast: it is to say that it is yours, not mine, that is, that another wrongs you by interfering with your possession of it. There are three such ways in which something can be mine or yours: you can be entitled to an object, be entitled to the performance of a specific deed by another person, or have what Kant calls "a right to a person akin to a right to a thing." Underlying these divisions is the intuitive idea that separate persons who are free to set their own purposes can interact in three basic ways. Sometimes they pursue their separate ends separately, which requires rights to person and property. Sometimes they pursue them interdependently. If the terms of their interdependent pursuit are set consensually, they give each other rights by contract. If they are set nonconsensually, their relationship is one of status.[13]

Property. In order to set an end for yourself, that is, to take it up as an end that you pursue, you must take yourself to have the power to achieve it. Your entitlement to set and pursue your own purposes parallels your ability to do so: you must be entitled to use the means that you suppose will enable you to achieve it. There are two ways in which you can be entitled to such powers. First, as we have seen, you have your own personal powers, which you have innately; that is, your right to them does not depend upon any act that you, or anyone else, have performed. The development of those powers may be the result of previous acts of yours or of others— you might have your exercise routine or your personal trainer to thank for your strength, for example. But your right to these powers, as against anyone else who might wish to use them, does not depend upon how you came to have them. Second, you might have powers that are external to you, as means at your disposal. Whether you can adopt a particular end will depend upon the powers and means you have at your disposal.

---

13. For a related, though distinct, explication of Kant's division, see Ernest Weinrib, "The Juridical Classification of Obligations," in Peter Birks, ed., *The Classification of Obligations* (Oxford: Oxford University Press, 1997), 37–56.

For Kant, property in an external thing—something other than your own person—is simply the right to have that thing at your disposal with which to set and pursue your own ends. Secure title in things is prerequisite to the capacity to use an object to set and pursue ends.[14] Secure title has two parts to it, possession and use. You have rightful possession of a thing provided that you are entitled to control the thing and exclude others from it. Thus you are wronged if someone else damages your property, or trespasses against it.[15] If your property is damaged, you are deprived of means you could have used to set and pursue ends. If your property is trespassed against, it is used in pursuit of ends that you have not set for yourself. Moreover, trespass or damage to it limits your freedom even if, as a matter of fact, you had no inclination (or even empirical ability at that moment) to pursue those particular ends, and even if you can think of no use to which you might put it. You are wronged because you are deprived of your ability to be the one who determines how the thing will be used. You have the right to use a thing if you are free to exploit it to pursue such ends as you might set, and do not require the consent of anyone else in order to do so.

Because of the connection between having things at your disposal and setting ends for yourself, Kant develops his conception of property as an account of its metaphysics, rather than as an account of its place in specifically human societies. In particular, Kant makes no reference to scarcity or need in developing his account. Although, for reasons that will become clear, the specific ways in which human societies protect property rights will depend in part on the particular circumstances, needs, and vulnerabilities of humans, the basic structure of property is a reflection of the connection between having means and setting ends.

If we think about property in the terms which Kant suggests, we come to a distinctive, and I think deeper, understanding of the relation between wrongdoing and human need and vulnerability. H. L. A. Hart once suggested that law and morality are likely to overlap in human societies, since

---

14. This does not rule out shared possession. If we own something in common, we have the right to exclude others, and determine its use together. But this must be a derivative case, because it presupposes the idea of exclusive ownership. See 6:251.

15. 6:248.

both are concerned, among other things, with avoiding injury to human beings in the ways in which they are most vulnerable.[16] So, Hart suggests, if we had an invulnerable armored exterior, like giant land crabs, and were able to extract nutrition from the air, we would not have a law of battery, or of murder, or much of our law of property. But for Kant, law and morality demand prohibitions on trespass as well as injury, and would demand them even if trespasses were unusual, or injury unlikely, because Kant understands wrongdoing as the interference with freedom, not with the setting back of interests. Hart's giant land crabs might have little temptation to trespass on each other, but if they did so, they would do wrong, because they would use one another for ends they did not share. More vulnerable beings, such as humans, are perhaps more likely to be attacked, and to attack each other. But for Kant, the structural reason for protecting person and property is the same, that is, to protect independence.

Much of the structure of rights to property parallels my rights with respect to my own person, since it too is something which I can use to set and pursue ends—indeed, I could not set or pursue ends without it. I do not have property in my own person; I just am my own person. The fact that my own person lacks the "mine or yours" structure of property explains the inherent limits on my possessory rights, so that, for example, I may not alienate my own person. Despite these differences, I have rights in my person like those I have in external things. Like rights in property, those rights are rights that I have as against all other persons. And like rights in property, they extend to both possession and use.

Property is a kind of rightful relation. It is also definitive of a distinctive type of wrong, the wrong of interference. If you damage my property, you do not merely set back my interests. You wrongfully limit my external freedom because you limit the means I have with which to set and pursue my own ends. You thereby violate my entitlement to use my means as I see fit. If you trespass on my property—use it without my permission—you limit my ability to set the ends for which it will be used. You thereby violate my entitlement to possession, that is, to have the thing subject to my exclusive choice. Because rights to person and property protect per-

---

16. Hart, "Positivism and the Separation of Law and Morals," *Harvard Law Review* 71 (1958): 622–623.

sons from others with whom they interact independently, the law of both persons and property consists in negative prohibitions: I am not allowed to injure or trespass against you or your goods. By contrast, contract and status create affirmative obligations, because they are cases in which separate persons interact interdependently.

Contract. Contract enables parties to modify their respective rights, so that one person is entitled to depend upon the specified deed of another. If you and I make a contract, each of us agrees to do something for the other, and each of us transfers the right to expect that deed to the other. We act interdependently and consensually. Through our agreement, I do not acquire an external thing, but your deed.[17] People may rely upon the behavior of others in a variety of ways; contract is distinctive because it creates an entitlement: you can demand that I perform, and a remedy if I fail to, because I have failed to give you something to which you have a right. Without a contract, you have not been wronged if your expectations are frustrated. In the case of a contractual right against you, I do not possess you. I possess only your power to bring about a specified outcome in the manner specified by our agreement.

As a rightful relation, contract also makes a distinctive type of wrong possible. I wrong you if I deprive you of a means—my performance—to which I have given you a right. Put slightly differently, the wrong consists in my failure to advance your ends in a way that you have a right to have me advance them. That interferes with your external freedom, because I had given you a right to a means—my future performance—and deprived you of it. It is coercive for the same reason.

Because I acquire your deed, I have a right in contract only against you. So I have no right against a third person who does something that prevents you from performing your part of the contract. I have only recourse against you. (Though you may have recourse against that person.) Again, although third parties may benefit from our completion of the contract, they have no rights in virtue of it. Precisely because contract is a way in which two of us may give each other rights, it has no bearing on the

---

17. 6:248.

rights of anyone else; for the same reason, two persons may not enter into a contract to limit the rights of a third.

Status. The third category, which Kant calls "domestic right," is made up of those relationships in which people interact interdependently but not fully consensually. The best way to think about this category is by considering the more general role of consent in private right. Consent is significant from the standpoint of external freedom because it can make otherwise wrongful acts rightful. But those acts can be wrongful in two very different ways. Sometimes consent makes an interaction rightful because one person permits another to do something that would otherwise be an interference with his or her person or property. I invite you to dinner at my home. Without my consent, you would be interfering with my property by dirtying my dishes or consuming my food. Having invited you, I render what would have been wrongful rightful. Our consensual interaction is bilateral: I invite, you accept. Having accepted my invitation, your use of my things and consumption of my food is an instance of my entitlement to determine how they will be used.

But consent does not only prevent the wrong of damaging or destroying another's goods. The other type of wrong that it is able to right is the wrong of use, which, from the standpoint of external freedom, we can understand as forcing a person to act for an end that she does not share. If you permit me to use your dishes at the dinner party, my use of them to pursue my own ends is not wrongful, for, by consenting to that use, you have made my use of your things one of your ends. There is no interference with your external freedom. But if I use you to pursue my ends in other ways, without your consent, I thereby wrong you. Suppose that I break into your home and eat dinner at your table while you are out. (I bring my own food, and clean up after myself.) I do not harm you in any way, but I help myself to a benefit to which I am not entitled. I use your property in pursuit of one of my own ends, an end that you do not share. In so doing, I wrong you. Of course, if you consent, I do you no wrong. But the wrong in question—the wrong that consent serves to make right— is depriving you of your freedom to be the one who sets the ends that you will pursue, or that will be pursued with your goods. I enlist you or your means in support of ends you do not share.

I should perhaps pause at this point to remark that it is easy to be seduced by the idea of consent, and to suppose that it is a self-standing source of moral significance. This appears to be the view of some libertarians, for example. But consent does not work that way at all. We don't worry about the lack of consent except where we are concerned with an action that would be wrongful but for the presence of consent. So if you want to know what is wrong with exploitative relationships, say, it is not that they are nonconsensual. It is that they are exploitative. It is just that consent can sometimes make a relationship in which one person determines what ends another person's means will be used to pursue nonexploitative. If an act is not wrongful, no consent is required. A wrongdoer does not need to consent to the redress to which his victim is entitled. Nor do we determine the nature of that redress by asking what the parties would have agreed to in advance. Instead, we need to ask what would right the wrong.

There are three limits on the ways in which people may treat each other. First, one person may not interfere with another's person or property without the latter's consent. Second, where one has, through contract, transferred one's right to something to another, one must follow through on that transfer. Third, one person may not enlist another in pursuit of his own ends without the latter's consent. To violate any of these limits is to coerce the other person.

This now brings us to the category of status. There are some situations in which one person is unable to consent to certain kinds of use. Of the examples Kant discusses, the case of children is the clearest. Kant notes that parents bring children into the world of their own initiative and without the consent of the children.[18] As a result, children are nonconsenting parties to a relationship in which they find themselves. Further, so long as they are children, they are not competent to consent. Nor are they competent to exit the relationship. Precisely because the children are nonconsenting parties, parents may not use their children in pursuit of their own ends. Instead, they are subject to a duty to act for the benefit of those children, where the benefit is understood in terms of enabling the children to become purposive beings. Parents have possession of their children, but

---

18. 6:280.

they do not have the right to use them.[19] Falling under the duty to act for the benefit of the children is the right to "manage and develop them" so as to ensure that they become fully responsible persons. A child's parent or other legal guardian can authorize things to be done to the child, such as medical treatment, so those acts are not wrongs against the child.

Relations of status enlarge the purposiveness of those in control of them by entitling them to make arrangements for others; because the power is nonconsensual, their purposiveness is restricted, so that they can only exercise that purposiveness on behalf of those in their charge. They also enlarge the purposiveness of those for whom others make arrangements. If I entrust you to manage my affairs while I am away, my purposiveness is secured because you make arrangements *for* me, in pursuit of my normal purposes. Your purposiveness is enlarged because you get to determine how my goods will be used, subject to the condition that they not be used for your benefit. Thus those who interfere with a status relationship wrong both parties to it. If someone takes it upon himself to see to your child's religious education without consulting you, he wrongs you by depriving you of the power to "manage and develop" your child as you see fit. He also wrongs the child by depriving her of your management. The child is entitled to be in that relationship, with you in particular, even if it should turn out that some other person could do a better job of it.[20]

The category of status is just the category of cases in which persons

---

19. 6:260. The difference between Kant's account and the common law approach at that time is striking. At common law, a parent was entitled to the services of his minor children. See *Dean v. Peel* 1804 5 East 45.

20. Kant writes that parents bring a child into the world "without his consent and on [their] own initiative" (6:280). The phrase "on [their] own initiative" might suggest that parents incur obligation because they cause the children, or that they voluntarily undertake the obligation, but neither can be quite what Kant means. Instead, the obligation is incurred simply because the parents take control of their children. If the parents die or abandon a child, then the person who takes the child in has taken control and is obligated to manage and develop the child. But an interloper cannot come along and seize the child upon its birth, because that would be a wrong against the mother, who takes rightful possession of a child simply by giving birth to it. Nonetheless, if the interloper does succeed in taking the child, then the interloper has obligations to the child structured by status, even though the mother has a right against the interloper to reclaim the child.

find themselves in a relationship in which one party is not in a position to consent either to the existence of that relationship or to modification of its terms. As a result, the other party is not allowed to enlist the nonconsenting party in the pursuit of his or her own ends. In this, the situation is no different from other cases of nonconsent. It is just a feature of the relationship that makes ordinary consent impossible, rather than, as in the ordinary case, consent simply being absent.

Many other examples fit this structure. The legal relation between a fiduciary and a beneficiary is one such case. Where the beneficiary is not in a position to consent or decline to consent, or the inherent inequality or vulnerability of the relationship makes consent necessarily problematic, the fiduciary must act exclusively for the benefit of the beneficiary. It is easier for the fiduciary to repudiate the entire relationship by resigning than for a parent to repudiate a relationship with a child. But from the point of view of external freedom the structure is exactly the same: one party may not enlist the other, or the other's assets, in support of ends that the other does not share.[21] Third parties do wrong if they take over the fiduciary's role, even if they do a good job.

Again, consider a different example of a relationship subject to exploitation, namely that between teachers and students. Is it appropriate for a professor to have her graduate students help her move house, or to ask them to volunteer to work in her garden? The answer, I take it, depends upon whether we think of these kinds of interactions as fully voluntary. Insofar as we do, it is just one person doing another person a good turn at the latter's request, and merely a coincidence that the two persons also stand in another relationship. But where there is a lot turning on that other relationship, we may worry about the quality of the students' con-

---

21. The "acting for another" structure of fiduciary relationships explains what is wrong with insider trading. The difficulty is not that it harms the shareholders of the company. Indeed, many economists contend that it makes capital markets more efficient, and so in the long run redounds to their benefit. Instead, the problem is that it is an abuse of the office held by the insider. The knowledge that an officer of the company has in virtue of an office is available for purposes of managing the affairs of the company in the interests of its owners. To use the office for private gain is using the company, which belongs to other people, for private gain. By contrast, any person outside the company can use whatever information he legally acquires as he sees fit, though of course that person does so entirely at his own risk, since, as Kant puts it, it is up to that person whether to believe it or not.

sent. We worry about it, not because it necessarily harms the students to help, but because it exploits the students.[22]

The problem illustrated by the teacher/student example is not that the transaction in question lies outside of the terms of the contract (implicit or explicit) between them. It is rather that the relationship of dependence in which the student has been placed (if it is one), albeit via contract,

---

22. Another example Kant gives of a status relationship is marriage. He represents it as a relationship structured by symmetrical asymmetry. Two persons each have possession of the other, and so neither may act for private (i.e., extramarital) purposes. This legal power is extraordinary because it includes the entitlement to engage in sexual relations. That poses a special problem because Kant argues for the conclusion, later endorsed by very different thinkers, such as Jean-Paul Sartre and Simone de Beauvoir, that human sexuality inevitably involves regarding a sexual partner as an object. (On this issue, see Barbara Herman, "Could It Be Worth Thinking about Kant on Sex and Marriage?" in Louise Antony and Charlotte Witt, eds., *A Mind of One's Own* [Boulder: Westview, 1994], 49–67.) Their arguments have typically focused on the purported phenomenology of sexuality. Kant makes no reference to such factors. Instead, his claim that sexuality involves one person treating another as an object reflects his more general view about sexuality as simply the form of human animality. He ordinarily conceives of humans as embodied purposive beings, capable of freely setting their own purposes. This characterization is in line with his characterization in the *Critique of Pure Reason* of the concept of a person (as of a rightful condition) as an "Idea of Reason," that is, a rational concept that we are required on moral grounds to apply to particular things encountered in experience. One of Kant's other examples of an idea of reason is the idea of a living thing with its characteristic life form. This, as he explains in the second part of the *Critique of Judgment,* is to be understood in terms of a principle of natural teleology (see *Critique of Judgment* [Indianapolis: Hackett, 1987], 377–384). Natural teleology is not an empirical principle, but rather a rational one through which we are able to find distinctive forms of order, through which the parts of an organism are subordinated to the organism as a whole. A human being is thus both a biological organism, a living thing that we can organize under ideas of teleology, and also, and at the same time, a rational being, which we have a moral obligation to regard as free and purposive, and which any other person has an obligation of right to treat as a person rather than as a mere object. These two ideas come together to generate what Kant regards as the distinctive problem about human sexuality: sexuality is just the form of human animality. The purposiveness displayed in animality is not the purposiveness of freedom. Instead, it is simply the "natural urge" which has its principle of unity in its own natural expression (see *Doctrine of Virtue,* 6:424). In this respect, it differs importantly from any choice made on grounds of freedom. The animal is attracted to its potential biological mate through a principle of natural teleology. But because teleological beings do not have free purposiveness, anything that is the teleological natural end of an animal is a physical object. Consent cannot serve to make this sort of interaction rightful, because the object of the desire falls under the idea of natural teleology rather than that of human freedom. Thus, when animals mate, it is their natural teleology working together, rather than the purposive agency of either.

makes the conferral of this sort of benefit an unacceptable term of the contract.

Kant's example of household servants has the same structure, as do cases of employment contracts more generally. An employee is required to advance the employer's purposes, and is not allowed to use the employer's premises or goods for outside purposes. Unlike someone con-

---

Kant's central claim, then, is not, as Allen Wood has suggested, that sexuality is typically exploitative in bourgeois society (Wood, *Kantian Ethics* [Cambridge: Cambridge University Press, 2008], 228–229, 235, and 238). Instead, the fundamental point is that sexuality is animality, and satisfying an animal, rather than free urge, involves treating the object of that urge as mere material, to be consumed. Other animal urges raise no parallel problems. The desire to eat, for example, takes food as its object, but food is merely a natural thing. Only animal teleology directed at a person generates the problem.

Kant's solution to this problem is marriage. An ordinary contract won't do, because if sexuality involves treating a person as a thing, it cannot be the subject matter of a binding arrangement between persons. Thus a prostitution contract is never enforceable. Since a binding contract must concern things the parties are entitled to do, sexuality cannot be made rightful by the mere agreement of the parties. Instead, a spouse can only be acquired by entering a form of relationship in which each spouse has possession of the other. Marriage is a more general unity of two persons, so that each spouse's purposes become the other's. Thus everything they do is an exercise of their joint corporate purposiveness. Even the "animal" urges to which they yield are subsumed within their broader relationship. The two basic wrongs against a marriage, adultery and abandonment, are violations of that possession; the possession is reciprocal because both spouses can be wronged in both ways. If that is what a marriage is, Kant has explained how sexuality within it could be rightful, since each spouse is entitled to make arrangements for the other. He has also explained how such a relation could be entered into consensually, because neither party consents to become a mere object. Finally, it shows why particular sexual interactions within a marriage must be consensual between the parties, as otherwise each spouse would not be making arrangements for the other.

There are a number of aspects of this account that might be thought to be suspect. Most significantly, it is not clear why the distinction between natural teleology and purposiveness belongs in a book called *The Metaphysics of Morals*, let alone how it can be applied so readily to particulars. Further, Kant's distinctions between "natural" and "unnatural" types of sexual activity reflect his conception of sexuality as animal teleology: the function of the sexual urge is the preservation of the species. Yet the *function* of an end could only be relevant to its matter rather than its form. Moreover, even if Kant's full characterization of sexuality is accepted, it does not establish that natural teleology cannot be rationalized by being taken up by a free person, and so turned into a form of reciprocal free purposiveness. A more Kantian alternative would be a sort of layering of rationality over animal teleology, as is suggested, for example, in Christine Korsgaard's *Self-Constitution* (Oxford: Oxford University Press, 2009). Perhaps the best way to read Kant's argument takes marriage to be the rational manner in which reproductive animality can be taken up.

tracted to perform a single task, an employee is subject to the employer's direction, and within that direction the employee's acts are imputable to the employer. That is why employers can be bound by contracts made by their employees, and can be held vicariously liable for the wrongs committed by them, but only insofar as the employee is acting within the terms of the employment relation. Although the arrangement is entered into contractually, its terms are given by the nature of the relationship itself, in which one person makes arrangements for another.[23]

We are now in a position to triangulate the category of status in relation to property and contract. In property, I have both possession and use of the thing. In contract, I have a limited right to the use of your powers for my purposes, but I do not possess you. In the third category, I have possession of you but am not entitled to use you for my own purposes. Let me perform the same triangulation in terms of the wrongs in question. The wrong in property is that of interfering with another's ability to set and pursue such ends as he has set for himself. The wrong in contract is failing to use your means in a way that you have given your contracting partner a right to have them used. The wrong in status is using another person to advance your ends. In so doing, you deprive that person of the freedom to set his own ends.

Relations of status arise in situations where consent is absent, impossible, or insufficient. The terms of those relations are governed by the freedom of the parties to them. As Kant explains in his discussion of public right, any arrangements one person makes for another are only consistent with the freedom of the other if that person could have consented to the arrangements that are made. The test of possible consent does not suppose that a person could only agree to whatever is most advantageous to him or her, but only requires that the capacity for possible agreement is bounded by each person's rightful honor. You could not consent to be treated as an object available for others to use in whatever ends they saw fit. You could, by contrast, consent to have someone manage your affairs in ways consistent with your continued purposiveness—to administer

---

23. On conceptual barriers to reducing fiduciary obligations to contractual ones, see Paul Miller, "The Fiduciary Obligation," doctoral dissertation, University of Toronto, 2007.

medical treatment to you while you are unconscious, to "manage and develop" you as a child, or to invest your retirement savings on your behalf.

Are wrongs against property, contract, and status the only possible types of wrongs against external freedom that one private person can commit against another? I believe that they are, and I will offer a brief and intuitive argument to show why. External freedom is a matter of being able to set and pursue your own ends. The only ways it can be interfered with is by interfering with either the capacity to set or the capacity to pursue those ends. As a private person, you can only interfere with another person's capacity to *pursue* ends in two ways—either by wrongfully depriving someone of a means she already has, or by failing to provide her with a means to that pursuit to which you have given her a right. You violate a property right by using or destroying the means a person already has; you violate a contractual right by failing to provide her with means—your action—to which you have given her a right. If her means are intact, you can interfere with the capacity to *set* ends in only one way—by making someone pursue an end she has not set for herself, either by using her goods without her permission or by using a relationship you have with her for private purposes.[24]

The argument that these three categories exhaust the possible interference with external freedom depends on the two premises which follow from the Universal Principle of Right but need to be made explicit. The first is that we are concerned here with the ways in which one private party may wrong another, not with whatever further powers a public authority can have to uphold a system of equal freedom.

The second is that harm, as such, is not a category of wrongdoing. In particular, interference with the successful attainment of a particular end is not an interference with external freedom. Harms and benefits—the advancing or setting back of the interests of a person—are only incidental to this analysis. Let me illustrate this with a pair of examples. Suppose that you and I are neighbors. You have a dilapidated garage on your land

---

24. Many apparent counterexamples actually illustrate this division. For example, some have suggested that such practices as advertising and religious indoctrination (perhaps especially when aimed at young children) interfere with freedom. They are controversial because people disagree about whether they fall into our third category.

where our properties meet. I grow porcini mushrooms in the shadow of your garage. If you take down your garage, thereby depriving me of shade, you harm me, but you do not wrong me in the sense that is of interest to us here. Although you perform an affirmative act that worsens my situation—exposure to light destroys my mushrooms—I do not have a right, as against you, that what I have remains in a particular condition. Although I do have a right to my mushrooms, which prohibits you from doing such things as carelessly spilling fungicide on them, I do not have a right that you provide them with what they need to survive, or that you protect them from things that endanger them apart from your activities. Thus you do not need to protect them from light by erecting a barrier unless your use of the land is the source of that light. Nor do you need to continue to provide a barrier that has protected them in the past. The distinction between depriving me of what I already have as opposed to failing to provide me with what I need does not turn on the difference between action and inaction. If I grow sunflowers in my yard and you put up a garage on yours, thereby depriving me of light, you harm me but do not wrong me, because all you have done is fail to use your land in a way that provides me with something I need.

These examples assume, as Kant does, a specific way of thinking about property in land, according to which it is a right to a specific region of the Earth's surface. The most fundamental, though also extreme, implication of this is that your decision to occupy, or fail to occupy, any part of the space making up your land raises no issues of the rights of others. As a result, they have no grounds to complain if you build on your land in a way that blocks something from reaching it, because, absent some prior arrangement, they have no right to a path across your land. Nor can they complain if you do not use your land to block some unwelcome force from entering it. But the point is much more general: others not only have no right that you use what is yours in a way that best suits their preferred use of what is theirs, they have no right that you use what is yours to preserve what they have.[25] Your right to your property does not place others under an obligation to take steps to ensure that what you have remains in

25. *Mayor, etc. of Bradford v. Pickles*, [1895] AC 587 (HL), and *Fountainbleau Hotel Corp v. Forty-Five Twenty-Five, Inc.* 114 So. 2d 357 (Fla. Dist. CA 1959).

its present condition. You only have a right that others not damage or destroy what is yours by using what is theirs in ways inconsistent with universal law. Your right to a thing must limit the ways in which others may interfere with what *you* own, but cannot extend to a right to require others to use what *they* own in ways that suit your particular purposes, and the preservation of what you own is just one of your purposes.[26]

Conversely, I may benefit from your shade (or light), and I do not need to secure your consent in order to derive that benefit. I can just help myself to it. Nor can you demand payment as a condition of my reaping that benefit, except in the sense that you can threaten to exercise your right to withdraw it unless I agree to pay. But my liberty to use it is not a feature of your implicit consent. It is just my good fortune.

Focusing on wrongs also identifies the rights that are at issue. A right is a restraint on the conduct of others, which can be identified by the deeds it proscribes. A property right is a right to possession and use of an object, that is, a restriction on the entitlement of others to use the thing (possession) or make it unusable (use). A contract right is a right to a specific deed on the part of another person, that is, a restriction on the entitlement of that person to use his powers in a contrary way. A status right is a right to a person "akin to a right to a thing," that is, a right to affect that person without his consent, and a corresponding obligation to avoid using the person. Relations of status are inherently asymmetrical,[27] and so can only be made rightful by restricting the freedom of the right holder to act for the purposes of the other person. Thus they generate interdependent rights and duties: the person who is entitled to make arrangements for another can constrain the conduct of anyone else who interferes with the possibility of doing so, and can be constrained to make those arrangements solely for the purposes of the other.[28]

---

26. Kant makes the connection between property rights and the occupation of space explicit at 6:262 and 6:268. My property right in land is the right to exclude others from the physical space that makes it up, and so cannot extend to limit what you do with your space.

27. This applies even to the case of marriage: each spouse makes arrangements *for the other*, and must do so in a way that does not subordinate the second to the purposes of the first.

28. Kant makes the same point in terms of the categories of relation: substance, causality, and community. These govern the "matter" of rights to external objects of choice. A person

These three types of wrong are, I have suggested, exhaustive of wrongs that interfere with external freedom. They need not be mutually exclusive. For example, in cases of fraud, one person might violate the freedom of another in each of the three ways. If I fraudulently sell you an unprofitable business, and, not realizing your mistake, you throw good money after bad, trying to make it profitable, I interfere with your freedom, because I mislead you into squandering your resources. As between us, it is as though I had destroyed those resources. But in the same case, I also enter into and breach a contract with you, and you are entitled to complain that I have failed to do that which I undertook to do, namely sell you a valuable business. Again, on the same facts, I use you in a circumstance in which your consent is vitiated (because you are operating under a mis-

---

could have a right to a corporeal thing (substance), another's performance (causality), or another person by being entitled to make arrangements for them (6:260). In the *Critique of Pure Reason*, trans. and ed. Allen Wood and Paul Guyer (Cambridge: Cambridge University Press, 2007), Kant introduces the "Table of Judgments" as forms of judgment, noting that a categorical judgment joins two concepts, a hypothetical judgment joins two propositions, and a disjunctive judgment "contains the relations of two or more propositions to one another, though not the relation of sequence, but rather that of logical opposition, insofar as the sphere of one judgment excludes that of the other, yet at the same time the relation of community, insofar as the judgments together exhaust the sphere of cognition proper" (A73–74/B99). The table of judgments is then brought to bear on possible experience under the categories of relation, substance, causality, and community. Applied to rights to external objects, the same classification yields the division property/contract/status: rights to objects/performances/making arrangements for others. Considered in terms of the form of the right, a property right is a right to independent choice, to an object considered as substance, and is a right that persists though changes in the object; a contractual right is a right to dependent choice, in which one person's choice is subject to another's with respect to some particular deed, so that the former is constrained to bring about some result for the latter; a status right is a right to mutual determination in the sense that one person is entitled to choose for the other and thereby bound to choose *for* the other. In choosing for another, a person is thereby precluded from choosing for himself. Thus the exclusion of a person in a relationship of status from using possession of the other for his or her own purposes is an expression of the relation of mutual exclusion characteristic of disjunctive judgments and so of relations of community in the *Critique of Pure Reason*. Kant also characterizes the property/contract/status division as referring to "a right to a thing," "a right against a person," and "a right to a person akin to a right to a thing," remarking that the three categories are generated by applying the distinction between rights to something and rights against to the distinction between persons and things. Those paired distinctions yield a fourfold distinction, but as Kant notes, there could not be a right against a thing, because a thing is not free and so not subject to obligation (6:357).

take I have created) and you can rightfully demand that I be deemed to have been acting on your behalf, and so disgorge my gains to you on the grounds that they were your gains all along. Of course, on particular facts, perhaps only one description will actually fit. But the fact that I have interfered with your freedom in one way does not mean that I have not interfered in another.

III. Coercion

Because each of these three types of wrong interferes with the ability of the aggrieved party to set or pursue his or her own ends, each of these wrongs against external freedom is inherently coercive. Of course, that wrongs are inherently coercive does not show that the prohibition of wrongs—a set of reciprocal limits on freedom—is coercive. Indeed, if everyone acts within those limits, and no one commits a wrong of any of the three types, no coercion occurs. Coercion enters the account in a different way.

As we saw in Chapter 2, Kant explains the idea of coercive enforcement in terms of the hindering of a hindrance to freedom.[29] If each person is entitled to use his or her powers to set and pursue his or her own purposes, the only legitimate restrictions on that purposiveness are imposed by the purposiveness of others. This system of mutual restriction entails that each person's entitlement to use means is restricted by the entitlements of others, and so the restrictions are part of the same system of equal freedom. At the level of innate right, hindering a hindrance can mean nothing more than what Kant calls "protective justice,"[30] that is, defensive force to repel another who attempts to touch you without your authorization.

Once acquired rights are introduced, both this minimal protective form of hindrance and a further, remedial form of hindrance become possible. You can grab your coat to prevent me from taking it, even though in so doing you frustrate my pursuit of my ends. You can refuse to aid me when I enlist you in one of my projects, so, for example, you can lock

---

29. 6:232.
30. 6:306.

your doors to hinder me from taking my afternoon nap in your bed. And if I am about to abuse a relationship in ways to which you are incapable of consent, I can be removed from that relationship, even if I prefer to remain in it. In each case, the fact that I wish to persist in hindering your freedom—the fact that I do not consent to be hindered—does not matter, because in each case our reciprocal freedom is being protected. The fact that I object to it does not entitle me to complain, because, as we have seen, consent is only relevant where the conduct in question would otherwise be wrongful. In these examples, however, allowing me to persist would be wrongful; hindering my wrong would not, so consent is not required. In the first instance, then, the idea of a hindrance of a hindrance is just the idea that norms of external freedom are supposed to guide conduct, but, being norms of external freedom, they can guide it externally.

This first, prophylactic sense of hindering a hindrance does not exhaust the possibilities of coercion. In each of our examples, the hindrance frustrates my achievement of a particular aim, but does not interfere with my ability to set and pursue my own ends. That is, at least in part, an artifact of the particular examples. But at least some prophylactic hindrances do not hinder external freedom.

The idea of the hindrance of a hindrance has a second, retrospective aspect to it as well. What is hindered in this case is not wrongful action but its impact on the external freedom of others. In an ideal world, no person hinders the external freedom of another, either because such hindrance doesn't happen or because, if it does, it is hindered directly. But sometimes a wrong will be completed, and if it is, its *effects* must be hindered in order to maintain the external freedom of the aggrieved party. If one person acts coercively against another, the latter is entitled to redress. So, for example, if I injure you or damage your property, you are entitled to compensation. You must be made whole, so that the embodiments of your external freedom are as they would have been had I not wronged you. The same applies if I fail to honor a contract I have made with you. You are entitled to be put in the position you would have been in had my choice—itself an embodiment of *your* freedom because I transferred it to you—been exercised as I was obligated to do. Again, if I manage to enlist you in support of my projects without your consent, I must surrender to you any gains I make as a result. I must do so because the use I made of your right to set your own ends must be treated as an embodiment of your freedom, and so given back to you. So, for example, if you invite tourists to explore the caves under your land, and lead them underground to the caves under mine, you must disgorge any gain you received from the use of my caves, even if I could not have capitalized on them on my own, and even if, had we entered into a contract, I likely would have agreed to let you use them on more favorable terms.[31]

Kant says that if another has wronged me and I have a right to receive compensation from the wrongdoer, "by this I will still only preserve what is mine undiminished."[32] In determining the appropriate remedy, right does not ask what parties would have agreed to, because they did not agree, and it would be inconsistent with the freedom of the aggrieved party to hold him or her to the terms of an agreement that was never entered into. Instead, right looks only to what the aggrieved party had prior to the wrong. Using another's person or property without his or her permission is never consistent with freedom for all. Because the property exists for the benefit of its owner, the only way to redress another's use of it is to treat that use as though it were done solely for that person's benefit. Another way of making the same point is to say that I am entitled to the proceeds of my property, since it is a means toward the ends I chose to adopt. Should you use my property in pursuit of ends I do not share, I am entitled to the proceeds of that pursuit, as I would have been had it been done rightfully, that is, on my behalf. The fact that you wronged me by acting in ways to which I did not consent cannot be used as a basis for depriving me of my right to the proceeds of my property.

In each of these examples, the wrong is redressed coercively, in just the same sense in which, in our prophylactic examples, the wrong was hindered coercively. That is, the redress is coercive in the sense that the wrongdoer does not need to make its redress one of his ends. Instead, the aggrieved victim is entitled to reclaim what is rightly his, regardless of what the wrongdoer might think. So, for example, I can reclaim my property from you, even if you took it by mistake. Moreover, I can require that you return it in the condition in which you took it. That is because my

---

31. *Edwards v. Lee's Administrator* 96 S.W. 2d 1028 (1936).
32. 6:271.

right to equal freedom just is my right to set and pursue my ends using the means to which I have a right, and keeping my property is a matter of being able to set and pursue my ends.

Because wrongdoing grounds redress, coercive enforcement of private remedies can also operate to deter wrongdoing, for deterrence is just the public manifestation of the prophylactic sense of coercion. If I am allowed to interfere with your freedom to protect my own—by locking my doors, or taking the bicycle you promised me—I am thereby allowed to operate on your capacity for choice indirectly. Other, less mechanical means can operate in the same prospective way. So if I honor my contracts, or keep my hands off your goods, because I fear that I will be made to disgorge my gains or repair your losses, your rights operate on my capacity for choice indirectly. Any indirect means of bringing my conduct into conformity with right will be acceptable, provided only that they be means that can apply to all, and do not interfere with freedom any more than they must to hinder the initial hindrance. That is just to say that the prospect of enforcing rights may be used to protect right.

If we think of the coercive rights inherent in the law in terms of restraint and redress, we have rejected the key elements of Mill's account of coercion as we considered it in Chapter 2. Recall that for the tradition for which I am treating Mill as spokesman, coercion has two key features. The first of these is that it interferes with a person's liberty, by imposing a cost on that person that he or she would not otherwise have borne. The second is that it is extrinsic to the wrong that it hopes to address.

We have rejected the first strand in Mill's account, which says coercion involves making a person bear a cost she would otherwise not have borne because we lack the relevant baseline. Against the background of norms of equal freedom, the person prevented from completing a wrong is not being made to bear a cost she otherwise would not have borne; she is just being made to respect the rights of others. The same point applies if the wrong is completed and the wrongdoer is made to pay damages or disgorge a wrongful gain. It is no doubt true that had we left the loss where it falls, or let her keep her gain, she would have kept something she must now give up, and so the enforcement of a right makes the wrongdoer bear a burden she would not have borne if the right had not been enforced. That is the wrong comparison. The appropriate baseline is not the having of the wrongful gain, but its lack. Again, the baseline is not the loss lying where it falls, but rather the loss lying where it belongs, that is, with the wrongdoer.

We have also rejected the second strand, which says that enforcement is extrinsic to the wrong. In cases of redress, the use of force restores a regime of equal freedom. Of course, it may also provide an incentive to the wrongdoer, or to other wrongdoers. From the point of view of equal external freedom it does not matter why people act in conformity with the demands of right, so long as they do so. Provided they do so, they do not interfere with the ability of others to set and pursue their own ends. But the point of coercive enforcement is not to provide such incentives, but rather, quite literally, to set things right. Perhaps the best way to see this is to think about the example where the wrong has occurred as a result of an honest mistake. I mistakenly take your coat, thinking it to be my own, having absentmindedly forgotten that I did not bring a coat this morning. You are entitled to reclaim your coat, even if I persist in my honest mistake. It would, I think, be peculiar to suppose that your right to forcibly reclaim your coat is to be understood in terms of its incentive effects. You are allowed to reclaim your coat, not because allowing you to do so will lead me or anyone else to be more careful in keeping track of whether he wore a coat in the morning, or even to be more careful in general in keeping track of his stuff. You get to reclaim your coat because it is your coat.

IV. Conclusion

The innate right of humanity does not presuppose the existence of means for setting and pursuing purposes other than each person's own body. Once the possibility that there are such external means is introduced, the Universal Principle of Right must be extended to make their use consistent with every person's freedom. That extension must be formal: if usable objects are to be used rightfully, people must have them available to use for whatever purposes they set, restricted only by the entitlement of others to use their external means as they see fit, rather than on the basis of the particular ends being pursued. Acquired rights require affirmative acts to establish them, but the form of the rights, including the ways in which they restrict the freedom of others, are conceptually prior to questions of their mode of acquisition.

CHAPTER 4

Private Right II: Property

THE THEORY OF PROPERTY is often thought to be a topic only of interest to libertarians or lawyers. Most recent political philosophy conceives of property as a sort of power the state confers on private persons as part of a broader distributive agenda, a sort of public law carried out by other means. Lockean theories of property stand in sharp contrast, seeking to ground property rights in the distinctive act of original acquisition.

Kant rejects both of these approaches. Against the "public law in disguise" model of property rights, Kant shows how it is a structure of rightful relations between private persons, the form of which can be understood without reference to the state. As we saw in the previous chapter, the possibility of a rightful relation with respect to property follows from the postulate of practical reason with regard to rights, which is supposed to show that it must be possible to have rights to things other than your own person or powers, insofar as these other things could be available as means for setting and pursuing your own purposes. For purposive beings, for whom having means is prior to setting ends, the entitlement to have something subject to their choice must be abstract, because it must not depend on the content of their particular choices. Your freedom to decide just is your freedom to use what is yours for your own purposes.

As we saw, it follows from this that insofar as having objects of choice as your own is consistent with the freedom of others, it is therefore rightful. Thus the *structure* of property rights—the basic rights of possession and use through which one person is entitled to constrain the conduct of others—can be explicated fully in terms of a "state of nature" without any reference to public law, but property rights are only enforceable in a rightful condition.

Kant's claim that concepts of property can be explicated in terms of the state of nature is not supposed to show that property rights are complete outside of a civil condition, or even that interference with the property of another is *prima facie* wrong in a state of nature. To the contrary, he says that "no one is bound to refrain from encroaching on what another possesses," in a state of nature, and that "those who intend to remain in a state of nature do each other no wrong" by interfering with each other's property, even though they "do wrong in the highest degree" by willingly remaining in a state of nature.[1] Kant also uses the concept of a state of nature to characterize a system of purely private interaction, to capture those aspects of right that, although they "take effect only in a public rightful condition, . . . are not based only on its Constitution and the chosen statutes in it: they are also conceivable a priori in the state of nature, and must be conceived as prior to such statutes, in order that the laws in the civil condition may afterwards be adapted to them."[2] In his lectures Kant refers to this second characterization of a state of nature as an "idea of reason," that is, a pure system of rational concepts of right.[3] It is in this sense, then, that property can be understood in terms of the state of nature: both its relation to freedom and the characteristic violations of it can be explicated without reference to positive legislation. That does not mean that property can be acquired, or its norms be applied to particulars or enforced in the absence of a rightful condition. It means only that the form of interaction in which property rights constrain the conduct of others does not depend on positive law.

---

1. 6:307.

2. 6:291.

3. Kant, *Lectures on Ethics*, trans. P. Heath (Cambridge: Cambridge University Press, 1997), 27:589.

Kant's argument that property is structured by "natural law" but can only be rightful in a public rightful condition stands in sharp contrast to many of the familiar themes of the public law model. One such theme contends that property is a "bundle" of disparate rights, with each stick in the bundle directed at a different purpose, and no principle to unify them.[4] Thus the various "incidents" of property, such as the right to exclude, the right to capital value, the right to use, are said to be separate powers that the law "grants" to owners based on some assessment of the balance of disparate interests. Kant does not explicitly consider the bundle theory, but his discussion of property contains the only possible mode of argument available to respond to it, by showing its unifying structure. As we have seen, his argument for the postulate of practical reason with regard to rights is that if you are physically capable of having means other than your person available to you for setting and pursuing purposes, consistent with the freedom of everyone, you can have a right to those means. Having things subject to your choice must be understood in terms of their being subject to your purposiveness, and so to your exclusive use of them. Your rights to property thus parallel your right to your own person, but because property is something that exists in a different location from you, your right to it can be violated when you are not in possession of it, and further, because it is separate, you can alienate it, either by abandoning it or by transferring it to another person via contract. Once property rights are understood as parallel to the rights each person has in his or her own person, the bundle metaphor falls apart. Your right to your own person includes many of the same incidents, but few are ready to conclude that it, too, is just a bundle.[5]

---

4. Wesley Newcomb Hohfeld, *Fundamental Legal Concepts as Applied in Judicial Reasoning*, ed. David Campbell and Phillip Thomas (Aldershot: Ashgate, 2001), 75; A. M. Honoré, "Ownership," in A. G. Guest, ed., *Oxford Essays in Jurisprudence* (Oxford: Oxford University Press, 1961), 107–147. Honoré treats "full ownership" as basic, and so resists this attempt to dismantle the concept of property wholesale. Instead, he explains how both private transactions and public law can allow a particular ownership claim to be dismantled "retail" in various ways.

5. The public law in disguise theory can be restated not as a thesis about entitlements, but rather as an attempt to debunk the entire idea of entitlements by presenting them as the products of brute political power. This mode of argument probably dates back to Thrasymachus in Plato's *Republic*. Many who would recoil from Thrasymachus's broader argument believe

The public law in disguise model is also sometimes put forward not as a claim about ordinary concepts of property, but rather as a claim about the entitlement of society as a whole to make decisions about the appropriate allocation of resources. From Kant's perspective, this suggestion does not even manage to be an alternative to his conception of private property. The power of the state to allocate land and chattels based on its priorities, and to determine the ways and terms on which they can be used, is a large-scale version of a property right. As Kant remarks against Grotius's claim that private property originates in a past agreement to divide up communal property, any such primitive community is not just a fiction but presupposes the very thing that needs to be explained. The concept of communal property would "have to be one that was *instituted* and arose from a contract whereby everyone gave up private possessions."[6] Otherwise the community would not be an owner, but would just be a usurper, with no power to divide "its" assets. Thus collective property raises the same questions as the theory of private property: why does this person or group have the power to decide, and limit the ability of private persons to use things in pursuit of their purposes? Those questions in turn resolve into the two issues that Kant's theory of property addresses: What powers does a person or group have in owning a thing? How can something that is not already owned come to be owned?[7]

---

that it can be deployed selectively, and the concept of property is a favorite target, typically supported by claims about the ways in which uses of resources have varied through human history. This factual assertion is irrelevant to Kant's view about the normative structure of property. Kant's claim that concepts of freedom have a rational basis is not a claim about their being obvious to every human being; grasping the full structure of something that is *a priori* is still a human achievement. Moreover, the claim that a normative concept can be grasped is not an assertion about the inevitable causal efficacy of grasping it.

6. 6:251.

7. A prominent variant on this argument claims that wealth, in particular, is created by social institutions rather than by individual labor; the role of those institutions is supposed to show that society is entitled to tax wealth. See, for example, Thomas Nagel and Liam Murphy, *The Myth of Ownership: Taxes and Justice* (New York: Oxford University Press, 2002). Such an argument provides a possible answer to the Lockean assertion that property rights are grounded in labor, but the terms on which it engages the Lockean argument also reveal its limits. It shares with that argument the premise that those who produce something have a right to constrain others in relation to that thing. The premise itself is indefensible, regardless of the scale on which it is supposed to operate.

Kant's specific way of rejecting the public law in disguise model does not commit him to accepting the broadly Lockean position that is often held out as the only alternative. Against that model, he rejects the aspect of property that Lockean theories suppose to make it prepolitical, namely its acquisition. The core of his argument, which will be considered in detail in Chapter 6, is that a purely unilateral act of acquisition can only restrict the choice of all other persons against the background of an omnilateral authorization, which is possible only in a condition of public right. This point is central to Kant's entire political philosophy, because it shows that what Lockean theories regard as the most straightforward private act presupposes a complete account of the nature of public, political authority. If property rights are only "provisional" outside of a rightful condition, it also follows that they are not enforceable.

The act of acquiring a piece of property is something that one person does on his or her own initiative, which changes the normative situation of others. Acts that were formerly permissible are now forbidden: if you acquire a piece of land, I can no longer use or interfere with it. Whether the act of acquisition places those others under an obligation or only a presumptive obligation, or simply authorizes the appropriator to exclude others from the thing acquired, it is a unilateral act through which one person changes the normative situation of another. As such, the acquisition of property presupposes an account of political authority, of how a merely permissible act can impose a normative constraint on someone other than the agent.

The focus of this chapter is not on the role of the state, but rather on the structure of property: the ways in which one person's property right constrains the conduct of others. All of this can be understood without reference to an omnilateral authorization. So, too, can the part of the theory of acquisition that can be characterized in a "state of nature," without reference to any political institutions. Kant's strategy is to first explain what it is to have a property right in a thing. His subsequent account of what it is to acquire property is simple and even boring, because it is the answer to a very simple question: how can something that is previously unowned make it into a system of property rights? The simple question gets a simple answer: an object becomes subject to somebody's choice when that person takes control of it.

The nature of a property right is structured by the basic requirement of a system of equal freedom in a world in which free persons can use things other than their bodies to set and pursue their purposes. That is why, as we saw in the previous chapter, property rights constrain others in ways parallel to the way rights to your own person constrain others. Your body is your person, and it constrains others because it is that through which you act, your capacity to set and pursue purposes, and any interference with your body interferes with that capacity. Your property constrains others because it comprises the external means that you use in setting and pursuing purposes; if someone interferes with your property, he thereby interferes with your purposiveness.

The same point can be made through the distinction, from Chapter 2, between a person's means and the context in which that person uses them. A changed context raises no issues of right, because it is the inevitable result of people's exercise of their freedom. A system of property is a system in which persons have rights to means others than their bodily powers, and others may not change those means or their availability. If you could not have a right to something in your absence, everything except your bodily powers would be mere context, subject to the choice of others.

The relation of property to setting and pursuing purposes underlies both its rationale and its structure. Freedom requires that external means that can be used in setting and pursuing purposes be available *formally:* an owner's entitlement to use them does not depend on the matter of the owner's or any other particular person's choice. For the same reason, a property right needs to constrain others even when the owner is not in physical possession of an object. Otherwise whether an object was available to the owner to set and pursue purposes would depend on the particular choices of others, and so violate the formality condition. As a matter of fact, you may be able to set yourself the end of making a mushroom omelet without having rights to objects that are not in your physical possession, but you could not have an entitlement against others to set yourself the end of making one. If there were no such rights, someone else would be entitled to take the eggs you had gathered while you were sautéing the mushrooms, and you would not be entitled to do anything to stop her. Your entitlement to set and pursue purposes would thus depend on the particular choices made by another. Again, the fact that some other person needs or wants what you have more than you do, could use it more effectively than you, or could gain from using it more than you would lose is of no significance. The simplest wrong against property is using what belongs to another without the owner's permission. Kant's account explains why this is a wrong without inquiring into the magnitude of the loss (if any) suffered by the owner, or the benefits the trespasser hoped to gain. Any account that focuses on specific uses—the matter of choice—must regard such a rule as wasteful, since it forbids a transaction that makes one party better off and the other no worse off. In the vocabulary of economic theory, a harmless trespass is a Pareto improvement: one person is made better off, and no other person is made worse off.[8] Perhaps a material analysis, focusing on need or wish, could generate a rule against trespass by reference to secondary problems about the resources people would waste in protecting their property, and so conclude that there are grounds for a general rule that sometimes prohibits people from doing harmless and even worthwhile things.[9] Kant's approach is different: the reason harmless trespasses are prohibited is that they violate the owner's right to determine how his or her property will be used.

By understanding property rights as a constraint on the conduct of others, Kant is able to undermine what he calls the "Guardian spirit" theory of property, according to which property is a special relation between a person and a thing. He refers to this as an "old and widespread view" which leads to the "deception of personifying things and of thinking of a

---

8. Pareto criteria are often couched in terms of voluntary transactions, but voluntariness enters the economic account as evidentiary rather than constitutive. Two welfare maximizers would only engage in a consensual transaction if each expected to gain by it.

9. As I explain in "Beyond the Harm Principle," *Philosophy & Public Affairs* 34 (2006): 215–245, a harm-based account faces parallel problems with harmless trespasses against persons, such as medical experiments performed on unconscious patients, or sexual assaults on drugged women that leave no trace. Harm-focused accounts must identify the grounds with prohibiting such actions in terms of indirect effects on other people, such as the climate of fear that they are likely to cause if word gets out, rather than, as the Kantian account does, on the fact that they are wrongs against their immediate victims. The appeal to the indirect effects is always treacherous, since it makes it an open question whether the best way to prevent those effects is to prohibit the acts themselves, or rather, to prohibit people from informing others about them.

right to things as being a right directly against them." He acknowledges that such a view is natural, and seems to have held it himself in his precritical phase.[10] But it leads to a deception because a right is always a constraint on the conduct of others. Your right to your own person is not a feature of your own relation to yourself. So, too, with property: your relation to the object that you own is not the core of the right; your entitlement to constrain others with respect to that object is. Understood as a form of self-relation, property could not be a constraint on the conduct of others, because any such constraint is a relation between persons, with respect to things. Nobody else is constrained by your relation to yourself. Your right to property is your right to limit the conduct of others in relation to particular things. It is an expression of your purposiveness in relation to the purposiveness of others, and so cannot be reduced either to your relation to the object you own or to the restriction on the conduct of others.[11] Thus Kant observes that "it is clear that someone who was all alone on the earth could really neither have nor acquire any external thing as his own, since there is no relation whatever of obligation between him, as a person, and any other external object, as a thing."[12]

The "mine or yours" structure that governs all acquired rights opens up two new questions that a theory of property must address. First, it

---

10. 6:269. In his handwritten notes in his copy of *Observations on the Feeling of the Beautiful and Sublime*, Kant appears to fall into that very deception: "The body is mine because it is a part of my I and is moved by my power of choice. The entire animated or unanimated world that does not have its own power of choice is mine in so far as I master it and can move it in accordance with my power of choice. The sun is not mine. The same goes for another person, therefore no property is a *Prioprietat* or an exclusive property. But in so far as I want to claim something as exclusively my own, I will presuppose that the will of the other is at least not opposed to mine, nor [is] the action of the other opposed to mine [67]. Therefore, I will carry out the actions that indicate what is mine, chop the tree down, timber it, etc. The other person tells me that it is his because, through the actions of his power of choice, it is as though belongs to his self." *Bemerkungen zu den Beobachtungen über das Gefühl des Schönen und Erhabenen*, AA XX, S. 66f, trans. Patrick Frierson, at http://people.whitman.edu/~frierspr/kants_bemerkungen3.htm (accessed October 7, 2008).

11. For an example of a theory of property in which the owner is dispensable, see James Penner, *The Idea of Property in Law* (Oxford: Oxford University Press, 1997). Penner begins with the "mine or yours" structure of property, but focuses exclusively on the restrictions on others. The Kantian objection to this approach is the converse of the objection to the Lockean one: property relates the choices of owners to nonowners, rather than relating either owners or nonowners to objects.

12. 6:261.

must explain how something can belong to a person when that person is not in physical possession of it. You are always in possession of your body, or, to be more precise, your body just is your physical person. Any wrong against your body is a wrong against you. The formal relation of having means to setting ends requires that any rights you have to things that *can* be separate from you apply when they *are* separate. Otherwise your freedom to use external means to set and pursue your purposes depends on what others decide to do with those means.

Second, it must explain how external objects of choice can be acquired. The theory of contract includes an account of how things can be transferred, but the theory of property requires, in addition, a theory of initial acquisition.

The first question, of how someone can have a right to a thing of which he or she is not in possession, marks the distinction between theft (or conversion) and battery. If I have my hand wrapped around an apple, you wrong me if you peel my fingers off it or wrestle it away from me, because you interfere with my person. That wrong is not sufficient for a wrong against a property right in the apple, because it provides no constraint on your conduct over and above the constraint already contained in my innate right to my own person. If I am holding a bowl of soup, you can come with a straw and drink the soup without interfering with my person. If I have a property right in the soup that is violated when you come with your straw, it must consist in some claim that is not directly connected to my person. More generally, because property is a relation between persons, if my ownership of an object is to constrain the conduct of others, the constraint must be separable from the constraint already inherent in my right to my own person. Because the right is separable from my right to my person, it can bind others even when I am not in physical possession of or even contact with the object of the right.

The distinction between physical possession and ownership resolves the first-order question about the nature of a property right: a property right is an entitlement to constrain the conduct of others with respect to an object by excluding them from that object. It sets up a new form of potential inconsistency between the freedoms of separate persons. If an external object is your property, it is subject to your choice, and so I must forbear from using it or interfering with it, even if my use or interference does not affect your person.

Because he conceives of right spatially, Kant treats property in land as the basic case of property. A right to property is a right to control a three-dimensional region of space. That is why you violate my property right by drinking the soup in the bowl I hold, even though you did not violate my right to my own person in so doing. To have a right to a piece of land is to have a particular location subject to your exclusive choice. Property in land, or "real property" as it is often called, is the right to constrain the conduct of others with respect to a specific location, including the possibility of constraining their occupation of the location, and what movable objects they bring to it. The postulate of practical reason with regard to rights already establishes that land can be subject to a person's exclusive choice. The analysis applies to property more generally, and is perfectly consistent with various complex forms of property, including owning shares in a company, land subject to mortgage, and money.[13]

Kant's normative resolution of the question of property rights also comes with a metaphysical exposition of the sense in which my act interferes with your entitlement to subject an object to your choice. Your basic right to your property is the right that you be the one who determines how it will be used. When, however, you are not physically in control of the property, because it is separate from you, you are not factually controlling it. So my interference with your right to property is not an interference with your factual physical control of it. Instead, I wrong you by interfering with what Kant calls your "intelligible" or "noumenal" possession of the object. Neither Kant's use of the word "noumenal" nor his introduction of it through the "antinomy of private right" is meant to invoke any ontological theses about some other world in which you are in factual possession of an object when you are not in factual possession of it in this world. Instead, the basic point is that in addition to thinking of things under the aspect of physical location and possession, as we do

---

13. The one case that goes by the name of property which Kant denies can be explained in terms of the concept of property is "intellectual property." Kant explains copyright as a non-proprietary right that an author has to "speak in his own name" (6:289). This account provides a more powerful interpretation of the familiar structure of copyright, including the idea/expression dichotomy, the role of the public, and the core exemptions for "fair use." See Abraham Drassinower, "A Rights-Based View of the Idea/Expression Dichotomy in Public Law," *Canadian Journal of Law and Jurisprudence* 16 (2003): 3–21; Jonathan Peterson, "Liberalism and the Public Interest in Art," doctoral dissertation, University of Toronto, 2007.

with respect to each person's innate right of humanity in his or her own person, we are also required—morally required, that is—to understand external objects of choice under normative principles of freedom. There is a nonphysical sense in which your property belongs to you, a sense that, like Kant's noumenal realm, can only be understood by abstracting away from the particularity of space and time. A postulate is required to make sense of this possibility, because the laws of freedom in question take objects in space and time as their subject matter: you have an entitlement to your pen, which is individuated by its empirical properties and location in space at any given time. Your intelligible possession of the pen brings the pen under nonempirical norms. The norms are nonempirical because they classify empirically individuated objects in terms of nonempirical normative features. That is why physical possession and ownership can diverge.

From this perspective, the theory of acquisition must be secondary. Any account of property needs an account of acquisition to complete it, even if the account of acquisition is not likely to regulate any but a tiny fraction of ordinary property transactions. In every system of property that we know, comparatively few unowned objects are up for grabs, and even those are typically located on land that is already private or public property. Despite a limited range of application, the theory of acquisition is systematically important. A theory of rightful rules of property presupposes that the owners of various things have genuine title to them. Even if title is typically acquired from some other person, the possibility of passing good title presupposes the possibility of initial acquisition, because any item of property could belong to someone other than its current owner.[14]

I. Acquisition

One of the most perplexing features of systems of property is the priority that they seem to attach to matters of timing: the person who got there first enjoys priority over latecomers. Even if it is supposed that the expenditure of toil grounds a claim in desert to the fruits of your labor, the

---

14. 6:259.

first person to toil on the object is the one who gets the chance to deserve its fruits. The difficulty with acquisition-based theories is that priority in time must enter them as a substantive normative principle. The Kantian alternative allows timing to matter, but only as the way in which objects make it into the system of property, without supposing that timing, as such, has any direct normative significance. If the theory of acquisition matters as only a theory of how particular objects become property, there is no reason to suppose that it must drive the rest of the theory of property.

By focusing on the structure of property rights and the ways in which they constrain the conduct of others, Kant's theory distances itself from the difficulties that bedevil acquisition-focused theories. Acquisition-focused theories represent the way in which property constrains the conduct of other persons as an implication of the way in which the owner acquired the property in question. On prominent interpretations of Locke, for example, the fact that one person has mixed his labor with an object (or, on other readings, made that object) creates a special relationship between a person and a thing, which others are thus bound to recognize and respect. In Hegel's otherwise very different theory of acquisition, the unilateral aspect of acquisition is brought out by contrasting property rights with contractual rights. Contractual rights are acquired bilaterally, and so bind only the parties to them, while property rights are acquired unilaterally, and so bind all others. Since others must respect my will, if I have "put my will" into an object in the requisite sense, others must respect my will as it is in the object.

There are two difficulties with the idea that my toil or will could bind others. One of these is the general problem about unilateral action binding others, to which we will return in Chapter 6. Kant does not deny that property can be acquired through a unilateral act, done entirely at the initiative of the acquirer. His argument is that a broader context of public right is required in order for one person's unilateral act to impose an obligation on another. Even though the *nature* of a property right can be explicated exclusively in terms of private right, unowned objects cannot be acquired except under the authority of a principle of public right. The familiar moral and legal idea that two persons cannot, through their agreement, change the rights of a third who is not a party to their agreement holds more generally: one person cannot, without more, change the rights of everyone else. Locke restricts the application of his principle to those occasions in which appropriation does not worsen the ability of others to provide for their own subsistence. Any such proviso fails to address the underlying difficulty. One person's ability to unilaterally place others under an obligation raises the same issue even if those who are obligated are no worse off in material terms. Indeed, this difficulty is the mirror image of the basic structure of a property right, understood as the right to exclude. I wrong you if I use your property without your authorization, and it is no answer to your complaint against me for me to say that you are no worse off in terms of your welfare or ability to provide for yourself. You are the one who gets to decide. A parallel point applies to the Lockean proviso: my entitlement to place you under a perfectly general obligation to refrain from using an object raises an issue about your freedom, not about your welfare. Any systematic justification of my entitlement has to address that issue, and restricting a justification to cases in which there is no material disadvantage does not engage the issue of freedom.

The second difficulty is most obvious in broadly Lockean theories which focus on toil or "sweat of the brow," but it is a general problem for acquisition-based accounts of property.[15] Kant notes that laboring on an object or piece of land does not give rise to a right as such. It is possible for someone to work on land or an object that belongs to another, and in so doing either work for the other or waste his own efforts. This might

15. For example, John Stuart Mill, in his *Principles of Political Economy,* writes of "the essential principle of property being to assure to all persons what they have produced by their labour and accumulated by their abstinence" (Book 2, chap. 2, §5). It is not completely clear that Locke himself has a fully "Lockean" theory in this respect, or whether instead his view marks less of a departure from, for example, Grotius's. For both Locke and Grotius, a theory of property begins with the assumption that the Earth is owned in common. Grotius argues that common land is divided up through a collective decision; perhaps Locke can be read as relaxing this requirement, and licensing acquisition whenever it does not worsen the situation of others. On this reading, Locke begins with a material principle in a way that is inconsistent with each person's right to be his or her own master. The grounds of severing property from the commons are also material, since they depend on whether others are made worse off, rather than on any freedom-based entitlement. Still, Locke also attaches great significance to the fact that each person owns and expends his own labor, and others have certainly taken such a message away from his theory. I am grateful to John Simmons for helpful discussion of this issue.

seem to be irrelevant, since the Lockean theory of acquisition focuses on things that are not already owned. Yet the point is more general: it must be possible for a person to waste his own efforts on something whether it is owned or not; improving something is only relevant if that thing is already yours.[16] If you own the object and improve it, you now own an improved object. If you already own it, no toil is necessary to establish your claim to it; if someone else improves something that you already own, then, absent special circumstances, you now own an improved object.

The distinction between improving something you own and frittering away your efforts is internal to the theory of property, and reflects the more general Kantian distinction between wishing and choosing. You can use whatever is yours, both your person and your property, to accomplish whatever purpose you suppose them to be suitable for achieving. One of the ways in which you can use what you already have is to pursue the purpose of acquiring something else. You can use your muscles to pick up a stick; now that you have the stick, you can use it to get at fruit that is out of your reach, and so on. Each time you successfully acquire something, you are the one who gets to decide how it will be used. Until you have acquired it, it is not subject to your choice; it is something you have chosen to pursue, but unless you succeed, it is just something that you wished for.

The means/ends structure of your *use* of objects is paralleled in your *rights* to objects; the right to have something as your own is the right to be able to have it as your means, that is, to decide the purposes for which it will be used. Using your other means for the purpose of acquiring that object is not sufficient for having it as your means. Your property right in the means that you already have constrains others to refrain from interfering with those means, but they are free to change the context in which you use those means as they see fit. That is just to say that they do not need to respect your wishes. All of this is to say that until you have acquired something, your intention to acquire it places no constraints on the conduct of others.

Kant's point about the priority of property to effort expended in improving it is particularly clear in the case of acquisition by capture. Locke

---

16. 6:265.

offers the example of a person who exerts toil chasing and tiring a hare, arguing that the expenditure of effort generates a property right in it, so that others may not come along and seize it. Locke is correct in the application of his own general account,[17] since the expenditure of effort in giving chase is a use of the chaser's labor. Supposing he has a right to that labor, the person who appropriates the exhausted hare interferes with that right. Kant's point is precisely to deny this, on the grounds that at least sometimes in seeking to acquire something, you simply fritter away your efforts. Since Roman times, legal systems have treated acquisition by capture as Kant does, for simple but systematic reasons.[18] The person who captures the fox or hare that I have chased does me no wrong, because he does not deprive me of something that I already had. I still have my horses, hounds, and bugle; I just failed to achieve the purpose I set for myself in using them. I no longer have my efforts; those were just squandered. Although the person whom the courts call the "saucy intruder" exercised his freedom in a way that caused my plan to fail, he did not deprive me of my toil any more than he deprived me of my horses, hounds, or bugle. My effort and toil were gone once I expended them. I could not have a right to my toil in a way that I have a right to my horses. The most I could have is a right to the *fruits* of my toil, but I could only have that right if I already have a right to exclude others from the object on which I toil. That is, the right to the fruits of my toil only applies if I already have a right to the object on which I work, and so cannot be used to generate a right to that object. The same point applies to the sugges-

17. John Locke, *Second Treatise of Government* (Indianapolis: Hackett, 1980), 20, §30.
18. Justinian, *Digest*, trans. Alan Watson (Philadelphia: University of Pennsylvania Press, 1985), Book 41, chap. 1, par. 5. The classic common law discussion, which considers the writings of Pufendorf, Grotius, and Barbeyrac, can be found in *Pierson v. Post* 3 Cai. R. 175 (1805). All of the classic discussions reject the Lockean view. Wild animals fall into the category of things that can only be acquired by being captured, because capture is required to subject them to a person's choice. Another example in the Anglo-American law of property is percolating water that flows under land, but not in a defined stream. You cannot take possession of percolating water, because you cannot take control of it. You can dig a well and take possession of the water in it and that you draw from it. Bees are another: see *Ferguson v. Miller* (N.Y. 1823) 1 Cow. 243 (1823). You can own the hive, so that anyone who takes honey from it wrongs you. You cannot own the bees, however, because you cannot take control of them. To be more precise, if you capture the bees in a container, you can own them, but while they remain wild, you cannot.

tion that laboring on a thing increases its value, so that the person who increases the value is wronged by those who appropriate the newly valuable thing. Conceptual difficulties attend any attempt to speak of a single act improving the value of an object. Insofar as flushing a hare out of the bushes increases its value, so does pointing it out, since each of these reduces the effort that others would need to put into capturing it. The difficulty is that any such contribution to the ease of others acquiring a thing is just a special case of a beneficial effect of your use of something that is already yours. You do not need to bring in special bees to pollinate your garden if I have planted the right plants; you do not need to first look for or flush the hare if I have spotted or flushed it first. However increasing the value of an object is understood, you do not have a right to the value you create unless you have a right to the things that bear the value. Instead, your right to the value follows from the right to the thing, and so cannot ground a right to a thing.

The difficulty for toil-based theories reveals a more general conceptual problem in the idea that a person has property in his or her own labor. If you have a property right in a thing, then you have a right to exclude others from using or interfering with that thing without your permission. From this perspective, it might seem unobjectionable to say that you have a property right in your labor, since others apparently wrong you if they interfere with your labor or use it without your permission. They certainly wrong you if they interfere with you, that is, your body. The problem comes in specifying what it would be for one person to use or interfere with the *labor* of another except by interfering with that person's body. If you stop me from cutting your hair, there is a sense in which you are interfering with my labor, but, since you are entitled to determine whether I cut your hair or not, you do not wrong me. I make your trip to the store a waste of your labor if I buy the last quart of milk before you get there, but this interference is not a wrong to you. *You* wasted your efforts; *I* just exercised my freedom. I wrong you if I interfere with your person—pushing you out of the way as you reach for the milk. The only way I can wrongfully interfere with your labor, then, is by wrongfully interfering with your person. More generally, whether my interfering with something you are doing violates your property in your labor depends on an independent specification of the permissibility of what each of us is doing.

The same problem applies to the idea of using another person's labor:

if I force you to work for me, I wrong you by using your person, and in so doing, it might also be said that I thereby appropriate your labor. It would be more correct, however, to say that I wrong you because I use you—I subject your person to my choice, contrary to your innate right to independence of the choice of any other private person. In the same way, I wrong you if I take something that belongs to you. If the thing that I take is something you have made, my wrong could be characterized as taking your labor. The problem is to specify this idea so that it is not just a paraphrase of the wrong involved in my taking the object. I wrong you if I take your property even if it cost you no effort to acquire it, and the claim that I have *also* taken your effort adds nothing to your complaint against me.

A further difficulty undercuts the suggestion that your right to your labor, or, as Locke puts it, your ownership of it, gives you a right to the fruits of that labor. As a general matter, the fact that something is an effect of something you own does not give you a right to it. If you landscape your yard, you might increase property values in the neighborhood, or attract beneficial insects that keep the mosquitoes in the yards of your neighbors at bay. Your neighbors who benefit from increased property values or insect-free yards do not need to pay you for the benefit they have received, because they have not deprived you of something you have a property right to. All they have done is take advantage of the effect of your exercise of something you have a right to. You do have a right to exclude others from these benefits—you might put up a tall ugly fence, so that nobody can see how beautiful your yard is, or a fine-mesh one to keep the insects in. You even have a right to warn your neighbors that you will put up a fence unless they pay part of the cost of your landscaping from which they will benefit. Both of these rights are simply the rights to *capture* the effects of what you own. If you fail to capture them, you have no claim against any other person who might take advantage of them. The same point applies to your toil: if the tired fox is the effect of your toil, you are entitled to capture it, but so is everyone else.

In the same way, if I grow mushrooms in the shade cast by your fence, you cannot claim a portion of my profits. If, however, you tell me that you plan to take down the fence unless I help you to repair it, I am free to accept or refuse your offer. The one thing you are not entitled to do is claim that I have wronged you because I have deprived you of the effects of something that you own. Exactly the same point applies to your ownership of your labor or, as it is sometimes more fashionable to put it, your self-ownership. You have a right to exclude others from your person, but it does not follow that you have any right to exclude others from the effects of the ways in which you permissibly use your person. Your right only protects what you already have, and so cannot generate a right to some further thing. Since you have no right against others to the effects of those things that you have a right to, your right to your own labor cannot generate a right to those things on which you expend it. If somebody else already owns the things on which you labor, then, unless you make arrangements with them, or if you mistakenly work on what is theirs and they freely accept the benefits you have conferred, you will simply fritter away your labor. If I clean your windows in the hope that you will pay me, I have no right to payment. If nobody else owns those things, you have used what you have—whether it is your labor or your hounds, horses, and bugle—to try to acquire something. Nobody is under any obligation to limit her use of what is hers so as to enable you to succeed in the purposes for which you are using what is yours. If you do already own the thing on which you work, you also own the improved thing after working on it. The work itself plays no role in establishing your claim.

If laboring on a thing will not establish a right in it unless you already have it, a different sort of unilateral act is required to make something your own. The only possible answer is the minimalist one: making something your means. We need only the transition itself, from subject to no person's choice to subject to *this* person's choice.[19] That is, the theory of

---

19. Kant characterizes the authorization as a "permissive law." Drawing on medieval and early modern uses of this term, Brian Tierney has argued that the permissive aspect of the law is that it grants permission to do something that would otherwise be wrongful. Kant's earlier use of the concept in *Perpetual Peace* might appear to conform to Tierney's interpretation, as he says that a permissive law allows a state to delay the full realization of a peaceful condition. See Tierney's articles "Kant on Property: The Problem of the Permissive Law," *Journal of the History of Ideas* 62 (2001): 301–312, and "Permissive Natural Law and Property: Gratian to Kant," *Journal of the History of Ideas* 62 (2001): 381–399. Joachim Hruschka has offered a reading that fits better with Kant's use in the *Doctrine of Right,* according to which the permissive law makes it possible for a merely permissible act, one that is neither forbidden nor required, to have consequences for rights. This concept plays a familiar part in other contexts. In a game such as chess, the rules create a system of permissions, through which particular moves can be imputed to the players. Hruschka argues that Kant inherited this tripartite structure from Achenwall, whose textbook he used when he taught courses on natural law. In

acquisition follows the structure of the theory of property: to acquire something is to make it your own. The Lockean claim that you must use an object to acquire it is mirrored in his doctrine of waste, according to which you lose an object if you stop using it. Neither is consistent with Kant's formal idea of purposiveness, which makes having means prior to setting ends. That is why Kant generates a doctrine of property rather than *usufruct*. Perhaps a consistent theory of the temporary right to use a thing could be made to depend on acquiring it by using it. The theory of property cannot.

Kant's account thus focuses exclusively on the transition in a thing's status from unowned to owned, that is, the transition from its being available to all to its being subject to one person's exclusive choice. The account is boring because the only factual precondition of rightful acquisition of an unowned object is empirical possession of that object. The act in question is simply bringing a thing under your control, so that you can now decide how to use it. Neither improving it nor putting your will into it is required. Improving it is not required because improving an object is only relevant once you have taken possession of it. Until you take possession, improving just fritters away your efforts. The same point applies to what Hegel describes as "putting your will" into an object, at least if this is understood as something different from simply taking possession of it. Wishing for a thing engages your will in a sense that is irrelevant; subjecting it to your choice—making it a means for setting and pursuing your purposes—is established only by taking control of it. Nothing more is required. All you need to do is take physical possession, and give a sign to

---

a later article Hruschka also shows the systematic role of permissions throughout Kant's theory of acquired rights. See Hruschka's *Das deontologische Sechseck bei Gottfried Achenwall im Jahre 1767* (Hamburg: Vanderhoeck und Ruprecht, 1986), and "The Permissive Law of Practical Reason in Kant's *Metaphysics of Morals*," *Law and Philosophy* 23 (2004): 45–72. See also Katrin Flikschuh, *Kant and Modern Political Philosophy* (Cambridge: Cambridge University Press, 2000), chap. 4. The change between *Perpetual Peace* and the *Doctrine of Right* may only be apparent. In the earlier work, Kant does not say that there is a permission to delay implementation of a peace treaty; he says that the prohibition of acquisition of territory by war or purchase can be delayed until there is a peace treaty. Thus in a state of war, acquisition by purchase or force is a permissive law, i.e. a way in which a state can acquire territory. Such acquisition is valid once peace is achieved because a peace treaty closes off all further dispute, and extinguishes all old claims, including those based on the wrongfulness of past acquisition through force.

others that you are doing so in order to have it as your means rather than just for a specific use. These steps are required because they are just the steps in subjecting a thing to your choice. You do not need to improve the object, because improving an object you are already in possession of is just subjecting it to your choice in some specific way. Unless it is already subject to your choice, however, the ways in which you change it—for example, by tiring it out—do not subject it to your choice. At most, they prepare it for subsequent use.

Taking control must be public, and so Kant says it requires giving a sign. If others could not determine that you meant to bind them, you cannot bind them. You can use something on a particular occasion without acquiring it or even intending to. You might use a stick to balance as you walk up a rocky path without making it your own. It is not that you acquire it and then immediately abandon it. Instead, you use it only while you are in physical possession of it. In so doing, you make no claim to subject the thing to your choice when you are not in physical possession of it. The second unilateral act (strictly speaking, the second aspect of the same unilateral act) is "giving a sign": you must make your appropriation of the object in question public, in the sense that others could be bound by it. If you are only using the stick to balance, you do not need to give a sign to others; the fact that you are in physical possession of the stick means that they cannot interfere with the stick while you are using it without thereby committing a wrong against your person. So no other person can grab the stick, making you lose your balance, but the wrong of so doing has nothing to do with the stick as such, and everything to do with the fact that you are currently holding it. On the other hand, if you give a sign, then the person who takes the stick from you wrongs you with respect to the stick as well, and so wrongs you by taking the stick when you put it down. It does not follow from the need for a sign that there needs to be a clear marker on every boundary line; only that in bringing the thing under control you make it apparent to others that you intend to make it your own.

II. Conclusion

Kant understands property rights as parallel to rights to one's own person, but distinct from them. By developing the parallel, he can explain what a property right is without attempting to ground it in a theory of acquisition; by developing the contrast, he can generate a theory of acquisition that explains how a rule of priority in time and unilateral action are appropriate to it. By setting things up in this way, his account captures the distinctive sense in which property rights are partly a matter of private rights between persons, but at the same time situates his argument that acquisition is only possible against the background of a public structure of rightful authority.

CHAPTER 5

Private Right III: Contract and Consent

THE SECOND TITLE of Private Right is contract. Contracts are essential to the operation of any legal system, because they are the legal means through which persons are entitled to make arrangements for themselves, and so to change their respective rights and duties. Kant's analysis of contract focuses on the way in which it enables separate persons to set and pursue their own purposes interdependently. The most familiar legal examples of contracts involve two persons making mutual undertakings for future performances: I agree to cut your lawn next Wednesday, and in return you agree to pay me. Kant introduces what he calls a "dogmatic division of rights that can be acquired by contract," which classifies the various ways in which two persons can organize their rights.

The main focus of this chapter will not be the specific legal manifestations of the idea of contract, but rather the underlying normative structure within which parties are entitled to change their legal relations with each other. That structure governs not only explicit contracts, but also, just as significantly, issues of consent. We saw already in our discussions of innate right and property rights that consent is fundamental to a system of equal freedom. I wrong you if I touch your person or use your property without your consent, but if you have consented, it is not that my wrong is somehow forgiven, but rather that it is no wrong at all. This general structure of consent is in one way completely familiar. Kant's discussion of acquisition by contract shows how this idea of consent is an expression of each person's entitlement to be his or her own master. Self-mastery, as we saw, is a contrastive idea: the idea that you are your own master is equivalent to the idea that no other person is your master. Contract and consent enable free persons to exercise self-mastery together. Moreover, the power to consent is already implicit in their respective rights of self-mastery: as the person who gets to decide what to do, you are entitled both to exclude others from your plans and to include them.

The Kantian conception of both contract and consent understands it as an expression of freedom, bringing both its familiar features and its familiar limitations into focus. Consent provides a complete defense to most torts and crimes against persons and property. Informed consent matters, for example, in medical contexts, because it provides a defense to what would otherwise be the tort (and crime) of battery. An adequate account of its role in all of these contexts must explain what consent is and why, so understood, it would provide a complete defense. Just as important, an account needs to explain the occasions on which it fails to provide a defense. Consent is not a defense if obtained through force or fraud; an account must explain why these always make consent defective. It is not a defense to a charge of murder in any jurisdiction, and it is only sometimes a defense to a charge of battery. An adequate account must explain why it is not available in these cases and also explain whether there is a principled way of identifying the exceptions to those exceptions—why, for example, in the context of sporting activities, victim consent can provide a defense to a charge of battery.

The account I will offer rests on two familiar ideas. The first is the distinction, central to all concepts of right, between wishing for something and choosing that thing. You choose something by taking up means to achieve it; you can wish for or want something that you either lack means to or for which you have means that you do not use. Your wishes do not need to form a consistent set, because you don't have to do anything about them. Your choices are different: you can only choose something if you have the requisite means, and so how you decide to use your means limits what you can choose; to choose to do one thing is thereby to forgo other conflicting uses of those means. The fact that I want something very badly is not sufficient for me to have chosen it, even if it has been offered to me on what others might think are favorable terms. I might be tempted by the savory treat or expensive toy in a shop window, but choose to resist the temptation.

The second is introduced in Kant's discussion of contract: the idea of a voluntary transaction between two people that engages both of their capacities for choice. The fact that I have decided to do something, even decided to do something involving you, is not equivalent to my having consented to doing that thing *with* you. The fact that you have decided to permit me to do something does not amount to your having consented to that thing unless something transpires between us. Neither your desire that I do some act *x*, my true belief about that desire, nor the combination of the two suffices for consent. Instead of merely *matching*, our choices must be *joined*.

Bringing these two ideas together, I will argue that consent is to be understood as two persons uniting their wills to create new rights and duties between them. In so doing, they make new means available to each other.

The account of consent presupposes the specific Kantian account of the wrongs to which consent is a defense. Consent gets its significance against the background of the basic right to independence that private persons have against each other. As we saw in Chapters 2 through 4, this basic right generates correlative duties that each person owes to others to refrain from using or interfering with another's person or property. These duties are relational: to violate these rights is not merely to do something wrong, but to wrong someone in particular; not merely to do something, but to do something to that person.[1] The mere fact that your act sets back my interest in some way does not make it wrongful, and so does not require my consent to make it rightful. Instead, every person owes each other person a duty to refrain from interfering with his or her person or property.

---

1. On this general theme, see Michael Thompson, "What Is It to Wrong Someone? A Puzzle about Justice," in R. Jay Wallace, Philip Pettit, Samuel Scheffler, and Michael Smith, eds., *Reason and Value* (Oxford: Oxford University Press, 2004), 333–384, and Stephen Darwall, *The Second Person Standpoint: Morality, Respect, and Accountability* (Cambridge, Mass.: Harvard University Press, 2006).

Interactions between persons are fundamentally changed by consent, because they create a new juridical relationship between the parties to them. If I consent to your use of my person (or powers) or property, *I* have decided how they will be used, and so your use of them is an exercise of my freedom. If I consent to your doing something that injures me or damages my property, the injury or damage results from the exercise of my choice. On Kant's strong reading of private rights to independence, "making arrangements" about another person—even touching a person or her property—is presumptively wrongful, unless consensual. In the same way, compelling another to perform an act or deliver property (or pay damages in lieu of performance) is wrongful unless a prior contract gives one person a right to performance or delivery. At the same time, in relations of status, in which one person makes arrangements for another, the arrangements are limited to those that the other could have consented to, had he or she been in a position to. The limits of possible consent will be important for understanding public right.

As we saw in Chapter 3, free persons can set and pursue their purposes separately, concerned only to avoid using or interfering with means that others have. They can set and pursue their purposes together only if they can connect not just their particular purposes, but their purposiveness. We pursue our purposes separately and in parallel if we both seek the same result, but do so independently of the other's pursuit of it. We pursue them together if one (or both) of us makes the other's particular purpose his or her own. If we do that, we unite our choices through a bilateral exchange of terms: one of us proposes something to the other, and the other accepts, each taking up the other's use of his powers in that way as his own. The bilateral aspect of this interaction does not require a bargain, whereby each of us expects to get something out of our arrangement, only that we have an arrangement. Kant's taxonomy of acquired rights thus requires him to distinguish between circumstances in which two persons voluntarily create a special relationship between them and the two other types of private rights. They are unlike property rights, which require a unilateral act for their acquisition, but are structured by the entitlement of each person to set and pursue his or her own purposes. They are unlike status rights because they are entered into and defined through the voluntary participation of the parties.

These familiar features of consent reflect its place in a system of rights, rather than a system of interests. I have the rightful power to make another person's use of my person or property an instance of my use of it, even if I later decide I don't want to, or judge that it would not be for the best, and even if it is not in my interest. All of this can be repackaged into the vocabulary of my long-term or higher-order interest in self-determination, so long as it is understood purely relationally: the only "interest" that matters to my rights is the interest in having no other person determine my purposes.

I. What Consent Is: Uniting Our Wills

Consent enables people to do things together by eliminating some of the legal consequences of doing those things. But consent itself is also something that must involve both parties.

The transactional nature of consent can be brought out by a contrast between two ways of thinking about the concept of contract, which is a special case of it. A contract is a consensual transaction, which changes the legal situation between the parties by engaging their wills in the appropriate way. A contract is often said to be an exchange of promises, and many commentators have sought to explain the binding force of contracts in terms of the binding force of promises. Different attempts to articulate the morality of promising lead to advocacy of various changes in contract law, to bring it more in line with the morality of promise.[2] It is not my purpose here to adjudicate between competing accounts of promising, because promises can create enforceable obligations to perform future acts only because people have the more general rightful capacity to make arrangements with each other that change those relations.[3]

---

2. See Charles Fried, *Contract as Promise: A Theory of Contractual Obligations* (Cambridge, Mass.: Harvard University Press, 1981), and Seana Shiffrin, "The Divergence of Contracts and Promises," *Harvard Law Review* 120 (2007): 708–753.

3. Kant assimilates "telling or promising them something" in his examples of things that have no bearing on questions of right, except where they wrong someone because they "diminish what is theirs" (6:238). This assimilation suggests that promising as such is not fundamental to the concept of contract, even though a forward contract will involve a promise, the breach of which will diminish what belongs to another.

Kant provides a fundamentally different way of representing the binding force of contracts. His focus is not on promises as such, but on *voluntary arrangements between people*. Many of those arrangements, especially the ones that get litigated, involve promises of future performance. The grounds for enforcing them, however, are not that they are promises, but that they are aspects of arrangements through which separate persons get together to vary their respective obligations. Again, although many contracts impose an obligation on one or both parties to perform an affirmative act, while familiar instances of consent grant only permissions, such contrasts are of no analytical significance. An obligation of right concerning future performance is a title to compel that performance, consistent with the freedom of the obligee, just as a permission granted through consent is a title to do something to another, consistent with that person's freedom. Arrangements between private persons are expressions of their respective freedom, and so, Kant argues, their enforcement is consistent with that freedom.

Kant uses the simple example of a present transfer of property to illustrate the conceptual structure underlying voluntary arrangements. Suppose I want to give you my watch. The physical transfer is easy to understand: I take it off my wrist and hand it to you. The physical transfer is not sufficient for the legal transfer of ownership. Having handed the watch to you does not extinguish my property right in it. The difference between merely handing it to you and transferring ownership is normative, not factual. Kant also points out that I cannot transfer it to you by abandoning it and having you subsequently acquire it. If transfer required abandonment, there would be a moment (even if infinitesimally small) during which the watch was unowned, and an interloper could come along and take it before you did, without wronging either of us. In the case of a small object like a watch, we might solve this as a *factual* problem by hanging on to it throughout the entire proceeding, so that the interloper would commit some sort of personal wrong against one or both of us by wresting the object from our hands. Any such solution would be limited to small objects. More fundamentally, the abandonment and acquisition account gives up on the idea that I give something *to you*, as you accept that very same thing *from me*.

To capture the idea that ownership moves seamlessly from me to you, without any period of limbo in between, Kant introduces the concept of a "united will" through which the transfer from me to you is continuous because it engages both of us. Kant notes that people making agreements often try to represent this continuity by physical acts that are continuous in the same way, such as shaking hands or breaking a straw. The basic idea, however, has nothing to do with the continuity of the handshake, any more than it has anything to do with the continuity of the physical transfer of a small object. Instead, the reason the watch becomes yours is that we create an entitlement *together,* that the watch becomes yours. I transfer it to you, and you accept it from me. We act together, because my act of transfer and your act of acceptance each takes the other's act as its object. It is not that I give and you receive without reference to the other— as Leibniz is reported to have contended that paternity was an accident in the father and filiation an accident in the son. My giving to you and your receiving from me are analytically equivalent. The interloper who takes what I am in the process of giving to you is a thief. He cannot say to me that I surrendered all my rights to the watch, and he cannot say to you that you did not have the watch yet, because the transfer of rights takes place seamlessly through our united wills.

Contrary to what is sometimes suggested,[4] Kant's example of a present transfer does not reflect the idea that either contract or consent must be analyzed in terms of a transfer of rights, or that all rights are modeled on property rights. To the contrary, Kant's analysis turns on the claim that the idea of an offer being accepted is required to make sense of how a physical transfer of objects can affect a transfer of rights. In a contract of transfer, something does get transferred, but Kant argues that we need the idea of a united will to understand how two people can participate in varying their respective rights.

By uniting our wills, we can transfer a right, even though neither of us on our own has means adequate to entitle us to transfer it. I might wish to

---

4. B. Sharon Byrd and Joachim Hruschka, "Kant on 'Why Must I Keep My Promise?'" *Chicago-Kent Law Review* 81 (2006): 47-74; Byrd, "Kant's Theory of Contract," *Southern Journal of Philosophy* 36 (1998): 131-153. Byrd's analysis draws on the *Naturrecht Feyerabend* student notes from 1784-85. There is reason to suppose that Kant's position on this issue changed in the decade between that and *The Metaphysics of Morals,* since he gives a very different account of slave contracts, beginning with *Theory and Practice.*

transfer my horse to you, but I cannot choose to do so unless I have means that I am entitled to use to achieve that purpose. I might abandon my horse in your stable, but you would not thereby acquire ownership of it. You might covet my horse, but you cannot unilaterally claim it as your own. As owner of the horse, I am entitled to do with it as I see fit, consistent with the rights of others, but making it become your property is not something I am entitled to do on my own initiative, because you have the right to refuse it. You might make acquiring it your end, but here, too, on your own you do not have rightful means sufficient to acquire. You do have the right to accept it, but that right is of no use to you except when exercised together with a corresponding purpose of mine to transfer it to you. Between us, we seem to have everything we need, but that is not quite right, because neither of us can accomplish our purpose except with the other. So even if I am eager to get rid of the horse and you are eager to acquire it, we still need to act together. Indeed, that is just the point about the interloper: I could abandon my horse in your stable, but any other person who was entitled to be in your stable could help him- or herself to the horse. I do not have means of my own sufficient to transfer it to you, nor do you have means of your own sufficient to acquire it from me. The most we can do on our own is abandon and acquire. Each of abandonment and acquisition is a unilateral act; our respective entitlements to freedom as against each other limit us to unilateral acts, because one person cannot unilaterally determine what purposes the other will pursue. I can physically transfer the watch without your participation, but you do not become its owner; you can physically relieve me of the watch without my participation, but you do not thereby acquire any entitlement to use it.

The only way in which you can acquire something *from me* is if we together make use of our respective moral powers.[5] That is where the united will comes in. Together we have the requisite means to make the transfer: I cease to have the horse and you come to have it, because we coordinate our respective means to achieve it, each of us allowing our

---

5. Kant analyzes contract formation into two "preparatory" and two "constitutive" moments. The former are required to fix the terms; the latter unite the wills so that one person's powers are subject to the choice of another consistent with the freedom of the first. See 6:272.

powers to be used to affect the transfer. The transfer preserves our respective freedom; not only do I direct the object to you; you accept it from me. When I offer it to you, I act unilaterally, and do not yet change our respective rights; when you accept my offer, both of our respective entitlements are engaged.

The unity of our wills does not presuppose any idea of our ability to act as a collective agent. Indeed, the very possibility of collective as opposed to merely parallel agency presupposes that we have already united our wills, so that we do not merely have a convergent purpose, which each of us pursues in the hope that the other's conduct will make it go smoothly. We act in parallel if I set up my souvenir table outside the cathedral in the hope that you will include it as one of the highlights of the guided tours you offer; we also act merely in parallel if you include the cathedral in your tour in the hope that my souvenir table will interest your tourists. To act together, we need more: to actually make arrangements to make our respective deeds and goods available to the other; that is, we need to unite our wills.[6]

Rather than some prior collective agent, the idea of a united will requires two separate persons, each of whom has moral entitlements in relation to all other persons, and each of whom exercises those entitlements in relation to the other in particular. Contractual and consensual rights create a new moral relationship between two persons so that one (or both) are entitled to act in ways that they were previously not entitled to act. This new relationship could only be consistent with the freedom of those two persons if both of them participate in its creation.[7]

---

6. On pain of regress, we could only do that if we don't first need to get together and plan for me to make and you to accept my offer. I don't need to say to you, "Why don't we get together and have me offer to cut your hair, and you accept my offer?" Instead, we need to be able to unite our separate wills in order to collaborate. I am grateful to Steve Darwall for discussion of this issue.

7. The juridical assumption of rightful honor, which, as we saw in Chapter 2, is the correlate of the innate right of humanity in your own person, generates a presumption that voluntary arrangements made between people will be bilateral in a further sense as well, because each person will be presumed to be acting for his or her own purposes, and so would not intend to restrict his or her freedom simply for the purposes of another. When agreements are made with respect to future performances, this will generate a version of the common law doctrine of "consideration," according to which a promise must normally be exchanged for

Kant's analysis makes no reference to what he calls the "matter" of choice, that is, the reasons that I might want to transfer my watch or horse to you. Presumably I have some motive for wanting to give it to you, and you some reason for wanting to take it, but the character of those motives plays no role in the account. All that is required is that I freely offer you the watch and you freely accept it.

A present transfer needs to be analyzed in terms of a united will, but a united will can create new rights, including rights to things that need not exist as fully determinate prior to the transfer. In the case of a transfer of property, it is certainly true that there is a right, that is, the property right, which is transferred, and that the transfer itself does nothing to alter either the form or the matter of right in any way. Other contracts may not concern rights that survive the transfer unchanged. For example, you can acquire by contract the right that I cut your lawn next Wednesday. Perhaps there is a way to analyze this as a transfer of part of my future freedom to you. There is no need to do so, however, because the analytical and normative work is done through our united will: we create a right on your part and the correlative obligation on mine that I cut your lawn next Wednesday.[8]

---

something of value in order to be legally binding. The same assumption governs the law of unjust enrichment. If you mistakenly pay my telephone bill, you can reclaim your money, because the law will not assume you meant to make me a gift. Kant notes important exceptions to this requirement. A present transfer of an object can be consistent with the transferor's purposiveness. It functions as a presumption because a person can make a gift, but can only enter into a binding contract to do so in a rightful condition (6:298). In many cases of consent, the situation is parallel to that of a present transfer, because one person undertakes responsibility for a particular act by another and can revoke that consent at any time.

8. Bequests might appear to allow one person to unilaterally change the normative situation of another in the way that I have suggested is not possible, since the testator makes the will while alive, and the beneficiary accepts the legacy after the testator's death. Kant characterizes it as a case of "ideal" acquisition because one of the parties to the transaction no longer exists. The issue arises because the testator makes the will while alive, but the beneficiary only has the power to accept the legacy after the testator's death, since the testator is entitled to modify the will at any time until his or her death.

Kant analyzes this as two contracts rather than one. The first contract simply grants the beneficiary an option, which he is free to accept or reject. The beneficiary can be deemed as a matter of law to accept the terms of this first contract in a specific and highly circumscribed sense: a third party, such as a trustee, acting exclusively for the benefit of the beneficiary, is

As in the previous example, the obligation can only be created if we have the requisite means. It is only together that we have the respective means that entitle me to give you the power to require me to cut your lawn. My obligation does not entail that cutting the lawn become my end in any robust sense. It requires only that my cutting it, and even your compelling me to do so, be a consistent exercise of my purposiveness.

The examples so far involve agreements that create obligations to do certain things. Other agreements create permissions as between the parties to them. If I undertake responsibility for your action—as I do if I make certain kinds of representations to you, or a contract to indemnify you under certain circumstances, or if I sign a waiver before you take me paragliding—we create your right against me and my correlative obligation. If I sign a waiver, you acquire a right (as against me) to expose me to danger; you do me no wrong even if I am injured.[9] My right to indepen-

---

entitled to accept the first contract on the beneficiary's behalf, and to hold it for the beneficiary until the beneficiary has the opportunity to consider whether to accept or reject the legacy. Although the legacy in itself cannot be treated as an incontrovertible benefit (because the beneficiary may choose not to become wealthy, or to own the particular pieces of property left to him or her), the option of deciding whether to accept the legacy is incontrovertible. As Kant puts it, "every human being would necessarily accept such a right (since he can always gain but never lose by it)" (6:294). Like other examples of incontrovertible benefits in the law, such as having your life saved, it is exceptional, and structures the law's readiness to impute a purpose to reach the conclusion that a third party is acting exclusively on your behalf. The physician who saves your life when you are unconscious can recover his fee because the law imputes to you the intention to stay alive, and concludes that the physician is carrying out that intention when you are unable to communicate it. The beneficiary is in a parallel situation: the beneficiary cannot accept or reject the legacy, as such, unless she is aware of its specific terms, but those terms are not determined until the testator dies. A third party acting on her behalf, can, however, hold the offer for her in the period between the testator's death and the beneficiary's learning of the legacy and exercising the option to accept or reject it. If she subsequently accepts the legacy, it functions as a further united will between the parties. This arrangement is also consistent with the freedom of the testator, because it enables him to dispose of his property as he sees fit, subject only to the acceptance by the beneficiary. Kant emphasizes that this double transaction is only possible in a public legal order in which the state can hold a legacy for the testator between the testator's death and a beneficiary's acceptance of a legacy; the testator can direct the legal system to offer the legacy to the beneficiary. (The same structure can be found in the rules surrounding third-party beneficiaries of contracts in the civil law tradition.)

9. One further difference between paradigmatic cases of contract and other consensual transactions is worth noting, though only to set it aside. Contracts, including those in which

dence ordinarily precludes you from touching me or putting me in the path of danger by doing such things as strapping me into the harness, opening the throttle on the motorboat, and releasing the tow rope attaching me to the boat. When I sign a waiver, those things become consistent with my background right to independence. Interacting with you on those terms is the way in which I, rather than anyone else, determine my purposes, because I have decided that my person and property may be used or endangered by you, in particular, in exactly these ways. In creating your right to do these things to me, we also create a new obligation for me, though my obligation is really just a reflex of your right. Since you are entitled to endanger me (and to touch me as you strap the harness on), I am under an obligation in the sense that my freedom is constrained; I may no longer treat your acts as aggression against me. It may be possible to gerrymander things so as to describe all of this as a transfer, but doing so draws attention away from the fact that the terms of our agreement serve to individuate the object of the agreement; as I give you an entitlement to my future performance, or take responsibility for your acts, I do not transfer something that exists fully determinate apart from our agreement.[10]

The transactional analysis of contract shows what is wrong with many prominent ways of thinking about consent. Like contract, consent is a transaction between two persons, in which they vary their respective rights by uniting their wills. Writers often divide between "attitudinal" and "expressive" accounts of consent, according to which consent is rep-

---

one person takes responsibility for the acts of another, typically bind into the future, while in familiar examples, consent can be withdrawn in the middle of the interaction that was consented to. If I have consented to have you cut my hair, and change my mind partway through, you must stop, and there are no residual legal consequences. If you did not violate the terms of my consent, I, rather than you, am responsible for the odd appearance that results. Despite these differences in familiar cases, the underlying structure is the same, since the respective rights and obligations are set by the express or implied terms under which the parties united their wills.

10. The familiar Hohfeldian picture of the parties to a transaction having particular powers must not mislead us here into thinking that the powers can be exercised separately. Even in cases in which there is a transferable object, my power to transfer it, and your power to acquire that thing through transfer, cannot be exercised independently of each other. They come as a matched set.

resented either as a mental state or as a performance.[11] Both approaches represent the question of whether someone has consented to something as a question about that person alone.[12] The appeal of these approaches may reflect a view of autonomy according to which a person is sovereign over the choices he or she makes, coupled with a disagreement about how to answer the factual question about what counts as a choice. A similar split animates the debate in discussions of distributive justice about what G. A. Cohen has called the "cut" between "brute luck" and "option luck," with some partisans supposing that option luck requires inner control, and others supposing that it requires some form of endorsement.[13] Partisans of both sides of those debates, like those on both sides of the attitudinal/expressive split, suppose that through a unilateral act of choice, a person opens up him- or herself to the vagaries of fate or the actions of others.

The difficulty with treating consent as a unilateral act in any of these ways parallels the distinction between abandoning something in another's presence and transferring it to that person. I can unilaterally abandon something (provided that I do so in a way that does not violate any right of any other person). I can only transfer something with the participation

11. See Peter Westen, *The Logic of Consent* (Burlington: Ashgate, 2004), 51; David Archard, *Sexual Consent* (Boulder: Westview, 1997), 3–5; Joel Feinberg, *The Moral Limits of the Criminal Law*, vol. 3 (Oxford: Oxford University Press, 1986), 173; Nathan Brett, "Sexual Offenses and Consent," *Canadian Journal of Law and Jurisprudence* 11 (1998): 69–88; Heidi M. Hurd, "The Moral Magic of Consent," *Legal Theory* 2 (1996): 121–146; Joan L. McGregor, *Is It Rape? On Acquaintance Rape and Taking Women's Consent Seriously* (Aldershot: Ashgate, 2005), 116; Alan Wertheimer, *Consent to Sexual Relations* (Cambridge: Cambridge University Press, 2003), chap. 7.

12. Peter Westen suggests that when I consent, you acquire a Hohfeldian "privilege," that you can do something that would otherwise be wrongful without any legal consequences. Analytically, the suggestion seems unobjectionable, but it simply packages the change in the legal situation—you can now do something you would not otherwise have been able to do—without explaining how it can be within my rightful powers to change your legal situation in this way. Westen's analysis mirrors the abandonment-and-acquisition account of contract, in that he identifies consent with a mental state or observable act by the consenting party, and says that this event causes a change in the other party's legal situation. This seems to bypass the fundamental question of how one person can change another's legal situation in the relevant respects. See Westen, *The Logic of Consent*, 91.

13. G. A. Cohen, "On the Currency of Egalitarian Justice," *Ethics* 99, 4 (July 1989): 906–944.

of another person. In the case of a transfer, this problem takes the form of a problem about the unwelcome gift. I can't give you my toxic waste unless you accept it. Even if I can *direct* my offer to you in a way that I cannot direct my abandonment of an object, you don't have to accept. The parallel problem for consent is that the fact that my unilateral act of offering something to you does not mean that you accept it, no matter how appealing you may find it.[14] Once I have offered, you can accept my offer by accepting the object on offer or performing the invited deed. Those are bilateral acts of acceptance, not unilateral acts.

The bilateral structure of consent presupposes that both parties are morally capable of doing their side of the transaction, and so that both are capable of acting on their own initiative. It requires only that both do act in the required and interlocking ways. I can *make* you an offer unilaterally, without any prior arrangements between us. Conversely, you can take up my offer without a prior arrangement between us regarding how you will respond. And you can decide which of several offers to take up without consulting all of the offerors.

Both my entitlement to direct offers as I see fit and your entitlement to accept or reject offers as you see fit are expressions of our respective rights to independence. The requirement that we unite our wills does not deny that fundamental fact, but builds on it to show that we can only do that if we are both involved. There is a sense in which your freedom is enlarged as soon as I make you an offer—you have an option you didn't have before, namely the option of accepting or rejecting the offer. The same point applies if I manage to accept your offer before you have made it, perhaps by signing the form consenting to a surgical procedure before I know whether I am eligible for it. My signing the form means that you can complete the offer/acceptance structure by scheduling the surgery. Understood in that narrow way, such an option can be represented as

---

14. The confusion of consent with abandonment reflects failure to distinguish two basic types of private rights. My rights to person and property hold against "all the world"; contractual rights hold only in relation to some other person. To abandon my right against trespass or harm, I seem to abandon it more generally, rather than targeting my abandonment to some other person. The Hohfeldian idea that rights *in rem* are bundles of rights *in personam* against indefinitely large numbers of people can redescribe this problem, but not solve it. I can only abandon an *in personam* right to the party against whom it holds, and so cannot do so unilaterally.

something that I can give you without any affirmative act on your part. That is because it is only an offer. Any contrary appearance grows out of the fact that in many situations you can accept the offer by acting on it, so that there is no intervening event in which you first accept the offer and then act on it. The normative structure still turns on your accepting my offer, not on the offer itself.[15]

As an entitlement merely to enter into legal relations with me, an offer is not a legal relationship. You might not want to enter into any such relationship with me. So if I offer to perform some service for you, or let you do something to me, you are entitled to decline, for *any reason whatsoever*. You are the one who decides what sort of consensual interactions you will enter into and whether the terms interest you. I can no more force you into such interactions by offering to enter into them than I can force you to accept property as your own by offering it to you as a gift. Perhaps you do not want a horse, because you think it will be expensive to feed. If so, you can just say no. Perhaps you don't want to be allowed to hold pieces from my porcelain collection because you are worried about being clumsy.

There are cases in which granting someone permission to do something might be thought to require no acceptance, since the permission seems to be an unqualified advantage to that person, something that he or she could have no grounds for refusing. This appearance is misleading, because concepts of right never deal in advantage. Suppose we are having dinner together and I reach for the check, hoping to pay for your dinner and in so doing to take responsibility for the order that you have placed. There is a straightforward sense in which having your dinner paid for is an incontrovertible benefit, since you receive something for free that you were prepared to pay for. Unlike a horse, the money already in your

---

15. In other legal contexts, the concept of reliance occupies what, for Kant, must be the same conceptual space as that of acceptance. If I make a negligent representation to you with respect to some particular transaction, and you rely on it to your detriment, I may be liable to you for the losses you incur. Although the concept of reliance appears to be factual—did plaintiff act on the representation?—the plaintiff's entitlement to act on the representation turns on the fact that defendant's representation is taken to be an undertaking or offer to create a legal relationship. By acting on the representation, plaintiff accepts, and so the extent of plaintiff's reliance is just the extent of the loss for which defendant has undertaken responsibility.

pocket or bank account costs nothing to maintain; unlike the case of my porcelain, you do not need to worry about damaging something of artistic value or historical interest. Nonetheless, from the standpoint of your private rights, you are entitled to reject my offer, and so to decline the benefit. Perhaps you worry about the symbolic significance of letting me buy you dinner, or do not like to accept gifts from people who have more (or less) money than you. Maybe you just want nothing to do with me. Or maybe you just don't choose to accept the benefit. My offer entitles you to decide whether to unite your will with mine, on whatever grounds you choose.[16]

The need for both offer and acceptance is even clearer in cases in which the offer amounts to one person asking another for permission to do something. If I ask you for permission to cut your hair, or pitch my tent on your land, you are entitled to accept or reject my offer. It seems odd to describe this as an enlargement of your freedom. Before I asked, you were entitled to decide who would touch you and what would happen on your land. You still have that right. What you have as a result of my offer is just the entitlement to take up the offer. That is not yet a new right that you have, but rather a feature of the context in which you choose, and I do not wrong you in any way if I change the context back, by withdrawing my offer before you have accepted it.[17] If you accept, your assent is sufficient for a united will, because it joins my offer. As a result, I can cut your hair, or pitch my tent, without wronging you. In none of these cases, however, can one party's action alone change the respective rights of the parties. Both offer and acceptance are required. Each can only do its work with the other.

Although the transaction could be repackaged so as to reserve the name "consent" for either offering permission or granting permission in response to a request, such an account would make consent unilateral in

16. I am grateful to Seana Shiffrin for discussion of this issue.
17. Under the Uniform Commercial Code, §2A-205 (2001), it is possible for someone to make a "Firm Offer" that cannot be revoked for a specified period of time. From Kant's perspective, the only way such a commitment could be consistent with the freedom of the parties is if it is analyzed into a separate contract which must be accepted by the other party. You must accept the irrevocable option I offer you in order to have a claim against me that I not revoke it.

name only. The basis of the change in the normative situation of the parties is the combination of offer and acceptance, rather than one of them considered apart from the other.

Again, a unilateral act on my part can factually *enable* you to do something without your participation—I can take down my fence so that you can wander freely on my land, leave my wallet in easy reach of your sticky fingers, or decide not to resist when you reach for my hair with your scissors. Each of those unilateral acts is an exercise of my rights to person and property. But none of these things, taken on its own, *entitles* you to do those things to me. Nor is a right conferred if I privately *decide* that I would be happy to have you on my land, or to give you my wallet. If I take down my fence, I no longer physically exclude any cattle, but my act does nothing to change the legal situation of either wandering cattle in general or yours in particular. Again, perhaps I know you need money desperately, and that you are too proud to accept a gift but not above stealing. I have not transferred the wallet or its contents to you, since, *ex hypothesi*, you would not accept a gift, and if you knew that I had left it out for you to take, your pride would prevent you from taking it. Again, some distinctions are in order: if I welcome your actions, I presumably *won't* complain. But that wasn't our question. Our question was whether you wrong me by so doing. And the answer to that question still seems to be "yes." Although it is true that I had no objection to your doing these things, you were not entitled to act on that truth.

Talk about a united will might be thought to make an illicit appeal to a set of unobservable or even fictitious events somehow standing behind the more familiar thoughts and actions of persons. But the idea of united choice, like the ideas of rights and obligations it aims to explain, is the rational structure through which what people actually do needs to be interpreted: for example, can you take this scratching of my ear as the making of an offer? The application of such concepts to particulars will inevitably depend in part on context and the expectations normal among the people involved, and it will also require the exercise of judgment. Sometimes a gesture is an invitation or the acceptance of one, sometimes not. Sometimes performing the invited deed is the most obvious way of accepting the invitation. The need for some sort of judgment and interpretation does not, however, change the significance of the idea of a united will. It structures the inquiry, since the question must be whether the parties have in fact agreed. Only through agreement can they act together, make their means available for specified uses consistent with their respective independence. At no point is the inquiry one exclusively about what one or the other party was thinking, because the thoughts a person may have had are indifferent to the distinction between wish and choice. The question must be whether the parties chose together, and what they chose.

Focusing on the transactional nature of consent also provides a principled basis for understanding what goes wrong with two familiar misconceptions about consensual interactions. The first of these identifies consent with risk-taking. The person who walks through a dangerous neighborhood at night takes a risk, but does not consent to any crimes or torts committed against him. After the fact, others might criticize his poor judgment, but the risk he took was the factual risk of injury, not the normative responsibility for the acts of another. One person's risk-taking does not entitle others to do anything they were not entitled to do before.

The second, more prominent misconception applies to consent as a defense in the criminal law, and interprets consent as a mental state on the part of the victim. A familiar line of argument holds that a mistake about consent exculpates a person from criminal liability, no matter how unreasonable the mistake might have been.[18] The proposed line of thought is simple: if the absence of consent is an element of many crimes against a person, then the person who mistakenly believes his victim to have consented did not have *mens rea* with respect to an element of the offense. As a general matter, lack of *mens rea* with respect to an element of an offense exculpates; the person who makes a mistake about consent is not guilty. All of this is correct, so long as the mistake concerns consent. The difficulty arises when it is sometimes concluded from this that if the person accused of a crime sincerely believes that the victim *wanted* him to perform the act in question, he lacks a guilty mind. What makes such "unrea-

---

18. Alan Brudner, "Subjective Fault for Crime: A Reinterpretation," *Legal Theory* 14 (2008): 1–38; Glanville Williams, *Textbook of Criminal Law* (London: Stevens & Sons, 1983), 137–138, both discussing *Director of Public Prosecutions v. Morgan* [1975] 2 All ER 347. All of these focus on cases of rape, and all turn on the suggestion that a mistaken belief about consent serves to negate *mens rea* with respect to an element of the offense, that is, the requirement that intercourse be nonconsensual.

sonable" mistakes unreasonable is that they are not mistakes about consent at all.

The transactional account shows the two flaws in this seemingly straightforward line of reasoning. To consent to another person's doing something to you is not to be favorably disposed toward it, but to *choose* it by uniting your choice with that person's so as to make that person's act consistent with your purposiveness. Whether you have consented does not depend on your settled attitude toward the act, but on whether you have chosen it by uniting your will with another person's. Thus consent requires both choice and a transaction between the parties.

Consent cannot be identified with wishing, because wishing does not require you to determine what ends you will pursue. You can choose something even if your wishes about it are ambivalent; there may not be a single answer to whether you wish for a certain interaction with another person, any more than there needs to be a single fully determinate answer to the question of whether you are wholeheartedly committed to anything you decide to do. The point here is not that your inner life is always an inconsistent blur; it is only that your ability to make arrangements with others does not depend on the lack of ambivalence on your part. You can consent to something with regret, and you can refuse to consent to something even though you want it badly. So the person who commits a crime believing that the victim has an inner wish that that act be performed does not have a defense, because the belief is about the wrong subject matter. Even if it were true, it would be irrelevant. Conversely, if the victim consents and then thinks better of it, but does nothing to indicate a change of mind, then the change is just a wish that consent had not been given, not a mysterious private act of withdrawing consent.

Even if the accused's belief is about some action performed by the victim, the action itself needs to be interpreted as making or accepting an offer, not as some sort of outer evidence of victim's inner thoughts. Suppose that someone is scheduled for a minor surgical procedure and the surgeon asks whether, while they are at it, the patient wishes to have some cosmetic surgical work done as well. Patient declines, but surgeon, thinking that patient was merely embarrassed over the prospect of cosmetic surgery that he wanted quite badly, decides to go ahead anyway. Suppose further that surgeon was correct about patient's secret wishes. Surgeon still commits a battery, even if patient is unlikely to complain, or will only complain out of the same embarrassment. Surgeon's correct belief about patient's wishes is not a belief about consent, so even if it is true, it is irrelevant. The same point applies if surgeon is mistaken about what patient wishes for.

Instead, in order for consent to be validly given, there must be a transaction between the parties. Someone can make a mistake about whether his or her offer was accepted by another person, perhaps because confused about conventional social cues, and perhaps another could accept an offer as a result of a similar mistake. Where there is nothing that could count as either an offer or its acceptance, beliefs about the person's wants are beside the point. The only thing that could count as consent is something that the parties do together, but that requires some sort of public act through which their choice can be united. As I suggested, there is one sense in which the public act, such as a handshake, merely represents the unity of purpose and simultaneity of choice, but there is another sense in which *some* public act is required for there to be unity of purpose and simultaneity of choice. People make mistakes about these things from time to time—what the precise terms of the interaction were, and so on. Some of those mistakes are reasonable, just as disputes can arise in good faith about the terms of any other agreement. Others are unreasonable, if they are understood as interpretations of what transpired between the parties—patient's refusal of the cosmetic surgery cannot be taken to be an act of acceptance. Surgeon might believe that patient is dissembling, and so have a different hypothesis about patient's true wants or wishes. That, however, is not a hypothesis about consent, understood as a transaction between the parties.

II. Why Consent Matters: *Volenti non fit injuria*

Understanding consent transactionally provides an immediate account of why it would provide the basis for a legal defense, both in tort and in the criminal law. The legal maxim *volenti non fit injuria* is a commonplace of liberal thought, and is often paired with another commonplace, Mill's "harm principle," operating to prevent the presumptive significance of harm to which the sufferer consented. The two sit together uneasily, however, because whatever exactly the proposed significance of harm, understood as some sort of setback either to welfare or to interests more broadly construed, it remains just as significant if the person suffering the harm consented to it. The harm principle rests on the idea that harm *is* ordinarily bad enough to outweigh exercises of freedom. Yet if protecting *you* from harm is sufficient grounds for limiting *my* freedom, it might be wondered why it is not grounds for limiting yours. Nor can the *volenti* principle say that the freedom of two people is enough to outweigh any harm that might result. You and I cannot make a voluntary arrangement that entitles us to harm third parties, claiming that somehow our two exercises of freedom somehow outnumber the harms to others we produce. The *volenti* principle requires the more ambitious idea that *you* have a special relation to any injuries *you* choose to undergo or risk. It does not say that your freedom somehow outweighs those harms. It prevents them from being wrongs at all, by changing the moral nature of the relationship between you and the person who injures you.

The transactional conception of consent traces the relevance of consent to the wrongs to which it provides a defense. If wrongs against persons violate their right to set and pursue their own purposes, consensual interactions are not wrongs at all, because they are consistent exercises of purposiveness.

By uniting your will with another person's with respect to a particular transaction, you can give that person powers over your person and property in a way that is consistent with your exclusive power to determine how they will be used. The *object* of the united will can be your deed, or your responsibility for another person's deed, but not an outcome considered apart from our capacities as purposive agents. You consent to my doing thus and so to you or your goods; I agree to bring it about that you receive the specified goods or services. When you tell me that it is fine for me to pitch my tent in your front yard, or tell your doctor to open you up and take out your malfunctioning appendix, you do not give me, or the doctor, a power inconsistent with your entitlement to determine how your person and property will be used. Instead, by consenting, you make my pitching my tent, or the physician's removing the appendix, an instance of your determining how your land or body will be used. You have the power to integrate my act into your purposiveness, since your entitlement to determine the purposes for which your person and property will be used is perfectly general, and so can incorporate the actions of another.

Once I have taken responsibility for your acts, I do not somehow forfeit the right to complain about them; that would be like supposing that I abandon my rights, which you then mysteriously acquire *de novo*. Instead, by performing your act you do me no wrong. I might be disappointed about my condition, but my disappointment does not generate a legal wrong. Since I have taken responsibility for it, it is just my problem. Absent some sort of defect in my consent, the situation is just the same.

The claim that I take responsibility for my own acts or for your acts when I make them mine through contract or consent is a normative claim about rights and duties, rather than a metaphysical one about my control over things for which I am responsible. When I sign the waiver before you take me paragliding, I am not asserting or acknowledging that I know everything about it; I am taking responsibility for what happens, including the parts that neither you nor I can control. Taking responsibility for things outside anyone's control might sound like willful gambling, but it is actually the most familiar feature of life as a person capable of setting and pursuing his or her purposes. To make something your purpose is to use your means to pursue it, even though you will normally have no guarantee of success, and no guarantee against unwelcome side effects. When you take responsibility for another person's action, you join your purposiveness with his or hers, again, normally with no guarantee of success or against side effects. When you do so, you are not wronged by what happens, because you've done what you always do—act in an uncertain world.

III. When Consent Does Not Matter

By consenting to something, you make another person's actions an expression of your freedom. Consent provides a defense, because an exercise of your freedom cannot be a violation of your freedom and so cannot be a wrong against you. There are some cases in which consent is not ordinarily thought to provide a defense. In some cases, consent is said to be defective: if it is fraudulently or coercively obtained, either it is not really consent, or if it is consent, it is not valid consent. In other cases, the wrong in question is thought to be beyond the power of individual consent. Consent is normally not a defense to a charge of murder or deliberate wounding.

These exceptions have an undisputed place in legal doctrine, but they also have considerable intuitive force apart from it. Defenders of legal moralism often bring out such examples to embarrass their opponents. Lord Devlin used the example of consensual murder to suggest that any coherent legal system must finally be rooted in the sensibilities of citizens, rather than their commitments to individual freedom.[19] Irving Kristol introduced the example of public gladiatorial contests to underscore what he saw as the necessary limits on freedom. Kristol contends that such contests would be objectionable, and any state should prohibit them, even if they could be shown to be fully consensual.[20] Defenders of Mill's harm principle, including Joel Feinberg, have sought to defuse such examples by emphasizing the indirect harm such public displays of brutality would cause.[21]

These exceptions pose an apparent challenge for the transactional account of consent, since that account purports to be formal, and so independent of substantive concerns about the value of activities being consented to, or the terms on which they are accepted. Other than fraud, the exceptions appear to be substantive (what Kant would call "material") rather than formal. The difference between material and formal principles has important implications for the scope of the limits on consent. If the availability of consent as a defense depends upon some public assessment of the worth of various activities, Devlin and Kristol are right, and the state may, if it chooses, prohibit activities considered degrading even when done by consenting adults, or, for that matter, when a person does them to him- or herself without anyone else's participation. If the exceptions can be given a formal analysis, neither degradation nor public assessments of value enter into them.

---

19. Patrick Devlin, *The Enforcement of Morals* (Oxford: Oxford University Press, 1965), 6.

20. Irving Kristol, "Pornography, Obscenity, and the Case for Censorship," *New York Times Magazine,* March 28, 1971.

21. Feinberg, *Harmless Wrongdoing* (Oxford: Oxford University Press, 1990), 128–129.

Consider force and fraud first. If consent is thought to be either a mental attitude or a public expression, the person who accepts or agrees to something under conditions of force or fraud has consented. The whole point of using force against someone or defrauding him is to get him to accept the terms in question. So the question of whether they have been accepted has an obvious answer. From this perspective, the only defect that could be involved in the use of force or fraud would have to be located in the way in which the acceptance was procured.

It might be thought that fraudulently obtained consent is not real, because in order to consent to something, you must understand what you have consented to and the terms on which you are consenting to it. If I knowingly but falsely told you that my paraglider was in good repair, and you agreed to take responsibility for any risks attendant on our glide, you consented to gliding in a safe glider, not a dangerous one, and so you did not actually to consent to what we did. The difficulty with this approach is twofold. First, people often consent to things that they do not understand fully, and that consent is valid. Again, the analogy with contracts is helpful. I might agree to invest in something in the expectation that its price will increase, when in fact all the signs point toward its price dropping. I might buy a painting at an auction, as a result of a mistake I made about the identity of the painter. I might agree to go paragliding with you because I mistakenly believe that there are no downdrafts unless there is a hill or tall building nearby. I have consented even though I was mistaken. The leading cases on negligent misrepresentation have exactly this structure. An auditor or public weigher certifies the reliability of some measurement or accounting. If the representation is carelessly made, the person making it is responsible for the losses incurred by the purchaser or investor, even though he or she undertook responsibility for acts done in reliance on the certification in the firm belief that the weights or accounts *were* accurate. That brings me to the second and more general difficulty: focusing on the way in which deceit interferes with wholehearted agreement leaves out the role of the deceiver.

Parallel considerations apply to force. People ordinarily consent to things because of the circumstances; someone will consent to invasive surgery to avoid illness or death. It does not follow from this that the consent is not valid. You may have an excuse in the criminal law if you were overwhelmed by circumstances and so might suppose that the overwhelming circumstances block the inference from your conduct to your agency or character. But that says nothing about the relation between you and the other person. In fact, in cases of necessity or duress, the person who is overwhelmed is typically supposed to be civilly liable to anyone who is injured. You don't go to jail for breaking into a cabin to save your life, but you are liable in tort for the damage you cause, because it is still something you did to someone else's property, even if you are not fully culpable. In cases of contracting or consenting where a lot is at stake, the agreement is still something you did. Force is different because of the role of the other person.[22]

Instead of focusing exclusively on the consenting party's situation, the transactional account must focus on the relation between the parties, in order to show that in cases of force and fraud, consent fails for lack of a united will. Both fraud and force stop the parties to an agreement from uniting their wills because the person committing either is already unilaterally determining how the other's means will be used. In cases of fraud, one person misrepresents the situation so as to get the other to agree, but the result is agreement without a united will because the parties lack common terms.[23] Agreements may also lack common terms in cases of mutual mistake, so that I think that I am agreeing to one thing, and you think we are agreeing to another. In such a situation, agreement fails for lack of common terms; for all of our negotiations, we were really just talking past each other. Fraud is distinctive because the willful misrepresentation of

---

22. There may be cases in which natural or social circumstances lead to so great a disparity of bargaining power that the contract will be judged to be unconscionable. It seems to me unhelpful to assimilate such cases to force cases for the same reason that it is a mistake to assimilate mistake cases to fraud. Instead, such cases reflect the underlying presumption created by the duty of rightful honor that a person does not intend to be a mere means for others. The standard juridical tests—the lack of donative intent and the absence of a functioning market in which exchanges take place—reflect this idea. On the idea that such factors underwrite a court's interest in protecting the integrity of its processes, see Seana Shiffrin, "Paternalism, Unconscionability Doctrine, and Accommodation," *Philosophy & Public Affairs* 29 (2000): 205–250.

23. Analyzed in terms of Kant's structure, the two "preparatory acts" of offer and assent are not completed, and so there are no terms on which to complete the "constitutive acts through which the parties unite their wills."

the situation *guarantees* that there can be no united will; the fraud does not suppose he shares a united will with his dupe. Of course the dupe thinks there is a united will and that there is an agreement. That is why he's a dupe.[24]

In cases of force, whether direct or threatened, a united will is impossible for a different reason. The problem is not that someone consents in response to an inducement, even an extreme one. People almost always agree to things in response to some incentive for inducement offered by some other person; I sign the waiver because I want you to take me paragliding; I consent to the surgery because I want you to remove my festering appendix. In cases of force, the incentive offered is one that the person offering it has no entitlement to offer, typically the other person's life or bodily integrity. Although self-preservation can be among a person's purposes—as consent in the medical context makes clear—parties can only unite their wills with respect to things to which they have rightful powers. In uniting their wills, the parties exercise rights that they have so as to create new rights and obligations. That is why you cannot unilaterally transfer something to another person; your entitlement to alienate and the other person's entitlement to accept need to be brought together. If I agree to do something in response to a threat, the person making the threat is offering something that he has no right to offer. Thus even if the terms are clear, they are not exercises of the respective rights of the parties.[25]

---

24. In principle this analysis could also apply if A consents to some interaction with B as a result of fraud by a third party, C, provided that B is aware of C's fraud. Although B does not perpetrate the fraud, common terms are lacking. If B is unaware of fraud, a court may provide A with a remedy of rescission of a foreword contract, but no court would grant A a remedy for trespass or battery against B, precisely because they had united their wills.

25. Analyzed in terms of Kant's structure, the two "preparatory acts" pose no conceptual problem because the terms are common, but there is a difficulty with the two "constitutive acts." In principle this analysis could extend to cases in which A consents to some interaction with B as a result of a threat by a third party, C. If B is aware of the threat, C's not carrying out the threat is an implied term of the contract, so B wrongs A by engaging in the interaction. If B is unaware of the threat, B does not wrong A by engaging in the interaction. A court may provide A with a remedy of recission of a foreword contract in such circumstances, but no court would grant A remedy for trespass or battery against B, precisely because they had united their wills.

IV. Material Exceptions: Slavery and Murder

Consent is not a defense to a charge of murder. In English law, at least since *Wright's Case*,[26] it is not a defense to a charge of deliberate wounding. In that case, the accused was asked by a beggar to maim him, to make him a more pathetic specimen as he asked for money. The court accepted the accused's description of the facts, but held that "on grounds of public policy," victim consent was not a defense in this case. In more recent cases, courts have held that in the case of a consensual fistfight from which death ensues, victim consent does not provide a defense. In German criminal law, in very limited circumstances, consent may reduce a charge of murder to one of manslaughter, but it does not serve to make the killing rightful.[27] These exceptions are familiar, and most people find them plausible and obvious. The same can be said for the limits to contract law that exclude slave contracts. Although some philosophers in the rapture of theses about "self-ownership" have tried to defend them, even those defenses have been halfhearted, typically limited by caveats about the requisite circumstances not applying, or competing values, extrinsic to issues of consent and contract, overriding them.

These material exceptions might seem to be in tension with the transactional account, as they seem to stop someone from taking responsibility for something for which he or she wants to take responsibility. Thus they may appear to be holdovers from paternalistic ideas of protecting people against their own poor judgment, or ideas about the wrongfulness of suicide. I want to suggest, however, that they are not only compatible with the account, but actually presupposed by it. I will do so by imbedding the examples in the broader conception of private interaction that underlies it. You cannot consent to your own murder or enslavement because it lies beyond your normative power for uniting your will with that of another.

For the transactional account of consent, consent is important against the background of a more general idea that private persons are free and

---

26. Co. Litt. f. 127 a-b (1603).

27. Although the best-known example of this doctrine involves the grisly case of a cannibal who advertised for the victim over the Internet and videotaped the entire proceedings, its more usual operation is in cases in which the killing took place on compassionate grounds.

equal *to each other* in the sense that each is entitled to pursue whatever purposes he or she might have, provided that this can be done in a way that is consistent with a like freedom for others to pursue their purposes. Within such a regime of equal freedom, people are independent, and able to do as they please. As a result, they are able to do as they please when it comes to interactions with others. Consent is fundamental to this picture, because it enables people to modify the boundaries that make their equal freedom with others possible, in light of their particular purposes. That is why consent serves as a defense. It enables one person to permit another to do what would otherwise be forbidden. In so doing, it lets each person determine the boundaries of his or her interactions with others. Moreover, it lets each person determine those boundaries in consultation or coordination with particular people, one at a time. So I can decide to consent to have you visit my home without thereby inviting everyone into my home; conversely (subject to antidiscrimination laws) I can invite the public into my business premises, but make an exception so as not to let you in.

Not every arrangement that two people might wish to make is consistent with this background of mutual freedom, because the background is structured by each person's innate right of humanity, which, as we have seen, is a right to independence of the choice of another. Kant's emphasis on the distinction between persons and things reflects the normative priority of the innate right of humanity. Thus in the Division of Rights in the Introduction to the *Doctrine of Right*, Kant notes that we cannot conceive of "the relation in terms of rights of human beings towards beings that have only duties but no rights."[28] He notes that this category is empty, for these would be "human beings without personality (serfs, slaves)." In the division of Acquired Rights, he notes that there are only three possible categories, rights to things, rights against persons, and rights to persons ("akin to" rights to things), because the fourth category, rights against things, is necessarily empty.[29] The distinction between person and thing is not put forward as a conceptual claim, but rather as an implication of the moral nature of rights. Rights always govern the interactions of free

28. 6:241.
29. 6:357.

persons. Among the rights that free persons can have is the right to vary their rights as against other persons by contract. As we saw in Chapter 3, contract belongs in the class of acquired rights, because if it is possible to do something for another person, it would be an arbitrary limit on freedom were people unable to have entitlements to performances by others. The power to contract thus constitutes an extension of innate right. At the same time, however, it is constrained by the duty of rightful honor, so that a contract cannot turn a person into a thing.

If consent is represented as a way in which one person through a unilateral act of choice becomes responsible for something, then the decision to become the slave of another might appear to be no different from any other decision. Provided that there was neither force nor fraud, it is just something someone decided to do.

Kant's objection to slave contracts rests on his broader understanding of contract, and in turn on his broader conception of the right to freedom under universal law. The possibility of two people uniting their wills presupposes each person's capacity for taking responsibility for actions. Thus the terms on which you unite your will with another's cannot presuppose the legal irrelevance of one of the two wills. Others can acquire your property or particular deeds, but not your person, because your person, understood as your entitlement to set your own purposes, forms the background against which you can take responsibility for deeds, whether yours or those of others. Put differently, two people can only act together in a way that is consistent with their freedom provided that they unite their purposes while preserving their separate purposiveness.

From this perspective, the problem with slave contracts is that slavery is the annihilation of legal personality: the slave becomes an object, fully subject to the master's choice. As such, the slave is incapable of undertaking obligations, because she has no rightful power to bind herself. Only the master has that power. Having purportedly transferred her capacity to be bound, however, she is no longer capable of being legally bound, and so has no contractual duties at all, so none to the master. A contract creates new rights and duties as between the parties to it; a slave contract purports to bind the slave, and at the same time dissolve her legal personality, so that she cannot be bound in her own right. Thus the slave who disobeys does not wrong her master, and so, although the master may be *able* to coerce her, the master could not be entitled to do so by way of enforcing a right. The slave has not deprived the master of anything, because a contract to transfer everything can transfer nothing.

The same argument can be stated in the vocabulary of the duty of rightful honor. As we saw in Chapter 2, like all duties relating to right, the "internal duty" of rightful honor restricts the ways in which a person can exercise his or her freedom to be consistent with the Universal Principle of Right. No rightful act on your part can bind you to a condition in which you are subject to another person's choice. So the limit on the exercise of your freedom must be the preservation of that freedom.

This argument for the incoherence of slavery contracts parallels the familiar Kantian "contradiction in conception" test in ethics in one way, but differs from it in another. When Kant argues in the *Groundwork* that the making of a lying promise could not be a universal law, his point is that such a law would require that all promises both be kept and not be kept.[30] The difficulty with slave contracts, however, lies not in the possibility of their universalization, but rather in the form of relation that they presuppose. You can only vary your rights and obligations in relation to another insofar as you are a being entitled to set your own purposes; a slavery contract both presupposes and rejects that entitlement. As Kant remarks, the moment you close such a contract, you are no longer bound by it.[31] Kant's point is not that you will be unable to meet such a contractual obligation; people who undertake contractual obligations they cannot meet are still bound by them. The problem instead is that a slave can have no legal obligations whatsoever, and so cannot have the obligation of obedience that is a supposed term of the contract. The master may think otherwise, as, indeed, may the slave. But the fact that the parties wish to create such a relationship does not show that they can make one, because their contract has inconsistent terms, and so cannot be the object of an agreement.

The idea that your right to freedom is inalienable follows from the rela-

---

30. Kant, *Groundwork of the Metaphysics of Morals*, 4:422.
31. In *Theory and Practice*, Kant makes this point by saying that a person "cannot, by means of any rightful deed (whether his own or another's), cease to be in rightful possession of himself" (8:293).

tion between each person's innate right of humanity and the normative structure of contract. A slave contract is incoherent because the slave is both a person and a thing, subject to an obligation to do the master's bidding, yet not a being capable of rights. The inconsistency between something's being both a person and a thing is not logical but normative. Kant does not try to ground the inalienability of each person's right to his or her own person in a conceptual claim that the concept of ownership cannot be reflexive; he shows that transferring your person is inconsistent with each person's innate entitlement to be independent of the choice of all others, which is a precondition of anyone's having the power to transfer rights.[32]

This analysis does not depend upon any substantive concerns about the vices of servility. Kant gives powerful expression to such concerns in his *Doctrine of Virtue*, but, as he remarks in the *Naturrecht Feyerabend* lectures, as a matter of right you can do as you want with your own person as far as right is concerned.[33] The servile person who always does the bidding of another may well suffer from self-inflicted immaturity, but is always nonetheless *entitled* to grow up.[34] The person who signs a slave contract is in a fundamentally different situation, having given up the entitlement to set and pursue his own purposes and to meet his own obligations, including those incurred under the contract. The slave contract gives up on the right to purposiveness, while the servile character is an exercise of that right, even if it is a debased and pathetic one. The idea that people are entitled to set and pursue their own purposes includes the entitlement to set and pursue them in pointless ways.

Slave contracts are sometimes said to be void on grounds of "public policy," but properly understood, that formulation simply underscores Kant's point. The relevant concept of policy here is not consequentialist.

---

32. G. A. Cohen accuses Kant of trying to "pull a normative argument out of a conceptual hat," in *Self-Ownership, Freedom and Equality* (Cambridge: Cambridge University Press, 1995), 212. Kant's argument for the distinction between persons and things is itself normative. There is a sense in which the problem with slave contracts reflects the problem with slavery itself, which lies at the heart of the Kantian account of each person's entitlement to independence of the choice of others.

33. Kant, *Naturrecht Feyerabend*, trans. Lars Vinx (unpublished, 2003), 27:1334.

34. Thomas Hill Jr., "Servility and Self-Respect," *Monist* 57 (1973): 87–104.

It focuses instead on the broader presuppositions of a regime of contract, according to which you can only alienate by contract what civilian legal systems call your "patrimony."[35] As we saw in Chapter 3, acquired rights always have a "mine and yours" structure such that, although a particular person has this right, it could coherently have belonged to another person. Property is the most obvious example of this structure: it is my horse, but if you had been the one who acquired it, you would have the same set of rights in relation to it. Actions have the same "mine and yours" structure: if I cut your hair, I might just as well have cut somebody else's hair, or you have had someone else cut yours. The structure of rights involved would have been the same. By contrast, your right in your own person could not belong to any other person. As we saw in Chapter 2, it is innate because it does not require an affirmative act to establish it; your right in your own person is something you enjoy simply in virtue of your humanity. It could not coherently require an affirmative act to establish it, because affirmative acts sufficient to establish rights presuppose persons capable of performing them antecedent to those acts. Your person, then, is the precondition of any entitlement you might give to anyone else, because it is your ability to give others rights in relation to your person, your

---

35. Other contracts that are said to be void on grounds of public policy also lie outside a person's patrimony. A contract to pay a bribe to an official is not enforceable, because the official does not have his office subject to his private choice, and so the performance or nonperformance of official duties is not subject to his choice. As a result, the official's choice cannot be united with that of another person with respect to conduct of those duties. A contract to vote for a candidate in an election is not enforceable for the same reason: a citizen's right to vote is not a private power to be used for private purposes. Some courts have held that a contract to convert to or practice a certain religion cannot be enforced. The right to vote, the powers of an office, and freedom of religion are all fundamentally different from your right to your deeds and possessions. The right to vote is something each person has in his or her capacity as a citizen; the example of officeholders is just a narrower case of this. The right to determine which religion you will practice is a further example with the same structure: the law will permit you to undertake and act on religious vows, but will not permit others to force you to do so, or to hold you to a contract to do so. The other prominent class of exceptions involves contracts to violate fiduciary duties, including both corporate directors (a private variant on the example of a bribe) and parents accepting inadequate child support for their children or opting out of their obligations as guardians in return for payment. In these examples, someone has possession but not use of either property or another person, and so cannot accept payment in return for failing to fulfill the concomitant duties.

deeds, and your property. The most you can do is to give another person a right to a particular use of your person or a particular deed. It is no accident, then, that any attempt to alienate it must fail, because you can only unite your will with another provided that your personality survives the union.[36]

Kant's brief discussion of slave contracts represents them in their purest form. Many historical instances of slavery and serfdom permitted slaves some legal powers. For example, under Roman law slaves could inherit, and enter into contracts that bound their masters. These differences do not render Kant's analysis irrelevant to these examples. Kant remarks that although you can give another person a right to a particular performance, and so to a use of one of your powers, you cannot alienate those powers. This restriction on alienating your powers is parallel to the restriction on alienating your person. Suppose I wanted to give you a right, not to have me do this or that service for you, but rather the right to permanently control the use of my arms. The difficulty with any such agreement is that it would limit my entitlement to exercise any other rights. So I could not sign a contract without your permission, or move (my arms) from one place to another. That in turn means that I am not allowed to do anything inconsistent with your directing my arms, and so my entire person is a mere object, even though I retain a variety of other legal powers, since you are entitled to determine whether I will exercise them or not. More generally, a form of slavery that reserved certain rights to the slave would give the master the right to determine whether the slave could exercise those rights by determining what the slave could do with his body. Since the slave is not entitled to decide whether to exercise his rights, the limited slave contract has an incoherent term. Gerrymandering

---

36. Defenders of "self-ownership" sometimes conclude that slave contracts are binding because a person is entitled to do whatever he wants with his own person. Such an account requires both an explanation of how a right can be transferred at all, which self-ownership theorists have yet to provide, and a specification of what is transferred when a person is such that the person can be transferred and still be subject to an obligation to the person to whom he is transferred—Kant's two issues. Although I cannot show that these could not be addressed, Kant's argument shows that the mere fact that someone might conclude that such a transfer was advantageous does not show that it can create a right in one person to own another.

the terms of such an imagined contract cannot solve this problem, because the underlying problem is that others can only assert a claim of right against you, that is, can only restrict your freedom, insofar as you are a free being, that is, your own master.

This brings us to consensual murder. Slavery is not the same as death, but it has been characterized as a form of social death.[37] From the standpoint of a system of equal freedom, the converse point is more relevant. Death is just a biological fact; murder, by contrast, is a form of biological slavery, since the murderer decides whether the victim will continue to exist. The reason that consent is not a defense to murder is the same reason that you cannot contract your way into slavery. In both cases, the possibility of people acting together in a way that is consistent with their respective freedom presupposes that they are able to maintain their separateness through that unity.[38] That is what makes the united will an exercise of their freedom. Thus the terms of the interaction and agreement must be consistent with the preservation of their separateness.

The difficulty for consent as a defense to murder thus turns on the distinction between murder (as biological slavery) and death as a mere biological fact. Consensual murder requires that one person taking the life of another is a term of the agreement, and so that one person relinquish any claim to resist with right the force that the other uses. As we saw, you can only agree to some action by another person by giving another person a right to do that thing, which is equivalent to undertaking an obligation to permit the other to do it. Victim cannot undertake an obligation to permit himself to be treated as an object; if he is an object, he can have no obligations. Thus the victim is both a person and a thing, which is normatively impossible.

This focus on the right that victim would have to give to aggressor underwrites the contrast between cases in which someone consents to being killed and those in which someone consents to participate in an activity

---

37. See John Rawls, *Justice as Fairness: A Restatement* (Cambridge, Mass.: Harvard University Press, 2001), 24. Rawls cites Orlando Patterson, *Slavery and Social Death* (Cambridge, Mass.: Harvard University Press, 1982).

38. Kant's own treatment of relations of status as ones in which one person has possession but not use of another person reflects the same requirement of maintaining separateness through unity.

that carries risk of death, even a significant risk, such as extreme skiing or freefall skydiving. In that sort of case, the terms of the united will do not presuppose the violation of their respective separateness. Even in sports where the risk is not merely of injury or death, but injury or death through the actions of an opponent, the parties consent not to one person doing something to another, but rather to two persons interacting in a way that foreseeably injures one or both of them, and from which one or both could die. Perhaps a consensual boxing match is more brutal than this description suggests. I do not mean to suggest otherwise, but only to note that the only way that it can be treated as a case of a consensual activity that results in injury is if it can be represented as a contest of strength, in which each boxer makes himself available as a target while trying to overpower the other, but neither grants the other the right to hit him when he is down.

A consensual fight to the death—Kristol's gladiatorial contest—is different. It cannot be represented as a consensual contest that carries with it a significant risk. Each of the gladiators in the example gives the other the power of life and death, and the winner is not declared when the loser gives up. Thus it is an arrangement in which the victim is turned into a mere thing, and so one to which the parties cannot agree.[39]

This may seem to be a misrepresentation of the gladiatorial contest, in which the entitlement to resist might appear to be a term of their agreement. But if one person cannot consent to being killed by another, then two cannot each consent to being killed by the other. Contrary to appearances, the gladiators do not have a right to defend themselves; the terms of the imagined contract would need to require that each agrees to be turned into a thing, and then the two things fight to the death, in the manner of animals that are sometimes made to fight to the death to entertain spectators.

In contrasting boxing matches with gladiatorial contests, I do not mean to be offering a brief in favor of boxing, or commenting on the best way to classify a consensual fight to the death in a less spectacular setting. The Kantian theory at the level at which I have sought to develop and defend

---

39. The problem is only exacerbated if we imagine that the arrangement involves a forward contract so that each gladiator's consent is irrevocable.

it is abstract, and speaks only to the factors relevant to classify particulars, without classifying any of them. The important contrast is between consenting to something that carries a risk of death, even a significant one, and consenting to death. The latter guarantees that the consenting party cannot be bound; the terms of the agreement provide the guarantee, so the agreement is not binding even if the victim survives.

The contrast between your person, which lacks the "mine or yours" structure of your deeds and possessions, also provides a framework for thinking about other cases in which consent is sometimes said not to be a defense, such as mutilation, including *Wright's Case,* involving the beggar who asked to be maimed so as to improve his earning prospects. Few would want to claim that consent was not a defense in many cases of one person permanently changing the structure of another's body. In addition to the obvious medical cases, cosmetic procedures including ear piercing and tattooing are wrongful if nonconsensual, but unobjectionable if consensual. Consensual mutilation looks different through something like the following chain of reasoning: your body simply is your person (that is why crimes against the body are "offenses against the person"); the "members" of the human body are not parts, but form an essential unity,[40] so that depriving a person of a body part deprives her of part of her general purposiveness. There is something appealing about this chain of reasoning, though perhaps also something implausible. Both the appeal and the implausibility reflect different considerations that might be brought to bear in determining whether maiming is, like tattooing, simply a way of decorating a person according to her highly unusual tastes, or whether instead, it is, like murder, a removal of purposiveness. At the level of abstraction at which the idea of consent as a united will operates, it provides no particular resolution of such questions, although it does show what is at issue in them.

The bar to consent as a defense to murder differs from the moral prohibition on suicide in the same way that the argument against slave contracts differs from the moral prohibition of servility.[41] Kant famously ar-

---

40. 6:278.

41. Because it does not depend upon the wrongfulness of suicide, the bar to consent as a defense to murder does not *automatically* preclude the legality of assisted suicide in cases in which a terminally ill person is incapable of taking his or her own life. Such cases might appear to be straightforward examples of consensual murder, in the sense that one person acts

gues in the *Groundwork* that a rational being could not adopt a maxim of self-love according to which a person makes it "my principle to shorten my life when its longer duration threatens more troubles than it promises agreeableness."[42] Kant argues that such a maxim could not be conceived as a universal law because it would violate its own presuppositions. Whatever its successes or limitations, this ethical argument against suicide has no bearing on rights, since it concerns only the relation between the end to be pursued and the means being used in pursuit of it. As Kant makes clear in the Introduction to the *Doctrine of Right*, the relation between an agent's ends and the means he or she uses doesn't matter for right; only the form of interaction with others does. So the wrongfulness of suicide does not enter the argument.[43]

---

through another, and so takes responsibility for the action of another of taking the life of the first. As such they seem to suffer from the incoherence that besets consensual murder. A significant hurdle to any attempt to distinguish them is generated by the familiar legal rule, in both civil and common law systems, that a person who acts to preserve the life of another is normally (though defeasably) deemed to be acting on the other's behalf and so commits no battery. A physician who treats an unconscious patient is entitled to payment for services; those injured trying to rescue another person (but not property) can recover in tort from those who created the initial danger. In these cases, the law treats each person as having the purpose of maintaining his or her continued purposiveness; this deemed purpose has been held to apply even to a case in which a physician revives someone who has attempted suicide. None of these doctrines would interfere with Kevorkian-type assisted suicide, in which one person provides another with a mechanism that enables the other to take his own life. Active cases would seem to require a different analysis, for the person who wishes to end his life is capable of doing so but chooses not to, wanting instead another person to do so. In such cases, it would seem that consent can be no defense. Perhaps an argument could be made consistent (though certainly not required) with Kantian concepts of right according to which an advance directive empowering an agent to act on a patient's behalf should patient be unconscious or otherwise unable to act for herself could include provisions not only for withdrawal of life support, but also for affirmative measures. If it could be shown that this is an instance of acting for the patient's purposes, in circumstances in which there is no possibility of future purposive action by the patient, perhaps it could be treated as an instance of one person acting as the legal guardian of another. But it would have to be restricted to such cases.

42. *Groundwork*, 4:422.

43. A corporation can consent to the annihilation of its own legal personality (through acquisition by sale, or going out of business) because that personality is derivative in two senses. First, a corporation is a structure of acquired rights through which individual human beings act. Second, a corporation does not have full personality because it is not entitled to use

V. Conclusion

Consent matters because it is a condition of free persons exercising their freedom together. Freedom in turn matters independently of the particular ways in which it is exercised: each person is entitled to set and pursue his or her own purposes, subject only to the condition that he or she does so in a way consistent with the entitlement of others to do the same. Such an austere account of freedom does not permit any assessment of different choices on the basis of some public index of their importance. Instead, it requires only that free persons be morally capable of getting together to change their respective rights and obligations.

---

its means to set whatever purposes it wishes. Its directors and officers are charged with acting for the purposes of its owners or, in the case of philanthropic corporations, its creators. They cannot set or pursue whatever purposes they see fit, and when dissolving the corporation advances the corporation's limited purposes, they may do so.

CHAPTER 6

Three Defects in the State of Nature

STATES CLAIM POWERS that no private person could have. Not only can they collect taxes and imprison wrongdoers; they can impose binding resolutions on private disputes, restrict agents on grounds of public health, and regulate other aspects of social life. Defenders of limited government insist that the state's power to do these things must be subject to fundamental restrictions. Prior to any question of what factors properly *limit* the exercise of those powers, however, is the more basic question of the justification of the powers themselves: how can an institution, whose offices are filled with ordinary fallible human beings, be entitled to do things to people, or demand things of them, that none of those same human beings are entitled to do or demand on their own? As Kant puts it, all positive laws are contingent and chosen *(willkürlich)* by the persons giving them. How can one person change the normative situation of others, consistent with everyone else's entitlement to be independent of the choice of another? This is the basic question of political authority.

In this chapter, I develop Kant's account of political authority as it is presented in his account of the transition from private right to public right. Those arguments are expressed in the social contract tradition's vocabulary of a state of nature and the need to exit it. Despite this common vocabulary, Kant does not follow Hobbes or Locke in focusing on the empirical defects of the state of nature, such as self-preference and limited knowledge. Kant's arguments are *a priori* because all internal to the concepts of acquired rights. Kant presents the state of nature as a pure system of private right, containing only the moral principles that govern interaction between private persons.[1] Understood in this pure form as a system of private rights without public law, the state of nature is morally incoherent from the standpoint of rights, in three distinct ways. First, the postulate of practical reason with regard to rights shows that acquired rights are a morally necessary extension of freedom. But, Kant will argue, it is impossible to acquire a right to anything in a state of nature. Second, rights are necessarily enforceable—a right is a title to coerce—but acquired rights cannot be enforced in a state of nature. Third, as aspects of a system of equal freedom, the application of private rights to particulars can only be determined in accordance with standards that are not unilateral exercises of the judgment of one of the parties to a dispute. But such objective standards cannot be established in a state of nature. Each of the defects in a state of nature is a conceptual problem concerning the internal requirements of a system of rights. Unlike the defects identified by Hobbes or Locke, they do not reflect human limitations; they apply "no matter how good and right-loving human beings might be."[2]

The remedy for each of the three defects is an institution that has moral powers that private citizens lack. Taken together, the three remedies are related as the three branches in a republican system of government are. The legislative branch is charged with making law, the executive with implementing and enforcing law, and the judiciary with applying it to particulars in cases of dispute.[3] The functions are distinct because only the legislature has the power to make law. It does so as the voice of the people, so that they rule themselves; Kant remarks that the people are "represented" by the sovereign, which means that they can only speak and act together through institutions. The executive branch does not make general rules, but takes up means to give effect to them. The judiciary resolves

---

1. Kant, *Lectures on Ethics,* trans. P. Heath (Cambridge: Cambridge University Press, 1997), 27:589.
2. 6:312.
3. 6:313.

particular disputes. Each is both coordinate with the others and subordinate to them, and "through the union of both each subject is apportioned his rights."[4] By the time Kant announces that the obligation to enter a rightful condition can be "explicated analytically" from the concept of right in contrast with violence, he has provided the resources to show why each branch is needed.

As he summarizes it in his lectures on natural right:

> *Justitia distributiva* determines right through a *lex publica,* applies it to each case, and enforces obedience. Renounce your intention to seek right according to your own judgment and leave it to the legislator to determine, to the judge to pass judgment, and give up your power with which you could force the other.[5]

The three defects are distinct, but have a parallel structure: nobody is under any obligation to defer to the deeds, claims, or judgments of others, unless appropriate institutions are in place. The distinctive powers that each institution must have require that those institutions differ in kind from any sort of private association. A private association can only have such powers as its particular members transfer to it. The powers to authorize one person to change the normative situation of all others, to enforce private rights in the name of all, and to impose closure on private disputes are all powers that no private person could have. The point of each argument is to show that these powers are morally required even though private persons lack them.

This chapter will focus on the defects of the state of nature as a system of pure private ordering and the form that any solution to all three of them must take. The next one will turn to Kant's argument that a state can solve them in a way that is consistent with everyone's freedom.[6]

---

4. 6:316.

5. Kant, *Naturrecht Feyerabend,* trans. Lars Vinx (unpublished, 2003), 27:1390.

6. Versions of each of the three defects have drawn the attention of commentators. To mention only some of these, the argument from unilateral action is considered in Bernd Ludwig, "Whence Public Right? The Role of Theoretical and Practical Reason in Kant's *Doctrine of Right,*" in Mark Timmons, ed., *Kant's Metaphysics of Morals: Interpretive Essays* (Oxford: Oxford University Press, 2002), and Katrin Flikschuh, "Reason, Right, and Revolution: Kant

I. Unilateral Choice:
Property and the Problem of Political Authority

The most general argument focuses on the problem of unilateral choice. Positive law requires a person, or group of persons, to formulate, apply, and enforce it. In each case, that person makes a choice, and the power to do so must be reconciled with the freedom of those who are bound by it. Kant's explanation of how such authorization is possible comes in the course of his discussion of the acquisition of property, but his solution to it applies to all political authority, including the power to make laws in pursuit of public purposes, to enforce laws, and to apply them to particular cases.

Kant's use of property as the central point of analysis provides a direct and powerful argument against the Lockean view that property rights are already fully conclusive in a state of nature. It might be thought to engage less fully with other accounts of private property. Many of these regard property as a conventional way of managing useful resources, or as a reflection of the choices made by a society. Although Kant does not directly address such views, his argument is directly relevant to them. The same form of question arises for any social convention or public policy choice as arises for initial acquisition of property: by what authority does the conventional practice bind people who were not party to it? From the standpoint of freedom, the claim that a certain conventional way of doing things works to everyone's advantage in the long run—however the truth of such a claim might be established—is not sufficient to show that any particular person is bound by it. As we saw in our discussion of Kant's theory of contract, others are not entitled to force you to participate in ar-

---

and Locke," *Philosophy and Public Affairs* 36, 4 (2008): 375-404. Assurance is central to Robert Pippin's analysis in "Mine and Thine? The Kantian State," in Paul Guyer, ed., *The Cambridge Companion to Kant and Modern Philosophy* (Cambridge: Cambridge University Press, 2006), 416-446, and Otfried Höffe, "'Even a Nation of Devils Needs the State': The Dilemma of Natural Justice," in Howard Williams, ed., *Essays on Kant's Political Philosophy* (Chicago: University of Chicago Press, 1992). Among those who focus on versions of the indeterminacy argument are Leslie Mulholland, *Kant's System of Rights* (New York: Columbia University Press, 1990), 284; Howard Williams, *Kant's Political Philosophy* (New York: St. Martin's, 1983), 169; Paul Guyer, "Kant's Deductions of the Principles of Right," in Timmons, *Kant's Metaphysics of Morals*, 23-64.

rangements that benefit you. More generally, the more artificial the rules of property are taken to be, the more pressing the need for an account of their authority is. If property rules are just the rules of a conventional game, they do not bind anyone other than a voluntary participant. Characterizing such arrangements as a choice "made by society" raises the question of society's entitlement to make that choice: what is the space of possible choices it might have made, and how could it bind anyone who neither participated in the making of the choice nor agreed to be bound by it? That is just to say that the question of society's entitlement to make a decision about how resources will be used presupposes some account of how a collective could have acquired the entitlement to determine how things will be used. But that is just a large-scale version of the question of initial acquisition: how does one person's decision bind others?

The discussion of property in Chapter 4 established Kant's arguments for several claims. First, Kant's account showed that it must be possible to have things as one's property, because otherwise the use of objects that can serve as means for setting and pursuing purposes would be forbidden or conditional on the particular purposes of others. That argument, as we saw, grounds the possibility of property in human purposiveness. It thereby precludes any requirement that all others consent to any acquisition. Such a requirement would make the use of a usable thing depend on the *matter* of other people's choices, and so subject everyone to the choice of each other private person.

Second, Kant argued against the thesis that property rights are to be understood as extensions of rights to one's own person. Variants of this thesis can be found in the otherwise differing accounts of property in Locke and Hegel. Locke's example of eating an apple involves explicit incorporation; Hegel's more abstract analysis in terms of putting your will into a thing captures the same intuitive idea. These accounts of property submerge the significance of acquisition for others, by representing the obligation to respect the property of another as an *instance* of the obligation to respect that person. As we saw, the Lockean/Hegelian strategy cannot explain why such acts of self-relation change the rights of others. Locke incorporates a "proviso" requiring that "enough and as good" be left for others through any appropriation. No saving clause of this sort can address the basic issue, however. Even if it restricts unilateral acquisition to cases in which doing so does not worsen the ability of others to provide for themselves, it fails to address the question of how one person can place another under an obligation. It may be worse to have others impose obligations on you if those obligations are onerous, but your right to freedom is at issue when others change your normative situation, even if you have other options so that the situation is not burdensome.

Third, Kant introduced an account of unilateral acquisition: the transition from an object's being unowned to its being owned depends on a unilateral act of appropriation. The acquisition of property is nothing more than the change in the status from being subject to the choice of no person to being subject to the choice of some particular person, its owner. The affirmative act required to acquire an object is simply taking control of it and giving a sign that you intend to continue controlling it.

Acquisition requires taking control, giving a sign, and bringing your act into conformity with a "general will." Although a person acquiring an object does so on his or her own initiative without consulting others, the *power* to do so requires an omnilateral will to make the unilateral act binding on others.[7] Kant thus treats initial acquisition as a special case of political authority.

If you acquire an unowned object, you do not need to consult everyone who could conceivably be affected; such a requirement would violate the postulate of practical reason with regard to rights. Instead, you are entitled to act entirely on your own initiative. This raises an obvious question: why am I bound by your unilateral act? Your innate right prevents me from interfering with your act, but the fact that I may not interfere does not mean that your act has further consequences for my rights.

Your act of acquisition casts a long shadow: you are entitled to exclude others from that object even when you are not using it. You are also entitled to dispose of it as you see fit, subject only to the requirement that you not violate the rights of others in so doing. You can give the fox to whomever you like, though you may not dump its rotting carcass on someone else's land without the owner's permission. Your right to exclude is established through your unilateral act, but the mere fact that you act unilater-

---

7. 6:262.

ally raises the question of how that action can bind me. As Kant puts it, a unilateral will is not a law for anyone else.[8]

The acquisition of property differs from other ways in which one person might be said to change the normative situation of another. If I wrongfully injure or interfere with you or your property, it is now permissible for you to claim damages from me. Such changes can (though need not) be thought of as changing your normative situation by creating new permissions to proceed against me. Your right to person and property is not changed, however, and, most significantly, you are under no new obligations. Your right to proceed against me is just your right to your person and property. Again, if I move from one place to another, I occupy space which is not available for your occupation while I am there. This change does not place you under a new obligation, but simply applies it to a different circumstance. In these examples, one person's act does not change any other person's obligations, but merely the way in which antecedent obligations apply. The acquisition of property is different: in acquiring a piece of land I make it unavailable to you even when I am not occupying it.

The normative issue is illustrated by considering other examples that John Simmons has suggested are analogous:

> I may make a legal will, unilaterally imposing on all others an obligation to respect its terms (which they previously lacked), for the very purpose of limiting others' freedom to dispose of my estate in ways contrary to my wishes. I may occupy a public tennis court to practice my serve, or we may take the softball field in the park for our game, unilaterally imposing on all others obligations to refrain from interference, and do so for the very purpose of enjoying our activities unhindered by such interference. Or I may rush to the patent office and register my invention, unilaterally imposing certain obligations of restraint on all others, for the very purpose of limiting others' freedom to likewise take advantage with their competing inventions. I may buy the rare stamp that many others are busy saving their money to buy, or I may organize a nature walk for children along trails many others use

8. 6:263.

to seek solitude. How different are the rights and obligations involved in these contacts from the right of the original appropriator to take unowned goods, unilaterally imposing obligations of noninterference in all others, for the very purpose of restricting their liberty to the free use and enjoyment of the goods? Not, I think, very different.[9]

Simmons is right that the appropriation of property is not the only unilateral act that changes the situation of others, and his examples make it clear that there are many ways in which it is morally acceptable for one person to do so. But the examples also underscore Kant's point about the need for omnilateral authorization in changing not only the situation of others, but their entitlements. Most of the examples could not even occur in a state of nature. So: making a will presupposes an antecedently and publicly established property right in the objects of the will. Kant also emphasizes that to affect a transfer by a will, there must be a public possessor, entitled to exclude others between the testator's death and the heir's acceptance of the legacy. That is, a "legal will" presupposes public institutions entitled to make the testator's choice binding. Both the "public tennis court" and "the park" presuppose public forms of property with standardized rules of access. Although we can take over the tennis court for our game, we are not allowed to build a house on it, and there are typically rules limiting the number of games in a row that we can play. Such public forms of property will be the topic of Chapter 8, but it is worth noting here that the entitlement to use public spaces is not a natural right that can be either exercised or even conceived in the absence of a rightful public authority, for there could be no such spaces without such an authority. (If there could be such rights without a public authority, they would be cases in which groups rather than individuals acquired unowned objects, and so just cases of first possession by a group rather than an individual.) However exactly we understand patent rights, they are validated through public statutory mechanisms, as the phrase "the patent office" suggests. You cannot register your invention with some other private person, who then grants you the right to prohibit others from making

---

9. A. John Simmons, "Original-Acquisition Justifications of Property," in *Justification and Legitimacy* (Cambridge: Cambridge University Press, 2001), 220.

substantially similar things, because that private person has no more right than you do to change the entitlements of others.

Simmons's remaining examples create no new obligations; they all illustrate each person's entitlement to exercise his or her freedom in ways that change the context in which others subsequently exercise theirs. Organizing a nature hike for children may disappoint the expectations or wishes of others, but it does not place them under any new normative requirements. Purchasing things that others had hoped to buy narrows the range of things that those others might do, but does not place any new obligations on them. Others were already under an obligation to refrain from interfering with the stamp that you wanted to acquire; they face no new obligations as a result of your acquisition of it. Only their hopes have been dashed. They are in the same position as against you that they were in as against the previous owner: they can still try to make you an offer to convince you to sell it to them, even if you do not actively invite offers.

The original acquisition of property remains distinctive because it does not simply change the world: it places others under new obligations. As we saw in Chapter 4, the basic structure of a property right is if one person owns an object, it is not part of the context which others may change in the exercise of their freedom. Your rights are not violated if people use, damage, or destroy things that are not your property, but they are violated if they interfere with your property in any way. The original acquisition of an object as property changes it from being something that others may use or change at will, or as a foreseeable side effect of their own activities, into something that others are under an obligation not to use, damage, or destroy; it thus places them under a new obligation.

Kant's specific account of the change that appropriation makes to the normative situation of others—that it renders them liable to coercion—is not required for his argument about the way in which property requires omnilateral authorization. The need is the same whether rightful acquisition is supposed to place me under an obligation, give you a power to forcibly remove me from your property, or limit my freedom in some other way. The philosophical literature on promising raises questions about how you could change your *own* normative situation through an act you perform on your own initiative. Kant's point is that the theory of property raises a deeper problem of how one person's act can place *an-*

other person under a new obligation. How can an act done entirely of your own initiative, to which others are not parties, have binding effects on them?

Kant's answer focuses on public authorization. As we saw in Chapter 4, the unilateral aspect of acquisition is not that *having* property is inconsistent with freedom. Nor is it that the acquisition of property narrows other people's range of options. Instead, it is the simple fact that one person changes the normative status of another. Kant's introduction of this point comes at the beginning of his explanation of acquisition in general, which he divides into a three-stage sequence:

> This *apprehension* is taking possession of an object of choice in space and time, so that the possession in which I put myself is *possessio phaenomenon*. 2) *Giving a sign (declaratio)* of my possession of this object and of my act of choice to exclude everyone else from it. 3) *Appropriation (appropriatio)*, as the act of a general will (in Idea) giving an external law through which everyone is bound to agree with my choice.[10]

The third member of this sequence is crucial to the argument for public right: it is only if my choice is exercised in light of an (ideally) publicly conferred power to appropriate that it could possibly be binding on others, apart from my physical possession of the object. As we saw in Chapter 3, a "permissive law" that entitles me to acquire things makes a merely permissible unilateral act have rightful consequences for others. However, it could only have this status provided that it is authorized by everyone, so that my unilateral act is also the exercise of a publicly conferred power. If the public authority is entitled to confer the power on me in the name of everyone, then my specific exercise of the power is also in everyone's name.

The role of the public does not turn property into a sort of instrument or by-product of public policy. The basic structure of property is governed by individual purposiveness; as a matter of private right, you can have external objects as your own because of the postulate of private

---

10. 6:258.

right. A public authority is required to authorize you to acquire things, because that changes the normative situation of others. But authorizing acquisition is not a discretionary purpose that a public authority might decide about based on some assessment of the desirable consequences or balance of benefits and burdens that will result. A public authority could not be entitled to prohibit all acquisition, as doing so would limit human purposiveness as such. It could, in principle, restrict initial acquisition in various ways—for example, setting aside areas as nature preserves for future generations—and it can impose conditions on properly recording acquisitions. Its power to do such things in particular cases, however, can only be exercised consistent with each person's entitlement to have external objects of choice as his or her own, so it cannot preclude all acquisition.

Kant's invocation of a general will to authorize private appropriation also differs from the view, put forward by Grotius and Pufendorf, which seeks to authorize appropriation in terms of a historical or hypothetical agreement by the people who own the Earth in common to permit people to divide it up. Such accounts incorporate a sort of primitive community of land, and so already presuppose some concept of ownership. As soon as any such content is presupposed, however, given the concept of property, a hypothetical agreement to divide up is not sufficient to bind the parties. Only an actual one could be. The difficulty is that any such common ownership could only function in the Pufendorf/Grotius argument if it was a form of private ownership by a group of persons. As Kant remarks, such a primitive community "would have to be one that was instituted and arose from a contract by which everyone gave up private possessions, and, by uniting his possessions with those of everyone else, transformed them into a collective possession [*Gesammtbesitz*]; and history would have to give us proof of such a contract. But it is contradictory to claim that such a procedure is an *original* taking possession and that each human being could and should have based his separate possessions on it."[11] The only form of common possession of the Earth prior to appropriation must be the "disjunctive" possession of the Earth's surface entailed by innate right, that is, that each person is entitled to be "wher-

---

11. 6:251.

ever nature or chance" has placed him or her, except in whatever place is occupied by another person. Persons who are in merely disjunctive possession of the Earth's surface, considered separately, are in a position neither to authorize anything nor to bind anyone.

The problem here is not just one of an incoherent imagined history. More fundamentally, an actual agreement in the distant past could only bind future generations if the parties to it had the authority to do so—which is just to say that the Grotius/Pufendorf model reproduces the problem of authorization it is supposed to address.[12] The ability of ancestors to place their descendents under obligation to respect private acquisitions is just an instance of the question raised by initial acquisition: how can their act bind later generations who are not parties to it? A hypothetical agreement based on perceived advantage does no better, because no private person has standing to force another to do what he or she *would* agree to unless he or she *has* agreed.

Kant's appeal to the idea of a united will makes the object of agreement the rule of law through political institutions, so that individual acts of rule-making are themselves instances of a more general law. The argument is not supposed to show that an agreement has happened, or even that it would be wise or prudent for people to enter into such an agreement so that it would happen under ideal circumstances. It shows only that a form of public authorization on behalf of everyone is required to underwrite private appropriation. Private property requires public right because they are both instances of a single, common problem, which has an irreducibly public element. Rather than trying to reduce the public to the private, Kant's argument shows that the private is only rightful in the context of the public.

The requirement of public authorization to underwrite private appropriation shows the acquisition of private property to be an example of the familiar features of legal systems that H. L. A. Hart describes as "power conferring" rules. Hart's own examples involve contracts and wills, which empower a person to change his or her *own* legal situation. Hart remarks

---

12. Locke's discussion of the failure of a father's consent to bind his son to political authority thus applies to the Grotius/Pufendorf account of acquisition. See Locke's *Second Treatise of Government*, §118.

that they empower people to act as small-scale legislatures.[13] Kant's example of property makes the legislative aspect of those rules especially clear: my appropriation can only change your legal situation if everyone, including you, has conferred a power on me to appropriate. My act of appropriation is thus a unilateral exercise of an omnilateral power, rather than a unilateral act. That is the point of the third moment in the three-stage sequence. However, if the third moment is presupposed by any possible act of acquisition—I unilaterally act *so as to bind everyone*—my act genuinely binds them only when the general will has authorized it.

The solution to the problem of unilateral will is, then, an omnilateral will, through which everyone authorizes appropriation. An omnilateral permission to appropriate makes private appropriation rightful, and so entitles a private person to bind others through a unilateral act. The act is unilateral, but the authorization for the act is omnilateral.

Kant does not deny that the people might come to recognize each other's claims to property or under contracts without an omnilateral authorization. He characterizes these as "societies compatible with rights (e.g., conjugal, paternal, domestic societies in general, as well as many others); but no law."[14] Members of such societies might well in fact accept rules and dispute-resolution procedures governing their interactions, but whether they accept them or not depends on the matter of their choices, that is, on the particular ends they happen to have. Such associations are purely voluntary arrangements from which any member might withdraw unilaterally if his or her particular ends were to change. The members themselves might not see things this way, and might think they are morally bound to recognize each other's claims, think it prudent to do so, or fear sanctions if they do not comply. None of these possibilities is sufficient to give either the rules or the procedures genuine authority, because there is no general entitlement to compel the members to accept them. Such societies are like the international order as Kant conceives it: each state has a right to withdraw from any alliance if it perceives that it is endangered by getting drawn into disputes between other members. We

---

13. Hart, *The Concept of Law* (Oxford: Oxford University Press, 1994), 26–42.
14. 6:306.

shall return to this contrast between voluntary and binding associations in our discussion of enforcement.

Kant's account solves the problem he identified with Grotius's view, according to which private holdings are grounded in some historical agreements to divide up the land. By focusing on the omnilateral authorization of a general power-conferring rule entitling people to acquire things as their own by taking possession of them, Kant does not need to presuppose a prior, collective form of property, and show that private property is consistent with it. The only thing that private property needs to be consistent with is freedom, and that can only be achieved through an omnilateral will capable of binding everyone.

Kant's argument about the need for omnilateral authorization of power-conferring rules focuses on the simple example of the acquisition of property. However, he gives further examples of cases in which a specific rule is required in order to make private rights systematically achievable, but the rule itself must be chosen by a competent public authority. That is, rules conferring the power of appropriation require a further "principle of politics, the arrangement and organization of which will contain decrees, drawn from experiential cognition of human beings, that have in view only the mechanism for administering right and how this can be managed appropriately."[15] These intermediate principles are required to confer the power, in this case of appropriation, in the same specific way on everyone. Thus what counts as taking control of an object will require some sort of further specification; that control is required can be established *a priori*. In certain familiar examples, such as holding an apple in your hand, the requisite act of taking control will be clear to the point of obviousness. However, when it comes to the appropriation of land, which, as we saw in Chapter 4, is control of a region of the Earth's surface, there can be no straightforward characterization of what it is to be in physical control of the land, only various possible but potentially conflicting accounts. Thus the legal system must choose something that counts as taking possession by taking control. In the same way it must choose something that counts as giving a sign. All of these lawmaking powers generate

---

15. Kant, "On a Supposed Right to Lie from Philanthropy," 8:429.

more specific rules so as to make the power-conferring rule governing acquisition clear enough to guide conduct.

To show the necessity of an omnilateral will to underwrite the private appropriation is not the same as explaining its possibility. Like the three branches of government that address them, the three branches of Kant's argument are coordinate, and the solutions are only possible taken together. Both the explanation of how a general will is possible and Kant's account of the authorization to force others into a rightful condition depend on the other two dimensions of political power, executive and judicial, so we must consider those before returning to it.

II. Enforcement: Why Equal Rights Require Assurance

The second problem concerns the enforcement of rights consistent with the freedom of everyone. Like the argument about property, it is driven by the tension between unilateral choice and freedom under universal law. Where the property argument focuses on the power to put others under new obligations, the assurance argument focuses on the entitlement to enforce existing rights, and does not "require a special act to establish a right."[16] Every right is a title to coerce and a part of a system of rights under universal law. Kant's argument shows that these aspects of rights can only be reconciled through public assurance.

To bring it into focus, put the other two problems aside and imagine that people have somehow acquired property, and that there is no controversy about exactly what belongs to whom. In this situation, without public enforcement, people lack the assurance that others will refrain from interfering with their property and, as a result, have no obligation to refrain from interfering with the property of others. The basic thought is that without such a system, nobody has a right to use force (or call on others to do so) to exclude others from his or her property, so nobody has an enforceable obligation to refrain from interfering with the property of others.

Kant introduces the idea of assurance in §8 of Private Right, arguing "I am therefore not under obligation to leave external objects belonging

16. 6:256.

to others untouched unless everyone else provides me assurance that he will behave in accordance with the same principle with regard to what is mine." Instead, rights to external objects of choice are only consistent in a civil condition, because it is "only a will putting everyone under obligation, hence only a collective general (common) and powerful will, that can provide everyone this assurance."[17]

Before turning to the details of the argument, it is worth remarking that a duty conditional on the conduct of others shows that the *Doctrine of Right* does not impose duties to do what you would do in ideal circumstances, regardless of the actual circumstances in which you find yourself.[18] Whatever the difficulties of this as an interpretation of Kant's *Groundwork,* no such principle applies to duties of right, because they always concern the claims that one person can enforce against another. You cannot have an obligation of right to accommodate yourself to the specific purposes of others; all obligations of right must be within a system of right "in accordance with universal law." The only obligation of right that you can owe to another person must be part of the system of reciprocal limits; they have no standing to compel you to do what you would have had an obligation to do had such a system been in place.

It is also worth remarking that the duty is one of right. Kant does not deny that there could be grounds of virtue for accommodating claims of others that would not be enforceable as a matter of right. Instead, the assurance argument shows that acquired rights are not enforceable in a state of nature, so that any attempt to enforce them is unilateral force that others may resist with right.

The assurance argument follows the broader structure laid out in the Introduction to the *Doctrine of Right*. As well as distinguishing between innate and acquired rights, and between public and private right, Kant provides what he calls a "division" of duties of right, which he expresses in terms of the "precepts" of the Roman jurist Ulpian, as they are recorded in Justinian's *Institutes.* Ulpian says that justice consists in living

17. Ibid.
18. Bernard Williams attributes this view to Kant in his essay "Moral Luck" in his *Moral Luck* (Cambridge: Cambridge University Press, 1981), 20–39. The same attribution is made in Isaiah Berlin's "Two Concepts of Liberty" in his *Four Essays on Liberty* (Oxford: Oxford University Press, 1969), 138n.

honorably *(honeste vive)*, not wronging others *(neminem laede)*, and giving each what is his *(suum cique tribue)*. Conceding that his interpretation involves a departure from narrow explication, Kant casts Ulpian's infinitives in the form of imperatives:

1. Be an honorable human being. Rightful honor consists in asserting one's worth as a human being in relation to others, a duty expressed in the saying "do not make yourself a mere means for others but be at the same time an end for them."
2. Do not wrong anyone even if to avoid doing so you should have to stop associating with others and shunning all society.
3. (if you cannot help associating with others), enter into a society with them in which each can keep what is his own.

The same division is said to organize duties of right into internal duties, external duties, and duties that "involve the derivation of the latter from the principle of the former by subsumption."[19]

The problem of assurance and its solution follow the pattern of reconciling the first precept with the second through the third. Kant's gloss on the third notes that "Give to each what is his" is absurd, "since one cannot give anyone something he already has." In its place, he suggests the paraphrase "enter a condition in which what belongs to each can be secured to him against everyone else."[20] The pattern of the argument is to show how rightful honor and the injunction against wronging others are only possible in a rightful condition.

As Kant formulates it, the assurance argument applies only to acquired rights. Your entitlement to use force to exclude others from your own person is consistent with your obligation to refrain from interfering with the person of another, because your right to self-defense is purely protective. That same right gives you a right to defend whatever is in your physical possession, since others can only dispossess you by touching or moving

---

19. 6:236. The details of this transition can be spelled out in a number of different ways. The simplest and most forceful presentation of it is still Julius Ebbinghaus's. For a succinct formulation, see "The Law of Humanity and the Limits of State Power," *Philosophical Quarterly* 3 (1953): 14–22.

20. 6:237.

you and so interfering with your person. Two people may have potentially conflicting rights to self-defense, but innate right does not give anyone a right to interfere with the person of another except to protect his or her own person. External objects of choice, including property, contractual, and status obligations, are different, because others are only entitled to compel you to refrain from their possessions if such an entitlement is consistent with your independence.

The assurance problem comes up because our entitlements in relation to things we are not in physical possession of are in tension with each other. The second precept requires you to refrain from taking what is mine. If you refrain from taking what is mine, without assurance that I will refrain from taking what is yours, then you are permitting me to treat what is yours, and so an aspect of your capacity to set and pursue purposes, as subject to my purposes. Exactly the same problem comes up for me: my rightful honor demands that I only refrain from using what you possess if I have assurance that you will do the same for me. So if either of us refrains from taking what belongs to the other without assurance, we restrict our choice on the basis of the other's particular choice, rather than in accordance with a universal law.

How frequently the absence of assurance will lead to actual conflict depends entirely on our particular ends—the "matter" of our choices. If I have trained guard dogs and weapons and you do not, I can simply help myself to your possessions, confident that you will be able neither to defend them nor to take mine. In so doing, I treat you as a mere means, because your entitlements are used in the pursuit of my ends. In this situation, your prudent course of action may be just to give in and let me treat you as a mere means. It is bad enough to have me pillage your goods, without making fruitless and dangerous attempts to do the same to mine. But the prudence of your course of action does not render it morally unproblematic. Whether you give in or not is simply a matter of my strength.

Other, more appealing motives might also lead someone to refrain from using things claimed by others. The sympathetic person might allow others to do wrong, forgiving their deeds out of a general philanthropy. Kant does not need to deny that such a person is empirically possible; the problem of assurance arises so long as no person is under an obligation to be sympathetic or assume that others are. A parallel point applies to the virtuous person, who will not have an undifferentiated sympathy for every aggressor or wrongdoer. Even the virtuous person, however, is under no obligation of either right or virtue to act on the assumption that others are equally virtuous. She is under an obligation of right not to allow others to treat her as a mere means.[21] Neither of us is under any obligation of right to assume that the other is virtuous.

Kant's remark that we do not need to wait for "bitter experience of the other's contrary disposition; for what should bind him to wait till he has suffered a loss before he becomes prudent?"[22] suggests that the experience will indeed be bitter. The assurance argument does not depend on any such premise, however. It may be prudent to use a strategy of tit for tat, waiting for the other to reveal a hostile disposition, before interfering with his or her possessions. What you are entitled to do does not depend on the particular choices of others. Obligations of right are always owed to other persons as parts of a system of reciprocal limits; a free being can only owe another person an obligation of right to accept a system of restrictions together with others; it follows that a free being can only be compelled to respect the rights of others under such a system of restriction. Where others do not restrict their conduct, they may not force you to restrict yours.

Kant invokes the Latin maxim *Quilibet praesumitur malus, donec securitatem dederit oppositi*[23] ("Everyone is presumed bad until he has provided security to the contrary"), not because of any views about the "radical evil" of human beings, such as those he defends in his *Religion*,[24] but

---

21. Kant's discussion of servility in the *Doctrine of Virtue* treats the general failure to stand on your rights as a serious vice. Although you have the rightful power to consent to acts by others, to make the purpose of every other person your own whenever they demand something of you is inconsistent with both rightful honor and virtue.

22. 6:307.

23. Ibid. Gregor mistranslates the maxim as "The party who displaces another's right has the same right himself." A better translation is found in B. Sharon Byrd and Joachim Hruschka, "From the State of Nature to the Juridical State of States," *Law and Philosophy* 27, 6 (November 2008): 605.

24. Kant, *Religion within the Bounds of Mere Reason*, 6:32, in Immanuel Kant, *Religion and Rational Theology*, trans. Allen Wood and George Di Giovanni (Cambridge: Cambridge University Press, 1996). In "From the State of Nature to the Juridical State of States,"

because the alternative is a merely material principle based on the particular motives of those you interact with. All they can force you to do is enter with them into a rightful condition, and that authorization obtains "no matter how good and right-loving human beings might be."[25]

The point can be made from the other direction, focusing not on interference but on the right to defend property. If I have no assurance that you will not interfere with my property, I am entitled to regard your attempt to reclaim goods from me as a unilateral use of force against me, which I may resist with right. The same applies to you: you may resist with right my attempts to exclude you from what is mine. As Kant remarks, in such a situation we "do each other no wrong" by feuding among ourselves, even though we "do wrong in the highest degree by willing to be and to remain in a condition that is not rightful, that is, in which no one is assured of what is his against violence."[26]

Kant's analysis of assurance thus differs from the more familiar Hobbesian problem of first performance of a mutually advantageous contract. The Hobbesian argument focuses on a strategic problem: nobody wants to be played for a sucker; absent assurance, nobody will ever perform, and contracts will be factually impossible. The Kantian argument focuses on a moral one: nobody can rightfully be compelled to serve the purposes of another unilaterally. Absent assurance, first performance of contracts is an instance of a much more general moral problem: any act done on the basis of another person's claim to an external object is an instance of serv-

---

Byrd and Hruschka attempt to relate Kant's argument to the "radical evil" of human beings in the *Religion*, and point to his endorsement, in the *Naturrecht Feyerabend*, of Thomasius's use of a related Latin maxim as a principle of moral philosophy (27:1340). On the interpretation developed here, no such hypothesis is required. Nor does the *Naturrecht Feyerabend* represent Kant's considered view on this issue. In it he rejects the *Doctrine of Right*'s central claim that the need to enter such a condition is an *a priori* requirement imposed exclusively by concepts of right. In the *Feyerabend*, Kant makes the opposite claim: "No man is obliged *a natura* to enter into civil society with the other. If I could take human nature to be just, i.e. as such a nature that cannot have the intention of harming the other, if I could posit that all human beings have the same insight into right and the same good will, a *status civilis* would not be necessary. But since the opposite is the case, everyone has the right to demand of others that they exit the *status naturalis*" (27:1381).

25. 6:307.
26. Ibid.

ing the purposes of another. It is *permissible* to serve the purposes of another, but each person is entitled to decide whom to cooperate with, so there can be no obligation to do so.

Without an obligation of right, nobody is under any obligations with respect to external objects of choice, and nobody is entitled to enforce any acquired rights they (suppose themselves to) have. As a result, all rights to external objects in a state of nature are merely *provisional*, because they are all titles to coerce that nobody is entitled to enforce coercively. A provisional property right is thus a right to use force to exclude others from an external object while you are in possession of it; although physical possession gives provisional title, in anticipation of a condition in which rights can be made conclusive,[27] your entitlement to use force is limited to the case in which interfering with your possession thereby interferes with your person. Any other use of force to secure an object against another is just aggression against that person, which can be resisted with right.

Private rights of enforcement are the cornerstone of Lockean political philosophy; Kant's premise that rights must form a consistent set under universal law preempts that entire line of argument. If I am entitled to coerce you, and you may resist with right, neither of us has a title to coerce consistent with our respective independence under universal law, so neither of us has a right, properly speaking.

If the problem is one of reconciling rightful honor with the duty not to interfere with others, the solution is to "enter a condition in which each can be secure in what is his," by means of "a will putting everyone under obligation, hence only a collective general (common) and powerful will, that can provide everyone this assurance."[28]

Only a "common and powerful will" can "provide this assurance" because only it can provide everyone with systematic incentives in relation to the possession of others. The incentive has two dimensions. First, it assures the private right holder that the right will remain intact, even if another violates it. Second, it makes rights violations prospectively pointless. If a right holder is assured of a remedy, others will not normally have

---

27. 6:257.
28. 6:256.

any incentive to violate rights, because a violator will expect to gain nothing and could possibly lose something through a violation.

First, as we saw in Chapter 3, a remedy in the case of the violation of a private right is not something new, but is rather simply the right itself, which survives the wrongdoing unchanged. If I take your pen without your authorization, you do not stop having a right to your pen. Your entitlement to recover it from me follows from the fact that your right survives the wrong against it. In the same way, if I destroy your pen, your right to have it replaced, or to the cost of replacing it, follows from the fact that your right to your pen survives the violation of it. So on the one hand, rights are vulnerable to wrongdoing; on the other hand, they survive any wrongs against them. The fact that you lose your physical possession of your property does not mean that you lose your rightful possession of it. The same point applies to contractual rights: if I breach my contract with you, you still have a right that I perform. This normative structure is familiar in informal contexts: if I am supposed to meet you at noon, and for whatever reason I am late, I still need to show up at 12:15. The reason I need to show up at 12:15 is just that I was supposed to show up at noon. My obligation, and so your correlative right, survives its own violation. Kant summarizes this thought when he remarks that the right to compensation for an injury just "gives me back what I already had."[29] Thus a publicly assured enforceable right to compensation can guarantee that your right will be effective, even if I violate it, because the object of the right will once again be subject to your choice. In the same way, if I use your property without your authorization, I can be compelled to surrender my gains to you, so that it is as if I had been using your property on your behalf. In either case, whether I damage what is yours or use it without your authorization, your right to have that thing subject to your choice remains effective, because my wrongful act has no effects on the rights of others. Against the background of such public assurance, you have grounds to refrain from interfering with my property. Each of us can respect what

---

29. In a civil action for a private wrong, the aggrieved party (or in cases of legal incapacity, his or her guardian) must bring a cause of action on his or her own initiative. The state will not step in to guarantee the outcome. This requirement simply reflects the more general feature of private rights: each person is always entitled to decide whether to stand on his or her rights.

belongs to the other without thereby allowing ourselves to be subject to the other's choice.

Second, because a public executive authority provides a remedy in cases of private wrong, it also provides an external incentive to refrain from wrongdoing by depriving wrongdoing of its point. The external incentive is secondary, but supports the assurance provided by the remedy itself. The point of the remedy is not to discourage others from committing similar wrongs; the remedy simply makes the aggrieved party's rights effective, by making factual possession correspond to rightful possession. Against the background of effective rights, however, any violation of rights carries potential disadvantages. If you use what belongs to another without authorization, you do not stand to gain; if you fail to look out properly for the security of others in their person and property, you will end up bearing a burden. These incentives are admissible under right, because right does not need to be the maxim of action. They are derivative of the underlying rights, because all they do is give effect to them. Their effects will sometimes be uncertain, since a private wrong can be committed carelessly or inadvertently, and might even occur despite the wrongdoer's best efforts. I may follow the coal seam under your land, disoriented because I am so far underground, and so trespass against your land and your coal. I may make a contract that, in changed circumstances, I am unable to honor. In these cases, your entitlement to a remedy guarantees that your right is effective in space and time. The further incentive makes no difference to *my* conduct, because an incentive can only guide me if I can recognize that it applies to a particular case. But the remedial aspect of the enforcement gives you all the assurance you need: you have what is yours, because if another wrongs you, you will be able to get it back. Private remedies secure private rights by ensuring that they will be effective in space and time. Norms apply even after they are violated, and coercive enforcement is just their effectiveness in space and time. Without that guarantee, rights are not secure, because whether they are effective depends entirely on the particular purposes of other persons.

When they are authorized by the state, these two incentives combine in a way that renders them consistent with rightful honor. If you act on the prudent consideration of *another private person's* threat advantage, you prudently give up on defending your rightful honor. By contrast, acting on the consideration of a threat issuing from a public authority is consistent with your rightful honor, because the incentive itself has been publicly authorized. Your self-restraint does not make you a means to any other private person's purposes.

From the need for assurance for acquired rights to be effective, Kant concludes that force may be used to bring the state of nature to a close. The right to defend your property can only be part of a system of rights if everyone has the requisite assurance:

> *Corollary:* If it must be possible, in terms of rights, to have an external object as one's own, the subject must also be permitted to constrain everyone else with whom he comes into conflict about whether an external object is his or another's to enter along with him into a civil constitution.[30]

Forcing someone with whom you cannot avoid interacting to enter a rightful condition with you is consistent with that person's freedom because it secures his or her rights. The person who resists wrongs you. By contrast, those who choose to remain outside a rightful condition "do each other no wrong" by feuding among themselves. There is no material wrong in interfering with each other's goods outside of a rightful condition because nobody has a right to exclude others, so there can be no wrong against persons. Instead, the wrong is formal, "wrong in the highest degree,"[31] because remaining in such a condition is inconsistent with anyone's having rights to external objects of choice. Thus everyone can be compelled to enter a condition in which rights are secure.

III. Indeterminacy

The third problem in the state of nature turns on the possibility of disagreement about rights. It combines aspects of the first two arguments, but it incorporates a general premise independent of them: general rules are not sufficient to classify particulars falling under them. If the applica-

30. 6:256.
31. Ibid.

tion of a rule or concept to some particular required a rule itself, the second rule would also require a rule governing its application, and so on, *ad infinitum*. If rules can be applied to particulars, then, it must simply be possible to apply them, without recourse to further rules.[32]

Kant's argument about disputes about rights differs from contemporary arguments that focus on political society as the solution to problems of disagreement about the good life or even about the demands of justice itself. Such arguments generalize Locke's idea of the "settling" function of law: to make official determination of questions that tend to generate disputes.[33] Like Locke, such accounts treat disagreement as an empirical fact. Where Locke thinks that people disagree about moral matters that have fully determinate answers, contemporary exponents of the settling function of law sometimes write as though questions about the basic terms of social life have no answers but somehow require them, so that institutions must step in to answer them.[34]

Kant's argument is fundamentally different. The source of disagreement is normative rather than empirical or epistemic. Disputes about rights reflect the two aspects of the concept of a right: on the one hand, it is an entitlement to restrain the conduct of others; on the other, it is a part of a system of freedom under universal law. Any entitlement to restrain the conduct of others must be an instance of a universal law rather than a unilateral judgment. If you and I cannot agree about the terms of our contract or the boundaries of our respective property, or about how to resolve our disagreement, neither of us can have rights that are part of a systematic set of reciprocal limits on freedom. Such disputes may or may not lead to actual fighting; if we are both intelligent and calm, we may see that we both stand to lose by raising the stakes.

If anything, empirical cases of disagreement may lead to more conflict, but they raise no issues of right. The person who "disagrees" with the claim that murder is prohibited, or that everyone is bound by law, or that each must refrain from the possessions of others, poses a certain

---

32. Kant, *Critique of Pure Reason*, A133/B172, A137/B176ff.
33. John Locke, *The Second Treatise of Government*, 66, §124.
34. Jeremy Waldron, *Law and Disagreement* (Oxford: Oxford University Press, 1999). Waldron attributes the same type of argument to Kant in "Kant's Legal Positivism," *Harvard Law Review* 109 (1996): 1535–1566.

kind of threat to the rightful condition, but the threat is factual rather than conceptual. No argument is likely to move such a person, but what is required is not an argument, just force, which is authorized by the fact that rights are being enforced. Such disagreements need to be contained by a rightful condition, but they do not need to be accommodated. Everyone has a right to interact with others on terms of equal freedom. Nobody has a right to exempt himself from such terms because he happens to disagree with them, because nobody could have a right, consistent with the freedom of others, to be bound only by laws that he happens to agree with.

Kant's indeterminacy argument, like the unilateral action and assurance arguments, is formal rather than empirical. Kant shows that rights are necessarily subject to dispute, not that they are always disputed. The application of concepts to particulars is always potentially indeterminate, and so requires judgment, as a result of which the classification of particulars is always, at least in principle, indeterminate. This general feature of concept application generates a special problem for right, because concepts of right govern reciprocal limits on freedom and so must apply to all in the same way. As we saw in the discussion of private right, there are some cases in which concepts of right completely determine the outcome of a dispute. No person can have a right that another person use property to accommodate his or her preferred purposes; no person who is not party to a contract has standing to compel its performance. In such cases, the complaining party is said to have "failed to state a cause of action," so the adjudication of the dispute cannot even get started. No question is raised about how to apply concepts of right to particulars. Only an unsupportable allegation about the concepts of right themselves is asserted. In other cases, however, even if it is agreed that concepts of right apply, there can be a dispute about how they apply to particular cases. In this latter class of cases, concepts of right do not always generate a single answer, but because they demarcate aspects of a system of reciprocal limits on choice, their application to particulars must be given a single answer in every case. Although their internal structure requires a single answer, neither the normative concepts nor the relevant facts nor any combination of them guarantees agreement. Again, different people may find the same things obvious, and so actually agree in a wide range of cases. Any such agreement is, from the standpoint of right, mere coincidence, and so rights are by their nature subject to dispute.

The general difficulty of applying rules to particulars raises a problem for rights in a state of nature, in which each can do no more than "what seems good and right to it." Equal private freedom presupposes objective standards of interaction. I do not merely need to do my best in avoiding injuring you; I need to exercise the reasonable care of an ordinary person. The meaning of the terms of a contract between two persons is not based on what one or the other of them thinks; nor is it created by some accidental overlap between the thoughts of each of them. Instead, the meaning is given by what a reasonable person would take it to be.[35] Objective standards are required because a subjective standard would entitle one person to unilaterally determine the limits of another person's rights. If I could avoid liability by trying my best, your right to my forbearance would depend on my abilities and judgments, and so be inconsistent with a system of equal freedom. If my contractual obligations reached only as far as I thought they did, your rights would depend on my judgment in a similar way. The point of objective standards in these contexts is not epistemic—it is not that our respective rights are fully determinate, but we have no way to discover them. Nor is it strategic: the risk of opportunistic behavior is secondary. Instead, objective standards of conduct are required by a system of equal freedom, in which no person's entitlements are dependent on the choices of others.

In these cases, equal freedom requires an objective standard, but such a standard cannot be exhausted by what either of us thinks about it. We can try to reduce the likelihood of disagreement by being more specific, but if the world changes in ways we had not anticipated, or if each of us judges in ways that the other had not anticipated, there is still room for good-faith disagreement. Again, in cases of property, Kant remarks that "the indeterminacy with respect to quantity as well as quality of the exter-

---

35. This objectivity is most obvious in common law systems of private law, but animates others as well. In French contract law, the terms of a contract are fixed by the subjective intention of the parties, but where intentions appear to diverge, a contract remains enforceable on the basis of legal principles. If one party to a contract is mistaken, the contract may be enforceable, if various normative legal requirements are met. I am grateful to Catherine Valcke for discussion of this issue.

nal object that can be acquired makes this problem (of the sole, original external acquisition) the hardest of all to solve."[36] Even if you and I agree that I have acquired something through my act, and that I am entitled to call upon the state's agents to enforce that right, we might still disagree about how much I have acquired, because neither the authorization to appropriate nor the title to enforce fixes the boundaries in space and time of my appropriation. A public authorization allows me to acquire things through a unilateral action, but it does not allow me to unilaterally decide the boundaries of that acquisition.

The indeterminacy in the application of concepts of right generates analogues of the problems of assurance and unilateral action. If I believe in good faith that the boundary between our property is in one place, and you, equally in good faith, believe that it is somewhere else, neither of us has any obligation of right to yield to the other. It may be prudent to yield, either because of force or because the subject of the debate is small enough to not be worth the trouble. To yield in such circumstances is, however, to fail to stand on our rights, because the resolution of our dispute depends on the content of our particular ends. More generally, neither of us needs to give in to the unilateral judgment of the other as to how to classify particulars. Unilateral judgment cannot be a law for another person.

The solution to both of these indeterminacy-generated problems is the judiciary: a body that has omnilateral authorization to apply the law to particular cases. The highest court's decision is final, not because it could not make a mistake, but because it has a public authorization to decide for everyone.

The court is empowered to exercise judgment in accordance with law. That does not mean that all questions of private right must be answered by a comprehensive civil code, only that the legal system as a whole authorizes officials to decide private disputes in accordance with concepts of private right. Private right can include (though it need not) a common law based on precedent, or (though it need not) a civil code that develops its concepts through a consideration of particular cases.

The three arguments are distinct from each other, but coordinate. The

---

36. 6:266.

assurance argument applies to external objects of choice, regardless of how they are acquired and whether or not their contours are determinate. Even if everybody knows who owns what, the assurance argument suggests that nobody has any claim to enforce a right to what she has, because any such enforcement will be merely unilateral, and so not part of a system of rights. The argument about unilateral choice applies to acquired objects of choice, whether or not they are determinate, and whether or not the obligations to respect them are conclusive or enforceable. The determinacy argument would arise even if rights are enforceable and can be acquired.

The three arguments generate three independent but coordinate branches of government: the legislature must authorize all acts that change, enforce, or demarcate rights; the executive must enforce rights in accordance with law, and the judiciary must decide disputes and authorize remedies, again in accordance with law.

Kant's solution to the three defects is institutional, and brings together the three branches: legislature, executive, and judiciary. Together, they comprise the sovereign.[37] They are coordinate insofar as they act together, but each is subordinated to the others because none can solve its own problem consistent with the realization of rights except in collaboration with the others.

The independence of each of the three arguments from the other two underwrites Kant's insistence on the independence of each of the three coordinate branches of government. A legislature and judiciary are not sufficient to render provisional rights conclusive, because to accept the authority of the legislature or the verdict of the court without assurance that others will do the same would be to allow others to treat you as a mere means. An executive and a court without a legislature omnilaterally authorizing the laws that they apply and enforce would simply be an exercise of unilateral choice by officials. And the legislature and executive without a court would leave rights subject to dispute. Taken together, the three arguments operate to establish three branches, which together are able to create a legal system that imposes closure on disputes about rights. Every legal question has a legally authorized answer. Thus neither the ex-

---

37. 6:316.

ercise of judgment nor the enforcement of the verdict is inconsistent with a system of equal freedom. Neither enforcement nor application is an instance of unilateral choice; and neither legislation nor adjudication involves submission to the will of another person.

Kant compares the three branches to the stages in a practical syllogism.[38] The major premise is the product of legislation, because it determines what conduct is prohibited, what conduct is required, and what "merely permissible" conduct has consequences for rights. Thus the activities of the other branches are dependent on law; the executive can only enforce the law, and the judiciary can only apply it. The minor premise is the executive branch, because it is the means available for giving effect to the legislation. Kant represents the judicial verdict as the conclusion, because he represents it as the making-determinate of the authorization to use force in the particular case. In a practical syllogism, the agent takes up particular means on the basis of a general principle; the verdict renders the general appropriately particular.

Although the arguments operate independently of each other, the argument about the legislative will takes priority over the others. Both the exercise of judgment and the enforcement of rights must be done in accordance with law, that is, in accordance with omnilateral choice. The only way that a judge or enforcer can be empowered consistent with right is through the act of a legislative will.

Failure to observe the proper separation prevents the executive and judiciary from solving the problems they are supposed to address. Kant's approach to the separation of powers thus differs from the familiar form of argument that starts by showing that some kind of state is required, and then goes on to explain the separation of powers within the state as a principle of inner restraint, so as to prevent usurpation and corruption. Locating different powers in separate branches staffed by separate officials reduces the likelihood of arbitrary uses of power. This mode of argument seems to have been prominent in the framing of the U.S. Constitution,

---

38. Like Aristotle, Kant understands the practical syllogism as the taking up of means, with an action as its conclusion, rather than as a series of inferences between propositions that happens to have action as its subject matter. For Aristotle's view of the practical syllogism, see *Nicomachean Ethics*, 1147 a27, and John Cooper's discussion in *Reason and Human Good in Aristotle* (Indianapolis: Hackett, 1986), 46ff.

and is often traced to Montesquieu's *The Spirit of the Laws*.[39] Philip Pettit offers a forceful contemporary articulation of this view when he defends the separation of powers on grounds that it reduces the risk of arbitrary exercises of power, in part by imposing general rules and in part by adding complexity to the business of government that makes arbitrary power more difficult to organize.[40] For both Montesquieu and Pettit the ultimate rationale for the *separation* of powers is the *dispersion* of power.

Kant's argument for the separation of powers is noninstrumental. Each of the basic things that states do must be shown to be made consistent with freedom before turning to any question of how various offices might be staffed or kept under control. Anything that the state does has to be properly authorized by law: the making of law, the taking up of means to give effect to the law, and the passive classification of particulars. Failure to separate the legislative from the executive function turns into a form of despotism, through which some rule over others. The failure to separate the judiciary from the executive and legislative branches creates another version of the same problem: a dispute can only be resolved consistent with the right of the parties if its particulars are brought under a general rule; if the rules can be changed in response to a particular case there is only force, not law. In *Toward Perpetual Peace*, Kant rejects Athenian democracy on the grounds that a form of government that does not distinguish legislative from executive roles is not a form of government at all *(unform)*. It cannot be thought of as a system under which people give laws to themselves.[41] Without enabling legislation, there is no distinction between an act of state and an act of members of the executive acting on their own initiative. In the *Doctrine of Right*, the parallel argument makes the more modest claim that failure to distinguish legislature from executive empowers the executive to act on its own initiative, and so not in accordance with law.[42] Kant's reference to the "practical syllogism" of the

---

39. Book 11, chap. 6.

40. Pettit, *Republicanism: A Theory of Freedom and Government* (Oxford: Oxford University Press, 1997), 174ff.

41. Kant, *Toward a Perpetual Peace*, 8:352.

42. As Ludwig has shown, the differences in formulation reflect Kant's application of the distinction between noumena and phenomena to public right, something that he does in the *Doctrine of Right,* but not in *Perpetual Peace.* See Bernd Ludwig, "Kommentar zum

three separate powers underscores this point: official action under the executive only counts as an action of the people as a whole, rather than the executive acting on its own initiative, if the powers of the executive are prescribed by law. As we saw in our discussion of assurance, it might be prudent to obey an unconstrained executive, but its use of force is no different from any other act of unilateral choice. All authority must come from law, because the only alternative is unilateral choice.

IV. Innate Right in the State of Nature

The three problems are distinct. Even if rules are fixed, they can be applied differently to particulars. Even if title is not in dispute, outside of a rightful condition, people need not abstain from the possession of others. And even if there is an enforcement mechanism and no dispute about particulars, without general legislation, one person's act of appropriation does not bind others.

Kant develops the three problems in terms of external objects of choice, that is, acquired rights. These rights are said to be "provisional" outside of a rightful condition. The innate right of humanity is not said to be provisional in the same way. It might be thought that the problem of determinacy does not come up in the same way with respect to each person's right to his or her own body that it can come up with respect to property or contract.[43] That is true of some, though not all, types of property. Horses and islands have clear boundaries, but the unilateral choice and assurance problems still arise. Nor are bodies always exempt from casuistical questions; in the *Doctrine of Virtue,* the second part of *The Metaphysics of Morals,* Kant introduces a series of casuistical problems about the body, including such matters as how a person should properly regard his or her hair. Parallel casuistical questions might come up with respect to interacting persons. If I shout loud enough to startle you when you stand on the edge of a cliff, but do not touch you, do I wrong you? This seems to be a question about our respective rights, which is not resolved

---

Staatsrecht (II), §§ 51–52; Allgemeine Anmerkung A; Anhang; Beschluss," in Otfried Höffe, ed., *Metaphysische Anfangsgründe der Rechtslehre* (Berlin: Akademie Verlag, 1999), 173–194.

43. Guyer, "Kant's Deductions of the Principles of Right," 62.

by some factual consideration about the number of molecules that my shout displaced toward you. I did not blow you over; I startled you. So the indeterminacy argument potentially comes up, in at least some cases.

Your right to your own person is not provisional, because of the two differences between that right and acquired rights that we saw in Chapter 3: your right to your own person does not require an affirmative act to establish it, and your person can never be physically separated from you. Thus neither the problem of unilateral appropriation nor the problem of assurance can arise. Your right in your own person is innate, so no affirmative act changes the rights of others. Your right in your own person is enforceable inasmuch as enforcing it is simply repelling others if they trespass against you; because your person is your body, to stand on your right to your own person is, at a minimum, to keep others away from it. Anyone who touches you without your authorization[44] hinders your freedom; to repel the trespasser is to hinder his hindrance. Kant characterizes the right to "forestall" a wrongful assailant as *"ius inculpatae tutelae,"* the right to blameless defense, and notes that there is no duty of right to "show moderation" in such cases.[45]

When faced with apparent aggression in a state of nature, a person is entitled to shoot first and ask questions later.[46] In a civil condition, the right to self-defense is much narrower. When self-defense serves as a defense to civil action for battery, the person who claims self-defense must establish it before a court; if the court rejects the defense on the grounds that it has not been proven, then the person who engaged in putative self-defense was just an aggressor. In a situation in which two people both believe themselves to be acting defensively, a court can find that one of them was wrong. The subsequent verdict of the court does not always

---

44. Parents and other (authorized) caregivers do not need express permission to touch children, because their duty to care for those children generates a right to do what seems to them required to "manage and develop" those children. Thus an infant can be carried, or an older child stopped from running out into traffic.

45. 6:235. At 6:306 Kant identifies "protective justice *(iustitia tutatrix)*" with *lex iusti*, which is in turn identified at 6:236 with the basis of rightful honor in the right of humanity in our own person, that is, innate right.

46. Kant makes this point about the right of nations in a state of nature to defend themselves against apparent aggression and even anticipated aggression (6:346).

provide a prospective guide to action when confronted with what you take to be an aggressor, but it does render defensive rights into a consistent set at the level of repair.

In a state of nature, the rights of several persons to defend themselves do not necessarily form a consistent set, because each is entitled to do "what seems good and right to it." Different people can act in inconsistent ways, even though each acts in good faith under the idea of the right of self-defense. Any two persons in a state of nature are entitled to defend themselves, and in defending themselves they have no perspective but their own from which to assess aggression. If you act on your right to self-defense in a state of nature, you do so on your own initiative, based on what seems good and right to you. People may sometimes commit aggression in the guise of self-defense, or have sincere but groundless beliefs about the dangers posed by others. But two people can also each act in good faith, each using force purely defensively against the other.

Actual legal systems refuse the defense of self-defense to an initial aggressor, and suppose that at most one of the two can be acting defensively. The other has, at most, some sort of excuse of mistake. This structure is not an accident of positive law, but rather a reflection of the normative structure of self-defense: your right to defend yourself only holds against an aggressor. Yet just as the question of who is an aggressor in a state of nature can be answered by nothing other than what seems good and right to the person defending himself, so, too, these higher-order constraints that require there be only one genuine justified defender can only be applied by the parties themselves. It is thus a structural feature of the situation that it is possible for each party to believe, in good faith, that the other is the sole aggressor. They each make inconsistent claims of right. However, once they have made inconsistent claims of right, there is no answer, apart from what seems good and right to each of them.

The idea that there can be no answer in a dispute about defensive force may seem surprising, because the question of who was the initial aggressor appears to be a purely factual one. But the question of whether defensive force is warranted is not equivalent to the factual question of who made the first move. Your right to defend yourself against an aggressor rests on your belief that someone is wrongfully attacking you, but in a state of nature only you are in a position to judge whether you are under attack, because you need not defer to anyone else. The entitlement to use defensive force is a reflection of the first Ulpian precept, rightful honor. To defer to the judgment of another about whether something is in fact a case of aggression is, again, to allow yourself to be treated as a mere means. If the other in question is an apparent aggressor, the difficulty with failing to defend yourself is clear. You also have an obligation (the second Ulpian precept) to avoid wronging others. The problem is that the two obligations do not form a consistent set. The other person's unilateral judgment must be both something to you via the second Ulpian precept—he thinks he is defending himself, and you must not wrong him—but also nothing to you, via the first—you don't have to defer to his judgment. Only positive law can guarantee a determinate answer to the question of who the aggressor was, because only under positive law can there be an "irreproachable" judge of such matters.

The imperfection of the right to self-defense does not, however, render that right merely provisional, because it is a conclusive authorization to coerce. Your right to repel those who invade the space occupied by your body does not require an omnilateral authorization. It is imperfect because it is not an authorization under universal laws, since any such authorization would have to be a member of a necessarily consistent set. The inconsistency in the right to self-defense in these cases is contingent, depending as it does on a factual question of whether the same or different things will seem "good and right" to different people. The problem, however, is conceptual: the idea of a rightful condition contrasts with "savage violence" because in the former, disputes are resolved by law, and in the latter, by force. How frequently force is used is entirely contingent, but that is exactly the point. Well-disposed and right-loving people might get into fewer disputes, but if so, it is still entirely contingent. You cannot be fully law-abiding without a lawgiver, no matter how "right-loving" you may be.

If rights to external objects of choice are not enforceable, then, as a specific case of this, contractual rights are not enforceable. This has two important implications for innate right in the state of nature. First, as we saw in Chapter 5, consent is a contractual (and so acquired) right, so it is not conclusive in a state of nature. As a result, the idea of consensual interaction is incomplete. Second, no contractual right to enforcement or protection is itself enforceable. If I am under attack by some third person, it is difficult to know what it would be for me to be either able or entitled to compel you to assist me while the attack is under way. That is, in the absence of assurance with respect to *external* objects of choice, I can have no assurance that you will keep your end of a mutual protection (or even nonaggression) agreement. The only assurance I could have that you would keep your contract to protect me is if I were entitled to a remedy were you to fail to do so, but no enforceable remedy is possible outside of a rightful condition.

The absence of enforceable rights to external objects of choice also means that you can have no remedial right if someone commits a wrong against your person. As a matter of private right, if somebody wrongs you, you are entitled to damages to make good your loss. However, the possibility of damages requires the possibility of conclusive title to whatever it is that will be transferred as damages. Absent such conclusive title, your right cannot be enforced retroactively. Nor can it be enforced prospectively by the prospect of damages. Thus your right to defend yourself is genuine, but if you fail to hinder a hindrance to your own freedom, it cannot be hindered after the fact.

These difficulties for innate right in the state of nature—indeterminacy, lack of conclusive defense or nonaggression agreements, and the impossibility of a remedy in cases of completed wrongs—do not make innate right provisional in the sense of being unenforceable. They do, however, stand in the way of its being what we might call "conclusively conclusive," that is, forming an integral part of a consistent system of rights. The fundamental feature of all rights is that they are parts of a system of equal freedom under universal law. In a state of nature, the indeterminacy of innate right and the impossibility of a remedy in cases of its violation mean that innate rights do not form a consistent set, which is just another way of saying that they do not, after all, fall under universal law. Although parallel considerations in the case of interacting nations lead Kant only to the conclusion that nations must bring their disputes before a court, in a civil condition the state must have the further power to bring innate right under universal law. Acquired rights can only be conclusive under universal law, and the universality of that law requires that innate rights also fall under universal law. If each individual were left with the power to do "what seems good and right" with respect to his or her own person, then each person would be entitled to resist with right the state's omnilateral claim to enforce acquired rights. Instead, the state must claim the power to define the objective standards governing each person's person, as well as the power to resolve disputes about wrongs against persons in accordance with law that has been laid down in advance. Thus although there is no direct argument from the innate right of humanity to the creation of a civil condition—no civil condition could be mandatory if acquired rights were impossible, because nobody would have standing to force another into one—systematic enforcement of acquired rights generates the state's authorization to make law with respect to innate right.

V. Conclusion

Kant characterizes the state of nature as a system of private rights without public right. The apparatus of private rights applies to transactions in it, but subject to three defects that make that application merely provisional. Each of the defects reflects difficulties of unilateral action. Objects of choice cannot be acquired without a public authorization of acquisition; private rights cannot be enforced without a public mechanism through which enforcement is authorized by public law; private rights are indeterminate in their application to particulars without a publicly authorized arbiter. Even the innate right of humanity is insecure in such a condition, both because no remedy is possible in case of a completed wrong against a person, and because even the protective right to defend your person against ongoing attack is indeterminate in its application. These problems can only be solved by a form of association capable of making law on behalf of everyone, and authorizing both enforcement and adjudication under law.

CHAPTER 7

Public Right I: Giving Laws to Ourselves

KANT'S CHARACTERIZATION of the three defects in the state of nature provides an account of why, in the absence of a "united and lawgiving will," conclusive private rights are impossible, and even the innate right of humanity in your own person is insecure. The arguments also show that a fully rightful condition must contain a separation of powers between legislative, executive, and judicial branches, because the resolution of disputes and the enforcement of rights must be done in accordance with prior law. Kant characterizes the need for a rightful condition as the "postulate of public right." Like the other postulates in the *Doctrine of Right*, it is both the conclusion of a normative argument and, at the same time, a postulate in Kant's technical sense of the term: an application of normative concepts to objects of experience,[1] in this case governments and their officials.

The arguments about the defects establish a negative claim: private

---

1. A postulate "does not augment the concept" to which it is "applied in the least" (Kant, *Critique of Pure Reason,* trans. Paul Guyer and Allen Wood [Cambridge: Cambridge University Press, 1998], A219/B266). Instead, it applies modal concepts to a concept already determined. I explain this point in more detail in the appendix.

interaction is morally incoherent without a public standpoint created through institutions. This chapter develops Kant's argument for the corresponding positive claim: a public standpoint, and so a rightful condition, *is* possible through institutions. Each of the defects in the state of nature requires an omnilateral authorization to solve it; solutions to the general problem of political authority and the problems of enforcement and classification of particulars are only consistent with the system of equal freedom provided that they are instances of an omnilateral will. Kant needs to explain how institutions can act omnilaterally. The first part of this chapter will provide Kant's solution to that problem, and show that the postulate of public right can be satisfied.

The second part of the chapter considers a further characterization Kant gives of a rightful condition in terms of the ideal version of it, which he calls "the idea of the original contract." Kant says that the state cannot make a law that the people could not impose on itself. What work is the idea of self-imposed law doing, and on what basis could the people decide between potential laws? This part also frames the general issue addressed in the next several chapters, each of which considers what Kant characterizes as the "effects with regards to rights" that follow from the nature of the civil union. Each of these reflects an institutional precondition of omnilateral lawgiving.

In the Preface to *The Metaphysics of Morals,* Kant concedes that "toward the end of the book I have worked less thoroughly over certain sections than might be expected in comparison with the earlier ones, partly because it seems to me that they can be easily inferred from the earlier ones and partly, too, because the later sections (dealing with public right) are currently subject to so much discussion, and still so important, but they can well justify postponing a decisive judgment for some time."[2] In developing Kant's position in the chapters on public right I draw on the earlier analyses in private right, from which the arguments might be "easily inferred." I have also taken account of more recent discussions of the same issues, both philosophical and juridical, which remain "subject to so much discussion, and still so important," two centuries later.

I. The General Will

A. Three Private Law Models of Political Power

The idea of people giving laws to themselves has taken three general forms in the social contract tradition, each of which reflects one of the standard ways in which private parties acquire obligations to each other. The first of these, which gives the tradition its name, is the idea of a contract, understood as a voluntary undertaking of a commitment, normally undertaken in consideration of something to be gained. Hobbes and Locke both emphasize aspects of this first idea. The second is the idea of cooperative fairness: those who benefit from their participation in a joint venture must bear their share of the costs of sustaining it. The third is the idea of authorization, whereby one person accepts responsibility for deeds done by another person. Hobbes represents the relation between the state and its citizens this way.

Kant's account of the reciprocal rights and obligations that private parties have in a state of nature makes each of these models inappropriate for an account of political authority. Any such model must presuppose the very thing that needs to be explained, that is, the transition from provisional to conclusive rights. You cannot transfer better title than you have. Outside of a rightful condition, all title is only provisional, so that any act of consent or transfer, implicit or explicit, will also be provisional. If private transactions do not give rise to enforceable rights, the contract to set up the state will not be enforceable either.

This difficulty is particularly clear if we focus on the idea of actual consent. As we saw in Chapter 5, consent is central to Kant's analysis of rightful relations between private parties, but its role in that account makes it unsuitable for an understanding of political legitimacy. Consent makes interactions between private parties rightful by making them exercises of the purposiveness of both parties. That role in private relations makes it unsuitable as a basis for public order. If we don't have conclusively rightful private claims without law, ordinary consent lacks its condition of application.

The same point applies to the idea that citizens authorize the state to act as their agent; you can only empower an agent to act on your behalf if you would be entitled to do those things. If people in a state of nature lack the authority to make, apply, or enforce laws, they cannot authorize the state to do so on their behalf. That does not mean that the state could not be entitled to do so; only that no datable act of authorization could be the basis of that entitlement.

Similar difficulties bedevil attempts to ground political obligation not in an actual transfer but in an idealized one, by appeal to a general moral obligation to contribute to a cooperative venture from which they benefit. On this view, the benefits of social cooperation, and the institution of a state, are such that everyone can be made to bear his or her fair share of the burden of providing them. The advantages of framing the issue in this way seem clear, because they require neither a specific occasion of agreement nor the private negotiation of the terms of that agreement.

This approach receives a particularly forceful statement in an early and still influential article by H. L. A. Hart called "Are There Any Natural Rights?" Hart later moved away from the paper's main argument, which closely followed Kant's claim that there is a natural right to freedom. The paper's abiding legacy has been Hart's introduction of what has come to be called "the principle of fair play," according to which,

> when a number of persons conduct any joint enterprise according to rules and thus restrict their liberty, those who have submitted to these restrictions when required have a right to a similar submission from those who have benefited by their submission. The rules may provide that officials should have authority to enforce obedience and make further rules, and this will create a structure of legal rights and duties, but the moral obligation to obey the rules in such circumstances is due to the co-operating members of the society, and they have the correlative moral right to obedience. In social situations of this sort (of which political society is the most complex example) the obligation to obey the rules is something distinct from whatever other moral

reasons there may be for obedience in terms of good consequences (e.g., the prevention of suffering); the obligation is due to the cooperating members of the society as such and not because they are human beings on whom it would be wrong to inflict suffering.[3]

Hart is right to treat enforceable principles of social cooperation as *sui generis,* and distinct from whatever principles prohibit the infliction of suffering. He is also right to argue that the obligation is owed to "the cooperating members of society" as members rather than to one or more of them considered severally. His formulation goes wrong at two crucial points, however: in his characterization of its scope ("when a number of persons conduct any joint enterprise") and in his treatment of political society as a special case of a more general obligation ("the most complex example"). Hart's formulation suggests that people can be compelled to abide by the rules of political societies as an instance of the more general moral principle according to which they can always be compelled to join joint enterprises from which they benefit. Hart does not explain how this principle can be reconciled with the right to freedom that forms the subject matter of the rest of his essay.

The difficulty with the broad principle according to which you can be made to pay for or otherwise contribute to the production of benefits you have received is not that it never applies. In some cases its morality seems intuitively plausible, even obvious. The person who refuses to do his or her fair share in some cooperative project is resented by the others, who are motivated by a sense that it is unfair that they should be contributing when someone else is unwilling to contribute. The person who always refuses to help clean up after the picnic, like the kid at the playground who refuses to take turns with the water pump or swing, is resented. Everyone else shows self-restraint, but this person does not.

A similar principle does seem to be at work in political life: the person who parks on the sidewalk, or regularly blocks it for his own convenience,

---

3. Hart, "Are There Any Natural Rights?" *Philosophical Review* 64, 2 (1955): 175–191. The same general idea may underlie Locke's doctrine of "tacit consent," according to which living in a state and accepting its benefits amount to consent. In a similar way, Locke's theory of property can be read as generating the right to exclude from the right to prevent others from benefiting from my efforts.

is resented, as is the person who uses government services but evades taxes. So it is natural enough to suppose that the same principle is at work in both the informal case and the legal case.

Despite its plausibility, as Hart articulates the principle, it is poorly suited to underwriting mandatory cooperation.[4] Robert Nozick's familiar counterexamples exploit this feature of the formulation: just because your neighbors make the streets more beautiful does not entitle them to compel you to join in their project. Nor do you need to refuse the benefit by closing your eyes as you walk past their houses.[5] The example, like the others that Nozick develops, has seemed to defenders of the principle of fair play to be beside the point. John Simmons attempts to repair the principle by limiting its application to "participants" or "insiders" in the scheme, suggesting that "one becomes a participant in the scheme precisely by accepting the benefits it offers."[6] Simmons illustrates the revised principle with the example of a person who refuses to join his neighbors in digging a well and then goes each evening to draw water from it. This person is a free rider, not because he has consented, but because he has taken benefits without doing his part to produce them. This revised principle is plausible, and makes sense of some of the informal examples—the kid at the playground gets a turn, taking advantage of the system of taking

---

4. In "Legal Obligation and the Duty of Fair Play," in his *Collected Papers* (Cambridge, Mass.: Harvard University Press, 1999), 117, Rawls endorses the principle of fair play and says that he "means to exclude the possibility that the obligation to obey the law is based on a special principle of its own." In *A Theory of Justice*, he restricts its use to participation in rule-governed activities. His disparate examples—marriage, promising, running for political office, playing a game—suggest that to have "voluntarily accepted the benefits" of an institution a person must have participated in it in accordance with its rules, rather than simply benefited from the participation of others. These examples suggest that Rawls does not suppose the principle to have as wide a scope as Hart suggests. Indeed, the case of officials, who choose to participate in government and so fall under the principle of fair play, is explicitly distinguished from that of ordinary citizens, who have what Rawls calls a "natural duty" to support just institutions. See *A Theory of Justice* (Cambridge, Mass.: Harvard University Press, 1971), 342–343. The duty to support just institutions is natural in the sense that it does not require voluntary participation or acceptance of benefits. I am grateful to Jon Mandle for discussion of this point.

5. Nozick, *Anarchy, State, and Utopia* (New York: Basic Books, 1974), 93–94.

6. Simmons, "The Principle of Fair Play," *Philosophy and Public Affairs* 8 (1979): 323–324.

turns, but then refuses to give up the swing, and so on—but, as Simmons points out, it does nothing to underwrite mandatory forms of cooperation such as the state. It says only that *if* you voluntarily participate in the cooperative arrangement by choosing to accept its benefits, *then* you can be required to "do your part" in producing or paying for the benefits. If you cannot refuse the benefits, however, then you cannot be compelled to contribute to producing them.[7]

Simmons's revision of the principle lends it some plausibility as a principle of private right, but dooms it as a principle of public right. As he formulates it, it is a social version of the familiar legal principle of unjust enrichment, according to which someone who freely accepts a benefit from another can be compelled to pay for it. As such, it is not specific to social cooperation. The relevant obligations hold, when they do, between any two private persons—if you dig a well and I draw water from it, I am required to pay you for it. The fact that a group produces the good is not essential to the analysis. As a principle of private right, however, the principle of free acceptance is even narrower than Simmons suggests. In particular, it does not apply to the case in which someone confers a benefit in the hope of extracting a contribution; I only need to pay for benefits I freely accept if those conferring the benefits *do not* do so in the hope of engaging in a transaction with me. If I do not honk my horn to signal my refusal of your services when you squeegee my windshield, you have conferred a benefit on me in the hope of reward; the fact that I am glad to have a clean windshield is irrelevant. I do not need enter into the arrangement you have proposed. As Baron Pollock famously asked in the nineteenth century, "One cleans another's shoes; what can the other do but put them on?"[8] We saw in our discussion of property that even if the Lockean premise that people own their labor is accepted, your efforts generate no right to the *fruits* of your labor unless you capture them successfully. For all of the same reasons, my willing acceptance of those fruits

---

7. Despite some initial plausibility, Simmons's example manages to dodge some difficult questions. Where is the imagined well? If it is on private property, then the free rider is also a trespasser, unless it is on the free rider's land, in which case the well diggers are trespassers, and he may claim their efforts as his own; if it is on public property, who authorized this particular use of it? Indeed, absent some *independent* principle of mandatory cooperation, how did the public property get established?

8. *Taylor v. Laird* (1856), 156 E. R. 1203.

gives you no claim against me in cases in which you direct them to me in the expectation of recompense.

As a principle of private transactions, Simmons's principle of accepted benefits cannot do the work that Hart wants it to, because it has precisely the difficulty that Hart sought to avoid, namely its requirement of voluntariness. Hart writes that the mistake of the classical contract theorists "was to identify *this* right creating situation of mutual restrictions with the paradigm case of promising; there are of course important similarities, and these are just the points which all special rights have in common, viz., that they arise out of special relationships between human beings and not out of the character of the action to be done or its effects."[9] The principle of unjust enrichment differs from the principle of promise keeping, but they are alike in requiring a transaction between the parties. That likeness prevents *either* from explaining mandatory cooperation: both are principles of voluntary interaction.

I cannot hope to canvass the literature seeking to defend the principle of fair play from Nozick's criticisms and Simmons's restrictions. I need not do so, however, because the entire debate has taken place on the mistaken grounds on which Hart set it out, by seeking to find a general principle applicable both outside and within the "most complex example" of political society. Hart takes himself to be capturing the truth in social contract theories of government, but instead he simply reproduces their core difficulty by supposing that a model taken from private relationships applies to authorizing the state. Outside of political society, there is no principle mandating participation in beneficial cooperative activities; within political society, the principle requiring people to do their fair share only applies if participation in political society can be shown to be mandatory on other grounds.

The problem for the benefit/burden principle as a basis of political justification is not simply that people may not have freely accepted the goods and services provided by the state, given that they have no real opportunity to reject them. As Simmons points out, that only shows that actual states do not satisfy its requirements.[10] The more significant problem is that it is the wrong test: others can only compel you to pay for or

---

9. Hart, "Are There Any Natural Rights?," 186.
10. Simmons, "The Principle of Fair Play," 336.

otherwise contribute to benefits you have freely accepted if we are *already* in a rightful condition in which people can be compelled to pay for or contribute to things, so any such obligation needs to be explained. In a private transaction, you can only make me pay for something from which you are entitled to exclude me. If the cooperators who create the benefit are not entitled to exclude me from the benefit, they cannot obligate me to contribute to it. The whole point of Kant's argument is to explain how provisional rights can only be conclusive in a rightful condition. The right to exclude is the core of that very problem.

Both the transfer and free acceptance models fail for another reason as well. Both seek to resolve the idea of a general will into a large series of bilateral relations between individuals and the state. Yet the question of how the state can have the power to enforce is really just the question of how there can be a state at all, how anything can count as an act performed or commitment undertaken by it. So we cannot presuppose the state as a party to it in explaining the contract.

More generally, the creation of a rightful condition cannot require a private transaction of any sort, because the rightful condition is the only context in which procedures can be valid, so that the legitimacy of an outcome depends upon how it came about. Thus the two clear problems with the idea that there is a contract to enter a rightful condition—first, that any such contract is merely "provisional" without a rightful condition, and second, that a contract by ancestors cannot bind their descendents—are manifestations of this broader problem. If procedures cannot be made authoritative, then the fact that people agree to something is not actually binding.

B. Persons and Offices

If people do not unite their wills through a series of private arrangements, in what sense can the actions of the state be said to be omnilateral, rather than just the unilateral acts of the particular officials making the decisions? The failure of the private law models of political authority raises a further issue as well. Both models aim to identify a bilateral relationship between each citizen and the state. In so doing they aspire to explain why a particular state has authority over a particular citizen, by showing that

that citizen has transferred some right to or received some benefit from that particular state. The failure of those accounts does not make that question go away; the fact that a state accomplishes something of great moral importance does not show who, in particular, it has authority over.

Kant's solution to these difficulties is not to find some other principle of private ordering, because no principle of private ordering can do the job. Instead, he works through the implications of the idea that "the best constitution is that in which power belongs not to human beings but to the laws."[11] His basic strategy is to show that a rightful condition can give authority to laws rather than human beings, so that the actions of particular human beings in making, enforcing, and applying laws can be exercises of public rather than private power, and so are instances of an omnilateral will. Institutions can do so because they incorporate a distinction between the offices they create and the officials carrying them out.

We have already seen part of the solution in Kant's claim, considered in the last chapter, that the incentive provided by a public authority is different from the incentive provided by another private person, and in his claim that the decision of the court is different from the decision of your neighbor. Neither of those arguments rests on any claim about the ability of officials to do anything more than act on their own best judgment, or to take the point of view of the universe.[12] Instead, both arguments focus on the way in which a publicly constituted role makes the provision of incentives or the exercise of judgment consistent with the rights of everyone. The legal rule solves the problem of assurance by providing each with the assurance that others have that incentive to respect everyone's acquired rights; a legally constituted court solves the problem of indeterminacy by interpreting objective standards from a standpoint that is not defined by the views of either party, not merely from the perspective of some other

---

11. 6:355.

12. Nor do they rest on the kind of claim made famous by Ronald Dworkin, according to which the positive law and morality taken together contain a single best answer to every legal question, and the task of the judge is to discover it through an interpretive exercise (*Law's Empire* [Cambridge, Mass.: Harvard University Press, 1986], 239). Dworkin's Hercules uses morality to render the application of positive law to particulars both determinate and morally appropriate. The Kantian judge, by contrast, applies positive law to particulars in order to make the relevant parts of morality apply to them.

private party. In so doing, the court acts consistently with the freedom of the parties, something that neither of them could do on his or her own.

The solutions to the problems of assurance and determinacy incorporate the idea of an official acting within his or her mandate. An official is permitted only to act for the purposes defined by that mandate. The concept of an official role thus introduces a distinction between the mandate created by the office and the private purposes of the officeholder. That distinction shows what it is for laws rather than people to rule, even though the actual ruling is done by people.

Focusing on the executive and judiciary might seem to simply push the same question back: the claim that lesser officials act for the state when they act within their legal mandates is only helpful if the legislature that confers those mandates is itself an omnilateral will. But the distinction between rule by laws and rule by human beings once more maps onto the distinction between an office and a person occupying it. All that is required for the legislative will to be omnilateral is for the distinction between public and private purposes to apply to it in the right way. As I shall now explain, the only public purpose that is relevant is the public purpose of creating and sustaining a rightful condition.

The clue to the application of the person/office distinction to the legislature is contained in the failure of the private law models of consent. As a principle of private right, actual agreement regulates interacting persons. However, in circumstances in which actual agreement is not possible, either because one person is incompetent to consent, as in the case of children or comatose patients, or because a person is unavailable to be consulted about particular matters, as in the case of a person who entrusts his affairs to another, one person can "make arrangements for another" consistent with right provided that the first does so subject to the formal constraints of relations of status. First, the person making arrangements must act so as to ensure the ongoing purposiveness of the one for whom the arrangements are being made, and second, the person making the arrangements is precluded from using the power to make those arrangements for his own private purposes. Even the power to ensure the ongoing purposiveness of another person can only be exercised on terms to which that person could consent; as we saw in Chapter 5, there are certain arrangements to which a person could not consent, as a matter of right, even if he found them advantageous. You cannot sell yourself into slavery, even if the proceeds could be used to care for others whom you care about more than your own freedom; you could not consent to participate in a public gladiatorial contest even if you were confident you would win, or if the prospect of your heirs receiving a handsome fee was more important to you than life itself. You can only make arrangements for yourself that do not allow others to treat you as a mere means. If you cannot make such arrangements for yourself, no other person could act on your behalf to make them for you. If a person cannot sell herself into slavery even in the expectation of a benefit, then parents lack the rightful power to sell their children into slavery, even if circumstances are such that those children would have a better life or be more likely to survive as slaves than as free persons.[13]

The structure of an official role parallels the structure of a person in a private relationship of status: an official is legally empowered to make arrangements for others, and is thereby prohibited from using his or her office for private purposes. Thus officials may neither take bribes nor award government contracts to their friends or family members. While the details of these restrictions require legal specification, their broad structure is clear: offices are for public purposes, and any power of choice they confer on their holders is public, not private. The distinction between an official's acting within his or her mandate and outside it does not depend on the official's attitude: legal systems can operate effectively even if many of their officials do not care about the law or justice, but only about doing their jobs and collecting their pay. The contrast between official duty and private corruption applies to such alienated officials in the same way that it applies to committed ones. The possibility of people living together in a rightful condition depends on external conduct, includ-

---

13. The deplorable situation of desperately poor people sometimes leads them to sell their children, and many commentators hope to block such contracts on the grounds that neither parents nor children had a real choice in the matter. See, for example, Debra Satz, *Why Some Things Should Not Be for Sale: On the Limits of Markets* (Oxford: Oxford University Press, 2008). Kant has a different explanation of why such contracts are not binding: nobody could have such a rightful power over another, though he certainly agrees that preventing such situations is a fundamental duty of the state under public right.

ing external conduct within the three branches of government, rather than on any person's attitude toward that conduct.[14]

The broad structure of making arrangements for another is present in each of the branches of the Kantian state. Each of legislature, executive, and judiciary changes the normative situation of private persons, and through the exercise of their powers, legislature and judiciary render persons vulnerable to coercion. As we will see in later chapters, the sovereign (legislature) also has the power to tax and to spend tax monies on the creation of public spaces, health, and national defense, and to make judgments about how to do these things effectively. We will also see that the fact that the power so exercised is not subject to private consent provides the ideal against which any such arrangement must be judged.

The state is thus in one important respect in a position parallel to a parent in relation to his or her child.[15] The state's entitlement to make arrangements for its citizens needs to be consistent with their freedom, even though that consistency cannot be secured by consent. Unlike the parental mandate to "manage and develop" a child, which covers whatever is required to enable the child to become a full member of adult society, capable of consenting to or refusing various private interactions, the state's mandate is much narrower. The parent guides a child to make it into its own master; the state creates a rightful condition in which each person can be his or her own master. Outside of a rightful condition citizens lack the conclusive rights required to create binding arrangements. So officials may take it upon themselves to act for them, but only in ways consistent with their freedom, that is, to create institutions capable of making law. It follows that the state's entitlement only extends to securing the rights of citizens, and never to advancing their private purposes.

When officials act within their roles, they act for the state; Kant also makes the stronger claim that they act for the people. This might appear to collapse back into a private law model by presupposing conclusive pri-

---

14. On alienated officials as a central topic for legal philosophy, See Scott Shapiro, *Legality* (forthcoming). Kant's remark that even a "race of devils" could solve the problem of right rests on the same idea (Kant, *Toward a Perpetual Peace*, 8:366).

15. For an analysis of the requirements this structure imposes on the state to be fair in addressing the competing claims of different citizens, see Evan Fox-Decent, "The Fiduciary Nature of State Legal Authority" *Queen's Law Journal* 31 (2005): 259–310.

vate rights as the basis for a civil condition. Kant's claim, however, is not that citizens actively entrust their affairs to the state, nor even that officials act for citizens considered separately. Instead, officials act for the citizens considered as a collective body. Kant introduces the term "people" as "a multitude of human beings";[16] taken together, they create what he characterizes in the *Critique of Pure Reason* as a "totality," that is, a plurality considered as a unity.[17] A multitude of human beings is a people just because institutions act for them; the institutions are the principle of their unity, and the acts of those institutions are the acts of the people. Kant's claim is thus not that each citizen has in fact consented to or transferred power to the state, nor even that the people have somehow united themselves and then transferred power to the state, but that the state, through its institutions, creates the people, because only through institutions can "a multitude of human beings" make itself into a people. So if a group of officials make, apply, and enforce law in a given region of the Earth's surface, in so doing they thereby unite the inhabitants of that region into a people. By becoming an agent for the people, the state creates that people as a moral subject to whom its acts can be imputed. The state's entitlement to rule does not depend on "whether a state began with an actual contract of submission (*pactum subiectionis civilis*) as a fact, or whether power came first and law arrived only afterward, or even whether they should have followed in this order."[18] What matters is that officials create a rightful condition; if they do, it is a rightful condition for the people in it. Kant can thus agree with Hobbes that a people is created by the institutions that act for it.[19] The existence of representative institutions—that is, institutions in which the officials act on behalf of the citizens considered as a collective body—makes it possible for the people to live together under laws *and so* to become a collective body.[20] Its status as a collective

---

16. 6:311.
17. *Critique of Pure Reason*, A80/B106.
18. 6:318.
19. Hobbes, *Leviathan* (Indianapolis: Hackett, 1994), 110 (chap. XVIII).
20. A representative acts on behalf of those he or she represents. Although election is the ideal way to select representatives, direct voting on all questions, or election of mere delegates who are not representatives, is a form of despotism. Kant thus concludes that a monarch could, in principle, represent the general will, as he says Frederick the Great at least claimed to

body is antecedent to any questions about its ability to rule itself through those institutions.

Powers exercised within a rightful condition provide the omnilateral will required to repair each of the three defects in a state of nature. Public acts are omnilateral because they are not any particular person's unilateral choice, but instead are exercised on behalf of the citizens considered as a collective body. They are also omnilateral in a further sense: a unilateral will always has some particular end, some matter of choice. The omnilateral will is different, because all that it provides is a form of choice, by providing procedures through which laws can be made, applied, and enforced. To return to Kant's initial example, when the state authorizes the acquisition of private property, it does not make the having of property, or the accumulation of wealth, its purpose. Its purpose is to enable individual human beings to have things as their own as against each other, in accordance with the postulate of private right. When the state acts to sustain a rightful condition, in the ways to be discussed in Chapters 8 and 9, it does not have the happiness of its citizens or the gross national product as its end; it only acts to preserve the formal conditions through which people can rule themselves. And when the state punishes criminals, the topic of Chapter 10, it does not do so to prevent harm or to see to it that wrongdoers get what they deserve. It simply upholds the supremacy of its own law.

Kant's account avoids the difficulties of the private law models because it does not suppose that creation of conclusive rights requires the exercise of conclusive rights. The creation of a rightful condition is *lege*, deemed by law, rather than the result of a particular affirmative act,[21] and Kant concedes that it begins by a deed of "seizing supreme power."[22] Once a state has established itself, nobody has standing to resist its creation or its claim to rule on the ground that he or she did not agree to it, because any such disagreement is the denial of an omnilateral will and so merely a unilateral act of refusal, and a unilateral will is never a law for

---

do, but that an Athenian democracy is necessarily a despotism because nonrepresentative. See *Toward a Perpetual Peace*, 8:352.

21. Kant identifies acquisition *lege* with omnilateral acquisition at 6:260.
22. 6:372.

others. So you are under an obligation, characterized in terms of the postulate of public right, which requires that "when you cannot avoid living side by side with all others, you ought to leave the state of nature and proceed with them into a rightful condition."[23] The rightful condition you have entered is the one that has authority over you.

Kant's solution to the problem of authority, then, is to show that official action, simply as such, is not an instance of one person's unilaterally choosing for another. His solution does not depend on any claims about an authority's ability to generate the correct result in every case, or even on the greater reliability of its chosen procedures, measured against some external criterion.[24] Whether you prevail in a particular civil trial may depend *in fact* on who the lawyers are, who the judge is, or who the jurors are. Whether the tax regime is the one that is most advantageous to you, or even to everyone, depends in part on particular decisions made by various officials, not all of which may be wise, fair, or prudent. So long as everyone acts in his or her official capacity, the result is authorized by law, and so is not arbitrary from the standpoint of freedom. Kant's account also explains the "content independence" of authority that has drawn the attention of many recent writers: the fact that different laws, or different

---

23. 6:307.

24. Joseph Raz's influential theory of political authority claims that an authority is legitimate if individuals normally do better at complying with reasons that apply to them independently by following it than by considering those reasons directly. See Raz, "Authority and Justification," *Philosophy and Public Affairs* 14: 1 (Winter 1985): 3–29. Kant's account is consistent with Raz's analysis so long as the idea of "reasons applying" is understood in the right way. For Kant, the only relevant reasons are duties of right, and the state's authority extends only to those duties, which cannot be coherently followed except in a rightful condition. All of the acts of a rightful condition, including the state's entitlement to decide how to achieve various public purposes, can be described as enabling people to "do better" at conforming to their duties of right. It is crucial to Kant's account that the authority is partly constitutive of the application of the underlying duties of right. Nothing in Raz's formulation precludes this, although his appeal to an analogy between political authority and technical expertise might be taken to suggest that the relevant reasons must be determinate apart from the exercise of authority, and the authority's role purely epistemic. The acknowledged role of authority in solving coordination problems by partially constituting their solution shows that Raz's account is more accommodating. Raz's political philosophy is opposed to Kant's because based on two further claims: that rights are based on interests that can be specified nonrelationally, and that law is a tool for achieving purposes that can be fully specified without reference to law. See *The Morality of Freedom* (Oxford: Clarendon, 1986).

official decisions, with different outcomes could *also* have been authorized by law does nothing to make the actual decisions lack authority, because the rule of law constitutes its authority by creating reciprocal limits on freedom through common institutions. Those institutions empower officials to decide authoritatively by deciding for everyone. Again, many details of legislation will depend on all kinds of factors that are accidental from the standpoint of right. However, provided that the legislature acts within its powers, the result is not merely unilateral.

Kant's account also explains why legal authority attaches to positive law in particular. Within a legal system, whether a given norm counts as a legal norm depends upon facts about official acts of lawmaking;[25] positive law is the alternative to each doing "what seems good and right to it." That is just to say that only positive law can solve the three defects in a state of nature.

II. The Idea of the Original Contract

Kant's account of the authority of public institutions shows how the postulate of public right can be satisfied by actual people filling humanly created offices. People "leave the state of nature and proceed" with others "into a rightful condition" simply by being subject to laws.[26] The postulate of public right lays out the minimal conditions for the existence of a rightful condition; it can be "explicated analytically from the concept of *right* in external relations as opposed to violence,"[27] because it contains only the requirement that institutions make, apply, and enforce laws. In a rightful condition, citizens know where they stand in relation to each other: each is secured in his or her rights because objects can be acquired and owned, and disputes resolved consistent with the freedom of all.

Kant also gives a further account of a rightful condition when he argues that every state must be understood, and assessed, in light of what he calls the "idea of the original contract." The point of the contract argu-

---

25. For this minimal definition of law's positivity, and a contrast between it and many other related claims, see John Gardner, "Legal Positivism: 5½ Myths," *American Journal of Jurisprudence* 46 (2001): 199–227.
26. 6:307.
27. Ibid.

ment is not to represent the state as the product of voluntary agreement between private wills, but to show the normative structure through which the exercise of public power is consistent with individual freedom. Although Kant introduces the term in his discussion of the unilateral nature of acquisition,[28] the full explanation appears in Public Right:

> The act by which a people forms itself into a state is the original contract. Properly speaking, the original contract is only the idea of this act, in terms of which alone we can think of the legitimacy of the state. In accordance with the original contract, everyone *(omnes et singuli)* within a people gives up his external freedom in order to take it up again immediately as a member of the commonwealth, that is, of the people considered as a state *(universi)*. And one cannot say: the human being in a state has sacrificed a part of his innate outer freedom for the sake of an end, but rather, he has relinquished entirely his wild, lawless freedom in order to find his freedom as such undiminished, in a dependence upon laws, that is, in a rightful condition, since this dependence arises from his own lawgiving will.[29]

The ideal case for thinking about a rightful condition is the one in which the people, considered as a collective body, unite to rule themselves, considered severally. No actual state could be fully congruent with this idea, because it is both abstract and normative, and so not equivalent to any set of empirical particulars. Instead, it "serves as a norm *(norma)* for every actual union into a Commonwealth (hence serves as a norm for its internal constitution)."[30]

In invoking the ideal case of a rightful condition as a model through which other, lesser cases are to be understood, Kant joins a long tradition of understanding the basic case of legality as the ideal one, and all lesser cases as defective versions of it.[31] In the *Critique of Pure Reason* he en-

---

28. 6:266.
29. 6:315.
30. 6:314.
31. See, for example, Thomas Aquinas, *Summa Theologiae,* Ia IIae90, in Aquinas, *Political Writings,* ed. and trans. R. W. Dyson (Cambridge: Cambridge University Press, 2002), 76ff.; John Finnis, *Aquinas* (Oxford: Oxford University Press, 1998), 219.

dorses this general strategy not only for thinking about legal systems but also for thinking about the concept of a virtuous person, and even concepts of living things.[32] In each instance, the parts are thought of as conditioned by the whole: virtuous acts are parts of a virtuous life, each of the branches of government has its function in relation to the whole that they together comprise, and the parts of a living thing are what they are in relation to the whole. In the case of living things, Kant's point in focusing on the ideal case is not to impute intentions to nature,[33] but rather to make sense of the ways in which living things are made out of inanimate matter, but subject to distinctive forms of generality. In the physical sciences, recalcitrant observations lead to revision of (some of) the generalizations they were supposed to test; in the case of living things, some failures to conform to expectations lead to the conclusion that the plant or animal in question is defective. The discovery of an injured or malformed horse with only three legs neither refutes nor qualifies the generality of the claim that horses have four legs, and the fact that almost all mayflies die before pupating neither refutes nor qualifies claims about the normal life cycle of the mayfly. Instead, such examples show that many living things are defective instances of their species.

In the same way, Kant follows the natural law tradition in treating the ideal case of a rightful condition law as analytically basic, and all actual cases as defective instances of it. He takes the general strategy of focusing on the ideal case to a higher level of abstraction because of a more general feature of normative concepts. To think of the way that something is supposed to be is always to compare it to an ideal of its kind. In the case of plants or animals, the ideal has both an *a priori* part—the idea of a prop-

32. *Critique of Pure Reason*, A318/B374.
33. Kant rejects the so-called design argument in the *Critique of Pure Reason*, A627/B655. The idea that teleology implies design is an instance of the same sort of reductive empiricist and utilitarian assumptions that lead Bentham and Austin to attempt to reduce rules to commands backed by threats. From Paley's example of the watchmaker, through Bentham and Austin's attempt to reduce rules to commands, to Mill's identification of the valuable with that which people are disposed to value, empiricist thought regards standards of correctness as in need of explanation, and psychological states as an unexplained explainer of them. Hume's readiness to invoke the concept of a rule places him in sharp contrast to the rest of the empiricist tradition. The Kantian tradition regards rational standards as basic and even psychological states as explicable only by reference to them.

erly organized living thing with a characteristic life form—and a part drawn from experience—the particular life form of a mayfly or horse. Without the *a priori* part, particular animals could not be thought of as alive,[34] but each individual plant or animal is understood in terms of the ideal realization of its own (empirically discovered) species. Investigation might reveal that the life form of some plant or animal has been misunderstood, and so requires revision.

Normative concepts are distinctive because their ideal case is entirely *a priori*. If a normative requirement fails to apply to what actually happens, that shows that something has gone wrong in the world. It does not reveal any defect in the requirement. The fact that experience has taught us that no actual human being has managed to meet all of the requirements of virtue is grounds for disappointment about human beings, not for revising the concept of virtue. In focusing on the ideal case, Kant is not suggesting that people should find fault with each other for every failure to meet it. The same purity that makes the ideal case of a norm regulative also makes it unattainable.

Principles of right have the same priority over actual conduct as other normative concepts: the fact that people often violate the rights of others is not a reason to revise the concepts of right, because they govern how people are entitled to treat each other, rather than describing how they actually or typically do. What actually happens can be relevant to what it is prudent to do, but not to normative requirements. That is why Lockean claims about the difficulties that human inclinations and limitations generate in a state of nature can at most show that it is advantageous to leave it, not that it is morally necessary to do so. Kant focuses on the pure case of a state of nature in identifying its three defects to show that a system of pure private right is normatively incoherent because it fails to meet its own internal criteria of adequacy.

The idea of the original contract extends the strategy of considering the pure case to public institutions charged with making arrangements for people, by articulating the structure through which the power to make

---

34. For a detailed defense of this claim, see Michael Thompson, *Life and Action: Elementary Structures of Practical Thought* (Cambridge, Mass.: Harvard University Press, 2008), Part One.

and enforce those arrangements can be consistent with freedom, and so fully legitimate. We saw in the previous section that institutions can create an omnilateral will because they incorporate the distinction between the mandate of an office and the purposes of the particular person filling it. An official acting within his or her mandate will often have room to exercise judgment in determining what it requires in a particular situation, or how best to carry out its purposes. In so doing, the official will both exercise judgment and take account of empirical and anthropological factors that might be relevant to those purposes. Any such judgment, discretion, or consideration of facts has to be exercised within the terms of the mandate; an official is not entitled to use public office to pursue private purposes, nor to make the world better in ways unrelated to his or her mandate. That is the sense in which officials are public servants: they act on behalf of the public. We also saw that the entitlement to make arrangements for others is limited to the arrangements that those others would have been entitled, as a matter of right, to make for themselves. The structure of making arrangements that others could have made for themselves includes not only the particular laws that the state makes, but also the "constitutional" law that creates the institutional structure through which some make arrangements for others. The postulate of public right entitles officials to make arrangements for citizens; the idea of the original contract represents citizens themselves as authors of the higher-order arrangement empowering those officials, so that all political power is exercised by the people themselves.

The ideal case serves as a standard because it provides the only consistent way of organizing the use of power to guarantee everyone's freedom under law. Institutions and their officials have a duty of right to act in conformity with it because they have a duty of right to act in conformity with every human being's right to freedom. Kant's argument does not say that since officials are making law, they should do the ideal version of lawmaking, or that in making law they are already committing themselves to some aspirational ideal of law. Such an approach is foreign to the Kantian project. The suggestion that the duty to rule in conformity with the idea of the original contract is a special case of a more general principle that requires you to do whatever you are doing in accordance with the standard internal to whatever you happen to be doing—as someone might imagine that the problem with making bad arguments is that person's failure to live up to the proper standards internal to argumentation, and so to somehow ensnare herself in some form of performative contradiction—would fault the person who failed to live up to the ideal with some sort of nonrelational, self-regarding failure of rational consistency, rather than a wrong against others. A state that makes laws inconsistent with the idea of the original contract is defective because it creates a condition that is not rightful, not because it violates a norm of inner consistency.

Laws can be defective from the standpoint of the idea of the original contract in two distinct ways. First, particular laws can be inconsistent with each person's innate right to independence. The state must eliminate these in order to make its laws fully rightful. Second, the form in which laws are *given* can be defective; a system that had excellent laws but in which legislation was not self-imposed would be defective in this second way. In a fully republican system of government, the people give laws to themselves through their chosen representatives, whom they have elected to act on their behalf, and the legislature empowers officials and courts to implement those laws and apply them to particular cases. The branches of government that solve each of the three problems must be separate. If the legislature could apply laws to particulars (though bills of attainder, for example), some people would simply exercise power over others, instead of the citizens collectively ruling over themselves severally.

Each of the possible defects in a system of laws generates a respect in which the state is under a duty to improve itself. The first problem generates a duty to improve its laws, the second a duty on the part of the state to improve its form of lawgiving, to bring it more nearly into conformity with the idea of the original contract, making the fulfillment of that duty a properly public purpose for which the state can both collect taxes and regulate other activities.

Both of these duties are internal duties of the state. Like the duty of rightful honor, no other person or institution has the correlative right to enforce them.[35] Like all duties of right, the state's duty to improve its laws can only be carried out by using means consistent with the Universal Principle of Right. Political change cannot be imposed from above, but

---

35. Bernd Ludwig has argued that because duties on the part of the state do not generate correlative rights, the state is subject to duties of virtue rather than right ("Kants Verabschiedung der Vertragstheorie—Konsequenzen für eine Theorie der sozialen Gerchtigkeit," *Jahrbuch für Recht und Ethik* 1 [1993]: 239-243). Ludwig's dichotomy between right and

must come from the people. The development of a more fully self-imposed form of lawgiving must ideally be self-imposed. In *Theory and Practice,* Kant characterizes freedom of speech as the "sole palladium" of the people's rights.[36] Political speech is the only medium through which both the improving and the improvement of institutions are fully in conformity with right. The right to complain of injustices in "matters of taxation, recruiting and so forth"[37] enables citizens to improve particular laws; the right more generally to speak in one's own name enables citizens to improve lawmaking institutions.[38]

---

virtue overlooks the possibility of internal duties of right (most significantly, the duty of rightful honor). As we saw in Chapter 2, an internal duty of right restricts the range of choice in light of the Universal Principle of Right. Each of the state's internal duties restricts *its* ability to act through its officials to those acts consistent with the rights of its citizens. Its only end, then, is to observe the restrictions presupposed by its basic mandate; its positive provision of, for example, public roads or support for the poor is just the restriction of its other activities to terms consistent with right. The only questions it faces are questions of how to give effect to a rightful condition. Its duty in answering those questions is to give effect to a rightful condition rightfully. Not only is the performance of these functions not assessed in terms of moral merit; the ends are not discretionary, and lack the "playroom" *(latitudo)* in relation to other ends characteristic of duties of virtue. See 6:233, and *Doctrine of Virtue,* 6:390; Barbara Herman, *Moral Literacy* (Cambridge, Mass.: Harvard University Press, 2007), 203–229; Hannes Unberath, "Freedom in the Kantian State," *Jahrbuch für Recht und Ethik* 16 (2008): 321–367. Public officials must figure out how to maintain and perfect a rightful condition. A permissive law permits them to rule even if their success at realizing the idea of the original contract is incomplete (*Toward a Perpetual Peace,* 8:347). Integrating the mandatory ends of a rightful condition with other purposes is prohibited, because the state has no other purpose but to be a rightful condition.

36. Kant, *On the Common Saying: That May Be Correct in Theory but Is of No Use in Practice,* in Gregor, *Practical Philosophy,* 8:304.

37. 6:319.

38. The characterization of official speech as private subjects it to a further restriction: an official could never be entitled to lie in an official capacity. (Kant makes a parallel point in his discussion of international right, where he rejects "underhanded means that would destroy the trust requisite to a lasting peace" [*Doctrine of Right,* 6:347]. In the case of international right, the difficulty is that an agreement to conclude a peace must include the intention to be bound by it; a rule permitting deception deprives the parties of the power to bind themselves through agreement.) Kant says that the liar makes "all rights that depend on contracts come to nothing and lose their force" ("On a Supposed Right to Lie from Philanthropy," 8:426). His point, as always, is transcendental rather than empirical; the destruction of trust is not a bad

III. Public Powers and Their Limits

Kant organizes his discussion of the powers of a state under the category of "effects with regard to rights that follow from the nature of the civil union."[39] He mentions six such effects: the prohibition on revolution, the state's status as "supreme proprietor of the land," its duty to support the poor, its right to establish offices exclusively on the basis of merit, its right to punish, and its right to control immigration on nonethnic grounds.[40] Each consequence is introduced as both an explanation of the powers that the state must be entitled to exercise and, at the same time, an instance of the supremacy of law over anything that claims to compete with it. The state's status as "supreme proprietor" and its consequent police power is the subject of the next chapter, the duty to support the poor and guarantee equality of opportunity of the following one, and punishment the one after that. In light of these powers I then turn to the question of

---

effect of lying; it is the fundamental presupposition of lying. Although deceit is not a wrong against the person deceived, it does "wrong in general," that is, what Kant goes on to call a "formal" rather than "material" wrong, or wrong in the "highest degree" (8:429). Like all formal wrongs, it is contrary to what Kant calls "the right of human beings as such," that is, the right to be in a rightful condition, one in which disputes are resolved by law rather than force (*Doctrine of Right*, 6:240; 6:308). The connection between a rightful condition and truth-telling follows from the more general requirement that the state can only make such arrangements for its citizens as the citizens could have made for themselves. The arrangements that people can make for themselves are limited by a requirement of truth-telling; as we saw in Chapter 5, you cannot unite your will with the will of someone who misrepresents the terms on which the wills are united. The fraud and his dupe do not share a united will. Truth-telling is the unconditional presupposition of possible agreement. That is the sense in which deceit makes rights founded on contract "come to nothing": it lies beyond any person's possible power of agreement. Applied to public right, the state's power to make arrangements is limited by the possibility of agreement. Where agreement is impossible, no arrangements can be made, and so, in the limiting case, the state cannot make a law that is inconsistent with the possibility of agreement at all. So any use of deception by officials necessarily involves making arrangements for citizens that the citizens could not have made for themselves. See Jacob Weinrib, "The Juridical Significance of Kant's 'Supposed Right to Lie,'" *Kantian Review* 13 (2008): 148-158.

39. 6:318.

40. Bernd Ludwig, "'The Right of a State' in Immanuel Kant's *Doctrine of Right*," *Journal of the History of Philosophy* 28 (1990): 403-415, argues that the numbering and ordering of the sections of Public Right reflect printer's errors which Kant was too preoccupied to correct. Among the changes is to have §50 become part F of the "General Remark" to Public Right.

revolution. The remainder of this chapter, however, is concerned with the general idea of the people giving laws to itself. Kant introduces this in hypothetical terms, and says that the state may not make laws that the people could not impose on itself.

As we have seen, it is a general principle that when one person makes an arrangement for another, the first cannot be entitled to make an arrangement to which the other could not consent. The Kantian sovereign makes arrangements for the people, that is, a "multitude of human beings" considered as a collective body. So the test of its lawmaking power must be the possible agreement of the citizens considered as a collective body.

As Onora O'Neill has argued, Kant's focus on what the people "could" choose differs from more recent contractarian theories that focus on what people in specified circumstances "would" choose, in order to best secure their own prospective advantage.[41] Although the distinction between what could and what would be chosen can be collapsed by insisting that people could only choose what is most advantageous for them, Kant's emphasis on possible choice focuses on the grounds for the individuals accepting the authority of the state, that is, to guarantee the systematic enjoyment of the right to freedom. You could agree to restrict specific exercises of your freedom, in order to guarantee its systematic preconditions, but the prospect of advantage could not entitle you to "throw away your freedom" in ways inconsistent with your general right to be your own master. No such act could be an instance of protecting your own capacity for choice. The same point can, once again, be made in the vocabulary of the duty of rightful honor: you lack the power to create any binding arrangement that presupposes that others may treat you as a mere means for pursuing their private purposes.

IV. The Power of the People to Bind Itself

Kant introduces the idea of a people giving laws to itself in his essay "What Is Enlightenment?" The arguments of that essay at first appear to

---

41. O'Neill, "Kant and the Social Contract Tradition," in François Duchesneau, Guy Lafrance, and Claude Piché, eds., *Kant Actuell: Hommage à Pierre Laberge* (Montréal: Ballarmin, 2000), 185–200.

have a religious character, and to be focused on getting religious matters right: "one age cannot bind itself and conspire to put the following one into such a condition that it would be impossible for it to enlarge its cognitions (especially in such urgent matters) and to purify them of errors, and generally to make further progress and enlightenment." This formulation appears to be focused on some basic interest in the doctrine of free faith. Kant reinforces this appearance when he goes on to say, "This would be a crime against human nature, whose original vocation lies precisely in such progress; and succeeding generations are therefore perfectly authorized to reject such decisions as unauthorized and made sacrilegiously."[42]

Kant's final qualification suggests that a different principle is at work: "The touchstone of whatever can be decided upon as a law for a people lies in the question: whether a people could impose such a law upon itself."[43] In the particular example, the difficulty with imposing a binding religious creed is not that each person would expect some disadvantage from it, nor that, taken in the aggregate, people would experience significant disadvantages. Such advantages or disadvantages could not be assessed *a priori*. Instead, a binding and enforceable religious doctrine would conflict with both the right of each person and the right of the people considered as a collective body. Each person is entitled to decide on his or her own what his or her purposes will be. That entitlement can be limited to reconcile each person's purposiveness with that of the others, but it cannot be limited on material grounds, that is, on the basis of some particular purpose, such as social stability or religious salvation, that many, or even all, people happen to share. Material purposes are, in the requisite sense, merely private, no matter how common they are. Each person is entitled to make what he or she will of what others say about any matter; any restriction on that entitlement could not be consented to. There is also a problem for the people considered collectively, for they could not decide in advance to preclude the possibility of making their condition more rightful; the "vocation" of human nature "lies in such

---

42. Kant, "An Answer to the Question: What Is Enlightenment?" 8:39. See also Jonathan Peterson, "Enlightenment and Freeedom," *Journal of the History of Philosophy* 46, no. 2 (2008): 223–244.

43. Ibid.

progress" in the ability of a people to give laws to itself. One generation could not "conspire" to render the next passive in relation to the laws that govern them.

Both of the uses of the idea of agreement in Kant's discussion of enlightenment figure in public right more generally. A state is required to act for public purposes, but prohibited from acting for private ones, and individual rights constrain the means that the state may use in pursuit of public purposes. Cast in the vocabulary of agreement, the test of whether the state is entitled to exercise a class of powers is whether the people must give itself such a power, whether a public authority having such a power is a necessary condition of the people binding themselves through law. Each of Kant's detailed arguments for specific powers follows this pattern.

Individual rights also constrain state power through the idea of possible agreement by restricting the means the state can use in pursuing public purposes to those consistent with each person's innate right of humanity. Further limitations can be generated by the systematic realization of rights, so that the state is also precluded from using means inconsistent with the possibility of citizens ruling themselves. Cast in the vocabulary of possible agreement, citizens lack the power to bind themselves to arrangements inconsistent with their own rightful honor, that is, ones in which they are treated as mere means, and from binding themselves to conditions in which they are merely passive in relation to the laws that govern them. A citizen does not have a right against the state that he be in a certain situation, considered apart from how it came about, only a right that the state not do certain things to him through its official acts. This restriction parallels the distinction in Private Right between wronging a person and changing the context in which that person acts. Rather than focusing on the effects of action or inaction, considered as such, it focuses on the means that are used.

The question of whether agreement is possible thus makes no reference to any matters of advantage. In particular, the ease or difficulty of keeping a potential agreement is not relevant to whether it is possible; Kant does not offer a version of Rawls's idea of the "strains of commitment." Rawls argues that a person could not undertake an obligation if he believed he would be unable to bring himself to carry it out. He argues that people choosing institutions from behind "a veil of ignorance" who did not know what social positions they would occupy would not agree to legally established slavery because they would foresee that if they turned out to be slaves, they would be unwilling to do the bidding of their masters.[44] Kant is concerned with the authorization to coerce, so it cannot matter whether someone would foreseeably lack an *internal* incentive to conformity with positive law. If something is wrongful, it can be prohibited, no matter how significant the contrary inclinations. As Kant observes in his discussion of the so-called right of necessity, the fact that in sufficiently dire circumstances wrongful conduct could not be prevented by externally given law does not make that conduct rightful or place it beyond the scope of legal regulation, even if it makes punishment pointless.[45] The foreseen ease or difficulty of compliance depends on the *matter* of choice. The argument against institutional slavery cannot be that rational persons would not take on a burden they expect to have difficulty in meeting, because questions of right are never questions about burdens at all. Instead, a rightful constitution could not institute slavery because it cannot make arrangements between private persons that those persons could not be entitled to make for themselves. If a person cannot bind him- or herself to a condition of slavery, neither can an official bind that person. No expected material advantage can override this.

Instead of advantage, possible agreement is limited by each person's innate right of humanity. Many individual rights are grounded in the "authorizations" that are "already contained" in the innate right to freedom; political rights are derived from the idea of the original contract. Freedom of expression follows from the innate right of humanity authorizing a person "to do to others anything that does not in itself diminish what is theirs, so long as they do not want to accept it—such things as merely communicating his thoughts to them, telling or promising them something, whether what he says is true and sincere or untrue and insincere; for it is entirely up to them whether they want to believe him or not."[46] The right to say what you think is a reflection of the more general point

44. Rawls, *A Theory of Justice*, 176ff.
45. 6:236.
46. 6:238.

that no person has a right that others conduct themselves in ways best suited to his or her preferred purposes. Short of depriving you of something you already have a right to, I can use my words as I see fit. Other aspects of right determine the ways in which one person can be wronged by another's words. Your right to a good reputation, which Kant argues extends even beyond your death, is one example. Others include the wrongfulness of fraud and even of speaking in another person's name by publishing a copyrighted book without the author's permission.

Innate right also governs the presumption of innocence and the burden of proof when someone is accused of wrongdoing. Each person's right to be "a human being beyond reproach" can be appealed to "when a dispute arises about an acquired right and the question comes up, on whom does the burden of proof fall, either about a controversial fact, or if this is settled, about a controversial right, someone who refuses to accept this obligation can appeal methodically to his innate right to freedom (which is now specified in its various relations), as if he were appealing to various bases for rights."[47]

Most significantly, innate right includes "a human being's quality of being his own master *(sui juris),*"[48] that is, the right not to be used for the purposes of others. This aspect of innate right means that people could not rightfully give themselves a law that made some official their master, and so precludes the use of public power to achieve merely private purposes. It also guarantees freedom of association. Part of your entitlement to set and pursue your own purposes is the entitlement to choose those with whom you will make arrangements, subject only to their entitlement to decline to enter into arrangements with you.

The right to independence of the choice of others constrains public officials because the people could not give themselves a master, that is, someone with unlimited discretion, or even someone who was empowered to make arrangements for them in pursuit of his or her own private purposes.[49]

The immediate basis of each of the right to freedom of expression, the

47. Ibid.
48. Ibid.
49. In *Roncarelli v. Duplessis,* [1959] S.C.R. 121, then Quebec premier Maurice Duplessis arranged the revocation of the liquor license of a restaurant owned by someone who had posted bail for Jehovah's Witnesses whom Duplessis had had arrested for proselytizing.

right to be beyond reproach, and the right to be your own master in innate right guarantees that a people giving itself a law does not have the rightful capacity to alienate or repudiate any of them. As a private person, you cannot sell yourself into slavery; so, too, free persons cannot "throw away their freedom" by making themselves inherently subject to reproach, or have their right to communicate their thoughts curtailed by anything other than the rights of other persons. Nor could they make themselves inherently subject to a calculus of material advantage, available to be used or disposed of on the basis of the net balance of consequences. The status of these rights as aspects of innate right does not mean that they do not require clarification and codification through positive law. It means only that such clarification and codification must be focused on those rights, and not subject to balancing against other potentially competing interests.

Innate right has the further implication that a people could not give themselves laws that are so open-ended that they effectively confer an unrestricted power on officials. A rule that created a broad set of presidential or royal prerogatives, to be used for whatever purpose the president or monarch chose, would be inconsistent with self-rule; a provision entitling the majority to impose bills of attainder regulating the conduct only of specific individuals would face the same problem. So, too, would a rule that instructed officials to make determinations on the basis of facts that they were not in a position to ascertain.[50] The same analysis captures the

---

Duplessis argued that the relevant legislation gave the manager of the provincial Liquor Control Commission the right to revoke licenses "at his pleasure," and so entitled him to do so on any grounds whatsoever, including political ones. Justice Rand, writing for the Supreme Court of Canada, held that as a matter of law, the legislature could not have conferred such a power on him, because "in public regulation of this sort there is no such thing as absolute and untrammelled 'discretion,' that is that action can be taken on any ground or for any reason that can be suggested to the mind of the administrator; no legislative Act can, without express language, be taken to contemplate an unlimited arbitrary power exercisable for any purpose, however capricious or irrelevant, regardless of the nature or purpose of the statute" (141). Rand does not use the vocabulary of the laws a people could give itself, but the broad structure of the argument is exactly that: a legislature could not have given that power.

50. This is the issue raised in *Little Sisters Book and Art Emporium v. Canada (Minister of Justice)*, [2000] 2 S.C.R. 1120, in which Justice Iacobucci held that the law governing obscenity lacked a rational connection to its declared purpose of protecting women against exploitation, because it empowered lower-level customs officials to prohibit the importation of any materials that they found distasteful.

difficulties of rules that grant discretion to juries to distribute punishments on the basis of extralegal factors. Persons concerned with their right of self-mastery could not find themselves under a law that made punishment depend on such factors, even if, in the abstract, they might expect a reasonable prospect of being advantaged by consideration of those factors.[51]

Other restrictions on the means that the state may use are imposed by the public structure of lawgiving, and the correlative requirement that citizens could not bind themselves to a condition of passivity. The defects of a binding religious creed provide one example. Restrictions on public political expression provide another. Free beings could not put themselves in a position in which they were prohibited from expressing their concerns about the rightfulness or even prudence of public laws.[52] Conversely, public officials may not deceive citizens.[53] These restrictions on the exercise of state power are indirect requirements of rightful honor. To be passive because of disposition or even circumstances is consistent with rightful honor; you are under no obligation of right to exercise your

---

51. In *McCleskey v. Kemp,* the United States Supreme Court upheld a Georgia death penalty statute, despite accepting evidence that the likelihood of execution for a black person who murdered a white person was four times as high as for a white person who murdered a black one. Rejecting the relevance of these factors, Justice Stewart focused on the fact that "discretion in the criminal justice system offers substantial benefits to the criminal defendant. Not only can a jury decline to impose the death sentence, it can decline to convict or choose to convict of a lesser offense. Whereas decisions against a defendant's interest may be reversed by the trial judge or on appeal, these discretionary exercises of leniency are final and unreviewable . . . a capital punishment system that did not allow for discretionary acts of leniency would be totally alien to our notions of criminal justice" (*McCleskey v. Kemp,* 481 U.S. 279 [1987]).

The application of this mode of reasoning to the particular case of racial discrimination in capital cases is appalling, but for present purposes less remarkable than the style of reasoning itself. Justice Stewart's characterization of the role of discretion moves from the claim that *some* wrongdoers *benefit* from the existence of discretion to the conclusion that it is consistent with the rule of law to give out such benefits on whatever basis officials or jurors wish to. Petitioner in *McCleskey* was complaining of a having suffered a form of unfair discrimination. It is no answer to such a complaint to say that *other* people actually benefit from that form of discrimination. Indeed, the whole point of calling it discrimination is to say that this discrepancy is legally arbitrary.

52. *Theory and Practice,* 8:298.

53. "On a Supposed Right to Lie from Philanthropy," 8:428.

rights, but rightful honor does not permit you to put yourself into an enforceable condition of passivity. A law prohibiting you from speaking your mind about public issues, or one that granted officials the right to deceive you, would make a condition of passivity enforceable against you.[54] Kant condemns a state in which "subjects . . . are constrained to behave only passively" as "the greatest *despotism* thinkable (a constitution that abrogates all the freedom of its subjects, who in that case have no rights at all)."[55]

The idea that the people are the authors of the laws that bind them is thus a formal rather than material idea. A material principle would insist that people have a particularly strong or even overriding interest in their innate right, and so would never agree to something likely to compromise it. Kant's formal principle focuses on the relation between innate right and legislation through the mediating idea of the authorization of coercion. The use of force is only rightful provided that it is consistent with the innate right of humanity; positive legislation is only legitimate if it could be a law that free persons could impose on themselves, where the test of the possible imposition is their rightful capacity to bind themselves, that is, consistency with their rightful honor.

V. Agreement

A familiar complaint against contractarian arguments is that all of the justificatory work is done by the premises from which the parties give themselves laws. Kant's use of the idea of possible lawgiving is vulnerable to this charge in one respect, since the lawgiving powers of people are governed by their innate right. As we have seen, Kant's point in introducing ideas of agreement is to explain how political authority can be consistent with the rights of those subject to it. Kant's answer is that one person can be entitled to change the normative situation of others only if the power to

---

54. Kant's notorious discussion of "passive citizenship" concedes that qualifications for voting can be consistent with a rightful condition, but require that each person be able to change from being a passive to an active citizen, precisely because such arrangements could not be made binding on individuals (6:314–315). See Jacob Weinrib, "Kant on Citizenship and Universal Independence," *Australian Journal of Legal Philosophy* 33 (2008): 1–25.

55. *Theory and Practice*, 8:290–291.

do so itself has an omnilateral authorization. Political authority, whether by a legislature, executive, or judiciary, is only legitimate provided that it can be understood as an instance of an omnilateral authorization. Talk about whether the people could give themselves a particular law thus enters not as either an algorithm or a heuristic for generating particular laws, but rather as a test of whether a particular law could have an omnilateral authorization. If a validly enacted statute could be agreed to, citizens are required to regard it as having received one. If it could not, it lacks the force of law. However, we will see in Chapter 12 that citizens are limited in their remedies when legislation is defective in this way.

By conceiving of the people as the authors of the laws that bind them, Kant provides a principled account of both the basis and the limits of state power. Because there is only one innate right, the right to freedom, all of the other, more specific restraints on government must be understood as aspects of that right, and so be reconciled with each other as aspects of it. If freedom of expression appears to come into conflict with the fundamental entitlements of equal citizenship—as is sometimes argued in the context of hate speech—any restriction on the former right must be justified as an expression of the underlying and more basic innate right of humanity that gives rise to both. The particular "authorizations already contained in" the innate right of humanity are not competing members of a disparate list, and any attempt to reconcile them must presume them to be capable of mutual adjustment. The task of judgment and justification requires specification of the incidents of innate right through positive law and the exercise of judgment in their application to particulars. That specification can generate a distinction between core and peripheral instances of a right, or between "high value" and "low value" speech, but the core of a right is just its systematic place in an articulated system of rights. Unlike the sort of balancing of interests that properly goes on in determining speed limits or tax rates—the subject of Chapter 8—reconciling different aspects of innate right does not weigh one thing against another, but rather adjusts each so as to work the various aspects of innate right into a coherent doctrinal whole.[56] The ineliminable place of both

---

56. Thomas M. Scanlon, Jr., "Adjusting Rights and Balancing Values," *Fordham Law Review* 72 (2004): 1477–1486.

judgment and doctrinal development reveals the affinity between legal reasoning in public right and private right: just as legal doctrines must be developed to bring general categories of right to bear on particular disputes, so, too, they must be developed to give effect to the basic right that provides the grounds of rights to be presumed innocent, freedom of expression, security of the person, and subjection to law rather than arbitrary choice. Like all rational concepts of right, both the innate right of humanity and the idea of the original contract require institutional realization to create a system of universal law that applies to particulars.

The difference between focusing on each person's capacity to bind him- or herself and focusing on each person's expectation of advantage generates a contrast between two very different ways of asking about hypothetical agreement. In a pair of recent articles, Thomas Pogge has argued that the social contract theory developed and defended by John Rawls ultimately collapses into a form of consequentialism, because it treats citizens selecting laws for themselves as recipients of those laws but not their authors in any robust sense. As Pogge puts it, "Understood as guides to the assessment of social institutions, contractarianism and consequentialism are for the most part not competitors but alternative presentations of a single idea: both tend to assess alternative institutional schemes exclusively by how each would affect its individual human participants."[57]

Without assessing the success of Pogge's charge against Rawls in particular, I want to suggest that his point certainly applies to many recent uses of the idea of hypothetical agreement. As Pogge frames it, the difficulty arises because parties concerned to maximize their prospective advantage can only do so by balancing competing advantages against each other. The point is not just that the parties in Rawls's "original position" reason instrumentally. It is rather that the basis for their choice of principles is to find the most favorable balance of benefits and burdens. The problem is in the question they are asked no less than in the manner in which they seek to answer it.

---

57. Thomas Pogge, "Three Problems with Contractarian-Consequentialist Ways of Assessing Social Institutions," *Social Philosophy & Policy* 12 (1995): 241–266, 246. See also Pogge's "Equal Liberty for All?" *Midwest Studies in Philosophy* 28 (2004): 266–281.

In laying his charge against Rawls, Pogge draws attention to Rawls's endorsement of strict criminal liability for possession of firearms in cases in which gun-related crimes are so serious as to pose a grave threat.[58] A contract-type argument is focused on the desirability of competing laws, framed exclusively in terms of their consequences. Liability without wrongdoing is defended on the grounds that "it might be accepted by the representative citizen as a lesser loss to liberty, at least if the penalties imposed are not too severe."[59] Pogge's point is that the use of the contract argument to assess this kind of situation reduces it to the sort of cost/benefit analysis characteristic of consequentialism.

Everything depends on how individual rights against the state are understood. In a footnote to the passage that Pogge discusses, Rawls, following Hart, identifies them in light of the general interest that persons have in being able to give effect to their choices. Thus Rawls suggests that the normal requirements of fault in criminal procedure are to be understood in just this way. The requirement that a person have the capacity and opportunity to avoid punishment makes the criminal law a system of choices, *because* citizens have an interest in being in control of their lives and so in being able to avoid punishment. Rawls later characterizes the priority of liberty in explicitly conditional terms: "The last point about the priority of liberty is that this priority is not required under all conditions. For our purposes here, however, I assume that it is required under what I shall call 'reasonably favorable conditions,' that is, under social circumstances which, provided the political will exists, permit the effective establishment and the full exercise of these liberties."[60] The conditions are ones that, as Rawls remarks, are met in normal conditions in advanced democracies. For Kant, how easily or frequently such conditions are met

---

58. Rawls's own treatment of this case uses it as an example of "nonideal" theory, and focuses in particular on the risk of social strife, perhaps even the breakdown of the social order. Thus in its particulars it may be closer to Lincoln's suspension of *habeas corpus* during the Civil War that to the cases to which Pogge assimilates it. If so, Rawls might wish to distinguish the question of what can be done to *sustain* a legal order from the question of what can be done in response to wrongful conduct within the legal order, and so avoid the generalization that Pogge wishes to draw from this example. If Rawls is able to do so, however, it does not follow that many who have sought to deploy similar modes of reasoning are also able to.

59. Rawls, *A Theory of Justice*, 242.

60. Rawls, *Political Liberalism* (New York: Columbia University Press, 1993), 297.

is not the central issue. Once the criminal law's fault requirements are understood as applicable only in favorable conditions, their application depends on how favorable conditions are, and favorableness in turn can only be assessed in terms of the likelihood of the requirements advancing the relevant interests. The interest that each person has in having effective choices is an interest he or she has apart from the state, because it is an interest that each person has, regardless of which factors advance or impair it. People concerned to protect such an interest will be just as concerned about protecting themselves against other persons as against state action. If the facts turn out the right way, the familiar prohibition on punishment without fault becomes fully fungible against other social costs. Any procedure will lead to wrongful convictions, but a decision to *dispense* with requirements of guilt does not simply accept wrongful convictions, but embraces them. The only question is which arrangements are most likely to protect the interest. The gain outweighs the potential loss, particularly if the loss is thought to be largely within an individual's control.

The possibility of balancing one person's right to be beyond reproach against the interests of others is the consequence of regarding rights as protections of things that matter to people apart from right, that is, from the more general instrumentalism that supposes that what matters morally can be specified without reference to legal concepts or institutions. Contemporary debates between "interest" and "will" theories of rights exemplify this instrumental conception of legal concepts, because they disagree about what rights are supposed to protect, but agree that they are supposed to protect something the value of which can be identified without reference to the concept of a right. Will theories focus on the importance to a person's life of shaping that life; interest theories, on whatever interests are important enough to justify burdening others with obligations.

As we have seen, Kant has a fundamentally different conception of a right. A right is not a tool for advancing or even protecting the interests or effective choices of one person by restricting the conduct of others. Nor is it a power to decide about a particular matter. It is an entitlement to independence of the choice of others under universal law. Each person's entitlement to freedom is simply the entitlement to a constraint on the conduct of others. The principle that no person be subject to another person's choice allows each person to be his or her own master, that is, to have no *other* master.

Applied to the level of legislation, each person's rights generate a basic constraint on the ways in which the state may act. Their application is unconditional because rights are not tools for securing a result that can be described independently of them. If rights are conceived as instruments, it always makes sense, at least in principle, to ask, "Is this a situation in which constraining the conduct of others in this way advances the interests it is supposed to?" even if the answer will typically be positive. The possibility of asking that sort of question makes the application of rights, or rules protecting them, conditional, because it depends upon whether the rule in question actually brings about the result desired. This sort of conditional analysis is potentially available with respect to exercises of the police power, so that it makes sense to ask whether a traffic rule should be enforced in unusual circumstances that the legislature overlooked in drafting the provision. If the Highway Safety Act contains no provisions regarding private citizens responding to emergencies, a court might well exempt someone from a penalty in those circumstances, on the ground that the case falls outside the rule's purpose or range of application. The situation is different with rights that have their root in the innate right of humanity: freedom of expression and the presumption of innocence, as well as the more general right not to be subjected to the private purposes of another. The systematic realization of those rights provides the only basis for the state to make, enforce, or apply law at all; any use of force contrary to them subjects one person to the private purposes of another.

This Kantian conception of constitutional rights as expressions of the innate right of humanity, rather than tools for protecting important interests, conceives of those rights as *unconditional* because their grounds are not based on any claims about the conditions that normally hold. There is thus no space for asking whether the conditions fail to apply because so much is at stake for others. The state could not give itself a law that the people could not give themselves; the people can only give themselves laws that are within their rightful power. Fundamental human rights are constitutional, then, because they are the conditions of the state *constituting* itself as an omnilateral will.

Although the particulars of Rawls's example of strict criminal liability might seem artificial, exactly this sort of tradeoff between security and individual rights against the state has been proposed as a response to terrorism. The Kantian focus on the innate right of humanity has found expression in several recent decisions by some of the world's leading constitutional courts concerning the use of extraordinary means in fighting terrorism. Kant does not consider the possibility of judicial review of legislation, and my use of these examples neither presupposes nor purports to develop a Kantian argument for judicial review.[61] I offer them only as illustrations of how the limits on the power of a people to give itself laws is to be understood, without considering here what body is competent to make such determinations.

A consequentialist interpretation of the idea of a social contract would have to find some common currency in which to balance each citizen's interest in being protected against terrorist attack with each citizen's interest in avoiding torture. It is often argued that torture should usually be prohibited, but would be appropriate where many lives are at stake because the state has a responsibility to prevent terrible things from happening, and that this responsibility overrides any limits on the acceptable means that may be used. If the government's choice is understood as a choice between torturing one person and permitting thousands or millions to die, it is hard to resist the suggestion that it must choose the former. Given the stakes, some have suggested that the use of torture is inevitable, and urged legal regulation and oversight of it.[62]

From a Kantian perspective, the problem with this form of reasoning begins with the question it tries to answer. The question of whether torture could be authorized by law concerns the state's lawmaking authority, not the rational or probable or even morally best course of action by a legally unconstrained actor in a specific situation, or even the appropriate

---

61. Kant says that the three powers in a state "jointly comprise" the commander that has power over its subjects (6:315). We saw in Chapter 6 that each of the three powers is required, as is their separation. It follows from this that a court cannot legislate. It does not follow that a court must be empowered to review legislation to ensure its conformity with law, but such a possibility is not precluded either.

62. Alan M. Dershowitz, *Shouting Fire: Civil Liberties in a Turbulent Age* (Boston: Little, Brown, 2002), 470–477.

response, after the fact, of a court to someone who has saved lives through the use of torture. Considering the use of torture in confronting terrorism, President Aharon Barak, of the Supreme Court of Israel, remarked, "We are aware that this judgment of ours does not make confronting that reality any easier. That is the fate of democracy, in whose eyes not all means are permitted, and to whom not all the methods used by her enemies are open. At times democracy fights with one hand tied behind her back."[63] In focusing on the question of whether such uses of force can be authorized by law, the only issue is whether the people over whom it is exercised could confer such a power on officials. People lack the authority to subject themselves to a power entitled to use a person for public purposes just because a lot else is at stake. And if they cannot rightfully subject themselves to such laws, they also cannot rightfully subject any dangerous noncitizens whom they have in their custody to them. Again, it might be thought that torture would only be used against someone who had been independently identified as a terrorist, so that anyone who would not reveal the location of a ticking bomb about to kill thousands is already a wrongdoer who has forfeited whatever rights he would otherwise have. Such a suggestion fails to constrain a contractarian/consequentialist argument for the legalization of torture because any wrongdoing on that person's part is incidental to its core analysis. Torture to extract information from a suspect violates the right to be beyond reproach. Like punishment for absolute liability crimes, a person's vulnerability to coercion would depend exclusively on the expected consequences of coercion, and not on what that person had done. Moreover, the dramatic example of a ticking bomb makes the use of torture seem pressing but at the same time drastically narrows the opportunities for investigating those consequences. Any legal license to torture would have to apply to someone suspected of involvement, even if, as it turned out, the person being tortured had not done anything wrong. Again, if the justification of torture turns on its expected results, it would extend to cases in which the terrorist is sufficiently strong-willed to be able to resist torture to himself but not to members of his family. The same point applies even if some

---

63. HCJ 5100/94 *The Public Committee against Torture in Israel v. The State of Israel*, 53(4) PD 817, 845.

way can be found to restrict the argument's application to those who have done wrong.[64] If the tradeoff between security and individual rights is quantitative, it does not matter whose rights are being sacrificed. Whether citizens concerned to protect themselves would in fact agree to such a thing would have to depend on how likely the various outcomes were (or on how likely they believed them to be), and so, it might be thought, torture could only be legitimate provided that the numbers were high enough.

The German Constitutional Court addressed a related question of whether the constitution could authorize the minister of the interior to order a hijacked airliner to be shot down if it was in danger of being used as a missile against a populated area.[65] The court held that such a law conflicted with the right of the passengers on the plane to human dignity, that legal system's correlate of the innate right of humanity.[66] The passengers cannot be used to save the people in the building. The court explicitly considered the possibility that they would consent to being killed in such circumstances, particularly if, since the plane is being used as a missile, their death is all but certain. They rejected that form of reasoning, even on the assumption that all of its premises are true. These premises may or may not be factually satisfied, and the minister of the interior may or may

---

64. In no case is the use of official force predicated on the idea that the wrongdoer has forfeited rights against force. The idea that wrongdoers forfeit their rights, like the related idea that rights have "thresholds," ultimately turns on the idea that rights are tools for protecting interests, whether in well-being or choice. Any attempt to connect such ideas to the model of a social contract will allow rights to be outweighed when enough other interests are at stake.

65. *Bundesverfassungsgericht* (BverfG), 1 BvR 357/05 vom 15.2.2006.

66. Strictly speaking, the right to dignity is not an enumerated right in the German Basic Law, but the organizing principle under which all enumerated rights—ranging from life and security of the person through freedom of expression, movement, association, and employment and the right to a fair trial to equality before the law—are organized. It appears as Art. I.1: "Human dignity shall be inviolable. To respect and protect it shall be the duty of all state authority." Art. I.3 explains that the enumerated rights follow: "The following basic rights shall bind the legislature, the executive, and the judiciary as directly applicable law." Other, enumerated rights are subject to proportionality analysis, through which they can be restricted in light of each other so as to give effect to a consistent system of rights. The right to dignity is the basis of the state's power to legislate and so is not subject to any limitation, even in light of the enumerated rights falling under it, because—to put it in explicitly Kantian terms—citizens could not give themselves a law that turned them into mere objects.

not be in a good position to assure himself that they are. The court's grounds for rejecting the reasoning do not depend on disputing the factual premises, however, but on the claim that the state is not entitled to make such a decision. The court is equally adamant in its rejection of the suggestion that the passengers would have agreed to it if they had been asked; the fact that it would be sensible for them to consent does not mean that they have consented. Their right to human dignity means that they cannot be conscripted into the project of the Ministry of the Interior any more than they can be conscripted into the project of the hijacker. The court concedes that matters might be different if the legal order itself were in danger. In cases of a defensive war, citizens can be conscripted into public purposes, the most familiar example of which is military service. Although death of civilians on a large scale is one of the familiar horrors of modern war, the mere possibility of such a death is not equivalent to the danger to rightful condition posed by war. As a result, even if war could justify conscription, including conscription to things with a significant risk of death, citizens could not consent to empower the state to use its citizens in this way to prevent a crime from happening.

The German Constitutional Court's reasoning reflects the underlying Kantian thought that the state's obligation to uphold a rightful condition and protect its citizens is unconditional, not simply because of some fondness for rules, but rather because the use of force is merely unilateral unless its authorization could proceed from an omnilateral will. People could only give themselves laws consistent with their innate right of humanity. As a result, the numbers cannot matter. If the state cannot order a person to stand in the path of a bullet that endangers an innocent person, it cannot order that person to stand in the path of a bullet that endangers many people. And if the state cannot order a person to do so, then it cannot exempt itself from such a prohibition in the case of a person who is likely to die anyway. The people give themselves laws not for their advantage, but for their independence, which they cannot trade against anything.

On the Kantian view, the fundamental test of any law is whether all could consent to it given their inner duty of rightful honor, or, what comes to the same thing, their obligation to take responsibility for their own lives. You couldn't agree to a law that suspended that obligation, even if you expected material gain, *because the state is never a tool for pursuing private purposes.*

VI. Immanent Purposes, Discretionary Implementation

Kant's understanding of the basic range of public powers is austere in one sense, yet permissive in another. The only powers a state may exercise are ones that fall under various aspects of its duty to create, maintain, and improve a rightful condition, and it may only do so in ways consistent with each citizen's innate right of humanity. Yet the range of powers that can actually be exercised under that duty seems capacious and open-ended. The constraint that all powers be derived from the duty to create a rightful condition—parallel to the way that the power of a parent to "manage and develop" the child is derived from the duty to raise the child into a responsible being—is a real constraint, but it does not preclude most of the familiar activities of modern states. Even substantial changes can be understood as falling under the duty: fundamental land reforms that abolish forms of slavery or serfdom are the creation of a rightful condition. Even things that seem less directly related seem easy to accommodate to the Kantian account. We shall see in Chapter 9 that preventing private dependence underwrites a variety of public activities, and also that nothing in Kant's account precludes overinclusive implementation. Kant makes space for even more state activity when he includes the state's right to "administer the state's economy and finances,"[67] and still more when he suggests in *Theory and Practice* that when the supreme power "gives laws that are directed chiefly to happiness (the prosperity of the citizens, increased population and the like), this is not done as the end for which a civil Constitution is established but merely as a means for *securing a rightful condition,* especially against a people's external enemies."[68] The only thing that is ruled out is organizing the state around private purposes. The only test imposed by the idea of the original contract is that it be possible to give public grounds of justification for such activities, that is, to relate them to the maintenance of a rightful condition.

67. 6:325.
68. Kant, *Theory and Practice*, 8:298.

The flexibility of the Kantian account on such issues reveals the underlying difference between it and both libertarian and utilitarian/egalitarian accounts. From Kant's perspective, the apparently intractable disagreement between the two extremes has the classic structure of an antinomy: the disagreements reflect a premise that both sides presuppose. The premise in question is that the purpose of political and legal institutions is to approximate a moral result that is perfectly determinate, even if imperfectly known, independently of them. A version of the same antinomy lurks in disputes between libertarian and utilitarian/egalitarian theories of the morality of property. The Lockean libertarian supposes property rights to be morally complete and fully determinate without reference to political institutions, and regards the state as a remedy to disagreements that, at least in principle, have complete answers. The utilitarian or egalitarian rejects the idea that anyone could have a morally basic right to property, and thinks that rules governing the dominion of particular persons over particular objects can only be designed so as to bring about a morally desirable result that can be described without any reference to anything like rules. As we saw in our discussion of private right, Kant conceives of private rights fundamentally differently. Their *structure* can be articulated without reference to legal institutions, but they do not apply to particulars outside of a rightful condition. Outside of legal institutions, property cannot be acquired conclusively, property rights cannot be enforced coercively, and disputes about them have no resolution consistent with the equal freedom of the parties. Again, although it can be shown as a general principle of private right that a person who is not party to a contract is not entitled to sue on it, or that a person who was deprived of the use of something to which he or she has no proprietary or possessory right has no claim against the person who damages the thing, in most cases concepts alone will not decide a particular case. Both the Lockean libertarian and a utilitarian/egalitarian see legal rules as trying to match something that is completely determinate without any reference to legal institutions. The Kantian sees legal rules as making determinate something that is morally binding but by itself partially indeterminate.

In the case of public right, the parallel antinomy concerns the use of public power. Although the libertarian insists that public power can only be used in the minimal ways that citizens have actively authorized, and the utilitarian or egalitarian thinks that it can be used to bring about good results (perhaps subject to certain constraints), they share a premise according to which a public authority's moral role is to bring about specific results that can be specified without any reference to a public authority. For the Lockean libertarian, the result is the protection of private rights to person and property, which are supposed to be fully determinate without reference to institutions charged with enforcing them. For the utilitarian or egalitarian, the morally relevant results are characterized differently and more broadly, whether in terms of welfare, prosperity, or a certain pattern of distribution. The structure of the account, however, is exactly the same: institutions are justified only insofar as they bring about results that can be specified without any reference to them.

The Kantian approach rejects the common premise, and understands public right as requiring institutions in order to give effect to the structural features of a rightful condition. The public purposes are contained in the idea of a rightful condition, but so, too, is the requirement that properly constituted public authorities determine how to implement them. In so doing, public officials have no alternative but to exercise judgment about the significance to attach to competing considerations, subject only to the constraint that they make only laws that the people could impose upon themselves.

VII. A Note on Public Right and the Right of Nations

The argument of Public Right shows why a rightful condition is required, and why even a defective one must be understood as falling under the idea of the original contract. In the conclusion to the *Doctrine of Right*, Kant announces practical reason's "irresistible *veto: there is to be no war*," either between human beings or between states.[69] The contrast between right and violence is presented as equivalent to the contrast between peace and war. From this it might be thought to follow that Kant should treat the cases of human beings and of states as parallel, and argue in favor of some form of world government, or at least a state of states. In this section, I want to briefly indicate Kant's basis for distinguishing the solution

---

69. 6:354.

to the conflict between individual human beings from the solution to conflict between states. My aim is not to offer a full development of Kant's account of international right, but only to show how the issue of the right of nations must be framed in light of the distinctively public nature of a rightful condition.

Kant's opening discussion of relations between states parallels his discussion of those between individuals in a state of nature. States are in a nonrightful condition, which is a condition of war, in which each can only do what seems good and right to it. To remain in such a condition is "wrong in the highest degree," and so nations must exit from the state of nature and organize themselves in accordance with the idea of the original contract. Both the structure of the argument and the obvious potential similarities have led many readers to suppose that Kant ought to favor a sort of transnational superstate, and even to authorize the use of force to create such a state.[70] That Kant rejects these solutions is apparent, both from his brief remarks in the *Doctrine of Right* and from his longer ones in *Perpetual Peace*. His grounds for rejecting them, however, are less clear. In the *Doctrine of Right* he says that the world state would extend "too far over vast regions," so that governing it "would become impossible."[71] In *Perpetual Peace* he appears to concede that a world government is rationally required before concluding that it would become a "soulless despotism."[72]

Many commentators have taken Kant's hesitation about the worldwide state of states to be based only on empirical considerations.[73] The contingency of such factors leads naturally to the thought that in the changed circumstances of the contemporary world, Kantian arguments are avail-

---

70. See, for example, Otfried Höffe, *Kant's Cosmopolitan Theory of Law and Peace*, trans. Alexandra Newton (Cambridge: Cambridge University Press, 2006), 193; Byrd and Hruschka, "From the State of Nature to the Juridical State of States." Pauline Kleingeld argues that a voluntary league of nations is an interim stage in the development of a world state with coercive powers in "Approaching Perpetual Peace: Kant's Defense of a League of States and His Ideal of a World Federation," *European Journal of Philosophy* 12 (2004): 304–325.

71. 6:350.

72. *Toward a Perpetual Peace*, 8:367.

73. See, for example, Jürgen Habermas, "Kant's Idea of Perpetual Peace, with the Benefit of 200 Years' Hindsight," in James Bohman and Matthias Lutz-Bachmann, eds., *Perpetual Peace: Essays on Kant's Cosmopolitan Ideal* (Cambridge: MIT Press, 1997).

able to argue for the irrelevance of the nation-state and, in particular, for the irrelevance of borders. Kant's rejection of a superstate is not empirical, however. Instead, it turns on the public nature of a rightful condition. Both a state of nature between persons and one between nations are contrary to right, and to remain in either is wrongful in the highest degree. The solutions are fundamentally different. Both Kant's rejection of a world state in favor of a "pacific league" or "permanent congress" of states that can be renounced by its members and his celebrated claim that republican states do not go to war with each other are reflections of his distinctive understanding of a state as a condition of public right.

Kant's discussion of conflict between states turns entirely on the right to engage in defensive war. Like individuals outside of a rightful condition, each state is only entitled, as a matter of right, to use defensive force against what it takes to be an aggressor. If that entitlement is to be part of a system of entitlements that could in principle be enjoyed by everyone together, it must, like other cases of defensive force, be subject to an objective standard; the issue of whether a particular use of defensive force is reasonable cannot be set unilaterally by either of the parties to a dispute. Neither has any claim of right to engage in acts of aggression against another. Each has only the right to defend itself, and, in determining whether to exercise this right, can only do what seems good and right to it. Since different things might seem good and right to different states, two states might each be entitled to act on the assumption that the other threatens it.[74] The problem is not that states will engage in aggression and claim self-defense, but that even if they act in good faith, their respective rights to self-defense may not be consistent.

In discussing conflict between states, Kant thus focuses on only one of the three defects he identified in the state of nature between persons. He offers an analogue neither of the assurance argument nor of the argument from unilateral choice. He does not suggest that one state may seize another's territory unless it has assurance that the other state will not seize its territory. Nor does he say that a state's acquisition of its own territory is somehow problematic because dependent upon a unilateral act. The absence of these modes of argument deprives Kant of the resources to ar-

74. 6:346.

gue for either an executive or a legislative international body. In *Perpetual Peace* he says that states in a pacific league submit themselves neither to public laws nor to coercion under them:[75] war arises between nations, but the problems to which public law and coercion are solutions do not apply. Instead, only the problem of determinacy arises, so only an analogue of a court is required.

The absence of arguments from coercion and assurance, and the corresponding absence of public law and coercive enforcement, reflect two differences between states and private persons. The first difference is that as Kant understands states, they do not have external objects of choice. The state does not acquire its territory; its territory is just the spatial manifestation of the state. That is why Kant joins other eighteenth-century writers in supposing that the state's territory is more like its body than like its property. The state is always necessarily in possession of its territory, just as a person is always in possession of his or her own body. Anyone who enters its territory without its authorization enters the state itself; should such a person overstay his welcome, he commits a wrong analogous to battery, rather than one analogous to theft. Although an act is required to establish a state, no act of acquisition *by the state* is required, and so the state does not acquire its territory. In juridical terms, it simply has it. As a result, there is no need for an omnilateral authorization of a unilateral acquisition. No "mine or yours" structure applies to it, so no assurance argument can arise. Each state's right against other states is purely defensive: to continue being the rightful condition it is, on its own territory. The same point generates Kant's claim in *Perpetual Peace* that no state can rightfully acquire another.[76]

The second difference is that a state is a public rightful condition. The public nature of the state limits the purposes for which it can act to those that are properly public, that is, sustaining its own character as a rightful condition. Because it is not entitled to set and pursue its own private purposes, but only public ones, it could never have grounds for going to war except to defend itself or to defend an ally whose defense was important

---

75. *Toward a Perpetual Peace,* 8:356.
76. Ibid., 8:344.

to its own self-defense, or to unite against a state that poses a general threat to the condition of peace among nations.[77]

The public nature of a rightful condition is most fully reflected in a republican system of government. Kant's famous claim in *Perpetual Peace* that republican states do not go to war against each other has been read as an empirical conjecture about how likely people who need to pay for wars are to vote in favor of them, and the ability of such states to engage in more productive forms of interaction.[78] It also has an *a priori* basis in concepts of public right, as a simple reflection of the fact that republican governments do not act for private purposes, and so have an internal limit on the ends they will pursue, and the means they will use in pursuit of them.[79]

If the only source of conflict in a state of nature between states is generated by the indeterminacy of the right to self-defense, then the solution is a partial analogue of a civil condition, but not a civil condition as such. Instead, the ideal is "a permanent Congress of states" which realizes the idea of "a public right of nations" through which nations establish a procedure "for deciding their disputes in a civil way, as if by a lawsuit, rather than in a barbaric way (the way of savages), namely by war."[80] Because each nation has neither private purposes nor external objects of choice, the analogue of a rightful condition among states has a court but neither

---

77. The distinctive moral status of states generates each of the three "definitive" articles for perpetual peace: it requires republican governments, in which the people act as a collective body rather than a mob; a federation of free states, which have "outgrown" the need to be under coercive law; and cosmopolitan right, which is limited to a right of hospitality (as opposed to colonialism) because it governs relations between an individual and a foreign state, rather than between the individual and the individual citizens of that state. See *Toward a Perpetual Peace*, 8:349–357. The same triad occurs in the *Doctrine of Right* at 6:311.

78. *Toward a Perpetual Peace*, 8:350. A prominent instance of this reading is Michael Doyle, "Kant, Liberal Legacies and Foreign Affairs," Parts I and II, *Philosophy & Public Affairs* 12 (1983): 205–235, 323–353.

79. 6:345. See also *The Conflict of the Faculties*, 7:86, in Immanuel Kant, *Religion and Rational Theology*, trans. Allen Wood and George Di Giovanni (Cambridge: Cambridge University Press, 1996), where Kant says that those who do not want justice do not want peace. See also George Cavallar, *Kant and the Theory and Practice of International Right* (Cardiff: University of Wales Press, 1999), chap. 4.

80. 6:351.

legislature nor executive. Such a court can resolve disputes about boundaries peacefully, but its resolution of disputes is only "as if before a court," because states can resolve their disputes peacefully by accepting the decision of a court as binding.

Kant writes that "this alliance must, however, involve no sovereign authority (as in a civil Constitution), but only an association (federation); it must be an alliance that can be renounced at any time and so must be renewed from time to time. This is a right *in subsidium* of another and original right, to avoid getting involved in a state of actual war among the other members."[81] Each has the right to defend itself, and to defend others, but no other state has an enforceable right that others put themselves in danger to defend it. The right to avoid getting involved in war is itself a reflection of the public nature of a rightful condition; the state can only enter into arrangements with other states that secure its status as a fully rightful condition, but no such arrangement could involve giving up the entitlement to do what seems good and right to it.

Perpetual peace is unattainable because the only rightful forum for establishing it is voluntary and can be dissolved. Its voluntary nature does not mean that it could not last a long time, even forever. It cannot, however, be perpetual, because it has no resources at its disposal to guarantee its own preservation. A rightful condition between persons may dissolve over the course of time, or even choose to dissolve itself,[82] but so long as it exists it must regard itself as existing in perpetuity, because as a matter of right, it has an entitlement to perpetuate itself, both by enforcing its own laws and by securing the conditions of a united will. No member of a rightful condition between persons is entitled to dissolve it. A permanent congress of states has no resources to perpetuate itself, and any member is entitled to withdraw from it.

VIII. Conclusion

Institutions can solve the three problems with the state of nature by incorporating a distinction between an official rule and the person filling it.

81. 6:345.
82. 6:333.

Officials can be required by their offices to act for purely public purposes of making, implementing, and applying law. If they act within these mandates, they act for the people as a collective body. In so doing, they also constitute the people as a collective body, and so provide the omnilateral standpoint that can solve the three problems. Those mandates also give officials moral powers that no private person could have. Both the powers and the constitutional restrictions on their exercise have their basis in the general requirement that officials could not have the power to make arrangements for the citizens that the citizens could not make for themselves. Instead, they must exercise their mandates consistent with each person's innate right of humanity and each person's status as a member of the united will.

A rightful condition between private persons is required to reconcile the purposiveness of a plurality of separate persons, consistent with each person's right to be his or her own master. A rightful condition between states has a task that is more limited but no less important: to reconcile the public nature of a plurality of states, consistent with each state's entitlement to be a condition of public right.

CHAPTER 8

Public Right II: Roads to Freedom

THE DEFECTS IN A STATE of nature that require a condition of public right arise exclusively at the level of private rights. It might be thought that they would therefore generate a state entitled only to enforce private rights, and unable to do most of the things that modern states do. Although some might celebrate such moral restrictions on state power, Kant takes a different approach. He argues that a rightful condition gives the state a series of further powers that no private person could have. The solution to each of the defects already incorporates distinctively public powers: the power to resolve disputes in accordance with law must be fully public if it is to be exercised at all. The same is true of the power to enforce binding resolutions of disputes, and the more general ability to make laws in accordance with an omnilateral will.

In addition to these powers, Kant supposes that the state has both an obligation and an entitlement to create certain kinds of distinctively public spaces, as well as a duty to support citizens incapable of supporting themselves, a duty to guarantee formal equality of opportunity, the right to punish, and the power to tax its citizens in support of all of these activities.

My focus in this chapter is on the class of purely public powers traditionally grouped under the state's police power. I examine them through the familiar, indeed paradigmatic, example of the powers of a public authority, the building and regulation of public roads. Traffic rules are often put forward as a clear case in which freedom is not an issue at all, and the only questions concern convenience. My aim is to use the same example to the opposite effect. I will show that they are instances of the state's status as "supreme proprietor of the land," which is in turn based on the systematic requirements of individual freedom, which depend on distinctively public spaces.

Traffic laws get almost no attention in political philosophy. Other dimensions of the liberal legal order—basic constitutional provisions, criminal law and punishment, taxation and property—are familiar topics of study and dispute. Traffic rules are neglected because of an implicit consensus about how to think about them: they are matters of convenience and coordination. The agreement about them in turn rests on the assumption that the main task of political institutions is to take account of competing interests and "balance" them against each other, on the basis of their importance. There is plenty of debate about how to balance interests fairly, about how to integrate fundamental interests into the balance, and about who gets to do the balancing. Against this background, traffic rules look so easy as to merit almost no notice. No fundamental interests are at issue, only convenience and the weighing of short-term inconvenience against longer-term congestion. The same understanding underwrites libertarian proposals to privatize roads based on the view that the market will do a better job of striking the appropriate balances. It also animates a favorite example in discussions of the obligation to obey the law: if traffic rules are based on balancing long- and short-term convenience, there is no point to waiting for a red light if the balance in the particular case is so different from the one that justifies the general rule.

As a familiar and largely benign example of lawmaking, traffic laws sometimes serve as an illustration of the claim that the main business of political life is balancing interests against each other. Consider two prominent examples.

Charles Taylor introduces the example of a traffic light in the course of a defense of a communitarian politics focused on the importance of substantive goods. He writes:

> Thus we could say that my freedom is restricted if the local authority puts up a new traffic light at an intersection close to my home; so that where previously I could cross as I liked, consistently with avoiding collision with other cars, now I have to wait until the light turns green. In a philosophical argument we might call this a restriction of freedom, but not in a serious political debate. The reason is that it is too trivial, the activity and purposes inhibited here are not really significant. It is not just a matter of our having made a trade-off, and considered that a small loss of liberty was worth fewer traffic accidents, or less danger for children; we are reluctant to speak here of a loss of liberty at all; what we feel we are trading off is convenience against safety.[1]

Taylor proceeds to contrast traffic laws with restrictions on religious freedom. Traffic lights restrict more actions per person per day than would prohibitions on public exercises of religion. Yet government restrictions on the exercise of religion are objectionable from the standpoint of freedom and traffic restrictions are not. From this he concludes that liberty only matters when the interests at stake are important.

Introducing his conception of the place of rights in liberalism, Ronald Dworkin uses the case of traffic rules to argue that there can be no right to liberty. He gives the example of driving the wrong way down a one-way street. His initial formulation of the point, in an essay in the *New York Review of Books*, makes the contrast clear:

> So, though the New York City government needs a justification for forbidding motorists to drive up Lexington Avenue, it is sufficient justification if the proper officials believe, on sound evidence, that the gain to the many will outweigh the inconvenience to the few. When individual citizens are said to have rights against the government, however, like the right of free speech, that must mean that this sort of justification is not enough. Otherwise the claim would not argue that

---

1. Taylor, "What's Wrong with Negative Liberty?," in *Philosophy and the Human Sciences Philosophical Papers,* vol. II (Cambridge: Cambridge University Press, 1985), 218.

individuals have special protection against the law when their rights are in play, and that is just the point of the claim.²

When the same example appears several years later in *Taking Rights Seriously*, Dworkin drives the point home, with a conclusion stronger than Taylor's:

> If we have a right to basic liberties it is not because they are cases in which the commodity of liberty is somehow especially at stake, but because an assault on basic liberties injures us or demeans us in some way that goes beyond its impact on liberty, then what we have a right to is not liberty at all, but to the values or interest or standing that this particular constraint defeats.³

As Will Kymlicka summarizes the upshot of their combined arguments, "Traffic lights and political oppression both restrict free acts. But any attempt to weigh the two on a single scale of neutral freedom, based on some individuation and measurement of free acts, is implausible."⁴

The examples pit freedom-based visions of the ordinary aspects of political life against a seemingly more realistic convenience- and compromise-based vision. The former view is rejected as hopeless, because it ignores the differences between trivial and significant interferences with freedom. An intuitive example is thus used to make a conceptual point: the concept of freedom can at most play a secondary role in

---

2. Dworkin, "Taking Rights Seriously," *New York Review of Books*, December 17, 1970, www.nybooks.com/articles/10713 (accessed February 18, 2009).

3. Dworkin, *Taking Rights Seriously* (Cambridge, Mass.: Harvard University Press, 1977), 271. Dworkin offers a version of the same argument in *A Matter of Principle* (Cambridge, Mass.: Harvard University Press, 1986), 189. Dworkin's claims may not be entirely consistent with his claims elsewhere in either book. As H. L. A. Hart points out, "Yet 'Hercules' (Dworkin's model of a Judge) is said not only to believe that the Constitution guarantees an abstract right to liberty but to hold that a right to privacy is a consequence of it." See Hart, "Between Utility and Rights," *Columbia Law Review* 79 (1979): 836.

4. Kymlicka, *Contemporary Political Philosophy* (Oxford: Oxford University Press, 1991), 141.

normative theory, because it requires some prior specification of important interests.[5]

Taylor and Dworkin do not agree about very much, but they take the same message away from the same example. In rejecting the idea of negative liberty (Taylor) or a right to liberty (Dworkin), they intimate, without ever quite arguing, that forcing people to do things, *as such,* raises no questions of justice, and can be done on the basis of a calculus of competing interests. So at least when it comes to questions of convenience both reject the Kantian idea that individuals are *sui juris* in favor of the idea that government is everyone's master. Each has his own list of exemptions from this sort of weighing of interests, things that it would be *wrong* to force people to do or refrain from doing, such as religious observance or political expression. Each also has his own account of what makes interests important, Taylor's focused on the good and Dworkin's on the systematic requirements of the state showing equal concern and respect to its citizens.[6] For both of them, the state must not burden especially important interests; force as such does not enter their analyses.

Traffic examples are well suited to motivating this interest-based conception of political life, because they seem consistent with a wide variety of positions about how benefits and burdens should be distributed, a comparably wide variety of positions about which interests are so significant as to be exempted from ordinary balancing, and various views about which institutions are best suited to answer such questions. The only remaining questions concern whether a rule or system of rules is most convenient or beneficial.[7] The example of traffic rules has a strategic and

---

5. Compare Hart: "A weighing of advantage and disadvantage must always be required to determine whether the general distribution of any specific liberty is in a man's interest, since the exercise of that liberty by others may outweigh the advantages to him of his own exercise of it." H. L. A. Hart, "Rawls on Liberty and Its Priority," *University of Chicago Law Review* 40 (1973): 550–551.

6. Equal concern and respect is the common theme running through Dworkin's argument in *Taking Rights Seriously* about insulating people from objectionable "external" preferences that others might have about their worth, and his view in *Sovereign Virtue* that focuses on the place of liberties in sustaining a system of equality of resources.

7. Hart attributes this argument to Sidgwick, and then, in a footnote, suggests that it is conceptually interchangeable with the "conflict between pedestrians' freedom of movement and the rights of automobiles" (Hart, "Rawls on Liberty and Its Priority," 538n and 546n).

rhetorical advantage over other examples, however, because it does not require supposing that all rule-governed aspects of social life are merely matters of convenience.

Although neither Taylor nor Dworkin uses this vocabulary, the provision and regulation of roads is an instance of what used to be called the "police power" enjoyed by the state.[8] For centuries the police power was widely recognized as one of the fundamental features of the legal order. It appears to have originated in the power that the head of a household had over its members.[9] Blackstone discusses it, as do Rousseau[10] and Kant.

Exactly what did and did not fall within the police power was subject to controversy, but its importance was not. One of the important tasks of modern political philosophy was to reconcile the important and ineliminable nature of the police power with the ideas of limited government. Like the despotic power of a traditional *paterfamilias,* the police power seems potentially to extend to everything.

My aim in this chapter is to use the example of traffic laws to cast doubt on the very idea of balancing benefits and burdens, and to defend the idea that state power is only justified to create a system of equal freedom. I will not defend the implausible claim that speed limits or the timing and placement of traffic lights can be deduced from some index of freedom and appropriate facts. As I shall explain, the expectation that any alternative to balancing must aspire to some such claim is itself symptomatic of everything that is wrong with the balancing picture. Nor shall I join Mi-

---

8. Dworkin does, however, discuss the *Lochner* case, which concerned the limits of the police power, and writes that "the vast bulk of the laws which diminish my liberty are justified on Utilitarian grounds" (*Taking Rights Seriously,* 269). Dworkin's later work invokes the idea of equality of resources as an alternative to utilitarianism, but it functions in a similar way: apart from constitutional restrictions, state action is justified insofar as it serves to approximate the results that would be reached in a frictionless system of equality of resources. See Dworkin, *Sovereign Virtue* (Cambridge, Mass.: Harvard University Press, 2000), 157, where he acknowledges his debt to the economic analysis of law, and writes of "the degree to which equality of resources secures its goal, which is to achieve a genuinely equal distribution measured by true opportunity costs." In an endnote to that passage, he suggests that the same instrumental analysis seems adequate to justify "traffic regulations, like one-way systems, that aim to protect convenience or efficiency rather than only safety or security" (483n24).

9. Markus D. Dubber, *The Police Power: Patriarchy and the Foundations of American Government* (New York: Columbia University Press, 2004), 3–80.

10. Ibid., 47–62.

chael Walzer in celebrating the claim that "the car is also the symbol of individual freedom."[11] Instead, I will argue that the state's entitlement to make traffic rules is rooted in its obligation to provide the conditions of equal freedom.

On the view I will defend, the fundamental rationale for the exercise of the police power is to create a regime of equal private freedom. In order to do so, the state must create and sustain the systematic preconditions both of the exercise of private freedom and of the conditions of its ability to provide them. It can compel citizens to do their part in creating and sustaining a rightful condition. The provision of these conditions is a distinctive case of *mandatory cooperation,* which is subject to distinctive normative constraints. In providing roads, the state is entitled make people contribute, both positively and negatively, to their provision, and to regulate them based on a variety of considerations. None of this, I will argue, requires any assumptions about the state having any more *general* power to make life convenient, or to force people to contribute to cooperative arrangements on fair terms. Nor does it depend on the idea that, *apart from the state,* people have a basic obligation to participate in beneficial practices, or even those practices from which they benefit. I will argue instead that the state's power reflects the fact that it is a public authority: its entitlement to obligate individual citizens reflects its obligation to act on behalf of the citizens as a collective body. The difficulties faced by the balancing picture are only compounded when it is joined to the common supposition that the state's entitlement to bind its citizens must be aggregated out of obligations of individual citizens,[12] by getting them to do things that they would have had fully formed and concrete obligation to do in the state's absence.

---

11. Walzer, *Spheres of Justice: A Defense of Pluralism and Equality* (New York: Basic Books, 1984), 115.

12. It is not surprising that both Taylor and Dworkin defend aggregative conceptions of political obligation. Dworkin emphasizes what he calls "associative obligations" which apply to each person, on analogy with obligations in other, smaller associations (*Law's Empire* [Cambridge, Mass.: Harvard University Press, 1986], 199). Taylor focuses on the need for each citizen to have a substantive connection with the state in order to motivate the "sacrifices" of political life, among which he includes military service and the payment of taxes ("Cross-Purposes: the Liberal Communitarian Debate," in Nancy Rosenblum, ed., *Liberalism and the Moral Life* [Cambridge, Mass.: Harvard University Press, 1991]), 159–182.

Kant himself discusses neither one-way streets nor traffic lights, but he offers an account of the irreducibly public nature of mandatory forms of social cooperation, which follow from the role of the state as "supreme proprietor" of the land.[13] Kant observes that the state, as supreme proprietor, is charged with the "division" of the land, rather than the "aggregation" of the state's territory from antecedent private holdings.

I will argue that rather than being the main business of the state, limited only through important interests, questions about the allocation of benefits and burdens arise only *within* public provision of the preconditions of freedom. If a government must provide something, it must provide that thing fairly, which will normally mean equally. Governments do not have a general power to force people into forms of cooperation either by making some bear burdens for the benefit of others or by making people bear burdens because those same people have received benefits. Both of these ideas—the utilitarian idea that someone can be compelled to contribute whenever others will benefit, and the "principle of fair play" according to which people can be compelled to contribute to practices from which they benefit—are inconsistent with the idea that people are free to determine what *their own* purposes will be. Neither the benefit to others nor the fact that you yourself receive a benefit is sufficient to compel you to pursue an end that you do not share. However, public provision does not require any such principle.

I will explain why the public provision of roads, and with them the traffic rules that regulate them, are a basic case of a public precondition for private freedom. Thus Taylor and Dworkin are right to suppose that traffic rules are important, and partially right in their supposition that benefits and burdens are relevant to determining what the traffic rules should be, as are considerations of fairness and convenience. They go wrong, however, in assuming that the relevance of benefits and burdens in such cases counts against a freedom-based account of political life.

Not every legitimate use of state power is an instance of the police power understood in these terms. Some traditional exercises of the police power—the provision of roads and public markets—are required to make private interactions fully rightful. Other traditional police powers are re-

---

13. 6:323.

quired to sustain a rightful condition against things that endanger it—national defense, public health (understood narrowly as the prevention of epidemics), and fire prevention. Other familiar forms of legislation are legitimate where directed at realizing the idea of the original contract so as to make public lawgiving more fully rightful.

I. Equal Freedom

Familiar objections to the idea of equal freedom target some idea according to which each person can do as he or she pleases. This idea of freedom, summed up with Hobbes's description that "every man has a right to everything, even to another's body,"[14] cannot be generalized, because it treats freedom as a specific sort of benefit. If you and I both have liberty with respect to my body, and our purposes differ, we cannot both enjoy our liberties at the same time. Which of us will enjoy it depends on various factual circumstances. Hobbes's version is extreme, but a milder version of the same point still exerts a powerful hold on the philosophical imagination. It is often said that any entitlement I have over *anything* limits your freedom with respect to it.

The Hobbesian account of freedom is the immediate target of Taylor's and Dworkin's use of the traffic examples. When conflicts arise, the underlying concept of freedom has no resources to resolve them; any resolution must be based on something *other* than freedom.[15] It has been concluded from this that such a conception of freedom cannot be generalized.

Recall Kant's characterization of the "one innate right."

> *Freedom* (independence from being constrained by another's choice), insofar as it can coexist with the freedom of every other in accordance

---

14. *Leviathan*, 80 (ch. XIV).

15. Robert Hale's *Freedom through Law* (New York: Columbia University Press, 1952), 4, opens with the example "Freedom to continue to drive while the light is red is restricted, but the restriction serves to enhance the general freedom of driving, which would otherwise be restricted by traffic snarls." As Lon Fuller points out in his review of Hale's book, the use of the term "freedom" plays no part in the analysis. Hale uses the vocabulary of freedom to talk about benefits and burdens. See "Some Reflections on Legal and Economic Freedoms—A Review of Robert L. Hale's 'Freedom through Law,'" *Columbia Law Review* 54 (1954): 70–82.

with a universal law, is the only original right belonging to every human being by virtue of his humanity.[16]

As we have seen, the claim that there is only one innate right generates the basic distinction between wronging a person and changing the context in which that person acts, as well as the broad structure of private right, and the requirement that public law be limited to the laws that people could impose on themselves.

I now want to argue that the same right to independence both generates and limits the state's ability to balance interests: government may only engage in "trading off safety for convenience," or take account of "the gain to the many outweighing the convenience to the few," in ways that are consistent with each person's right of humanity to independence from being constrained by another's choice. In particular, state power may not be used to subject one person to the choice of another, even if "the activity and purposes inhibited here are not really significant."

As we saw in Chapters 2 through 5, a system of restrictions on the means available for each person to use requires a specification of the relevant means. As a matter of your innate right to freedom, you have your own bodily powers, subject to your choice: you alone are entitled to determine what you will do with your body. You can also have acquired rights: things other than your body that belong to you but could, in different circumstances, have belonged to some other person. Your person and your acquired rights exhaust the means that are subject to your choice. In particular, absent affirmative arrangements you have made with particular persons, you have no right to have *other* people use their means in ways that are favorable to your preferred use of yours. Each person is entitled to use what he or she has, consistent with the entitlement of others to do the same. You get to decide what you will do with what is yours. I get to decide what I will do with what is mine.

We also saw that this set of restrictions on the means that a person may use restricts each person's freedom in light of each other, so that we are each entitled to use what we have as we see fit, and neither of us is entitled to determine how any other person will use what is his or hers. I cannot use what is yours without your permission, because that would limit your

16. 6:237.

freedom by drawing you into purposes that you have not chosen. I also do not get to use what is mine in a way that will deprive you of what you already have. At the same time, each of us is completely free to use what we have in ways that will change the world in which the other uses what he has. You can cut down your own trees, depriving me of shade that I value, but you cannot cut down trees on my land. Nor can I plant trees on yours. Each of us has an absolute right to exclude the other from our land, and neither of us can be compelled to use our land in ways that accommodate the particular uses the other chooses. We retain our respective independence precisely because neither of us is subject to the choice of the other, either directly or through one's having an entitlement to determine how the other's land will be used. The only restraints on our respective use of our own land prevent us from making the other's land unusable.

The Kantian account of the right to freedom focuses on the freedom that one private person has against another: no private person can be compelled to serve the private purposes of another. Nor can a private person be compelled to serve the private purposes of several (or many) other private persons. If you do not need to accommodate the wishes of one person, adding a dozen, or hundred or thousand or million, does not change your rights.

This focus on what people already have and the concomitant irrelevance of the wishes of others might seem to make the Kantian account of freedom just as vulnerable to the traffic example as the Hobbesian one. Suppose that you are out walking (or driving, or boating) someplace that you have a right to be—not on some other person's private property, for example. I interfere with your freedom if I take it upon myself to force you to paddle on a particular side of the lake, walk in a particular part of the field, etc. On the Kantian account, the interference is no less objectionable if my demands turn out to save you time overall. So, too, it might seem, in the case of traffic rules: I cannot require you to modify your route, even when you will benefit in the long run. You get to decide both what your priorities are and how to advance them; you can't be compelled to follow my advice, even if it is correct. Nor can you be compelled to accommodate the convenience of others, because you cannot be forced to provide them with a context that suits their particular purposes. Others cannot circumvent these requirements by providing you with a benefit that you did not request and demanding that you help to produce it. The Kantian account thus precludes itself from each of the familiar accounts of traffic rules: none of your long-term convenience, the convenience of others, or collateral benefits you receive entitle other private persons to compel you to enter into cooperative activities with them.

The failure of any Kantian principle of private right to justify traffic rules is not the end of the road. Mandatory cooperation requires a distinctive principle of public right. The key to the Kantian analysis is that the state, acting on behalf of the citizens as a collective body, has legitimate powers that neither individual citizens nor any group of them have apart from it. As we saw in the previous chapter, the only way the state could have these powers is if they can be regarded as exercised on behalf of the citizens, and that requirement in turn is understood in terms of the possibility of the citizens giving such laws to themselves.

The Kantian approach shows how enforceable principles of social cooperation are *sui generis,* and distinct from whatever further principles govern the obligations of private persons to each other: everyone can be compelled to do his or her part, as identified by public rules. Principles governing mandatory cooperation only apply when mandatory cooperation is required by a system of equal freedom. Such a system both requires and enables each person to take responsibility for her own life, deciding which ends to pursue in light of the means she has, consistent with the entitlement of others to do the same. The systematic protection of individual private freedom is only possible under public law, and public law must guarantee its various conditions. One of these, I shall now show, is a system of roads.

II. Taking Roads Seriously

Suppose, then, we have a system of equal private freedom, and nothing more. Each person has a right to his or her own person and property, and no person is under an obligation to use his or her property to accommodate the particular wishes or needs of others. In such a system, we may suppose, all external resources—everything that could be subject to some person's exclusive choice—is privately owned, by individuals or groups of persons. Land is a conspicuous, and important, example of property.[17]

Consider a system in which all land is privately held. Land can be subject to a person's choice, and no other private person has any basis in the system of private freedom to complain of another's acquiring a piece of unowned land. For analytic purposes, it does not matter who holds these parcels of land, or what their size is. They could be equal or unequal in size; they could be held by private individuals or by worker cooperatives, or by separately incorporated government corporations,[18] or some combination of these. The structural problem has the same form, regardless of size and the nature of the natural or artificial persons owning them. So as to exclude any extraneous considerations about benefits and burdens, you can suppose that the plots of land are equal in size and quality, and so equally well suited to whatever purposes their respective owners might have.

The problem arises because each owner is entitled to determine what happens on his or her piece of land, and no other private person, natural or artificial, has any say in it, except with the owner's approval. Suppose that you and I are the two owners: each of us gets to decide what happens on our own land, but not what happens on the other's. Each of us can complain if water, unusual insects, a bad smell, or excessive noise from the other's property reaches our own in a way that interferes with our ability to use it. Neither of us can complain about what takes place entirely on the other's land, however. If you build a tower that blocks my sunlight, I have no grounds to complain, because I have no right that you occupy your land in a way that lets me have a path for sunlight across it. If you use pesticides, I can complain if they spill onto my land, but not if the bees from land on the other side of yours no longer reach mine. I have no claim to a path across your land.

---

17. Kant treats it as the basic case because control over property is control over a specific location, and any right to use any particular object on that location is thus subject to control over the location. Nothing in what follows depends on that feature of his argument.

18. Tony Honoré's celebrated essay "Ownership" begins with what he characterizes as a standard list of the incidents of property. As his wry but overlooked footnotes point out, the incidents can all be found in the law of the Soviet Union, in which property was owned by separately incorporated state enterprises. See A. M. Honoré, "Ownership," in A. G. Guest, ed., *Oxford Essays in Jurisprudence* (Oxford University Press, 1961), 107–147.

Your general right to decide what happens on your land includes the right to determine who enters your land. From the perspective of our respective rights in the situation, my entry onto your land is just a particular instance of something happening on your land, that is, one of the things about which you get to decide, but I do not. As between any two private persons, the right to exclude just is the right to private property. You can only go on my land with my permission; I can only go on yours with yours.

Property in land has the further feature of being immovable. The point is not that earth-moving equipment cannot change the topography of a particular piece of land, but rather that the subject matter of the property right in a piece of land is not its accidental topographic features, but its location. Any two pieces of land are numerically distinct, even if they turn out to be qualitatively and quantitatively indistinguishable, equal in size, drainage, annual rainfall, soil type, vegetation, and so on.

This uniqueness of land has an important systematic implication: to get from one location to another, you need to traverse all of the locations in between. Unless two pieces of privately owned land are adjoining, to get from one to another, you must cross some other piece of land, owned by another person, who, as a matter of private right, is entitled to exclude you from it.

The problem presents itself in an extreme form for any landowner who is surrounded by others: to get off your land, or get back to it after you've left, you need the permission of your neighbors to cross their land. The situation is actually worse than that, because even if your immediate neighbor lets you pass, it may be that to get where you are going, you need to cross the land of the next neighbor, the one after that, and so on. Having what the law calls an "easement of necessity" across the land of your immediate neighbor is no help unless you can keep going once you get to the end of your neighbor's plot. This is particularly apparent if you have left your land, and now cannot get back to it because you cannot get to your immediate neighbor's land.

The uniqueness of land thus has the surprising implication that as a matter of private right, your neighbors are entitled to trap you on your land, or, once you are off it, keep you off. The problem is not that your neighbor gets to stop you from doing something that you would like to do, or narrows your range of options. Rights to private property always stop other people from using things to which they have no right, because they allow the owner to set the terms on which the property can be used by others. My freedom is not violated because you will not let me drive your car or graze my cattle on your land, no matter how badly I might want or even need to do either. I have no right against you that my options be broad.

Instead, the problem with being landlocked arises because your neighbor's control over the region of the Earth's surface separating you from your destination can prevent you from entering into voluntary interactions with others. Suppose that you and I want to do something together—spend the afternoon discussing philosophy, trade horses, or whatever else. In a system of pure private property, each of us is landlocked by our immediate neighbors, and so by the series of neighbors, however long it might be, separating us from each other. Our ability to enter into a private transaction of whatever sort is subject to the choice of those who happen to occupy the space that separates us. Their property right gives them a power to block our consensual interaction. This limitation on our freedom is not made up for by the fact that each of us may have a similar power in relation to some other person or persons.

The difficulty here is not that you and I are unable to interact in ways that we might wish to. That is a problem to which no *general* solution is possible; the fact that we live too far apart may be no less of an impediment, but it raises no special issues about our right to be independent of the choice of others. We are entitled to use our means as we see fit, not to have whatever means we might require to get what we wish for.

Our problem is different. It is not just that we are unable to get together when we want to; *somebody else* gets to decide whether we are allowed to. When parents tell their children whom they may associate with, the children can at least take comfort in the fact that they will outgrow their tutelage (and if it provides no comfort, the parental authority remains rightful because it is exercised over children). Things are different if a stranger is entitled to tell us whether we can interact. No such comfort is possible. We are subject to his choice—he is entitled to restrict the interaction we may engage in, simply because of where he happens to live.

The problem arises because land is immovable, and thus unique. The fact that you are unwilling to let somebody use your chattels for their preferred purpose is just an example of each person's getting to determine how his or her property will be used. As we saw, the basic structure of private right entitles each person to determine how she will use what belongs to her, and so restrict any other private person from having a claim to require her to use it in some particular way, or make it available for another's use.

Land is special, because as an embodied rational being, you have to do anything you do somewhere. Any two people who want to do something together need to get themselves to the same place.[19] To get from any point to any other point, you have to pass through every intervening point. If other persons control any of those points, then you need the permission of each of the intervening owners to join your friend.

Private ownership of land does not simply foreclose some particular purpose that you might happen to have, but also forecloses the entire formal class of purposes involving voluntary interactions with others. The problem is formal, because it does not depend on the particular purposes for which any two persons might wish to interact, but rather on the fact that they are subject to a third (or fourth or fifth) person from whom they must secure permission to interact.

The sense in which the problem is not a reflection of some specific purpose is revealed by its generality. Every person is subject to it, because every person needs the permission of his or her immediate neighbors to interact with anyone else. The uniqueness of land makes a system in which all land is privately held a system in which each person is subject to the choice of his neighbors. It is not that some particular person is unable to pursue a project he wishes to if, as it turns out, some other particular person refuses to accommodate it. Instead, every person is systematically subject to the choice of others. Voluntary cooperation between any two persons who are not immediate neighbors requires the permission of those who occupy the space between them. It also prevents the condition from being fully rightful because it is in conflict with each person's right to associate with others as those others see fit, which, as we saw in Chapter 2, is simply an aspect of "a human being's quality of being *his own*

---

19. Telecommunications won't help, because the point applies to your signal. The right to occupy your land includes the right to build on it, including building a tower that a signal (or helicopter) cannot pass through. See *Hunter v. Canary Wharf Ltd.*, [1997] 2 All ER 426 (HL).

master (sui juris.)"[20] As we saw, the right to be your own master is contrastive: no other person is your master. A neighbor who is entitled to decide who you can associate with would be your master.

The problem of being landlocked is structural, and does not depend on the sort of factual considerations that Hume and Rawls describe as "the circumstances of justice." It does not depend on material scarcity, because the normative difficulty arises even if your plot of land is large enough to see to your needs, or your imagination is so limited that you do not realize that it is not and so have no inclination to leave it. Nor does it depend on the limited benevolence of others, or on worries that your neighbor will be mean-spirited or a busybody. Perhaps your neighbors would be happy to let you through, either in the expectation of future benefits from you or out of the goodness of their neighborly hearts. Like the possibility that your land is so commodious, or you are so timid, that you would never want to leave your land, this possibility fails to engage the issue of freedom that is at issue. The problem is that your neighbor is *entitled* to do this, and so it is up to your neighbor to decide whether you enter into voluntary transactions with others with whom you wish to transact. Such dependence is not repaired by the fact that you can do the same thing to your other neighbors.

Nor does the problem depend on any hypotheses about how likely people are to work out a mutually advantageous solution, or concerns about the resources that would be wasted as people haggle over whether to permit others to cross their land. The problem would be the same, even if there were empirical grounds for supposing that enterprising people would buy land in promising locations and build roads, and that they would attach only financial conditions to access. The source of the problem is the *entitlement* to determine whether one person can enter into voluntary arrangements with another, not the terms on which such an entitlement would be exercised, or the price for which it would be waived.

The solution to this problem is obvious: roads, understood as a system of public rights of way, guaranteeing that there is a path from every piece of privately held land to every other. With a system of roads in place, everyone can enter into voluntary transactions with whomever they wish,

20. 6:238.

without being subject to the choice of any other person. The rights of way need to be public, rather than endlessly many private easements, precisely because access must be guaranteed to everyone in order to reconcile property in land—ownership of a location—with freedom. The system as a whole must make it possible to get from any piece of land to any other. A public right of way can cross private property, but it must be public in the sense of being open to all as a matter of right, rather than available only to some specific person or group of persons.

If roads are understood as public rights of way, required by the systematic features of private landownership, the familiar examples of traffic rules are cast in a different light. Taylor's and Dworkin's examples represent a road as though it were a natural free space, on which everyone is entitled to come and go as he or she pleases. The state is then depicted as an extrinsic agent that steps in and places limits on this natural freedom, for the sake of overall convenience. Taylor and Dworkin don't view this limitation of freedom as objectionable, but their representation of it raises the question of just what sort of arrangement we are being asked to imagine. Are roads like the high seas, uninhabitable zones that are available for all to traverse? Or are they somehow a residue of an original commons, the bit of land that has not been appropriated? Neither model has much to recommend it. The first, "high seas" reading requires the roads be uninhabitable; if this assumption is dropped, it turns into a version of the "commons" reading, which conceives of the road as simply unowned, in which case anybody who wants to could come along and claim it as his or her own property. Perhaps the "commons" reading can be modified to conceive of the road as a sort of residue left over from private appropriation, subject to some sort of Lockean proviso to guarantee the sort of access that roads provide. If so, then its residual status requires rules of use and access, provided by Taylor's "local authority" or Dworkin's "government." Although the details of those rules need to be fixed by a public authority, that there are such rules constitutes the system of roads. Neither model provides any way of thinking of the road as a free space which the government steps in to restrict.

It is not as though the road is already there, and then the rules are subsequently imposed. The road and the public rules regulating it come as a package. Both are constituent parts of a system that guarantees the accessibility of each piece of private property from each other one. Being told that you cannot drive the wrong way down Lexington Avenue or that you must stop for a red light does not *take* something away from you that you already had; taken together, the road and the rules governing it *give* you, together with everyone else, an entitlement to get from place to place, so that you can interact with whomever you wish to, on whatever terms you and those with whom you interact choose. It follows that the roads will be available to all, but no private person will have either the right to exclude others or the right to use the road for whatever purpose he or she pleases. Indeed, as we shall see, many offenses against both traffic rules and other police ordinances consist in one person's privatizing a part of a public space, claiming it for his or her particular purposes to the exclusion of other members of the public. *Public* terms of access to roads are just structural features of public guarantees that there will be no *private* terms of access to other persons except those set by those persons themselves.

As parts of a system of public provision, the rules of the road are neither rules of private law nor rules of criminal law. They are not rules of private law, because you can violate them without wronging anyone else in particular. You might convince the police officer who gives you a speeding ticket that you weren't actually endangering, let alone injuring, anyone. You get the ticket anyway for violating the rules of public provision. Again, a law requiring you to stop for a traffic light on a deserted road[21] seems pointless from the point of view of harm: it doesn't reduce the likelihood of collisions, and the claim that it helps form good driving habits sounds forced. The law is enforceable because it is one of the terms of public provision of roads. You can be compelled to do your part. What your part is depends on what the public authority has decided. Mandatory licensing and insurance requirements for operating a motor vehicle are also specific to public roads.[22]

Traffic laws are also not rules of criminal law. They typically have no *mens rea* requirement, and can be violated unintentionally or inadver-

---

21. M. B. E. Smith, "Is There a Prima Facie Obligation to Obey the Law?" *Yale Law Journal* 82 (1973): 950. See also William Edmundson, *Three Anarchical Fallacies* (Cambridge: Cambridge University Press, 1999).

22. The nature of traffic rules also makes road accidents a potentially misleading set of examples for thinking about tort law more generally.

tently. The right to be beyond reproach precludes traffic offenses of absolute liability, but to violate a traffic rule a user of the road need not realize that he or she is breaking the law. Moreover, the ground of their enforcement is different from that of the criminal law. Theorists of the criminal law sometimes use traffic rules as examples of what they call "regulatory crimes" or crimes *mala prohibita,* as opposed to "true crimes," *mala in se.*[23] Such a classification is fine as far as it goes, but potentially misleading insofar as it suggests that the laws in question *regulate* an ongoing activity that exists apart from the regulation. The road, as a physical stretch of tarmac with various markings on it, could exist apart from its legal status as a highway, as could all of the cars and drivers on it. The same physical object could have been somebody's driveway, subject to the owner's unique choice. Its status as a highway, however, is constituted by the rules that integrate it into a general system of roads providing access to everyone.[24] Modern legal systems take the basic case of property in land to include the heavens above and the earth below, down to the center of the Earth, where we are all neighbors.[25] So at least in principle the requisite rights of way could be flight paths over or deep tunnels under land.

The example of roads reveals a formal structure to the public task of

23. Like so much else in contemporary criminal law theory, this way of demarcating the police power from "true crimes" appears to have originated in Paul Johann Anselm Feuerbach's Bavarian criminal code of 1813. Philosophers often confuse Feuerbach with his son Ludwig, and the elder Feuerbach is now mostly remembered as the guardian of the wolf-boy, Kaspar Hauser, thanks to Werner Herzog's 1974 film. In his time, however, he was the leading figure in the development and theory of criminal law. Unlike Bentham's codification project at around the same time, Feuerbach's became the basis of modern German law and later codification efforts throughout the world. Feuerbach argued that violations of police ordinances attracted only "disobedience penalties" rather than punishments. See Dubber, *The Police Power,* 76–77. Dubber also notes that Feuerbach doubted that police powers could be systematized.

24. I suspect (although I will not develop or argue the point here) that the public nature of roads is also relevant to at least some of the less controversial forms of "paternalistic" legislation, such as seat-belt or helmet laws. Like the familiar examples of limits on freedom, the familiar examples of paternalism—the ones that many liberals swerve to avoid—take place on public roads. See Peter de Marneffe, "Avoiding Paternalism," *Philosophy & Public Affairs* 34 (2006): 68–94.

25. Strictly speaking, Kant limits property rights to what a person can control, so the owner does not acquire a space higher (or lower) than anyone could go. But whatever technology would enable others to cross your land at great heights or depths would also enable you to fly or tunnel, and so extend your right as far as they could go.

making the exercise of private rights systematically consistent. Although the same formal structure does not arise in every legitimate use of public power, it does govern the traditional public power to maintain and regulate public markets. A public market is a place in which private persons can meet to offer each other incentives, and decide whether to accept the incentives offered by others. Just as private ownership of land potentially restricts the ability of each person to enter into voluntary transactions with others, so, too, would private ownership of market spaces. As guarantor of private rights, the state claims land for public markets and regulates the activities that take place in them so as to guarantee the systematic conditions of private freedom. The requirement that the state do so is abstract, and requires the same kinds of specification that the provision of public roads does.

III. Public Provision

The structural argument for roads does not show how roads should be constructed, maintained, or paid for. It shows only that rightful private property in land has public preconditions. It does not fall on any particular landowner to make his or her land available to any particular neighbor, or to any private person seeking to get from one place to another. A system of private property with mandatory private permissions would produce the mirror image of the same difficulty: your entitlement to use your land as you see fit would depend upon the choice of those who prefer to use it as a path for getting from one place to another. Unless you happen to be in a particularly unfortunate location, this might make little difference to your actual use of your land. The difficulty is structural, however: the private choices of others would *entitle* them to determine how you could use your land. I do not require your permission to enter into a consensual transaction with a third party. Nor do you require the permission of everyone who might wish to cross your land before erecting a structure on it or planting a garden on it.

Familiar methods of road provision suggest that the structural argument is implicit in their rationale. For example, homestead acts typically required homesteaders to clear the road along their land; the seignorial system in rural Quebec did not require the building of roads, but did require that all subdivision of land be done perpendicular to the St. Lawrence River. Modern land-use law requires a developer subdividing land for building and sale to build a road connecting all of the building sites and to cede it to the municipality. In most jurisdictions, property owners pay municipal taxes for the upkeep of local roads, but other roads are paid for through more general tax revenues collected by higher levels of government. Gasoline taxes are popular, giving expression to some idea that people who use the roads should pay for their upkeep in rough proportion to their use of them. Government-owned lands do not need to be accessible. If a road is blocked or washed out, those who are unable to use it are entitled to trespass on adjacent private land under the doctrine of public necessity.[26] Getting from one place to another falls under public law rather than private, so an individual owner's right to exclude is limited by the systematic requirements of private landownership. Long before antidiscrimination law, innkeepers were required to serve all users of public roads, and were exempted from Sabbatarian laws.

The differences between these examples are much less interesting than their similarities.[27] All rest on the same pair of ideas: no piece of privately

---

26. The leading common law case is *Taylor v. Whitehead* (1781) 2 Dougl. 745 99 E.R. 475 (KB).

27. In rural parts of some countries, such as Norway, *allemannsretten* gives everyone the right to cross the uncultivated or frozen land of others and collect "berries, mushrooms, or flowers" for personal consumption, but not to go near buildings or cross cultivated land. As the prefix *allemanns* suggests, these are public rights of way. These ancient systems solve part of the problem. They allow people to move from one place to another but impose limits on what a traveler can *move* from one place to another. The right to collect berries, mushrooms, and flowers parallels the rights in other systems to collect such plants from public lands and the side of a highway. However, their modern forms, which are sometimes bruited as examples of different conceptions of property, are importantly different. In Norway, *allemannsretten* are explicitly incorporated into the Act of 28 June 1957 No. 16 Relating to Outdoor Recreation. The declared purpose of the act is "to protect the natural basis for outdoor recreation and to safeguard the public right of access to and passage through the countryside and the right to spend time there, etc., so that opportunities for outdoor recreation as a leisure activity that is healthy, environmentally sound, and gives a sense of well-being are maintained and promoted." The modern versions of such laws effectively convert uncultivated or frozen land more than 100 meters from a building into public parks, subject to the same sorts of restriction that public parks typically have. See "Act of 28 June 1957 No. 16 Relating to Outdoor Recreation," www.regjeringen.no/en/doc/Laws/Acts/Outdoor-Recreation-Act.html?id=172932 (accessed December 6, 2008).

held land can be landlocked, and the protection against this difficulty is the public provision of public rights of way. There are obvious differences between making each person clear and maintain the portion of the road in front of his or her land and the collection of taxes to cover the costs of building roads. The account I have developed so far provides no resources for deciding between them. That is not to say that there are not plenty of different arguments that might be brought to bear. Some arguments concern efficiency: which way of organizing the costs will consume the fewest resources? These are detailed factual questions, the answers to which depend in part on whether private landowners will typically hire specialist companies to do the job for them. Will the increased cost of corner plots, bordering on two roads, have negative effects on economic development? Others concern consistency: will consistent standards be maintained if road building and maintenance are subject to the shifting fortunes of particular landowners? Still others concern fairness: should people pay for road access in proportion to the amount they use roads, or in relation to their proximity, or equally? All of these considerations are potentially relevant to deciding the issue. Considerations of efficiency reflect the necessarily public nature of public purposes. Public officials are entitled to tax private activities to secure resources for public purposes, but they are not entitled to claim more private resources than they judge in good faith to be necessary for those purposes. To collect more would be to tax private persons for something *other* than a public purpose. Anything that is not public is private, so any such taxation would be contrary to right because in pursuit of a private purpose. Consistency and fairness matter, because the provision of roads is a case of mandatory social cooperation. The relevance of either does not depend on the state's having an open-ended mandate to establish efficient or fair allocation of benefits and burdens. The state has *neither*. It simply has an obligation to provide roads on terms consistent with the freedom of its citizens. So Taylor is partly right when he says that the decision to put in the traffic light is a matter of "trading off safety for convenience," and Dworkin is right to say that decisions about one-way streets bear a lower burden of justification than do restrictions on speech. Their mistake lies in supposing that the grounds of these decisions, and the state's entitlement to make them, have nothing to do with freedom. The state only has the power to consider convenience as part of its obligation to secure the conditions of equal freedom.

The concession that a number of factors are potentially relevant to deciding how roads are to be paid for will seem, from a certain perspective, to be an abdication of the responsibilities of normative theory, which, it might be thought, is supposed to dictate to political processes and institutions, rather than listen to them. Kant is certainly committed to the idea that "right must never be accommodated to politics, but politics must always be accommodated to right."[28] The only question is how this commitment is to be interpreted. For Kant, it means only that the fact that the demands of right are unpopular or inconvenient can in no way condition what right demands. It does not follow from this that right, even ideally, provides a template for every detail of social life, or mandates *a priori* a unique resolution of every conceivable dispute. Among the unfortunate but abiding legacies of Bentham's utilitarianism is the view that an account of the legitimate uses of state power is incomplete or hopelessly indeterminate if it does not answer the sort of question, or at least specify which facts would be sufficient to answer it, even if there is uncertainty about them. For Bentham, institutions are tools for approximating a moral result that could, in principle, be fully specified if there were no institutions. Their only role, then, is to gather information, or coordinate behavior, more effectively than individuals might be able to do if left to their own devices. From such a perspective, the optimal design of the provision of government services depends entirely on factual questions, and so has a determinate answer apart from any institutions. From Kant's perspective, however, the point of institutions is to act on behalf of the public, that is, the citizens considered as a collective body, providing things that must be provided publicly—a forum for dispute resolution, public codification of law, and public enforcement, as well as the conditions of the publicity of those institutions, including public roads. From this perspective, the only normatively interesting claim is that institutions must be created, and that the officials of those institutions must be empowered to exercise their judgment about how to carry out these mandatory public purposes. Officials act within their mandates if their decisions also reflect

---

28. Kant, "On a Supposed Right to Lie from Philanthropy," 8:429.

judgments about what people will find more pleasant or convenient, or what will make citizens find particular rules sensible or fair. The Kantian approach does not regard it as an unfortunate limitation that actual human beings will be given these jobs, because it does not suppose that their task is to match what an omniscient being, taking the point of view of the universe, would do in all of its particulars. Nor does it give them detailed criteria to apply. That there must be the requisite institutions can be established *a priori:* this is the respect in which politics must conform to right. It does not follow that there is a pre-institutional answer about what they should do in every conceivable case that comes before them. The Kantian approach provides a framework that tells officials how to think about questions of public provision, rather than what to think about them. It also provides a framework for citizens to engage in democratic deliberation and processes, the task of which is for the citizens to give themselves laws that are consistent with their lawmaking powers.

IV. Doing Your Part: The Structure of Mandatory Cooperation

Violation of a public space consists in failing to do your part, by failing to contribute, either positively to sustaining it, or negatively by taking up part of it for private purposes.

The basic terms of public provision are dictated by the fact that it is mandatory. We have seen that the Kantian answer to the question of when cooperation is mandatory focuses on the preconditions of sustaining a condition of equal private freedom, in which no person is subject to the choice of another. Roads are a central example of this, and everyone can be compelled to contribute to them. A further question asks: on what terms can a free person be compelled to contribute to those social projects to which he or she can be compelled to contribute? The Kantian answer to this second question demands reciprocity: in sustaining a condition of private freedom, we are all in it together.

The Kantian answer to the first question does not yet tell us what the relevant principle of contribution is. Kant's political philosophy has additional resources, however, that generate a principle of contribution. As we saw in Chapter 2, Kant identifies a basic "internal" duty of rightful honor, expressed by the saying "Do not make yourself a mere means for others but be at the same time an end for them." This obligation follows from the innate right of humanity that each of us has in his or her own person, and guarantees that you can have no more specific obligation that presupposes that you can be bound to act exclusively for the purposes of another. In the context of mandatory social cooperation, if you do your part but others do not do theirs, they have treated you as a mere means, because you have contributed to the achievement of their purposes. You set out to do your part; rather than doing theirs, they took advantage of your efforts.

No parallel principle applies to private cooperation: whether, and on what terms, you confer a benefit on another person is entirely up to you. If things turn out differently than you had expected, and you bear a disproportionate burden, you have no claim against your contracting partner. It was up to you to protect yourself. Your responsibility, and the consequent lack of a cause of action, reflect the right of every self-determining being to voluntarily enter into binding arrangements with others on whatever terms he or she sees fit. Kant remarks that to require us to limit our contractual arrangements in light of some extrinsic conception of fairness would be to treat us like children, because we are free persons, each of us entitled to set and pursue our own purposes.[29] The role of voluntariness is explicit in cases in which people negotiate terms, but it is no less important in cases in which a buyer simply accepts a seller's offer, and in cases in which someone accepts something he or she knows to be valuable without asking about the price. If you order the special in a restaurant without asking its price, you have to pay for it. As Kant puts it, in voluntary private transactions, equity is "a mute divinity that cannot be heard."

The priority of private ordering cannot apply in cases of mandatory cooperation. Negotiations toward mutual agreement can only take place against the background of the entitlement of either of the parties to decline to cooperate at all. You can be held to what you agreed to because you did not have to agree to it. If you had no choice—if someone makes you an offer you can't refuse—you cannot be held to its terms. Where cooperation is mandatory, agreement on terms is not even possible. As we have seen, Kant argues that there is only one type of mandatory cooperation: you are under an enforceable and unconditional obligation to enter

---

29. Kant, *Naturrecht Feyerabend*, trans. Lars Vinx (unpublished, 2003), 27:1360.

and remain in a rightful condition, and to provide for its conditions; as such, you cannot attach terms to doing what you can already be forced to do. The only respect in which everyone can be thought to have set the specific terms is by having their representatives participate in the making of public law. Important though this is, it is not a sort of second-best approximation of private bargaining toward agreed terms. You have no entitlement to refuse to enter a rightful condition if you do not think the terms favorable enough, and neither does your representative. The most the representative can do is exercise judgment about how to achieve and sustain a rightful condition. To do so may sometimes require a weighing of interests and compromises, but that is not enough to turn it into a large-scale version of a private contract, not even a crude approximation of one.

So mandatory cooperation cannot treat terms of interaction as reciprocal because they are voluntary. Instead, there is a more direct requirement of reciprocity: everyone must do his or her own part; the person who fails to do so violates reciprocity by taking advantage of the cooperative efforts of others, like the one who fails to keep up his end of a contract. From this perspective, the "free rider" wrongs his fellow citizens by taking advantage of their efforts. The free rider may claim—and it may even be true—that he would rather do without the rightful condition and go it alone. That claim is beside the point, because the obligation to enter a rightful condition is unconditional, that is, it does not depend upon any particular person's subjective assessment of the benefits it will yield. Others are entitled to treat the creating and sustaining of a rightful condition as one of the free rider's purposes, quite apart from what he may have to say about it. Thus they can rightly complain that they are being required to work for the purposes of another, or that they are being used by the free rider, and they can make this claim even if the free rider's failure to contribute costs them nothing.

The mandatory character of such cooperation generates a presumption in favor of an equal division of its burdens. Kant suggests that legislation that "goes against the law of equality in assigning the burdens of the state in matters of taxation, recruiting and so forth"[30] is defective. Citizens

---

30. 6:319.

are entitled to petition against such laws, because equal division is the basic case of mandatory cooperation. If everyone must do his or her part in jointly providing public spaces, those parts will be equal unless there are positive grounds for differentiation.

The requirement that contribution in cases of mandatory cooperation be reciprocal is diffuse and open-ended. What exactly it requires in a particular case will often be unclear, even after some public decision has been made about how to measure the relevant burdens. This is not a problem for a principle of public law, however, because explicit legislation is required in order to determine the respective obligations of citizens to contribute. Any requirement of reciprocity will also need to be systematic, in exactly the same way that the system of public rights of way must be understood as systematic. It may be beyond the legitimate power of a public authority either to make traffic rules or to have a tax regime that distributes burdens in a grossly inequitable way, but it is plainly within its power to place specific burdens in ways that turn out to confer burdens and benefits unequally in particular cases.

Focusing on the example of roads provides a useful reminder that many other examples in which citizens can be required to bear burdens for the sake of benefits that they may not enjoy directly need not be understood in terms of some more general calculus of benefits and burdens. In particular, it is often said to be the task of the state to provide what economists describe as "public goods," such as public health and national defense. These are often characterized in terms of two features: if the goods are produced, everyone benefits, and it is difficult or impossible to exclude those who refuse to contribute from enjoying the benefits. These features lead to positive externalities, that is, those who participate confer benefits on those who do not. A rational agent considering whether to participate would conclude that she would do just as well taking advantage of the efforts of others. As a result of these problems of collective action, in particular free riding, these goods are not produced in adequate amounts by private actors in the market. Thus the state is said to have a role in their production.

I do not mean to question the standard analysis of these goods in terms of collective action by rational agents on its own terms. The difficulty is with grounding mandatory cooperation or public provision in terms of benefits, burdens, or externalities. We saw already in our discussion of private right that externalities as such generate no issues of right; I do not need to pay you for the customers that come into my restaurant because of your nearby hotel, or the bees that pollinate my flowers because of your garden. The mere fact that problems of collective action may lead to an undersupply of a certain good, relative to people's willingness to pay for it, does not underwrite mandatory contribution. The mere fact that a group of people are not able to coordinate to guarantee the production or preservation of something that they value does not entitle them to use the coercive apparatus of the state to compel others to join them in their efforts at producing it. Religious conformity or modest dress may be difficult to maintain without state support, but neither the difficulties posed by temptation nor the collective action problems that result underwrite state action.[31]

Instead of analyzing public health or national defense in terms of benefits and burdens, it is better to assimilate them to the example of roads. They are required to sustain a rightful condition. People can be compelled to contribute to genuine national self-defense quite apart from whether they personally stand to benefit from it. Perhaps some people would see their lives change little if their state were conquered by a hostile neighbor, as Kant's life changed little during the Russian capture of Königsberg.[32] Such people can be compelled to contribute, not because they have accepted a benefit of national defense, but rather because it is

---

31. Thus Charles Taylor seeks to defend Quebec's language laws banning, among other things, visible signs in languages other than French with the contention that "political society is not neutral between those who value remaining true to the culture of our ancestors and those who might want to cut loose in the name of some individual goal of self-development" (*Multiculturalism and "The Politics of Recognition"* [Princeton: Princeton University Press, 1992], 58). Taylor eschews the technical vocabulary of rational choice theory, but his argument can be put in exactly those terms: the preservation of French language and traditional Quebecois culture, especially in urban Montreal, is a public good in the economist's sense, and everyone has incentives to undermine its provision. Taylor argues that in such a situation, a majority of citizens may act together to preserve "the ways of their ancestors" against the incursions of some "ideal of individual self-realization" by prohibiting signage in languages other than French. The example is specific, but Taylor's way of framing it is perfectly general: a majority may use the state to force others to provide them with a benefit they seek. The Kantian objection to this form of argument is clear. See ibid., 52–59.

32. Manfred Kuehn, *Kant: A Biography* (Cambridge: Cambridge University Press, 2002), 118.

the defense of their nation, understood juridically, that is, as their system of laws.

Another familiar public power, public health, has a similar structure. The state's mandate to protect public health follows from its mandate to see to its own preservation. Thus the citizens can be compelled to pay taxes to support public health, and a particular citizen can be compelled to pay even if he or she has the financial wherewithal to take private precautions against plagues and epidemics, or is so elderly that public health measures will add little to his or her expected life span.

V. Public Spaces and Police Powers

I now want to use the example of roads to show that a core exercise of police powers is to prevent people from misappropriating public space for private purposes. Along the way, I will take a detour through Kant's own brief list of police powers, which he sums up by saying that the government's "business of guiding the people by laws is made easier when the feeling for decorum, as negative taste, is not deadened by what offends the moral sense, such as begging, uproar on the streets, stenches and public prostitution."[33] Kant's remark sounds like it is from another age, as his examples may appear to be,[34] but the underlying principle is one of public provision on fair terms.

In the common law, the traditional example of a public nuisance is blocking a public road. The person who puts a pole across the road commits a public nuisance and is subject to a public law penalty, even if he does so in the pursuit of some socially useful purpose. In limited circumstances, private parties who are affected by the public nuisance have standing to sue, but the public nuisance is not an aggregate of private

---

33. 6:325.

34. By the standards of his times, Kant's list is strikingly spare. Feuerbach's much longer list includes, *inter alia,* failing to sweep the sidewalk on Saturday, unauthorized placing of a flowerpot, skating on thin ice, unauthorized river bathing, and making public statements "gravely insulting the admiration of the highest Being." Other entries on the list sound much closer to Kant's own list: failing to make a timely appearance at the water pump in case of fire, operating a coach at excessive speed, obstructing a narrow street with a cart, begging, establishing a chemical laboratory in one's kitchen. Given the breadth of the list, it is not surprising that Feuerbach despaired of finding a unifying principle for the police powers. See Dubber, *The Police Power,* 75–76.

nuisances. Instead, it is an interference with the rights of members of the public, that is, private citizens coming and going as they please, making use of the road, a right that they enjoy as members of the public. The ground for prohibiting a public nuisance is just that it interferes with these rights.

Blocking a road is a private appropriation of a public space. As such, it is objectionable even if it has no significant effects on anyone else. If I block only one lane of traffic, by parking illegally, others may still be able to get where they are going. Perhaps I have just slowed things down. If traffic is unusually light, maybe I haven't even done that. Yet the state can still ticket or tow my car, because I have claimed the public space for private purposes. If I am ticketed, the fact that I caused no harm is irrelevant; the fact that I used the road in the wrong way is sufficient.

In such cases, rather than a limitation imposed on one person for the convenience of others, the basic principle is one of mandatory cooperation: everyone has to do his or her part in the provision of the public right of way. The state is required to provide public rights of way; its obligation to do so authorizes it to decide how to do so. The obligation is not self-applying, and the public authority, acting on behalf of everyone, is entitled to decide how to provide roads, and what terms of use to specify. The person who violates the terms of use—parking during rush hour, going the wrong way down a one-way street, or ignoring traffic lights—interferes with this mode of public provision. In this sort of situation, it makes sense to ask "What if everybody did that?" because the basic principle of public provision is that everyone has to do his or her share. Any bad effects are secondary.

Kant's eighteenth-century examples have the same structure. Kant's first example is begging, an activity to which his opposition, both personal and political, is well known. As a struggling young scholar, Kant sold some of his books to make sure he would never depend on charity; as a more established professor, he never gave money to beggars, but when he passed one gave money to the community treasury.[35] His argu-

---

35. Reported in John H. Zimmito, *Kant, Herder, and the Birth of Anthropology* (Chicago: University of Chicago Press, 2002), 90. For Kant's attitude toward begging as an individual vice, see Kant, *Lectures on Ethics,* trans. Peter Heath (Cambridge: Cambridge University Press, 1997), 27:606, 27:706.

ment for state support for the poor turns on the ways in which private charity in general, and begging in particular, subjects the needy to the private choice of people of means.[36] The grounds for exercising the police power to control begging are different. The beggar doesn't merely block the street by loitering. He actively seeks to draw passersby into his purposes—that is the whole point of what he is doing. Kant characterizes begging as "closely akin to robbery,"[37] because of the manner in which the beggar demands something of passersby. A normal market interaction consists in one person offering an incentive to another, which the other then decides whether to take up. The only thing the beggar offers to do is to stop thrusting himself into the passerby's affairs in return for a contribution. As a matter of private right, it is up to the passerby to decide whether to pay any attention to the beggar. As a matter of public right, however, the beggar does wrong by appropriating public space for private purposes. Again, stenches become a public problem when they invade public spaces. If everybody emptied slop buckets into the street, the streets would be either impassable or passable only with extreme effort. The person who does it has failed to do her share in keeping the streets passable, even if there is no reason to think that others will fail to do their part, and so no actual blockage is created in the particular case. The slop dumper claims a prerogative that others could not all claim. Slop buckets are a thing of the past, but the same point applies to littering and pollution. Kant's example of noisy crowds also fits this model. Noisy neighbors are a private nuisance; noisy crowds in public spaces, a public one.

These examples all occur in public spaces. Their universal practice would make those spaces unavailable to the public, or impede public use of the space. Either way, violators "offend the sense of decorum as negative taste" because they claim more of the public space for themselves than anyone is entitled to claim, and so preclude the possibility of everyone's doing his or her fair share.[38] A public nuisance stops you from en-

---

36. 6:325–326. See also Chapter 9.
37. 6:326.
38. A parallel analysis extends even to Kant's example of public prostitution *(venus vulgavaga)* and more generally to what used to be called "offenses against public morals." In each case, the key term is "public"; the issue is not one of corrupting others by setting a bad example, but one of interfering with public spaces. The police power does not extend to activities going on in private. Claims that street prostitution blocks sidewalks or interferes with traffic

joying your privilege as a member of the public to access public spaces without having anyone else draw you into his or her private purposes. The fact that I do not like or approve of what you do in public plays no part in the analysis, no matter how upsetting I might find your conduct.

The Kantian analysis also explains the familiar idea that public speech is largely exempt from the police power, even when people find the speech inconvenient or troubling, and the related thought that a political rally is not the same as a crowd of carousers. Political speech is addressed to members of the public as such and, as we saw in Chapter 7, is a fundamental aspect of public right because it is the tool through which the state can bring itself more nearly into conformity with concepts of right in a way that is not itself inconsistent with those concepts.[39] In cases in which speech is public and political in this way, the only police restrictions that apply automatically are the familiar neutral limits on time, place, and manner, that is, ones that stop speech from interfering with the use of public spaces.

The distinction between activities that interfere with public spaces and those that offend does not on its own give much guidance about how to apply it to particulars. As a result, it provides no conceptual guarantee that officials will not be inappropriately selective in identifying interferences. It is not a simple or mechanical matter to draw a line between the apparently public purpose of speaking in your own name and a private purpose of drawing another into a private transaction. Some examples are clear: advocating for a change in government policy is public; trying to sell someone a watch or convince him to give you a gift is private. Because the Kantian approach focuses on rational concepts, it provides the conceptual framework within which cases need to be classified, but does not classify them. Given the role of public discourse in enabling the state to perfect itself, there is a structural pressure to err in the direction of classifying things as public. Most examples are mixed; a homeless camp set

---

may be made in bad faith, but if they were true, their regulation would be within the police power. The only basis for "offences against public morals" focuses on the way in which such conduct interferes with the right every citizen has to access to public spaces.

39. Kant, "What Is Enlightenment?" in Gregor, *Practical Philosophy,* and Jonathan Peterson, "Enlightenment and Freedom," *Journal of the History of Philosophy* 46, no. 2 (2008): 223–244.

up in a public park both occupies public space for a private purpose and at the same time seeks to remind members of the public of a situation that they might prefer to forget about. Volunteers soliciting for a charity both ask for money and address passersby about matters of public concern. A department store–sponsored holiday parade is both a commercial venture and a cultural event. These examples show that pure cases of private speech are comparatively rare, and that most speech has a public dimension. That said, the point of the Kantian analysis is to explain how the state is entitled, as a matter of right, to restrict private speech and action insofar as it interferes with the ability of members of the public to use public spaces.

The Kantian account's provision of conceptual resources rather than detailed prescriptions might strike some as an abdication of responsibility. I hope the arguments of this chapter have suggested a different conclusion. The failure to eliminate the need for judgment is a vindication of Kant's conception of the ambitions of political philosophy, not a weakness in it. The most that normative philosophy can do is provide a principled account of the tasks of the various powers within a liberal state. In specifying what officials must do, a normative theory cannot guarantee that they will do it well. Still, the Kantian approach has the clear advantage of articulating a principled account of the basis and limits of the police power. Rather than starting with an image of a paternalistic government charged with making people happy, and then introducing a list of exceptions, the Kantian account shows that the public use of power is only legitimate in the service of individual freedom.

VI. Conclusion

At the beginning of this chapter, I noted that the interest-based approach to state power typically focuses on three questions: how competing interests should be balanced against each other, which interests should be exempt from ordinary balancing, and which persons or institutions should be charged with doing the balancing. I have presented a different way of thinking about the legitimate use of state power, focused on the conditions of freedom rather than interests.

From the perspective of the interest-based approach, the freedom-based approach is oddly silent on the first question, because it supposes that it only comes up in the context of mandatory forms of social cooperation. In that context, it says nothing about benefits, only that burdens should be borne equally, but provides no guidance about how to measure burdens. The freedom-based strategy will seem to shunt many of the most difficult issues off to the third question: the people's representatives must figure out what the burdens are, and what it would be for people to bear them equally. Having rejected the interest-based strategy, it cannot claim that those representatives are likely to weigh the interests more accurately, or balance them in a better way. It can claim only that a public authority is just that: it is public, constituted by the citizens as a collective body, and it is an authority; that is, *within* its mandate, its decision is binding apart from its merits, solely because it is the decision of a competent public authority. The department of transport can forbid you from driving uptown on Lexington Avenue or make you stop for a red light, neither because it has weighed all of the interests correctly, nor because it has better information than some other agent, but simply because the legislature has delegated those questions to it.

The freedom-based approach also rejects the second question in the form in which it is posed by the interest-based strategy, because it denies that the state has a general mandate to balance interests, and so does not set aside a special class of interests that are exempt from ordinary balancing. Instead, it requires that the same innate right of humanity that structures the state's police power also serve as its limit. In setting up the institutions and services that are required for a system of equal freedom, the state must not use means inconsistent with its citizens' innate right of humanity. All of this could, with some distortion, be translated into the vocabulary of interests: in order to justify the use of coercive power by the state, freedom, understood as independence of another person's choice, is the only interest that matters.

CHAPTER 9

Public Right III: Redistribution and Equality of Opportunity

THIS CHAPTER WILL consider two further issues Kant addresses through the idea of the original contract: what he characterizes as the duty to support the poor, and his argument for formal equality of opportunity. Recent political philosophy, including political philosophy that characterizes itself as "Kantian," has often represented these ideas as outmoded, and sought to replace them with more robust ideas of material equality. Kant's grounds for rejecting these more substantive ideas rest on his understanding of the nature of political society as only entitled to use force to create and sustain a rightful condition. Kant's narrow conception of the legitimate uses of state power does not preclude many of the activities that modern liberal states have taken to improve opportunities for people who are disadvantaged. It does, however, preclude the familiar suggestion that such programs as universal public education and health care are unstable stopping points on a path to a more thorough equalization of benefits and burdens in general. The rationale for such programs is immanent in the requirements of a rightful condition, rather that extrinsic to it.

I. Two Consequences for Rights: The Duty to Support the Poor and Equality of Opportunity

Kant treats the duty to tax people of means in order to support the poor and the duty to guarantee equality of opportunity separately from his discussion of the police power. The structure of his argument for each is also different from the argument for the police power. It does, however, share one important feature. Here, as throughout Kant's discussion of public right, the nature of the power in question can only be understood in terms of its basis. Rather than focusing on some desirable outcome—for example, that all citizens have equal or even adequate resources at their disposal—and supposing that the desirability of the outcome underwrites the state's entitlement to take steps to bring it about, Kant works in the opposite direction. The state intervenes in distribution and guarantees equality of opportunity as mandatory means of sustaining a rightful condition, not in the service of any valuable end outside the state. In the same way, rather than focusing on the efficiency gains of a system in which careers are open to talents, Kant focuses instead on the requirements of a rightful condition.

Kant's focus on identifying the basis of each public power reflects two central themes of his broader project in political philosophy: his division between duties of right and duties of virtue, and his conception of law as something other than a tool for achieving independently desirable moral outcomes. The significance of these distinctions is particularly evident in the case of economic redistribution. Many recent political philosophers, such as Joel Feinberg and Onora O'Neill, argue that the state properly belongs in the business of economic redistribution because individuals acting on their own are ineffective in meeting their own individual obligations of charity.[1] The state steps in as a coordinating device, telling people their respective burdens so that all may discharge them effectively. Even if the state does not do an especially good job of determining the appropri-

---

1. Onora O'Neill, *Constructions of Reason* (Cambridge: Cambridge University Press, 1989), 231; Joel Feinberg, "The Moral and Legal Duties of the Good Samaritan," in his *Freedom and Fulfillment* (Princeton: Princeton University Press, 1992). For an account that reads Kant as making such an argument, see Allen Rosen, *Kant's Theory of Justice* (Ithaca: Cornell University Press, 1993), chap. 5.

ate burdens or their distribution, its demands still carry moral weight, because they are in the service of an antecedent moral obligation.[2] From Kant's perspective, this form of argument would provide the wrong basis for any form of state action, even if both its premise and its conclusion were true. The difficulty reflects Kant's distinction between right and virtue. Duties of right are enforceable, but concern only the relation of choice between persons, and so do not depend on effects considered in the abstract. Duties of virtue can never be coercively enforced, because they can only be discharged by acting on the appropriate maxim or rule of action. If you pay your taxes merely because you are legally required to, your act of doing so still carries no moral worth, and so does not in fact discharge your imperfect duty of making the needs of others one of your ends. The person who pays taxes that support the poor because he wants to avoid penalties for tax evasion is like the *Groundwork*'s example of the shopkeeper for whom honesty is the best policy for keeping customers. That taxpayer's deficiencies do not rule out the possibility that a different taxpayer could be virtuous by paying taxes, provided that he or she does so only in order to help those in need. Nor does Kant's focus on maxims prevent groups of people from coordinating their charitable activities to make them more effective. But it does mean that a group of people cannot compel nonmembers to aid them in the project of enabling the members of the group to act more virtuously. For Kant, the moral status of an action is never measured solely by its effects, neutrally specified. As a matter of private right, an action is wrongful only if it interferes with means belonging to another person. Neither causing harm nor failing to confer a benefit is a wrong on its own. Failure to give to those in need does not wrong them at the level of private right. In matters of virtue, actual effects are irrelevant for a different reason: the end for which you act matters, but the result which you produce only matters in relation to the maxim on which you act. Nobody has a general obligation of either right or virtue to bring about a specific result, so no obligation could be discharged merely by bringing about such a result if it is brought about in the wrong way. So the

---

2. Tony Honoré argues that this explains the moral obligation to pay a tax even if it is unjust, provided that its proceeds go toward morally required goods. See A. M. Honoré, "The Dependence of Morality on Law," *Oxford Journal of Legal Studies* 13 (1993): 1–17.

state's power to redistribute cannot be traced to some antecedent obligation on the part of the wealthy to bring it about that the needy receive more than they have. Instead, the state's duty to support the poor must itself be a freestanding duty, something that the state must do in order to be a rightful condition at all.

II. Redistribution

Contemporary philosophical debates about economic distribution have tended to polarize around two positions. One broadly Lockean argument, more recently associated with Robert Nozick's *Anarchy, State, and Utopia,* focuses exclusively on private interaction, and supposes that the moral character of and constraints on the relation between the individual and the state can be no different from those between any two private parties, individual or corporate. The other, broadly egalitarian argument, often attributed to Rawls,[3] both by critics and by self-described followers, proposes an equally reductive view, but proceeding in the opposite direction, so that relations between private persons are structured to secure the requirements of distributive equality.[4]

Kant's emphasis on both the innate right of humanity and fundamental principles of private right might seem to place him squarely in Nozick's Lockean camp, and to leave no space for economic redistribution.[5] If the

---

3. Although incorrectly.

4. Kant's argument differs from familiar contemporary approaches which trace the power to tax to the causal role of society in producing all wealth. See Nagel and Murphy, *The Myth of Ownership: Taxes and Justice* (Oxford: Oxford University Press, 2005). This view incorporates a social version of the Lockean idea that a person's claim to an object depends upon the toil he or she has exerted in creating or acquiring it. It is also like the Lockean position in that it supposes that *society* acquires a sort of absolute dominion over the things *it* has produced.

The Kantian approach must reject such an argument, both because it seeks to establish a right of ownership on the basis of causation, rather than a system of equal freedom, and, more significantly, because it treats the state as a private party, free to dispose of its assets as it sees fit. If the state has a claim on it because it produced it, it might just as well use it for some publicly selected purpose other than achieving a just distribution.

5. See Wolfgang Kersting, "Kant's Concept of a State," in Howard Williams, ed., *Kant's Political Philosophy* (Cardiff: University of Wales Press, 1992), 164; Thomas W. Pogge, "Is Kant's *Rechtslehre* A Comprehensive Liberalism?" in Mark Timmons, ed., *Kant's Metaphysics of Morals: Interpretive Essays* (Oxford: Oxford University Press, 2002), 149; Bernd Ludwig,

only possible grounds for redistribution presuppose either that the Earth belongs to everyone in common or that private rights are tools for achieving desired outcomes, Kant would have to oppose redistribution, since he rejects both of those claims. The supposition that a focus on property and freedom of contract reduces the state to just another private actor animates Nozick's version of Lockean political philosophy, which represents the legitimate state as an organization created by private persons for distinctive private purposes. We saw in Chapters 6 and 7 that Kant's conception of the social contract is fundamentally different, because he rejects the idea that private rights are conclusive outside of a rightful condition. Nonetheless, the two might be thought to be similar in at least this respect: the state's normative rationale is rooted in a series of problems regarding private interaction. Institutions charged with making, applying, and enforcing laws are required so that separate persons may enjoy their respective private freedom in a way that forms a consistent set. Problems of exclusive appropriation, assurance, and disagreements about right require distinctive institutions to solve them. We also saw, in Chapter 8, that public institutions and spaces are required to make private rights systematic.

Given the private nature of the problems the state is called on to solve, it might seem natural to conclude that the institutions could not possibly do anything more than that; to do so would be to usurp their basic roles. Indeed, if the state is represented as acting for its citizens, its mandate is necessarily limited. Again, even if the state must exercise its police power to secure the systematic conditions of freedom, that role may have redistributive effects, but it has no redistributive purpose.

The requirement that it act for its citizens does limit the state's man-

---

"Kants Verabschiedung der Vertragstheorie—Konsequenzen für eine Theorie der sozialen Gerchtigkeit," *Jahrbuch für Recht und Ethik* 1 (1993): 239–243. In "The Great Maxims of Justice and Charity," in her *Constructions of Reason* (Cambridge: Cambridge University Press, 1989), 219–233, Onora O'Neill limits right to the prevention of force and fraud, and grounds other state activities in virtue. Howard L. Williams, *Kant's Political Philosophy* (New York: St. Martin's Press, 1983), 195–198, argues that Kant grounds the duty to support the poor in an ethical concern unrelated to right. Allen Rosen concludes the duty that is "taken over from the people" is one of benevolence. See Rosen, *Kant's Theory of Justice* (Ithaca: Cornell University Press, 1993), 189.

date, but it also generates the duty to support the poor. The key to Kant's argument for the state focuses on the need for a united legislative will. As we have seen, the idea of a united will not only serves to make unilateral appropriations rightful; more generally, it explains the possibility of one person changing the normative status of another through word or deed. Thus the actions of the executive branch must be authorized by law, because the enforcement of rights, either retrospectively or prospectively, can only be rendered consistent with the rightful honor of those against whom force is used if it issues from an omnilateral standpoint. In the same way, the resolution of disputes could only be consistent with the rightful honor of the parties to the dispute if the arbiter is authorized through an omnilateral will. The state, through its officials, speaks and acts for all. Otherwise it could not solve any of the problems of unilateral choice or judgment that plague the state of nature. Any powers a state has must be traced to its claim to speak and act for all. Both its task of economic redistribution and its guarantee of equality of opportunity can be traced to this claim. The institutions that give effect to a system of equal freedom must be organized so that they do not systematically create a condition of dependence.

III. What Is Poverty?

Kant argues that provision for the poor follows directly from the very idea of a united will. He remarks that the idea of a united lawgiving will requires that citizens regard the state as existing in perpetuity.[6] By this he does not mean to impose an absurd requirement that people live forever, or even the weaker one that it must sustain an adequate population, or make sure that all of its members survive.[7] The state does need to maintain its material preconditions, and as we saw in Chapter 7, this need generates its entitlement to "administer the state's economy and finance."[8] The state's existence in perpetuity, however, is presented as a pure nor-

---

6. 6:326.

7. Allen Wood argues that Kant's focus in his discussion of the duty to support the poor is based on the fact that physical survival is a precondition of the exercise of agency. See *Kantian Ethics* (Cambridge: Cambridge University Press, 2008), 196.

8. 6:325.

mative requirement, grounded in its ability to speak and act for everyone. That ability must be able to survive changes in the state's membership. You are the same person you were a year ago because your normative principle of organization has stayed the same through changes in the matter making you up. As a being entitled to set and pursue your own purposes, you decide what your continuing body will do. That is why your deeds can be imputed to you even after every molecule in your body has changed, and even if you have forgotten what you did. The unity of your agency is created by the normative principle that makes your actions imputable to you.[9] In the same way, the state must sustain *its* basic normative principle of organization through time, even as some members die or move away and new ones are born or move in. As we saw in Chapter 7, its unifying principle—"in terms of which alone we can think of the legitimacy of the state"—is the idea of the original contract, through which people are bound by laws they have given themselves through public institutions.[10] The state must have the structure that is required in order for everyone to be bound by it, so that it can legitimately claim to speak and act for all across time. The requirement of unity across time is clear in the cases of legislation by officials: if the official's decision were only binding while a particular human being held office, a citizen would be entitled to regard laws as void once the official's term ended. Because each person is master of him- or herself, one person is only bound by the authority of another through the idea of a united will. So the idea of a united will presupposes some manner in which it exists through time. Past legislation, like past agreement, can only bind those who come after if the structure through which laws are made is one that can bind everyone it governs.

The solution to this family of problems is a self-sustaining system that guarantees that all citizens stand in the right relation to each other and, in particular, do not stand in any relation inconsistent with their sharing a united will.

The most obvious way in which people could fail to share such a will is through relations of private dependence through which one person is

---

9. Christine Korsgaard, "Personal Identity and the Unity of Agency," *Philosophy & Public Affairs* 18 (1989): 106.
10. 6:315.

subject to the choice of another. A serf or slave does not share a united will with his or her lord or master, so these forms of relationship are inconsistent with a rightful condition. Yet the same relation of dependence can arise through a series of rightful actions. The problem of poverty, on Kant's analysis, is exactly that: the poor are completely subject to the choice of those in more fortunate circumstances.

Although Kant argues that there is an ethical duty to give to charity,[11] the crux of his argument is that dependence on private charity is inconsistent with its benefactor and beneficiary sharing the united will that is required for them to live together in a rightful condition. The difficulty is that the poor person is subject to the choice of those who have more: they are entitled to use their powers as they see fit, and so the decision whether to give to those in need, or how much to give, or to which people, is entirely discretionary.[12] So long as there are a variety of unmet wants, private persons are entitled to determine which ones to attach priority to.

Because Kant represents individual freedom and dignity through purposiveness, each person is entitled to set and pursue his or her own purposes. Yet that entails that no person in need has a claim of right against any other specific person based exclusively on that need. In the Introduction, Kant insists that right focuses on the form of choice rather than its matter, and so "it does not signify the relation of one's choice to the mere wish (hence also to the mere need) of the other."[13] Kant's cold equation of need with wish reflects the more general project of restricting the use of force to the reconciliation of private freedom. As we saw in our discussions of private right, Kant's arguments do not turn on the factual vulnerability to suffering, but rather on a juridical vulnerability to wrongdoing. By setting things up in this way, Kant precludes the possibility of a private right to charity. The entitlement under right that no person needs to accommodate him- or herself to the specifics of another person's purposes is perfectly general, and so applies to even the limiting case of the other person's minimal purpose of keeping alive. This is why Kant denies that

---

11. Kant, *Groundwork of the Metaphysics of Morals*, 4:423.

12. That is why Kant describes the duty to give to charity as an "imperfect" duty: although you have an obligation to make meeting the needs of others one of your ends, it is up to you to judge which people to help and which of their needs to meet, and to determine whether you have met them adequately.

13. 6:230.

there could be a right of necessity, entitling one person to kill or steal from another so as to keep himself alive.

Kant's case for conceiving of private rights in this way has been elaborated and defended in earlier chapters. His emphasis on the form of transaction rather than the particular end another person has is a direct implication of the idea that each person is entitled to use his or her means to set and pursue his or her own purposes, independently of the choice of others. Your entitlement to set and pursue your own purposes, however, means that you alone are entitled to determine what those purposes will be, and your entitlement to do so does not depend upon the particular purposes of others, but only on the entitlements of others to use their means to set whatever purposes they have. Private right protects each person's purposiveness by protecting each person in what he or she already happens to have. As such, it has no space for recognizing a person's wish that she had something that she lacks, and no way of distinguishing a need from a wish. Such wishes, like any other wishes, concern the matter of choice. The same point applies to acquiring further means. Each person is entitled to use his or her own means to acquire things he or she currently lacks; no person is required to make his means available to another to aid such acquisition, because no person is ever required to make his means available for another person's purposes. The conclusion that I do not wrong you by failing to help you when you are in need is thus a special case of the more general claim that each of us is entitled to set and pursue our own purposes. It precludes any encumbrance of freedom based on a particular purpose, however pressing that purpose might be.

It might be thought that other, seemingly more commonsensical ideas of rights of necessity, and concomitant duties to aid, might either solve or preempt the problem Kant articulates for private charity. In support of this, examples of legal systems that do indeed enforce rights of necessity or duties to rescue might be brought forward, and the Kantian approach rejected as nothing more than a reification of some particular system of private law. Matters are complicated by the fact that the legal systems that do impose duties to rescue, with or without a correlative right of necessity, entitling a person in peril to freely use the property of another in order to preserve his own life or the lives of others, incorporate two features that doom them as models of duties of charity more generally. First, these doctrines always include a duty on the part of the person using or destroying the property of another to compensate the owner.[14] When the emergency is over, the person must pay for the property used or destroyed. Such legislation is of limited use as a model of a more general duty to aid those in need, because a private duty of charity is not a duty to let someone else use your money or property on the condition that she repays it in future. A duty to make your goods available for emergency use is not the same as a transfer of those goods to others. Second, duties to rescue typically sound in public law. The Kantian argument for poverty relief sounds in public law, and addresses a problem of dependence that is necessarily invisible to private law. Jurisdictions that enforce a duty to rescue presuppose either the Kantian argument or some analogue of it.

Indeed, the problem of dependence that the Kantian argument addresses follows from the absence of a private duty to rescue. The freedom of donors to set their own purposes without attention to the needs of others gives them discretion over whether to respond to claims of need. That discretion generates a problem of dependence. In a state of nature, even without enforceable property rights, one person could be factually dependent on the generosity of another. Perhaps the remaining fruits on a tree are too high for me to reach, but you are able to get them. In that sense, I would be dependent on your generosity, and I would have no claim of right against you. Nonetheless, you would not wrong me from the standpoint of right if you failed to help me, as you would not deprive me of my ability to use my own means for my own purposes. All you would do is fail to provide me with a favorable context in which to use those means. In this respect, then, my dependence on you, such as it is, is merely factual, because it depends on the particular ends I happen to have. The fact that these are natural ends of self-preservation is not relevant. If I could only reach the fruits I wanted (or needed) by having you crouch down so I could stand on your back, you would be under no obligation to bow down for me, and I would not be dependent on you in a way that was inconsistent with our respective moral independence. My factual dependence on you is normatively no different from the sort of factual dependence that is inevitable as each person uses his or her means

---

14. "German Civil Code," www.gesetze-im-internet.de/englisch_bgb/index.html (accessed October 7, 2008).

to set and pursue his or her own purposes, and in so doing changes the context in which other people are able to use their means.

In the civil condition, the situation of private dependence is changed in two respects. First of all, property rights become conclusive, so that one person is entitled to exclude another, and call upon the state's assistance in doing so, from objects that the first is not in physical possession of. In a state of nature without enforceable property rights, those lacking property do no wrong by using or consuming anything that is not in the physical possession of another person. In a civil condition with enforceable property rights, objects that are privately owned are not available for others to use. On its own, this problem is not sufficient, since it concerns only private relations between private persons. Since entering a civil condition does not change the nature of those rightful relations,[15] neither the fact that things other than your person are not available for others to use nor the absence of any duty to make them available creates a wrongful relation between you and others who might wish for access to those means. Like your entitlement to your own bodily powers, your entitlement to your property means that no other private person can require you to use it in a way that best suits his or her preferred purposes. A special case of this is that you need not make your means available for others to use, regardless of what their purposes might be, even in cases of self-preservation. As a matter of private right, the dependence of one person upon another is merely factual.

The second problem, however, is specific to public right. The condition of public lawgiving, including lawgiving that makes the acquisition of property binding on others, and lawgiving that makes rights to external objects of choice enforceable, is a united will. Although the united will is itself an idea of reason, we saw in Chapter 7 that the state can only make arrangements for a person that that person could have agreed to, consistent with his or her rightful honor. Anything that could not be the object of agreement cannot give rise to enforceable private rights, including enforceable property rights.[16]

---

15. 6:307.

16. For a related but somewhat different interpretation of this part of Kant's argument, see Ernest Weinrib, "Poverty and Property in Kant's System of Rights," *Notre Dame Law Review* 78, no. 3 (2003): 795–828.

Kant's central claim is that the dependence of one person upon another inherent in private charity is inconsistent with those people sharing a united will. In private right, people can only make arrangements for themselves that are consistent with their rightful honor; in public right, the state can only create an arrangement between people that is consistent with it. An arrangement in which one person's entitlement to use anything is entirely left to the discretion of others is inconsistent with rightful honor, so it could not give rise to enforceable rights. Therefore, the only way that property rights can be made enforceable is if the system that makes them so contains a provision for protecting against private dependence.

Kant's argument that discretion is inconsistent with people sharing a united will echoes Rousseau's argument in *The Social Contract* that extremes of poverty and wealth are inconsistent with the people giving themselves laws together.[17] Where Rousseau is sometimes taken to be making a factual claim, Kant is plainly making a normative one: a social world in which one person has the rightful power of life and death over another is inconsistent with those persons sharing a united will, even if the situation came about through a series of private transactions in which neither did the other wrong. Kant's approach also contrasts with Fichte's. For Fichte, institutions to provide for the poor are a precondition of poor people's being members of the social contract at all.[18] Without such institutions, poor people are outside the contract, and so entitled to help themselves to the property of others. Kant does not discuss this formulation of the argument, but his general rejection of a private right of necessity provides grounds for either rejecting it or construing it in a very specific way. Kant rejects the supposed right of necessity on the grounds that a person cannot acquire a right based on his or her specific circumstances. As we will see in Chapter 10, in certain limited cases, circumstances are potentially relevant to the state's claim to punish the violation of a right. That analysis can only apply provided that there is a genuine violation.

---

17. Jean-Jacques Rousseau, *On the Social Contract*, in *The Basic Political Writings*, trans. Donald Cress (Indianapolis: Hackett, 1987), 170.

18. J. G. Fichte, *Foundations of Natural Right*, trans. Michael Baur (Cambridge: Cambridge University Press, 2000), 185. Kant thanked Fichte for sending him the *Foundations*, though it is not clear whether he actually read it. See his letter of December 1797, in *Correspondence*, trans. Arnulf Zweig (Cambridge: Cambridge University Press, 1999), 12:221.

For all the reasons that there is no duty to make one's means available for the purposes of another, there can be no private right to avail oneself of another person's person or property, for such a right would entail a correlative duty. Fichte's argument about exemption from the social contract seems to suggest that the possibility of enforceable rights depends on circumstances. Kant's own arguments focus not on the possibility of exemption, but rather on the fundamental presuppositions of a united will.

The problem is specific to property, because if property rights are not enforceable, each person is at liberty to help himself to whatever he wants, and so to what he needs. It may turn out that a person cannot meet his needs in a state of nature, but the ability to use external objects of choice to meet them is a natural matter, not subject to the choice of another. By contrast, once property rights are enforceable, the ability to use external objects that are not your own is subject to the choice of others. This is not always a problem, but it is in the special case in which a person's entitlement to use her own person is subject to the choice of another. Since your ongoing purposiveness just is your person, your right to use your own person to secure your own person's continued purposiveness depends on another. This dependence is not simply a function of the particularity of another person's choices about how to use her means. Instead, it is also a function of the united will, which makes property rights enforceable and so gives her the right to decide how they will be used. A free person could not authorize a situation in which his or her entitlement to set and pursue purposes could be entirely subject to the choice of another. The omnilateral will's power to make law is restricted by the laws the people could give themselves; they could not authorize a situation in which some are completely beholden to the choice of another.[19]

Although Kant does not put the point in these terms, a spatial formula-

---

19. This interpretation of Kant's argument differs from Paul Guyer's claim that a system of property rights "must allow each participant at least an opportunity to maintain his or her own existence at least equivalent to what he or she enjoyed under the original common possession; otherwise it would be irrational for anyone to freely consent to the transfer of rights, and it would indeed be a violation of the duty to strive to maintain one's own existence." Where Guyer's interpretation makes the argument turn on a concern for self-preservation and an analysis of rational advantage in pursuing it, the interpretation defended here makes it turn on the duty of rightful honor. See Guyer, "Kantian Foundation for Liberalism," in his *Kant on Freedom, Law, and Happiness* (Cambridge: Cambridge University Press, 2000), 254.

tion of the argument makes it more vivid. If all land is privately held, then any person who does not own land would only be entitled to be anywhere at all with the permission of the person who did own the land. The innate right to occupy space, which is the basis of all further rights, would be totally surrendered in such a situation. We saw in the last chapter that the spatiality of private property requires that there be roads joining any two parcels of land, and various other forms of public space are certainly possible. The possibility of walking the King's Highways, as beggars did in Britain in earlier centuries, is no solution for people lacking land, because, as we also saw, blocking a public road is inconsistent with public right. If private owners are entitled to exclude from their land, and nobody is allowed to live on public highways, the poor could find themselves with no place to go, in the sense that they would do wrong simply by being wherever they happened to be. They would be entirely subject to the choice of those who owned land. Free persons lack the moral power to join with others to give themselves laws that create such a possibility, even if there were reasons to think it unlikely it would ever happen. The person who is entirely dependent on the grace of another to occupy space, or to use physical objects, is not merely lacking in self-determination, or somehow on the losing end of the bargain that makes up the social contract, having perhaps given up more than he gained. The contract cannot be represented as a bargain that the parties enter into in the expectation of advantage, and the poverty-stricken person as opting out because it is not advantageous enough. Instead, the person who can only occupy space with the permission of others has no capacity to set and pursue his own purposes. As such, the person in need is like a slave, and the contract creating such a situation is, like a slave contract, incoherent.

The spatial version of the problem illuminates actual cases of poverty and need because the juridical significance of biological survival is that it consists in a person's keeping control of his or own person. Death, as such, is of no direct significance to right; your own person, like everything else, is subject to natural deterioration. But if another person is entitled to determine whether you will maintain control of your own person, you are subject to that person's choice in exactly the same way as the person who cannot occupy space except through the grace of another. Each is entirely subject to the choice of another.

The spatial version of the problem also illustrates its systematic structure: those who have no place to go without the permission of another are not merely frustrated in the pursuit of some specific purpose, not even the purpose of self-preservation. All property rights prevent people from doing things that they might have otherwise been free to do, because a property right entitles the owner to determine how the object in question will be used. The sort of factual dependence that is thereby created raises no issues of right. Poverty, as Kant conceives it, is systematic: a person cannot use his or her own body, or even so much as occupy space, without the permission of another. The problem is not that some particular purpose depends on the choices of others, but that the pursuit of any purpose does.[20] If all purposiveness depends on the grace of others, the dependent person is in the juridical position of a slave or serf.

The parallel between charity and slavery may seem surprising. Slave owners are often thought of as cruel and immoral, and those who give charity as benevolent and gracious. To understand either slavery or charity in this way is, however, to focus on the matter of choice instead of its form. The conceptually possible cases of a slave who is well cared for by her master, and another who is happy with his status, remind us that the moral outrage of slavery is not that it is cruel or that it diminishes welfare, any more than that it is inefficient because of supervision costs. The moral outrage of slavery is the way in which one person is subject to the choice of another; not only that what the slave must do, but that what he or she may do, and whether he or she may even continue to exist, is solely at the discretion of the master. Kant's argument shows that depending on private charity to meet even a person's "most necessary needs"[21] is no different from slavery along these dimensions. The mendicant, like a slave, depends on the specific choices of another person, or on the combined

---

20. A similar point applies to patents, the point of which is to give their holder a monopoly on the use of a certain invention, thereby entitling that person to set the terms on which others may use that type of thing, even if those others invent it independently. I will not develop or even speculate about a Kantian theory of patent law, but only note that if a system of patents is to be consistent with public right, it could allow patent holders to attach terms to the use of types of things, but could not allow everything to be patented so that someone could be precluded from using his or her person or property *in any way* without the permission of others. The standard features of patent law—requirements of originality and nonobviousness, limited terms, and forms of mandatory licensing—provide forms of protection against such a possibility.

21. 6:326.

choices of the various passersby who decide whether to favor him in the course of the day. To depend on the grace of another is inconsistent with rightful honor, because it reduces a person to the status of a thing.

The problem of private dependence on charity is institutional, because it is a consequence of the creation of enforceable property rights. So any solution to it must also be institutional, in order to make enforceable rights consistent with all citizens sharing an omnilateral will. Moreover, the institutions in question are not private institutions, but rather public omnilateral ones that make the right to exclude rightful by protecting against dependence. Rather than either creating private charitable foundations or depending on voluntary associations of religious people to provide for needy members of the community, Kant argues that support for the poor must be provided through taxes.[22] Taxes do not enter to fill whatever gap might remain should either charitable foundations or religious groups fail in their mandate. The point instead is that depending on such organizations is inconsistent with the basis in right for a duty to support the poor. Endowed foundations are inconsistent because, as Kant puts it, it is better that each generation takes care of its own poor; among those who share a general will, those who have property must provide for those who lack it. Religious organizations are rejected for a further reason: from the standpoint of right, religious organizations must be considered purely private, and the fulfilling of religious obligations must be understood as instances of people pursuing purely private purposes. Whether the purpose of following religious edicts is to improve the chances of salvation, or whether religion is understood (in a more Kantian way) as a private association whose members unite to strengthen themselves in relation to the moral law, Kant supposes that the key to religion is the way in which it structures an individual person's adoption of particular ends. Kant also writes that the state must keep an eye on religious organizations, because they claim to respond to an authority higher than the state that may conflict with it.[23] Such a claim requires close supervision because, again, no matter how philanthropic its ends, the role of a religious organization is fundamentally private, rather than being public

22. Ibid.
23. 6:327.

in the ways in which a system of public right is necessarily public. Because of their private nature, religious responses to charity remain mired in problems of dependency, even if, when successful, they enable people to become independent. Here, as everywhere else, the result alone is not sufficient; the means used to pursue it must be consistent with rights, and, Kant argues, dependency is never consistent in that way.

The public solution is taxation to provide for those in need. Taxation by the state is consistent with the freedom of those who are taxed because they "owe their existence to an act of submitting to its protection and care."[24] The sense in which they "owe their existence" to the state is formal rather than material: their wealth consists entirely in their entitlement to exclude others from their goods, which in turn is consistent with equal freedom only when consistent with formal conditions of the general will.

This argument for economic redistribution is *internal* to the idea that acquisition must be authorized and disputes resolved through public procedures that can be accepted by all. Absent institutions of public justice, the rich person's claim to exclude the poor one from his or her property would just be a unilateral imposition of force. Those who have property have the right to exclude provided that their holdings of property are consistent with a united will shared by all—that the system of private rights really is part of a system of equal independence of free persons. Where that system turns into a system of dependence, it fails to be an omnilateral will because its citizens could not agree to an enforceable system inconsistent with their innate right of humanity.

Kant's antipathy to private charity might be thought to stand in tension with his claim in the *Doctrine of Virtue* that each human being has a duty to make others happy. Yet his claim about how needs must be met through public rather than private action leaves plenty of scope for private actions. One person can make the happiness of another his or her end in circumstances where the other is not in fact in need. Charitable support for arts and culture, sports and recreation, and countless other activities to make other people happy is consistent with Kantian right, and so an appropriate exercise of Kantian virtue. Indeed, virtuous people could even make it their maxim to contribute to public schemes of provi-

---

24. 6:326.

sion. What would not be an appropriate exercise of Kantian virtue would be to scale back programs of public provision, so as to create more needy people to whom others, in more comfortable circumstances, might respond charitably. To do so would treat those abandoned to the generosity of others as a mere means toward the moral improvement of other, more fortunate people. To fail to set up institutions to care for those in need would do the same thing by omission. Where an individual fails to act on another's behalf, no wrong is committed. Where the state fails to do so in this sort of situation, however, no general will can be formed.

IV. Most Necessary Natural Needs

Kant's narrow focus on "most necessary natural needs" does not have to limit redistribution to what is required for biological survival. The Kantian argument is formal and procedural rather than substantive. In particular, it does not specify the *level* of social provision, whether it covers merely biological needs or considerably more.[25] Nor does it provide detailed criteria for identifying cases of wrongful dependence. It does, however, provide the framework within which to think about such problems.

Although Kant focuses on the example of support for the poor, the force of his argument is concerned with the structure of the general will. As a result, it requires actual institutions to give effect to it—to set appropriate levels and mechanisms of aid and introduce forms of regulation where necessary. As a philosophical account it is supposed to show what means are available to the state, consistent with the freedom of all; it is not supposed to micromanage social policy. In private right, questions about the limitations period for adverse possession, the standard of care in the law of negligence, or the proper speed limit in rural areas can only be answered through the exercise of determinative judgment by a properly constituted public authority. The same point applies here. The requirements of a general will constrain the form of possible answers, but not

25. The idea of the original contract imposes a broader duty on the state to create the full conditions of citizenship, to prevent the state itself from being a form of despotism and thus dependence. The narrow argument about the duty to support the poor focuses on preventing the conclusive right to exclude others from private property from becoming a system of dependence. It goes to the matter of the laws rather than the form of lawgiving.

their substance. Any answers need to be consistent with equal freedom, so they cannot introduce mandatory forms of cooperation merely on the grounds that they will produce an aggregate increase in welfare. Nor can citizens assert private rights which apply against other private persons as a bulwark against the public requirements of sustaining a rightful condition. But within the appropriate structure, the answers must be imposed by the people themselves.

Instead, *The Metaphysics of Morals* says only that provision must be made so as to preserve independence. The principle of right focuses exclusively on the relation between the choice of the person of means and that of the one in need, and requires that provision be public rather than private. A further "principle of politics" brings that structure to bear on particulars, taking account of the particular society to which the principle of right is to be applied, and guides officials in determining the level and manner of provision. The resulting forms of public provision will in turn reflect economic and political features of a particular society, provided only that they are carried out without violating any person's innate right of humanity. In the past, societies with large amounts of habitable but uninhabited land could make it available for homesteading, but could not rightfully deport poor people to those regions. To switch to a more modern example, if illness and medical expenses regularly lead citizens to fall into conditions of dependency, a state can act proactively to provide publicly funded universal health care. Different countries have adopted different mechanisms to implement this solution, and whether forms of elective surgery are included depends in part on assessment of what is economically or politically feasible in a particular country at a particular time. Here, as elsewhere, the Kantian response must be that use of public power is both justified and restricted by the requirements of creating and sustaining a system of equal freedom under self-imposed laws, but that those requirements demand certain institutions but do not dictate specific results. Democratic politics has an ineliminable place in determining such matters, because the purpose of public institutions is to make the requirements of right apply systematically, not to discover some detailed blueprint that exists apart from those institutions.

Again, if a public authority concludes that workers accept unsafe and unhealthy working conditions because those are the only terms on which they can survive, it can regulate those conditions. The power to do so resides in the state's task of making sure that its citizens can share a general will, rather than in a paternalistic concern to protect people from dangers they freely undertake. That is why such legislation is completely consistent with permitting people to undertake exactly the same dangers in the course of recreational activities or high-status careers.

Kant's approach to the problem of redistribution thus reflects his more general conception of each person as responsible for his or her own life. That idea of responsibility, as we have seen, is framed through ideas of right and obligation; you alone are entitled to determine what purposes you will pursue, subject only to the requirement that others have the same entitlement, and the further systematic requirements imposed by the joint satisfaction of those first requirements for a plurality of persons. The cases in which you are not responsible for your choices are not identified by the nature of your mental deliberations as you make the choices, nor by the ease or difficulty with which others might make similar choices, but by the structural and relational aspect of those circumstances, that is, the fact that you are entirely subject to the choice of another. The solution in those situations is not to indemnify you for what you did as a slave or mendicant, but to provide the background conditions in which no one will ever be a slave or mendicant. In the same way, the rationale for freeing the slave or providing for the mendicant is not that had they been prudent, they would have insured themselves against such contingencies;[26] it is that persons concerned to preserve their independence could not consent to laws that would consign them to a condition of dependence. It bears repeating that the grounds of nonconsent do not depend on any assessment of rational advantage or aversion to risk; they depend instead on the grounds for entering a rightful condition at all: to preserve their freedom under laws. Thus nobody could consent to laws that could make it possible for him to lose his freedom through a rightful act.

---

26. Dworkin, *Sovereign Virtue*, 65ff.

V. Formal Equality of Opportunity

Kant also defends a doctrine of formal equality of opportunity. In the past century, the idea of formal equality of opportunity has often been represented as occupying some sort of unstable middle ground. Libertarians reject it, because they suppose that the state has no business regulating the content of private transactions, and they seek to analyze all transactions, even those involving the state, as fundamentally private. If an employer wants to hire someone on whatever grounds, libertarians suppose that this is legitimate. The standard libertarian unease with the concept of anything distinctively public carries the same form of reasoning to other contexts, including the state. If citizens are viewed as hiring the state, then it is no different from any other private actor, and is entitled to discriminate as it sees fit.

Criticisms from the opposite direction are more prominent in philosophy than in political life, but they, too, view the idea of formal equality of opportunity as morally arbitrary. As Will Kymlicka summarizes what he characterizes as the liberal egalitarian consensus, "no one deserves to be born handicapped, or with an IQ of 140, any more than they deserve to be born into a certain class or sex or race. If it is unjust for people's fate to be influenced by the latter factors, then it is unclear why the same injustice is not equally present when people's fate is determined by the former factors. The injustice in each case is the same—distributive shares should not be influenced by factors which are arbitrary from the moral point of view."[27] Merely formal equality of opportunity is thus arbitrary, because it limits the effects of legal institutions on distributive holdings. Yet for Kymlicka, the only conceivable reason to limit the effects of legal institutions on distributive shares is that race and class and sex are beyond a person's control, so a person's "fate" should not depend on them. That the state is involved in producing the dependence on arbitrary factors is no part of his analysis. On this point, Kymlicka endorses Ronald Dworkin's characterization of formal equality of opportunity as a "fraudulent" ideal. Once we see this, it is suggested, *all* other factors that are beyond a

---

27. Kymlicka, *Contemporary Political Philosophy*, 56.

person's control—both her talents and the circumstances in which she finds herself—should also be prevented from influencing distributive outcomes. Some have pressed these ideas still further, insisting equality requires that people be insulated from the choices of others,[28] or that that the full realization of equality of opportunity demands that parents refrain from differentially conferring benefits on their own children,[29] even if it is also sometimes said that implementing such a proposal would either be impractical or conflict with other values. The underlying ideal that is said to be the true crystallization of the idea of equal opportunity is the removal of all aspects of natural contingency in determining a person's fate in life.

The Kantian defense of formal equality of opportunity depends upon framing the issue differently. Kant's understanding of private right already precludes a systematic focus on whether factors are beyond a person's control. As a matter of private right, each person is entitled to use his or her means to set his or her own purposes, and does not need to use them in a way that best accommodates the purposes of some other private person. Each person's exercise of freedom will change the context in which others choose, and yet be outside the control of those others. A system of public right that sought to systematically cancel the effects that one person's choices had on others, simply on the grounds that they were not chosen by those others, would preclude the exercise of private freedom.[30]

If people are thought of merely as beneficiaries of possible laws, it is natural enough to suppose that the benefits should be given out on the basis of what people deserve, and so to strive to eradicate the effects of

---

28. G. A. Cohen, "On the Currency of Egalitarian Justice," *Ethics* 99 (1999): 906–944.

29. See, for example, James Fishkin, *Justice, Equal Opportunity, and the Family* (New Haven: Yale University Press, 1986); Morris Lipson and Peter Vallentyne, "Equal Opportunity and the Family," *Public Affairs Quarterly* 3 (1989): 29–47; Harry Brighouse and Adam Swift, "Parents' Rights and the Value of the Family," *Ethics* 117, 1 (2006): 80–108.

30. There is a further conceptual question of whether such a possibility could even be described for a plurality of persons. If you consider one person in isolation, there seems to be no problem with drawing a line between things that are within that person's control and those that are outside it, and providing some form of indemnification for the latter. However, the extent to which each person needs to be indemnified is beyond the control of all of the others, and so providing such indemnification introduces new factors beyond each person's control, on which, nonetheless, his or her distributive share depends.

anything other than desert. Like the utilitarian who supposes that social institutions should be designed so as to maximize overall benefits, Kymlicka advocates designing them so as to equalize them, except where people have decided to take risks. Such an approach locates the familiar moral distinction between what a person does and what merely happens at the level of each individual, focusing on that individual's choices rather than the circumstances in which he or she acts. From the standpoint of possible beneficiaries, there can be no possible distinction between legal and nonlegal factors that determine how benefits or burdens fall. Like the utilitarian ideal, the luck-egalitarian ideal Kymlicka articulates can be specified without any reference to legal institutions. Whether individuals or institutions are better positioned to realize it is an open question.[31]

As we saw in Chapter 7, if people are thought of instead as the authors of the laws that bind them, the same distinction between what is done and what merely happens applies at the level of the legal system itself, as the distinction between the limitations created by the legal system and those that are instead the result of either nature or the exercise of freedom by other persons. From this perspective, legally imposed restrictions do pose a special problem: a people cannot give itself laws to which its members could not consent.

Kant's discussion of equality of opportunity needs to be understood in these terms. It takes as its immediate focus the eighteenth-century question of hereditary nobility. Kant's treatment divides into several parts. The first focuses on the requirement that the state determine for itself how official positions will be filled, rather than leaving it to some idea of a nobility that asserts a claim that it is somehow prior to the claims of a rightful condition. This portion of the argument parallels an argument he makes against entailed estates: both hereditary nobility and entailed estates in land—which include private land holdings, religious orders, and philanthropic organizations, such as hospitals and universities—have the conclusive entitlements they do only in the context of a rightful condition. Thus they can assert no claim prior to it. If the state allows heredi-

---

[31]. Unsurprisingly, G. A. Cohen combines luck egalitarianism with the claim that institutions have no special place in the theory of justice. See *Rescuing Justice and Equality* (Cambridge, Mass.: Harvard University Press, 2008).

tary titles to lapse, it does not wrong those who would otherwise have inherited them, because any entitlement attaching to a hereditary title could only be rightful if authorized by law. In the same way, entailed estates, both within families and within religious orders, can be dissolved, turning them into ordinary private property, because the entailment is, once more, only rightful under law. These arguments are specifically directed at positions that are seldom seriously entertained, and so may seem to be of largely historical interest.

The second set of arguments focuses on the fact that "talent and will" cannot be inherited. Here Kant's argument looks as though it rests on a hypothesis about the extent to which the ability that makes someone suitable for office depends upon genetics or familial factors. So understood, the argument not only violates Kant's own claim to be providing a metaphysics rather than an anthropology of morals but, further, seems oddly unmotivated. Many people claim that intelligence and ability *are* largely hereditary, and many of those who deny such claims concede that they are partly hereditary. Kant explicitly denies that he is making such an argument of prudence.[32] Instead, the argument focuses on right. In arguing that "talent and will" are not such that they can be inherited, he is focused on the juridical concept of inheritance.[33] A parent cannot decide to give his or her child abilities appropriate to public office in the way that a parent can decide to give a child a piece of property. The word "cannot" here is juridical rather than empirical: a parent might well be able to develop some of a child's abilities in particular ways. What the parent cannot do, however, is give a child an entitlement to be qualified for this or that.

The third argument is the most significant, and of the most enduring interest. It focuses on the incoherence of citizens legislating a hereditary nobility. It provides grounds for prohibiting hereditary nobility even if it could be shown that, as a matter of fact, such a system would produce government that was less costly, more efficient, better organized, or less vulnerable to corruption. Citizens still could not give themselves that form of law, because, as Kant puts it, to do so would "throw away their freedom."[34] The freedom at stake is not the ability to pursue advantage

32. 6:329.
33. Ibid.
34. Ibid.

effectively. In favorable circumstances, that ability might be enhanced by a hereditary bureaucracy. Instead, it is the innate right of humanity, that is, the right to independence of the choice of another.

The problem with hereditary nobility is that free citizens could not consent to a system in which the availability of someone to serve in an official capacity depended on an innate legal classification. Such an arrangement is defective from the standpoint of right for two reasons: "What a people (the entire mass of subjects) cannot decide with regard to itself and its fellows, the sovereign cannot also decide with regard to it."[35] The people considered as a collective body ("with regard to itself") cannot agree to limit the available supply of candidates for public office. Second, the people considered severally ("with regard to its fellows") cannot give up the entitlement to be judged on the basis of their own acts. As we saw in Chapters 2 and 7, the entitlement to be judged on the basis of what you have done is an aspect of the innate "right to be beyond reproach," which in turn generates the burden of proof, not only when accused of wrongdoing but when being considered for public office, and so not to be disqualified except on the basis of something you have done. The same right, transposed, shows what is wrong with "the anomaly of subjects who want to be more than citizens of the state, namely born officials (a born professor perhaps.)"[36] The only way someone could be assigned a juridical status is on the basis of an affirmative act. Even the status of candidate for a particular position in government requires a public lawful act. This opens up two possibilities, each of which is contrary to public right: first, the status could be treated as innate, and so antecedent to any act of legislation. That possibility is contrary to public right because of the supremacy of law. The other possibility is that the existence of such qualifications is established through an affirmative piece of legislation. That possibility is contrary to public right because the people considered as a collective body could not impose such a law on itself. Nor could the people considered severally.[37] The result is formal equality of opportunity.

35. Ibid.
36. Ibid.
37. The idea that each person has an equal claim to the Earth's resources looks like a different rationale for the claim that distributive shares should be equal. We have seen that Kant rejects the idea of collective ownership of the Earth in favor of the idea that prior to appropriation, the Earth is occupied disjunctively, but unowned.

Kant's explicit argument focuses on formal equality of opportunity in the distribution of state offices, and so might seem insufficient to ground even formal equality of opportunity in private interaction, permitting, for example, employers or landlords to discriminate on the basis of race, religion, sex, or sexual orientation. Kant makes no explicit mention of such examples, but the argument about the relation between property and poverty can be combined with the argument about formal equality of opportunity to generate a prohibition on such discrimination. The duty to support the poor is grounded in reconciling the enforceability of private property with the rightful honor of each citizen. The state cannot make an arrangement for a person inconsistent with his or her rightful honor. Therefore the state cannot set up a system of property that would allow one person to become fully subject to the choice of another. If the people could not give itself a law mandating the distribution of offices on the basis of birth, then it also could not give itself a law setting up a system of private property that gave private persons the unrestricted power to use their private property to establish one. The word "unrestricted" is essential here, because there is no *a priori* argument to show exactly how such a requirement must be realized, or exactly how far it should go.

The impossibility of a people giving itself a law that mandates full material equality does not, however, stand in conflict with many of the familiar programs that liberal democracies have introduced, such as universal and publicly funded education. Those programs are often characterized as egalitarian in their focus, and there is some truth in that characterization, so long as they are understood as contributing to equal republican citizenship, not as unstable stopping points justified only because they provide a fair approximation of material equality.

Within Kant's framework, the rationale for such programs is different, but both more familiar and more compelling. Education is both an effective means of achieving some basic public purposes, although in principle a contingent one, and also, at the same time, a necessary means of a rightful condition perfecting itself. It is thus required both by a principle of politics, based on empirical features of the human situation and by a principle of right. A principle of politics designed to give effect to the principle of right in a specific society can embrace publicly funded education on two distinct grounds. First of all, an educated population provides advance protection against poverty and the dependence it creates. Publicly funded universal education is an investment in preventing future individual dependence. Second, the state's ability to maintain itself also depends on its maintenance of its own material conditions. Those conditions are varied, but include protecting it "both internally and against external enemies,"[38] and so providing education needed to strengthen and stabilize the economy. (The same rationale could also provide a further ground for public provision of health care, on the ground of its long-term stabilizing effects.) The state also requires an educated population to fill out the narrower aspects of its mandate. Its ability to resolve disputes depends upon private persons trained in the law; its ability to manage the economy so as to sustain itself as a rightful condition depends upon private persons with requisite skills and abilities to develop novel opportunities, and, where necessary, to adapt to change.

Publicly funded education can also be justified more directly in principles of right, both at the level of rights as between private persons and at the level of public right considered more generally. As we saw in Chapter 7, a condition of public right includes your right to speak in your own name, including the right to address not only those near you but the public. Others do not need to pay attention to you, but they must be the ones who decide for themselves whether to pay attention. Further, every citizen must be able to stand on his or her rights, both against other private persons and against the state. Each of these aspects of a rightful condition demands both literacy and civic education.[39] Details of the implementation of this requirement depend on empirical and anthropological factors.

The idea of the original contract provides a further rationale. Education is the principal means through which a rightful condition can bring itself more nearly into conformity with the idea of the original contract, through which the people more fully give laws to themselves. Even if relations between private persons could be rightful under a despotic system

---

38. Kant, *Theory and Practice*, 8:299.

39. In *Political Liberalism*, 199–200, Rawls discusses religious groups that seek to limit the influence of public education on their children. He argues that children of such groups must know their basic constitutional rights. Kant's program in civic education is more ambitious: children must be educated to become capable of making arrangements for themselves.

of government, the form through which the laws are given to them is defective against the standard of the idea of the original contract. A fully republican system of government sees to it that the people rules itself, and taxes itself, through its representatives, but this in turn requires reflective citizens and voters, capable of accessing proposed laws and candidates for public office. Kant remarks that the duty to "make the kind of government suited to the idea of the original contract" can only be discharged in accordance with concepts of right. As a result, even improvements from that perspective must be self-imposed. A change in a state's constitution "cannot consist in the state's reorganizing itself . . . as if it rested on the sovereign's free choice and discretion which kind of constitution it would subject the people to." Such a mode of change "could still do the people a wrong."[40] Constitutional change from above seeks to enable the people to rule themselves by depriving them of the ability to do so. The only way that a rightful condition can improve itself is by cultivating educated and reflective citizens, which is just to say that it can only do so through education.

None of this is to say that public education guarantees reflective voters and citizens; the Kantian claim is only that the only way that the process of the state bringing itself into conformity with concepts of right can be done in accordance with those very concepts is through an educated population that imposes laws on itself. A theory of the legitimate uses of state power cannot guarantee that the uses of those powers will in every instance bring a state more nearly into conformity with right, any more than it can guarantee that legitimate uses of public power will be prudent ones.

For each of these reasons, the state has an interest in seeing to it that its citizens are educated. Like any other legitimate state purpose, public education is an instance of mandatory social cooperation, to which all can be required to contribute. We saw in the last chapter that the basic principle of public provision is that in cases of mandatory cooperation in sustaining a rightful condition, the state must see to it that burdens fall equally. Where cooperation is mandatory, people cannot negotiate specific terms, because none can withdraw from the agreement. In such situations, the

40. 6:340.

only terms to which all could agree are ones that place the burdens of cooperation equally. Applied to the case of education, the legislature alone is competent to determine how exactly to characterize the requisite burdens and corresponding benefits, as well as how to interpret its mandate for equal distribution. These matters are obviously controversial in any particular case. At the same time, the state cannot provide education only to the children of educated parents, even if that would be more efficient. Public provision must satisfy the condition of formal equality of opportunity. Formal equality of opportunity in publicly provided education means education for all.

This rationale for public education provides a further instance of the powers of a public authority, which entitle it to place requirements and regulations on private citizens. Parents can be compelled to send their children to school; citizens can be required to pay taxes to support educational institutions.

Kant thus has the conceptual resources to explain why public provision of the means to full participation in society is both a legitimate state interest and, just as importantly, something that must be provided equally. He can do so without importing any assumption that the state must act in ways that will bring about some state of affairs that can be characterized as desirable apart from it, and without attributing to the state any right or duty to make its citizens happy. Its only duty is to protect their freedom.

VI. Cosmopolitan Right, Cosmopolitanism, and the Scope of a Rightful Condition

Kant's arguments for the duty to support the poor and equality of opportunity focus on the requirements of sustaining a rightful condition. Even if the arguments are accepted on their own terms, they might strike contemporary readers as somehow outdated. The extremes of poverty in the contemporary world are a global problem, which is often thought to have its roots in the unequal opportunities created by a system in which wealthy countries control their own borders. So long as the state is understood as an instrument for achieving purposes that make no essential reference to it, this challenge has merit; Kant does not claim, and could not credibly claim, that a world of separate states is an effective way of meeting needs or equalizing opportunities on a global basis. His argument has a different structure: both equality of opportunity and providing for those who are unable to meet their own needs are internal requirements of sharing a united will. Those outside a particular civil condition do not share a united will with those inside it, so no argument from the preconditions of the united will can lead to any more specific claims. The citizens of a country do not require the permission of outsiders to unite themselves into a rightful condition, or to meet the requirements of their own united will. Thus as a general matter states are entitled to exclude outsiders, because doing so does not interfere with any of their rights. It may disadvantage them, but Kant's account must frame the issue in terms of rights rather than advantages.

Instead of being governed by the public right of a state, relations between a state and human beings who are not its citizens are governed by "Cosmopolitan Right," which is limited to a right of "universal hospitality."[41] Every person is entitled to visit another state, as an incident of each person's right to be "wherever nature or chance has placed him," which itself follows from the "disjunctive" possession of the Earth's surface.[42] Since everyone has a right to occupy that surface, and the surface itself is a closed sphere, human beings must "put up with" being close to each other. A visitor may propose terms of interaction to residents, offering, for example, to engage in commerce with them. Residents are free to accept or reject such invitations as they see fit.[43]

By restricting cosmopolitan right to the right to visit, Kant rejects the more expansive versions of cosmopolitan right that had been put forward in early modern defenses of European colonialism. His rejection is rooted in the distinctively public nature of a rightful condition: individuals who go to another nation must take account of its status as a rightful condition. They are not entitled to regard its inhabitants as a state of nature, and their own settlement of its land as the setting up of a rightful condition. Instead, the host nation alone is entitled to decide whether to accept them as settlers.[44]

---

41. Kant, *Toward a Perpetual Peace*, 8:357.
42. 6:262. See also *Toward a Perpetual Peace*, 8:358.
43. 6:338.
44. 6:266, 6:353.

To give effect to this right of hospitality, states must allow visitors in, allow them the right of transit to otherwise inaccessible states, and enter into arrangements with other states to enable the civil resolution of private disputes about rights between their respective citizens. Such "Private International Law" is a precondition of people being able to have things as their own when they visit other countries.[45] Your claim as a citizen of the world is not to be a citizen of whichever country you choose, let alone of every country, but to visit without being met with hostility, with respect to either your person or your acquired rights.

Restrictions on your right to reside in another state do not compromise your cosmopolitan right, because they limit only your ability to achieve what you wish, rather than your ability to use what you have to set and pursue your own purposes. Kant's equation of need with mere wish explains why the fact that some countries are much wealthier than others does not, without more, constitute a wrong against the residents or citizens of the poorer countries.[46] Although citizenship is a hereditary status, it is not objectionable, so long as every human being is a citizen of some country. The cosmopolitan analogue of the duty to support the poor is not world citizenship, but the division of the world into states in a way that guarantees that each person has a home state to return to.

The right to refuse visitors or attach terms to their visits has one internal limit: a state can only turn a foreigner away if it can do so "without destroying him." In ordinary circumstances, to be refused entry to a country is simply to need to return to some other country, however difficult your existence there might be. The state, through its officials, can decide whether to admit you. Whatever decision they make is fully consistent with right, provided only that it is open to you to return to your home state. Your home state is the place on the Earth's surface where you can be in a rightful condition with others. It is also the place where you can demand as a matter of right to have some space that you do no wrong by occupying, and to the support of your fellow citizens if you cannot provide for yourself.

---

45. 6:344.

46. If the history of colonialism has produced the disparity, there may be grounds for reparation, but that is not the issue here. On Kant's opposition to colonialism, see 6:266, and Sankar Muthu, *Enlightenment against Empire* (Princeton: Princeton University Press, 2003).

If your own state will not take you back, because it has stripped you of your citizenship, or you cannot safely return because its rulers are making war on their own people in some other way, the right of any other state to exclude you runs up against its own internal limit. Your ability to do anything at all—to use your own bodily powers or whatever personal property you have with you—is entirely subject to the choice of the officials of the state you seek to enter. As a foreigner, you do not need to share a general will with the officials, or with the legislature that sets their mandate, but any power they exercise over you must finally be consistent with your innate right of humanity in your own person, which includes the right to "disjunctive" possession of the Earth's surface, the right to be wherever nature or chance has placed you. Just as property in land is consistent with this innate right provided that it does not give another person the right to decide whether you may occupy space, so, too, the establishment of national borders is consistent with your innate right provided that you have someplace else to go.[47] Only if you have nowhere else to go does the state's right to restrict your entry make you subject to the choice of another. So the officials have to let you stay, simply in your capacity as a citizen of the world. Once you are in, you are subject to their laws, and so to the preconditions of lawmaking powers, even to the point of being provided for if you are unable to provide for yourself, and being entitled to become an active citizen rather than merely a passive resident.[48]

VII. Conclusion

The state enters Kant's account as the solution to problems of private interaction, but it can only solve those problems by occupying a distinctively public standpoint, through which its acts can be acts of everyone. That requirement, in turn, generates novel powers and obligations: the power to tax and redistribute to prevent enforceable property rights from

---

47. See John A. Simmons, "Human Rights and World Citizenship," in his *Justification and Legitimacy* (Cambridge: Cambridge University Press, 2001), 195–196.

48. The dependence of the right of hospitality on violence in your home state helps to make sense of two of the perplexing features of refugee law: the distinction between economic migrants and refugees, and the "safe third country" provisions. The cruelty and hypocrisy with which these criteria are applied in practice make them neither irrational nor illusory.

generating new forms of dependence, and the obligation to provide formal equality of opportunity and public education. These novel powers and obligations are grounded in the public character of a rightful condition, rather than in either human needs or the private duties of human beings among themselves. Although these powers are ultimately grounded in each person's innate right of humanity, they are internal requirements of a rightful condition and do not apply outside of one.

Despite Kant's vigorous defense of a world made up of separate states, each entitled to accept outsiders only as visitors, he also provides an account of the right of refuge as a right of world citizenship. If you cannot go to your home state without being met with violence, any place of safety becomes your home, because, as Robert Frost put it, "they have to take you in."

CHAPTER 10

Public Right IV: Punishment

KANT'S DISCUSSION of punishment has probably generated more scholarly attention than any other aspect of his legal and political thought. Much of that attention has focused on Kant's endorsement of a retributive principle; recent discussions, drawing on a groundbreaking article by Sharon Byrd,[1] have sought to integrate Kant's retributive principle with his explicit references to deterrence. A successful integration of deterrence and retribution is of interest both to Kant scholarship and to legal philosophy more generally, in that it promises to bridge the divide between the two intuitive ideas that animate both popular and scholarly discussions of punishment. One of these says that punishing criminals is a way of preventing crime, the other that criminals should be punished because they have committed crimes. Many have sought to make these ideas consistent with one another.[2] My aim, which I will claim that Kant shares,

---

1. B. Sharon Byrd, "Kant's Theory of Punishment: Deterrence in Its Threat, Retribution in Its Execution," *Law and Philosophy* 8 (1989): 151–200.

2. H. L. A. Hart's theory of the criminal law is a clear example; many discussions of Kant's theory in the wake of Byrd's article provide others. See, for example, Thomas E. Hill Jr., "Kant's Theory of Punishment: A Coherent Mix of Deterrence and Retribution," in *Respect, Pluralism, and Justice: Kantian Perspectives* (Oxford: Oxford University Press, 2000),

is more ambitious: to argue that, properly understood, each of them requires the other.

Both deterrence and retribution are sometimes conceived as extrinsic goals that a system of punishment should try to achieve: either the reduction in certain kinds of harmful acts or the matching of suffering to wickedness. Each of these results could conceivably be brought about in ways other than a legal institution of punishment. Each might also, at least in principle, justify punishing someone who had not broken any law. The conflict between these instrumentalist versions of both retribution and deterrence is yet another instance of the antinomy generated by instrumentalist conceptions of law. Both suppose that the legal institution is in the service of results that make no reference to legal institutions as such. A Kantian does not need to deny that both the prevention of crime and the matching of virtue to happiness[3] (and so, conversely, of suffering to wickedness) are valuable results, but neither could justify the use of force except as authorized by law. Unless the right to punish is inherent in the idea of a rightful condition, no good consequences could authorize it. If it is inherent, its justification does not depend on those consequences. A Kantian account must analyze punishment as a fundamental aspect of legality, and show how each of deterrence and retribution is partially constitutive of a system of equal freedom under law.

In the Introduction to the *Doctrine of Right,* Kant identifies right with the authorization to use coercion. We saw in earlier chapters that Kant does not understand coercion primarily in terms of the making and carrying out of threats, but instead in terms of reciprocal limits on freedom. Although Kant's account of punishment does focus on the making and carrying out of threats, that focus is another instance of the more general Kantian claim that the authorization to coerce follows from the fact that coercion can be understood as a hindrance to freedom, and the enforcement of rights as the hindering of those hindrances. I will explain Kant's

---

173–199. Although Byrd has inspired compatibility accounts, her view provides the resources for reading Kant's own account as making the two aspects of punishment equivalent.

3. In the *Critique of Practical Reason,* 5:110–114, Kant identifies happiness in accordance with virtue as the "highest good," the hope for which should structure all moral thought. But he denies that any person is entitled to take it upon him- or herself to bring about such matching. See Hill, *Respect, Pluralism, and Justice,* 186–188.

conception of retributivism as an expression of this idea, arguing that punishment is nothing more than the supremacy of law; I will bring deterrence under the same principle, arguing that the supremacy of law requires that the prospect of enforcement be capable of guiding conduct. I will show how Kant generates each of these aspects of punishment as an *a priori* feature of public law, rather than as a response to potentially destabilizing features of human nature.

Deterrence and retribution are united through Kant's view of punishment as something that can only be done by a superior; he also emphasizes the way in which the distinctive feature of crime is the way in which the criminal seeks to exempt himself from the law. Bringing these strands together, I will argue that the criminal exempts him- or herself from public law, and is liable to punishment simply because public law cannot permit unilateral exemptions. Punishment is the guarantee that public law is effective in space and time. The deterrent effect of the prospect of punishment is not something separate from this guarantee. Instead, for public law to be effective in space and time is for it to provide assurance to all by creating an incentive to compliance by announcing in advance that attempts to violate it will fail. The threat of punishment is thus the announcement that public law will remain supreme. The prospective threat and retrospective applications of punishment are thus not an aim to be pursued and an extrinsic constraint on its pursuit; they are equivalent.

Before developing my own account, I should briefly situate it in relation to Byrd's important discussion. Those familiar with it will recognize significant similarities between our accounts. Like Byrd, I understand Kant's treatment of punishment in the context of his broader concerns about legality, and thus accept her claim that "punishment as coercive deterrence follows from the necessary nature of law within Kant's theory of justice."[4] I also agree with her that it is a nonaccidental feature of punishment that it prospectively serves to guide conduct, and much of my argument will develop these ideas in ways that I take to be consistent with Byrd's treatment of them. Aside from differences of emphasis, my remain-

---

4. Byrd, "Kant's Theory of Punishment," 153.

ing disagreement with her may be largely verbal.[5] It concerns her further claim that the deterrent aspects of punishment require an instrumental analysis. Byrd characterizes civil society "as a means necessary to the end of individual freedom,"[6] punishment as "instrumental in nature,"[7] and criminal law as "an instrument to preserve civil society."[8] To characterize something as a means or instrument suggests that it serves to achieve something that might exist apart from it. Where Byrd writes of means or instruments, I will argue that Kant posits an identity: civil society *is* the systematic realization of individual freedom, required *a priori* "however well disposed and right-loving human beings might be."[9] In turn, the criminal law is an integral part of civil society, for it is nothing more than the supremacy of public law against opposing individual wills, should there turn out to be any. The enforcement of its prohibitions is itself equivalent to the prohibitions themselves.

I. Wrongs and Remedies

The idea that enforcement upholds a right that has been violated reflects the specific sense in which rights both are and are not vulnerable to wrongdoing. A wrong is, on the one hand, a violation of a right, and rights are, as reciprocal limits on freedom, themselves vulnerable to violation. This vulnerability is not merely factual and empirical, although its particulars will often have a factual and empirical component. In Chapter 2, we considered H. L. A. Hart's suggestion that law and morality overlap in their content, prohibiting, for example, crimes against persons and property, because of the specific facts of human vulnerability and need.[10] We

---

5. Byrd's article has generated its own literature. For example, Jean-Christophe Merle criticizes Byrd on the grounds that her conception of deterrence is insufficiently independent of her account of retribution. See "A Kantian Critique of Kant's Theory of Punishment," *Law and Philosophy* 19 (2000): 311–338. What Merle sees as a defect, I regard as a strength.

6. Byrd, "Kant's Theory of Punishment," 154.

7. Ibid., 156.

8. Ibid., 198.

9. 6:312.

10. Hart, "Positivism and the Separation of Law and Morals," *Harvard Law Review* 71 (1958): 622–623.

saw that for Kant, the basic law of persons and property does not depend on factual vulnerability to harm or injury, but rather on juridical vulnerability to wrongdoing, that is, to the violation of reciprocal limits on freedom. Hart's invulnerable beings could commit batteries against each other, if one were to touch another without permission. They could also commit wrongs against the property of others. Hart's empirical speculations are potentially relevant to the *inclination* of such beings to commit crimes, but the ground for prohibiting crime is not that it is tempting, but that it is wrongful. Rational beings who occupy space are vulnerable to wrong if they interact.

At the same time, although right is by its nature vulnerable to wrong, it is also, in another sense, immune to it. If one person wrongs another, the wrongdoer deprives the victim of something to which the latter is entitled. The right, however, survives. As we saw in Chapter 3, in simple cases of conversion or theft, the fact that a thief takes your book deprives you of physical possession of it, but the thief does not deprive you of your right to it. That is why you have a claim to recover it from the thief. If the thief destroys the book, you have a claim to damages, precisely because your right survives the wrong against it. The thief takes what is yours willfully, but if another person destroys your book wrongfully but not willfully, that person also fails to destroy your right to the book. By contrast, if your book is destroyed without any wrong, there is no longer an object to which you have a right, and so you have no claim against any other person.

In Private Right, Kant treats the first aspect of enforcement as so obvious as to barely merit mention. In distinguishing the payment of damages from the acquisition of something new from another person by contract, Kant remarks that if another "has wronged me and I have a right to demand compensation from him, by this I will still only preserve what is mine undiminished but will not acquire more than what I previously had."[11] The compensation simply gives me back what I had all along, because my right to what I had survives any wrongs committed against it. If I damage your vase, you do not cease to have a right to it. So, too, if I

---

11. 6:271.

break your arm: you still have, as against me, a right to your arm, intact. That is just to say that you have a right to cancel the consequences of my wrong, and so a right to compel me to compensate you by giving you back what you had before. The prospect of liability may well lead me to watch what I do around your vase or arm in future. The basis of liability, however, is just your right to what you had all along. Damages make that right effective in space and time, precisely because the object of the right was your power to determine the use of that thing in space and time. You had a right that your vase be subject to your choice; I violated that right in space and time, and so can be compelled, consistent with our respective freedom, to restore to you your effective right in space and time. If my wrongdoing has destroyed the object of your right, the payment of money does so because money is, as Kant elsewhere explains, the "universal *means by which men exchange their industriousness with one another.*"[12] That is, it can be used to acquire objects from others with which to set and pursue your purposes.[13]

The combination of vulnerability to wrongdoing and immunity from it is a reflection of Kant's central idea that laws of right are normative laws of freedom governing beings in space and time. The *normative* basis for supposing that we have the familiar juridical obligations to respect the rights of others that we do—to avoid interfering with other people's bodies, keep off their property, and honor our contracts—is to be found in the directly normative arguments of the Introduction and Private Right. Those normative arguments in turn provide the basis of our entitlement to suppose that human bodies, the bits of matter that make up property, and agreements fall under laws of freedom. You can compel me to pay you, because in so doing you simply get back what was yours all along: my failure to pay hinders your freedom by depriving you of something to which you have a right; coercing me to pay gives you the very thing to which you had a right, thereby hindering my hindrance of your freedom.

---

12. 6:287.

13. I develop a Kantian account of private damages in detail in "As If It Had Never Happened," *William and Mary Law Review* 48 (2007): 1957–1995.

II. Punishment

I now want to explain how the formal structure just outlined applies to Kant's account of punishment. A crime violates a public law; as such it is legally void. The commission of a crime neither changes the law nor exempts the criminal from its application. Instead, the law remains normatively unchanged—it still governs conduct. Yet the criminal has factually violated the law; punishment makes the law remain effective in space and time. The law remains effective if it is supreme. Kant contends that punishment is something that only a superior can do to a subordinate.[14] The rationale for punishment is simply the upholding of the relation between superior and subordinate, that is, between the state, as representative of public law, and a private citizen.

We saw in Chapter 7 that the legal system constitutes the people, which Kant defines as a "multitude of human beings" considered as a unity. They are unified through public law, which alone can provide an omnilateral standpoint from which reciprocal limits on conduct are authorized on behalf of all. The authorization of those limits includes an authorization of their enforcement, both prospectively—what Kant calls "protectively"—and retrospectively, that is, punitively. These two authorizations are not separate components, analytically detachable from each other. Neither is justified by hypotheses about how dreadful conditions would be in its absence. As we saw in Chapters 6 and 7, *positive* law, including institutions of legislation, adjudication, and enforcement, makes private rights effective in space and time, by creating a standpoint through which omnilateral public law replaces unilateral private choice. Public law constitutes a system of equal freedom in which no person is subject to the choice of another by generating omnilateral institutions to create, apply, and enforce law.

The possibility of enforcement is crucial to this account, because enforcement hinders hindrances to freedom, both prospectively and retrospectively. We saw in Chapter 6 that public law makes private rights conclusive by providing everyone with assurance that others will comply; it assures everyone that others will have an incentive—a reason for taking an

14. 6:347.

interest in an action—to comply. A parallel point applies to public right: institutions make public law effective protectively and prospectively by providing an incentive to conform with law; that is, they prevent people from violating the law. They do so *retrospectively* in those cases in which wrong is committed, and the same law guarantees that the wrongful acts do not change the rights of their victims or the entitlement of the legal system to govern conduct. The prospective and retrospective fit together because the external incentive to conform with the law is just the law's guarantee that any violation will be legally nothing, its guarantee that rather than earning the criminal the exemption from the law that he seeks, it will exclude him from the aspect of the law that he has violated. By announcing in advance that the law will make a wrong fail, the law also provides a prospective incentive against it by announcing that the criminal will be burdened in the very way he hopes to succeed.

If people were to be so "well disposed and right-loving" that they had no inclination to violate the law, the incentives provided by law would be empirically unnecessary, but they would still be legally required.

The prospective and retrospective applications of public law are thus not an aim and a constraint on its pursuit, in the way that Hart, for example, supposes that the aim of punishment is to discourage crime, and the principle of its distribution is to make the law a system of individual choices.[15] Instead, the threat is one of retributive punishment—that the supremacy of the law will be upheld. Announcing penalties in advance enables the law to guide conduct; carrying out the threatened punishment upholds the law even when it is violated.[16] These two aspects of

---

15. H. L. A. Hart, "Legal Responsibility and Excuses," in his *Punishment and Responsibility* (Oxford: Oxford University Press, 1968), 28–53.

16. I am not sure if I am disagreeing with Byrd here. She distinguishes her way of combining deterrence and retribution from Hart's distinction between the justifying aim of punishment and a principle governing its distribution. However, her discussion of the retributive principle as a limitation on the ways in which crime prevention can be pursued sometimes presents it as a limitation on the pursuit of an independent public purpose. See, for example, "Kant's Theory of Punishment," 195. Drawing on Meir Dan-Cohen's distinction between "decision rules" and "conduct rules," Byrd suggests that the deterrent aspect of punishment serves to guide conduct of citizens by threatening unwelcome consequences should they violate the law, but the retrospective and retributive aspect of the criminal law guides officials in dealing with those who have committed crimes (Dan-Cohen, "Decision Rules and Conduct

punishment are not only mutually supporting but mutually constituting. That is why each can be represented as prior to the other. The retrospective application appears conceptually prior to the prospective, because it determines the content of the threat that can be made; the prospective application appears conceptually prior because retrospective application does nothing more than uphold the law's entitlement to guide conduct externally.

In this section I will begin with the retrospective aspect of punishment. The basic idea is simple, but each part of it requires explanation: the criminal, through her crime, chooses to exempt herself from one or more of the prohibitions contained in public law. She thus asserts a form of what Kant calls "wild, lawless freedom." The crime does not change the law normatively—violations do not change what people are entitled to do—but it is a case in which the law's guidance of conduct is ineffective. In every case of a crime, the law has partially failed to create a system of equal freedom by constraining conduct. The punishment restores the supremacy of the law because it deprives the criminal's deed of its effect. It does so by turning the criminal's maxim—the principle though which he makes "such a crime his rule"[17]—against him: where he sought exemption, he receives exclusion, so that the law remains supreme.

III. Crime and Public Wrong

Kant's discussion of punishment is contained in a "General Remark," the subject of which is "the effects with regard to rights that follow from the nature of the civil union."[18] Punishment is discussed in the fifth of either five or six subsections to the General Remark. The other subsections

---

Rules: On Acoustic Separation in Criminal Law," *Harvard Law Review* 97 [1984]: 625-679). Byrd writes, "Similarly punishment is *threatened* to induce compliance with criminal law norms or to deter violations, but is *executed* according to the demands of justice stated in the principle of retribution, because the actor violated the norm." Although the deterrent threat and the retributive principle are addressed to different persons, it does not follow that they are normatively distinct principles in the way that rules of conduct and excusing conditions arguably are.

17. 6:321.
18. 6:318.

contain the prohibition on revolution, the state's role as the "supreme proprietor" of all land, the duty to support the poor, the power to grant offices, and the power to regulate immigration and emigration. We have seen the basis of some of these already, and will turn to the issue of revolution in the next chapter. For now, a further unifying structure is significant: each contains an example of the supremacy of the legal order. In each case, the legal system contains an answer to those that challenge its supremacy. The revolutionary claims to speak for the people, but not through its institutions, and the prohibition on revolution turn on the requirement that the people can be a people only by giving itself laws through institutions. The state's claim to be supreme proprietor of the land overrides the competing claims of corporations, churches, and estates to hold land in perpetuity independently of public law, and entitles it to burden private claims in order to uphold the systematic requirements of a rightful condition. The public law duty to support the poor displaces the power of churches to claim that as their vocation, and relegates them to the status of purely private associations with no political authority. Offices are distributed by the state because inherited offices violate the "natural division" between sovereign and people. The state's power to regulate immigration reflects the priority of public law over any claim of an ethnic or linguistic group that claims to be prior to the state.[19]

Kant's engagement with questions of crime and punishment must be understood as an answer to a different, individual challenge to the supremacy of public law. The criminal is punished because he has committed a crime. A crime, in turn, is a "transgression of public law that makes someone who commits it unfit to be a citizen."[20] In a footnote to his discussion of revolution, Kant explains that "any transgression of the law can and must be explained only as arising from the maxim of the criminal (to make such a crime his rule); for if it were to derive from a sensible impulse, he would not be committing it as a *free* being and it could not be imputed to him."[21] The criminal's maxim is the rule on which he acts,

---

19. Thus Kant argues that the lord of the land has the right to "encourage *immigration* and settlement by foreigners (colonists), even though his native subjects might look askance at this" (6:338).
20. 6:331.
21. 6:321.

and, like any maxim, must have the form "use these means in order to achieve this end." The wrongfulness focuses on the means the criminal has used, because external wrongdoing always consists in using prohibited means: private wrongs against person and property involve either using means that belong to another or acting in ways that deprive another person of means to which he or she is entitled. Kant's use of the vocabulary of maxims to make this point might suggest that something more than means is at issue. But Kant's elucidation of the concept of right in the Introduction to the *Doctrine of Right* makes it clear that "no account at all is taken of the *matter* of choice, that is, the end each has in mind with the object he wants."[22] Thus a crime is objectionable from the standpoint of right purely on the basis of the means that are used, regardless of the end pursued. Kant's examples of crime all turn on the use of wrongful means: theft, murder, burglary, rape, and counterfeiting;[23] in each case, the wrongfulness of the crime is identified through the means used rather than the end pursued. In each case, the criminal uses means that he knows to be prohibited. The criminal's ends are ordinary, and might be pursued in other contexts through acceptable means. The use of those prohibited means (with the exception of some instances of counterfeiting)[24] also typically wrongs someone in particular, and the victims would also have a private right of action against the criminal. But the distinctively criminal aspect of the wrong is the use of publicly prohibited means.

The criminal uses means that are inconsistent with a system of equal freedom, and that inconsistency provides the grounds for prohibiting those crimes: theft, murder, and counterfeiting are inconsistent with a system of equal freedom under universal law, and so they must be prohibited under public law. Kant writes that "counterfeiting money or bills of

---

22. 6:230.

23. Counterfeiting contrasts with "fraud in buying and selling, when committed in such a way that the other could detect it" (6:331). The latter is merely a single wrongful transaction; counterfeiting of money or bills of exchange is inconsistent with the very possibility of universal exchange, because money is never particular.

24. Rousseau gives the example of a person who gives counterfeit money as a gift. The recipient is not deprived of anything, and so is not wronged, but the counterfeiter still does wrong. See Jean-Jacques Rousseau, *Reveries of a Solitary Walker,* trans. Peter France (New York: Penguin, 1984), 65.

exchange, theft and robbery, and the like are public crimes, because they endanger the commonwealth and not just an individual person."[25] The emphasis on the danger to the commonwealth recurs in his discussion of theft, when he writes, "Whoever steals makes the property of everyone else insecure."[26] These claims all go to the grounds for prohibiting theft, counterfeiting, and the like: they are inconsistent with the possibility of property; since part of the state's role is to make property claims conclusive, it must prohibit crimes against property. None of these enters Kant's account as an empirical claim about the inevitable or even probable effects of crime. Instead, they enter as claims about the normative structure of property. As we saw in Chapter 4, a property right is a right to an object that can be physically separate from its owner but still subject to the owner's choice. Theft violates the basic norm of property: the thief seeks to remove an object from the owner's choice merely by physically separating it from the owner. If you were entitled to do that, there could be no property. That is why theft is a wrong against the owner whose property is stolen.

The ground for *punishing* theft, however, is not the fact that the thief chooses to violate the basic norm of property. Instead, the grounds for punishment reflect the fact that his choosing to do so must be understood as choosing to exempt himself from the authority of the law. Kant writes that "any transgression of the law can and must be explained only as arising from a maxim of the criminal (to make such a crime his rule)." His rule may be one of exemption, "without formally renouncing obedience to the law." Such self-exemption need not expressly repudiate the law in the way that Kant supposes that a revolutionary or regicide does—it is not, as Kant says "*diametrically* opposed to the law."[27]

The criminal's choice of means is inconsistent with the rule of law and so with a civil condition, because she unilaterally determines which means are available to her, rather than accepting the omnilateral judgment of public law. She thereby asserts a claim to what Kant elsewhere calls "wild, lawless freedom." The inconsistency parallels the inconsistency between

25. 6:331.
26. 6:333.
27. 6:321.

theft and property, but does not merely replicate it. The structure of a civil condition is that omnilateral public law replaces unilateral private judgment. Through their representatives, the citizens as a collective body give themselves laws, together. No private person is entitled to make, apply, or enforce laws. Only officials acting in their official capacities are entitled do so. Much of the matter of these laws is dictated by innate right or private right: public law "contains no further or other duties of human beings among themselves than can be conceived" in a state of nature; "the laws of the condition of public right accordingly have to do only with the rightful form of their association."[28] In making crime her rule, the criminal violates not only the "duties of human beings among themselves" that make up the *matter* of most familiar crimes, but also the rightful *form* of public law, because the criminal's "rule" is one of unilateral exemption from omnilateral law. If unilateral choice could cancel omnilateral law, there could be no omnilateral law.[29]

Crime is a public wrong because of its inconsistency with the claim of public law to protect those rights. In the concluding note to Private Right, Kant introduces a distinction between what is formally wrong and what is materially wrong.[30] His immediate concern is with acts that are formally but not materially wrong, such as remaining outside a rightful condition. His analysis of crime shows that some acts can be both *formally* and materially wrong.[31] Formal wrongs "take away any validity from the concept

---

28. 6:307.

29. It is perhaps worth contrasting Kant's view with the prominent version of retributivism developed by Herbert Morris. Morris portrays the criminal as taking unfair advantage of the self-restraint of others by exempting himself from a rule that others follow. See Morris, "Persons and Punishment," *Monist* 52 (1968): 475–501. Kant sees that the rule of law is not a set of discreet burdens that people accept in return for their expected benefits; it is just the condition of the consistent enjoyment of freedom.

30. I am grateful to Jacob Weinrib for convincing me of the importance of the concept of formal wrongdoing throughout the *Doctrine of Right,* both in general and in the discussion of punishment.

31. Kant uses the distinction between form and matter at several different levels. Every material wrong can also be characterized in terms of its formal aspect. In the case of theft, the material wrong is taking a particular piece of property belonging to another person. Its formal aspect consists in acting on a maxim that is inconsistent with property as such. More generally the form of private right does not attend to the matter of the things to which private persons have rights, but only to the form of their interaction, so that as far as the principles of private

of right itself and hand everything over to savage violence, as if by law, and so subvert the right of human beings as such."[32] The right of human beings as such is the right to freedom with others under universal law; the repudiation of the possibility of reciprocal limits on freedom in favor of "wild, lawless freedom" is contrary to it. The criminal "hands everything over to savage violence" in the same way that the thief "makes the property of everyone else insecure." Both the criminal wrongfulness of his act and the ground for punishment rest on formal aspects of his rule of action: the incompatibility of theft with property grounds criminalizing theft as a matter of public law; its incompatibility with publicly given law grounds its punishment. A crime is a violation of the very possibility of a *system* of equal freedom, because the criminal becomes a law unto himself. His principle of action permits him to exempt himself from the public legal regulation of conduct and resolution of disputes. As such, he is like the person who chooses to remain in a state of nature: he asserts his own "wild, lawless freedom" against the claims of the state, even if he does so "by way of *default* only."[33] So a crime is wrongful both against its victim and against the public: it is inconsistent with the rights that private persons have against each other; *and* it is inconsistent with the right of the citizens, considered as a collective body, to uphold their respective freedom by giving themselves laws together. Every crime will, by its nature, "endanger the commonwealth,"[34] because the commonwealth itself is nothing more than the possibility of the citizens giving themselves laws together.

That is why the criminal is discussed together with the revolutionary, the entailed estate, the church, the hereditary nobility, and even the people, considered culturally rather than juridically. Each claims a priority over public law, and so a wild, lawless freedom within a specific domain,

---

right go, everyone is entitled to keep what is his or hers, regardless what it might (materially) be, and anyone who deprives another of what is his or hers commits a (formal) wrong. A similar hierarchy of formal/material distinctions can be found in the *Critique of Pure Reason*, A266/B322, and in Kant's *Lectures on Logic*, ed. J. Michael Young (Cambridge: Cambridge University Press, 1992), 75, 589, 598, and 616.

32. 6:308.
33. 6:321.
34. 6:331.

because each supposes that the principles of social order should be something independent of principles of the rule of law.

IV. Hindering a Formal Wrong

If every crime is wrongful because of its incompatibility with the form of public lawgiving, it can only be hindered through a response that upholds the form of public lawgiving. In the case of the particular wrong against some victim, it is up to the victim who has been wronged to decide whether to claim a private remedy—whether, that is, to stand on his or her rights. The wrong against the form of lawgiving requires a different public and mandatory response, rather than a discretionary private one.

A civil union enables people to give themselves coercive laws together. The only way they can do so, however, is by giving laws to themselves externally. In characterizing the executive power of the state as "irresistible,"[35] Kant is making a conceptual claim about the nature of executive power. Anything you do contrary to sovereignty is without legal effect. If you wrongfully take something from another person, it does not become yours, and damages restore it to its original possessor. The state prevents you from exempting yourself from the law by providing you with a contrary incentive; if you ignore the incentive, the state restores its own authority by hindering your hindrance of the system of equal freedom by removing the legal effect of your exemption.

Normatively, the law remains supreme even in the face of violation. Kant's technical vocabulary places norms in the noumenal realm, in the sense that they are outside of space and time. His claim that the law necessarily survives its violation noumenally does not rest on any assumptions about some other, parallel world in which all laws are always obeyed. Instead, it is an application of the more general feature of norms: they govern what ought to happen rather than what does happen. You have a right to your pen, even if I take it out of your possession, and the state has the right to prohibit theft, even if I steal it. Just as your right to your pen—your entitlement that my conduct be restricted by your normative claim—survives its violation, so too does the state's right to tell me what to do—

---

35. 6:316.

its entitlement to restrict my conduct by its normative claims. Empirically, however, a hindrance to freedom can be hindered by an equal and opposite force. Punishment hinders the juridical effect of wrongdoing by upholding the aspect of right from which the criminal sought to exempt himself.

The analysis of upholding the supremacy of law in the face of exemption works most straightforwardly in Kant's example of theft. The thief exempts herself from public law by exempting herself from the law's claim to regulate property. The way to make it the case that the crime did not change the law is to turn the criminal's own maxim against her. Having sought to exempt herself from the rule of law as realized in the law of property, the criminal finds herself excluded from the system of property, prohibited from having any external objects subject to her choice.

If the nature of crime needs to be understood formally rather than materially, so does Kant's retributive claim that "whatever undeserved evil you inflict on another within the people, that you inflict upon yourself."[36] As a result, the thief must be understood not merely to have deprived some particular person of some particular piece of property, nor even simply to have acted contrary to the system of property. Instead, she has acted contrary to the people's power to give themselves laws. She made self-exemption her rule by making the violation of a particular public law her rule; her act must be made into an act of self-exclusion from that aspect of the system of public law from which she exempted herself.

Normatively, the law survives any wrong against it. In the world of space and time, however, the wrong has an effect, and the only way to restore that supremacy of law is to restore its effectiveness, so that the violation is without legal effect. The wrongdoer violated the law by violating some particular prohibition; to restore the supremacy of the law, that very prohibition must be upheld. The crime is an illicit exemption from an aspect of the law's supremacy; the punishment excludes the criminal from that very aspect of its protection.

The thief's specific maxim—the specific way in which she uses prohibited means—must be turned against her because an individually asserted unilateral exemption from the law is juridically impossible: a per-

---

36. 6:332.

son cannot act so as to exempt herself from the law. Instead, she must be taken to have chosen something else. Her maxim is one that is contrary to freedom under public law. The only way the state can recognize and respond to her maxim is by treating it as its own mirror image, as the criminal's exclusion of herself from the very same public law. The thief's specific maxim is of the form "all property is entirely subject to my choice," that is, "there is no property to me." The punishment inverts the maxim from a challenge to the authority of public law to an exclusion from it: the thief is held to the implications of her own maxim, and so is excluded from the system of property: there is property, but not for her. Property persists, because the criminal cannot eliminate it unilaterally, but she can exclude herself from it through her unilateral act. In willing that the property of another be subject to her choice, the criminal is taken to have willed that there be no property for her, since her maxim is inconsistent with the possibility of property. The use of force that responds to this must be the objectification of the maxim, the turning of the criminal's maxim against itself. The criminal wants to be exempt from the rule of property by making the law of property nothing to others; the punishment exempts her in a different sense by making the law of property nothing to her. She makes a rule only for herself; the law responds by limiting its application to her alone. Her hindrance to freedom is thus hindered by sealing it off.

What exactly does it mean to exclude the criminal from the system of property? It would not be enough for the thief to lose whatever property she had. That would be a merely material response to a formal wrong; it would restrict her participation in the system of property by its particulars, and so would not address the formal incompatibility of her self-exemption with the law. Instead, the exclusion requires that no external object be subject to her choice; she would not be allowed to acquire anything and would only be able to use things with the permission of others. Thus others determine the purposes for which her powers can be used.

The example of theft makes Kant's account of punishment analytically clear, but it is potentially unrepresentative. It is one thing to say that the thief exempted herself from public law in general by violating the law of property in particular, and so is excluded from the system of property, unable to own anything. Other wrongs violate aspects of public law that are more difficult to represent as self-contained components of it. A person who commits a crime against another person's body violates the victim's innate right; public law protects innate right. The person who violates another's innate right cannot be excluded from the "system" of personal protection, and turned into an outlaw, whom others may attack at will.[37] Crimes against persons can only be punished in a way that avoids making "the humanity in the person suffering it into something abominable."[38] Conversely, the criminal cannot be subjected to a punishment that is inconsistent with the humanity of the official carrying it out. "Thus the principle of *lex talionis* must be honored in its spirit."[39]

Kant gives little guidance as to how this might be done, but the formal nature of criminal wrongdoing generates the perspective from which this issue can be addressed. Because every crime is formally a self-exemption from public law, exclusion from the system of freedom must be the appropriate punishment. The seemingly self-contained nature of property is not only unrepresentative but misleading in this respect. The underlying retributive principle requires excluding the wrongdoer from participation in the civil society constituted by public law insofar as he has sought to exempt himself from some aspect of public law. Every form of punishment will thus be a form of exclusion from full participation in civil society.

The "spirit" of *lex talionis* is thus the requirement that self-exemption be hindered by exclusion. Indeed, as Kant's own discussion of theft makes clear, the only way to exclude someone from the system of *property* is to physically confine him. The most obvious way to exclude someone from a system of *freedom* is also through physical confinement.[40] The appropriate quantum of confinement—the length of the prison term—must

---

37. In one troubling passage, Kant is prepared to grant the ruler the power to exile a subject and make him a *vogelfrei* (an outlaw who is "free as a bird") within the state's boundaries (6:338).

38. 6:333.

39. 6:363.

40. In principle, a monetary fine could also serve as a punishment, insofar as money is the general *"means by which men exchange their industriousness with one another."* As such it can be treated as an approximation to a measure of purposiveness. Kant is wary of fines, however, precisely because of the role of money in exchange, which might lead someone to regard it as merely a price, and so as potentially worth paying. See 6:287 and 6:332.

be proportional to the gravity of the wrong. In assessing the gravity of the wrong, the particular public law the criminal violated provides an appropriate measure, for the material wrong is the precise manner in which the criminal has committed the formal wrong. Thus the principle of *lex talionis* must *always* be honored in its spirit.[41] The particularity of the criminal's choice of means is only significant inasmuch as it is the material way in which the criminal sought to exempt himself from public law. Excluding him from participation in the system of freedom created by a rightful condition addresses the public aspect of the wrongfulness; the particularity of the matter can only be specified in light of it. Kant's preferred example of property illustrates this point: the thief is excluded from property by excluding him from freedom under law.

V. Deterrence

Punishment upholds the supremacy of the law in space and time. Just as an individual right is normatively immune from wrongdoing, so, too, is the rule of public law. However, it is empirically vulnerable to wrongdoing, in the sense that a crime violates the law's supremacy in space and time because every time a crime is committed, public law has failed to guide conduct. As Kant observes, the criminal is punished *"because he has committed a crime."*[42] I now want to argue that the law's supremacy is nothing more than its ability to guide conduct prospectively. Your private rights are effective in space and time just in case the things to which you have a right are subject to your exclusive choice. Public law is effective in space and time just in case it hinders those acts inconsistent with it, by shaping conduct prospectively.

Public law can guide conduct externally only by providing incentives to conformity. The incentives are external, and indeed, the only possible incentive is that of having actions that hinder the system of freedom them-

---

41. The supposition that a normative theory of punishment must generate a mechanism for determining proportional punishments is yet another instance of the instrumentalist view that supposes that the only task of legal institutions is to discover something that can be specified without reference to them. For Kant, a scale of seriousness of crimes requires legal development.

42. 6:331.

selves hindered. Ordinarily, a criminal takes an interest in committing a crime in response to some incentive, that is, some hope of achieving something. The criminal law hinders the crime prospectively by announcing in advance that if a crime is committed, it will be hindered retrospectively. In so doing it provides an incentive to conform with law, which can compete with the criminal's other incentives. The law is effective if and only if conduct inconsistent with it will be hindered, whether prospectively through an incentive, or retrospectively by upholding it.

If punishment is nothing more than the effectiveness of law in space and time, Kant's seemingly extreme remarks about the need to punish are cast in a new light. Outside of a rightful condition, only "protective right" is available as a hindrance—you block the aggressor who is about to interfere with your person, and the prospect of defensive force provides a potential incentive to refrain from aggression. In a rightful condition, the prospect of remedial force also provides a possible incentive. Both protective and remedial force are only possible incentives, because they are fully discretionary on the part of the person exercising them. A person defending himself may follow the recommendation of ethics and "show moderation" against a wrongful assailant.[43] The person who is entitled to a remedy in accordance with strict right may listen to conscience and decline to claim it, or think that she would achieve her purposes better in some way other than reclaiming what is hers. More generally, a private person may decline to stand on his or her rights for any number of reasons, and so the prospect of protective or remedial force must be merely possible.

The prospect of punishment is different, because it must provide an incentive if the law is to be effective in space and time. Moreover, it must provide the incentive *systematically*, and thereby provide everyone with an assurance that each of the others will act in conformity with their rights. Again, as we saw in Chapter 6, Kant argues that in private right, you are under no obligation to refrain from interfering with the property of others unless you have assurance that they will do the same with yours. Instead, rights to external objects of choice are only consistent in a civil condition, because "assurance requires omnilateral public enforce-

---

43. 6:235.

ment."⁴⁴ Assurance under public law mediates between each person's entitlement to stand on his or her own rights and the rights of others: to refrain from the possession of others when they do not do the same allows them to treat you (and what belongs to you) as mere means in pursuit of their purposes. The only way to reconcile these is to provide everyone with the assurance that everyone else has an external incentive for conformity with the rights of everyone else. People may have a variety of incentives for such conformity, including morality, sympathy, and concern for reputation. Each of these may lead to acts in conformity with law, but they fail to provide assurance because their overlap with the requirements of law is contingent in any particular case. Only public law, with the threat of punishment, provides the requisite assurance, by providing an incentive that is available even when others fail in a particular case. In his lectures on natural right, Kant makes the same point, remarking that there are only two possible incentives to conform with law as such: the ethical incentive of respect for the law as such, and the juridical incentive of systematic coercion. Only these incentives can lead someone to conform *to the law*, rather than to do the things that the law requires.⁴⁵ Only the availability of public enforcement can assure others that a person will conform to the law, and so only systematic enforcement can assure everyone with regard to everyone else.

As the upholding of public right, punishment is not discretionary; although the sovereign has the right to grant clemency, Kant characterizes it as the "slipperiest" right of all, because it "does wrong in the highest degree."⁴⁶ In exceptional circumstances, clemency can be granted (though not in cases of crimes of subjects against each other) "to show the splendor of his majesty."⁴⁷ Even when permissible, however, it is done outside of the law, and is strictly speaking inconsistent with the existence of a rightful condition. That Kant should take such a harsh stand against clemency is unsurprising; to fail to punish the convicted criminal is to permit him to exempt himself from the rule of law, and so to set up his

---

44. 6:255–256.
45. Kant, *Naturrecht Feyerabend,* trans. Lars Vinx (unpublished, 2003), 27:1326–1328.
46. 6:337.
47. Ibid.

own "wild, lawless freedom."[48] As a private person, the criminal can be thought to have merely exempted herself from the law to achieve a private purpose. The sovereign cannot exempt itself in pursuit of a private purpose because the sovereign is not a private actor; the sovereign is the omnilateral will, and its only purposes are those inherent in the idea of the original contract. So the sovereign has no discretion over the ends that it will pursue, and so does not have means in the way that a private person has means subject to his or her choice in setting and pursuing ends. To fail to punish, then, would be to treat its coercive power as an instrument to be used for discretionary purposes, and so to do wrong in the highest degree by renouncing its own principle, even in the form of a single exception.

The fact that punishment is not discretionary does not commit Kant to any specific position about what public resources should be devoted to crime detection, or where those resources should be focused. Like all questions about public provision, it is the responsibility of the legislature to address such questions, guided, as elsewhere, by a principle of politics taking account of anthropological factors and empirical circumstances, but always framed by issues of right.

Kant's much-discussed remarks about the supposed right of necessity also reflect the role of punishment in making the law effective. Discussing the example of a shipwrecked sailor pushing another off a plank that can support only one of them, Kant writes that the sailor acts wrongfully, and

---

48. 6:316. Kant's notorious remark about the moral requirement that a society disbanding itself execute any murderers among its members follows the same reasoning: "for otherwise the people can be regarded as collaborators in this public violation of justice" (6:333). The claim follows from his analysis of the relation between a prohibition and punishing those who violate them: for the people, that is, the citizens as a collective body, to fail to punish a convicted murderer would be for them to acquiesce in his choice of means, that is, to subject the rule of law to the criminal's choice. The need to follow through, then, is not merely, as Byrd contends, a duty of virtue to follow through on an intention that has been announced. Such a failing could only be a personal failing on the part of the sovereign (although personal to the office, not the person or persons who occupy it), of a piece with familiar weaknesses of sovereigns like the breaking of election promises and defaulting on the national debt. Neither of these is a wrong in the highest degree. If the threat of punishment is understood as justified by its expected results, the failure to follow through on a threat makes the sovereign ineffectual, and perhaps even renounces a commitment, but does not renounce concepts of right.

so is culpable, but lies beyond the reach of punishment under public law because "a penal law of this sort could not have the effect intended, since a threat of an ill that is still *uncertain* (death by a juridical verdict) cannot outweigh the fear of an ill that is *certain* (drowning)."[49] Kant's point here is that in circumstances in which the law cannot guide conduct, it cannot carry through on the punishment. If the punishment just is the upholding of the law's supremacy, then in circumstances in which the law is necessarily incapable of guiding conduct prospectively, it has no supremacy to uphold. To turn the criminal's maxim back against him would fail to uphold the law's supremacy. The sailor who shoves the other off the plank remains a law unto himself because public law cannot give effect to the system of equal freedom in such cases. The only means available to it are means internal to the system of equal freedom, that is, the enforcement of the law. Enforcing the law by punishing the drowning sailor who saves himself at the expense of another sailor's life could never provide the right kind of incentive to conformity. Any coercive incentive the law can offer must be more uncertain than immediate death, and could not (consistent with right) be anything more severe than death. In such circumstances, the law is necessarily incapable of providing an incentive. Kant's claim is not that no *other* incentive could dissuade the sailor; even if the particular sailor's idiosyncrasies might lead him to moderate his conduct, they could not provide a legal assurance to others. Assurance requires that each person know that the law provides others with an omnilateral and significant incentive to conformity. Here the law's only means for providing the incentive is the threat of death, which *must* be ineffective. The sailor who frames the issue in terms of life and death will respond to a more urgent and certain version of the same incentive. In such circumstances, the state has no means at its disposal with which to uphold the law.[50]

49. 6:235–236.
50. As Dennis Klimchuk has argued, Kant's claim about the plank is not that the threat will fail empirically, but rather that it must fail conceptually. Other incentives might lead the sailor to refrain from dislodging the other, but the threat of execution cannot, simply because the prospect of losing one's life now cannot be outweighed by the prospect of losing it later. See Klimchuk, "Necessity, Deterrence, and Standing," *Legal Theory* 8 (2002): 349.

VI. Conclusion

Kant's legal and political philosophy is presented as an *a priori* system, which is meant to apply to finite embodied rational beings, without any reference to the malevolence or defects of human nature or the difficult circumstances in which humans find themselves. His theory of punishment poses an apparent obstacle to the *a priori* status of his account. Crimes are typically the product of bad people or difficult circumstances. In spite of the roots of crime, I have argued that Kant's account of punishment is required because of the nature of freedom, rather than the imperfections of free beings or the world in which they find themselves.[51]

I have argued that deterrence and retribution are not merely compatible but mutually require each other. In so doing, I have sought to provide an account that is both true to Kant's texts and, at the same time, resolutely noninstrumentalist. Retributive punishment does not serve to see to it that the wicked suffer as they deserve to; nor does punishing one person serve as a deterrent in order to prevent others from engaging in unwelcome behavior. Instead, punishment is nothing more than the su-

---

51. It might be thought that the Kantian approach closes the gap between the rule of law and separate values at the cost of precluding the possibility of international criminal law being used to punish people who are morally guilty but legally innocent. There is no international public authority or omnilateral authorization of such law because there is no world state.

International criminal law is perhaps in some tension with Kantian rule-of-law conceptions of punishment. Yet it is even more resistant to instrumental analysis. States feel legal pressure to introduce international legal instruments articulating the requirements of international criminal law, reflecting the underlying Kantian ideal of doing justice through law. International criminal law is not interchangeable with vigilantes exacting comparable punishments; it insists on trials and procedure. Even more significantly, the uncontroversial examples of the application of international criminal law have two features that make them distinctive. First, they involve conduct such as genocide that is "diametrically opposed" to the possibility of a rightful condition, rather than opposed to it "by default" (6:322). Second, they typically involve officials who commit crimes while claiming to act with legal warrant but, from a Kantian standpoint, have no legal grounds on which to assert such a claim. An official who acts outside his actual legal authority acts privately; an official who acts outside his possible legal authority, by murdering civilians, also acts privately. As such, he is just a common criminal who happens to have been involved with a highly organized group. Like the kingpin mobster, his desire to set himself outside the limits of law makes him more culpable. We will see in the next chapter that the Kantian theory has a more general way of framing the issue of wrongdoing by "officials" of failed states.

premacy of the rule of law. Prospectively, it guides conduct by threatening to make actions contrary to law pointless; retrospectively, it makes any such actions pointless, depriving them of their legal as well as their factual effects. The principle of punishment is thus the guarantee of freedom in space and time, the hindering of hindrances to freedom.

CHAPTER 11

Public Right V: Revolution and the Right of Human Beings as Such

KANT'S FOCUS on the social contract as an "idea of reason" solves a certain problem about any actual existing set of institutions. Both the entitlement and the obligation to think of the government as a representative of the united general will follow from the need to look at any sort of particular institutional realization of law as an imperfect version of the fully specified idea of law. Thus there is at once a standard through which particular legal institutions can be judged, that is, the standard of a system of equal freedom under laws, and, at the same time, the conceptual apparatus to suppose that the state can be entitled to rule despite its imperfect realization of that standard. The basic case for understanding political legitimacy is the case in which the people considered as a collective body rule themselves considered separately, through laws that they give themselves together. As an idea of reason, the original contract provides an ideal version of the pure rational structure of a state, and any actual set of institutions will fall short of it. But Kant provides a way of thinking of these shortcomings as grounds for improving the state, rather than grounds for rejecting its right to rule. These differences in turn reflect the fact that the possibility of the state's ruling rightfully does not depend upon the state's approximating some condition that could be achieved without it. For utilitarian theories of political morality, for example, law is a useful instrument for achieving morally desirable outcomes that can be *specified* without any reference to it, even if they could never in fact be *achieved* without it. For Kantians, without institutions to make, apply, and enforce law, relations between persons could never be fully rightful. Thus, as Kant lays out the possibilities in the figure following the "Division of the Relation of Law to Duty," the duty of right generates not only the right of humanity in our own person, but also the right of human beings as such, that is, the entitlement of every human being to live with those others with whom he or she interacts in a rightful condition.[1] Those who act contrary to the right of human beings as such do wrong "in the highest degree."

Kant's solution to that problem, however, is often thought to come at too high a price, since it has two implications, both of which Kant seems alarmingly eager to embrace. The first is that although the state has duties to its citizens, the citizens have no correlative rights to enforce them. Thus the people must "put up with" unequal burdens of taxation, irrational regulations, and so on. Their only recourse is to "petition" for change, rather than to bring it about forcibly. The second is that everyone is always under an obligation to "obey the authority that has power over you."[2]

Kant's insistence that citizens must obey their governments and have no right to take up arms against it is often said to be objectionable, and is sometimes said to be shown by experience to be objectionable. We have already seen Kant's systematic answer to the philosophical anarchist, who doubts that authority could ever be legitimate, and so doubts that an official could ever be entitled to make a choice that binds others. Even the most basic private rights presuppose a public authority. So there can be no general objection to authority as such, or to institutions vesting authority in individuals.

A more interesting objection initially appears more moderate. It does not deny the possibility of legitimate state authority, but rests instead on the distinction between good and bad exercises of authority. Yet that seems to be exactly the distinction that Kant wishes to reject. Even sym-

---

1. 6:240.
2. 6:372.

pathetic readers express reservations about Kant's absolutism. Wolfgang Kersting writes that "Kant's imagination proves to be very limited, if we measure it by our historical experience. In view of the vileness of state terrorism which our century has produced and never tires of producing, Kant's anti-revolution and anti-resistance argument seems naïve and over-optimistic. But we cannot blame Kant for not having anticipated the political pathology of the 20th century."[3] Christine Korsgaard argues that when institutions are bad enough, the virtuous person will rebel against legitimate but unjust institutions.[4] Others have sought to limit the reach of Kant's argument to protect only republican systems of government against revolutionary fervor.[5]

The anti-revolutionary argument takes several forms. In *Theory and Practice* Kant argues that a constitution can never include a provision giving the people a right to revolution. That argument can be characterized as an argument against a *legal* right to revolution. Some readers have found this argument overly legalistic, and have argued that considerations about what can and cannot be contained in a constitution neither address nor purport to address the question of a moral right to revolution.[6] The second argument focuses on the wrongfulness of the people's inquiring "with any practical aim into the origins" of legal institutions. Kant seems ready, almost eager, to concede that force came first and law only later, and that it would not be better for law to have come first.[7] This argument

---

3. Kersting, "Kant's Concept of a State," in Howard Williams, ed., *Kant's Political Philosophy* (Cardiff: University of Wales Press, 1992), 163.

4. Korsgaard, "Taking the Law into Our Own Hands: Kant on the Right to Revolution," in Christine M. Korsgaard, Andrews Reath, and Barbara Herman, eds., *Reclaiming the History of Ethics: Essays for John Rawls* (Cambridge: Cambridge University Press, 1997).

5. See, for example, Sharon Byrd and Joachim Hruschka, "The Natural Law Duty to Recognise Private Property Ownership: Kant's Theory of Property Rights in His Doctrine of Right," *University of Toronto Law Journal* 56 (2006):217–282, esp. 241–244; Kenneth Westphal, "Kant on the State, Law, and Obedience to Authority in the Alleged Anti-revolutionary Writings," *Journal of Philosophical Research* 17 (1992): 383–425. For a criticism of these attempts to save Kant from his own argument, see Katrin Flikschuh, "Reason, Right, and Revolution," *Philosophy & Public Affairs* 36, 4 (2008): 375–404, and "Sidestepping Morality: Korsgaard on Kant's No-right to Revolution," *Jahrbuch für Recht und Ethik* 16 (2008): 127–145.

6. Thomas E. Hill, Jr., "Questions about Kant's Opposition to Revolution," *Journal of Value Inquiry* 36 (2002): 283–298.

7. 6:318.

can be characterized as an argument from the irrelevance of history. The third argument is potentially the most troubling, as it focuses on the fact that the revolutionary necessarily acts unilaterally, and so can never be justified. Call this the argument from unilateral choice. The first two arguments are comparatively limited in their reach; the third argument appears to lead to the conclusion that every government is legitimate.

I will consider these arguments in turn. I will argue that they are successful in relation to the issues they consider, and lead to a robust conclusion about the possibility of revolution, according to which the people must simply "put up with" unfair and burdensome regulations, and that Kant is also right that the use of extralegal force can never be justified as an expression of the popular will.

The claim that Kant's arguments succeed on their own terms depends, however, on a careful analysis of just what those terms are. Kant draws a distinction between the basic grounds for entering a rightful condition and the internal criterion for assessing and, where appropriate, improving an existing rightful condition. The first grounds are articulated in the postulate of public right: "When you cannot avoid living side by side with all others, you ought to leave the state of nature and proceed with them into a rightful condition."[8] Only a condition in which laws are made, applied, and enforced through a public authority can make the differing rights claims of separate persons consistent. Only by distinguishing the making of law from its application can any official act be said to be a properly legal action; as we saw in Chapter 7, the separation of lawmaking from application and enforcement is required in order to distinguish between people and a mere mob. Only if the people are represented through legal institutions can they act together.

In Chapter 7 we saw that the second, internal criterion for assessing a rightful condition is contained in the "idea of the original contract."[9] In *Theory and Practice*, the original contract is said to "bind every legislator to give his laws in such a way that they could have arisen from the united will of a whole people and to regard each subject, insofar as he wants to be a citizen, as if he had joined in voting for such a will."[10]

---

8. 6:307.
9. 6:315.
10. Kant, *Theory and Practice*, 8:297.

Kant's arguments against revolution rest on the difference between the postulate of public right and the idea of the original contract: a state is under a duty to bring itself more nearly into conformity with the idea of the original contract, and the people are "authorized at least to make representations against" laws that are not in conformity with it.[11] The state's internal duty does not correspond to a correlative right on the part of the people, which is just to say that the people may not use force to bring the state into conformity with it.[12] If the state violates this duty, the people do not have an enforceable remedy, and so must "put up with" oppressive legislation. Their only recourse is to "oppose this injustice by complaints but not by resistance."[13]

Thus the anti-revolutionary arguments are all supposed to show that although the state must always strive to improve itself, by bringing itself more nearly into conformity with the idea of the original contract, the people may not violate the postulate of public right. That minimal standard is a precondition of any freedom under law; the state's entitlement to rule depends only on its providing a rightful condition at all. The inviolability of the postulate of public right does not have the objectionable implications sometimes attributed to it.

I. Constitutional Incoherence

The first, "legalistic" argument turns on the claim that no one can sit in judgment of the sovereign, on the grounds that the person who could do so would be the sovereign, and so, either the real sovereign, or subject to having still *others* sit in judgment, generating either a regress or a contradiction, since under such an arrangement the supreme authority would both be and not be the supreme authority. Thus a constitution that reserves to the people a right of revolution necessarily contains a contradiction. This argument is often discussed independently of the other parts of Kant's argument for the state, and unsurprisingly, it strikes many readers as too legalistic to be of much interest. However, Kant's point in making it needs to be understood in the broader context of his argument for the

---

11. Ibid., 8:298.
12. Ibid., 8:304.
13. 6:319.

state. As we saw in Chapter 6, that argument turns on the problem of unilateral choice, and the need for authoritative institutions to make choice omnilateral. In order for the power to resolve a dispute to be anything more than yet another unilateral use of force, the arbiter of the dispute must be able to make a decision on behalf of the parties to the dispute. In the case of a revolution, however, someone presents himself as outside the legal order, yet entitled to resolve a dispute in relation to it. In those terms, the revolutionary's position is incoherent. From the claim that the revolutionary is not entitled to be judge in his own case, Kant draws the surprising conclusion that the sovereign *is* entitled to be judge in his own case.[14]

Kant's focus on the incoherence of a constitutional provision permitting revolution is a claim about the supremacy of law. For example, it does not preclude a constitutional provision establishing judicial review of legislation and administrative action, so that a constitutional court is charged with determining whether the law is one the people could give to themselves. As we saw in Chapter 7, in the past half-century, many of the world's leading constitutional courts have taken a distinctively Kantian turn, focusing on the means available to a state and making the right to dignity, understood as the right to independent purposiveness, the organizing principle for rights analysis. From Kant's perspective, empowering a court to determine whether the state or one of its officials has acted within its constitutional authority simply imposes a higher level of closure on the system as a whole. The supremacy of the legislature resides in its lawmaking powers; it is entitled to make public law as that the people could have given to themselves, not to make general rules for private purposes. The judgment as to whether a particular law is in keeping with those powers must be decided on the basis of a legally conferred power to do so.[15] That requirement can be satisfied through judicial review. As

---

14. 6:319.

15. In the same way, the conformity of legislation with the requirements of innate right can be assessed against a legislative enactment such as the British Human Rights Act. In this context, Lord Hoffman's remarks are instructive: "Parliamentary sovereignty means that Parliament can, if it chooses, legislate contrary to the fundamental principles of human rights.... The constraints upon its exercise by Parliament are ultimately political, not legal. But the principle of legality means that Parliament must squarely confront what it is doing and accept the political cost. Fundamental rights cannot be overridden by general or ambiguous words.... In the absence of express language or necessary implication to the contrary, the courts therefore presume that even the most general words were intended to be subject to the

a result, the court does not stand outside the law, and so does not constitute a counterexample to Kant's point about the revolutionary. The revolutionary claims to speak for the people as they are apart from representation through institutions, and that is the possibility that Kant must rule out.

The argument that the sovereign must be judge in its own case can thus be recast as the claim that there can be no extralegal test of the legal system. Since the legal system imposes closure on disputes, no person acting outside of an official legal capacity could ever have standing to impose closure on the dispute. That is just to say that it could not give the people a right to judge in their own case.

It does not follow from this first argument that officials cannot act outside their authority, or that the highest authority deciding a question cannot make a terrible decision, or even one inconsistent with innate equality. The test, as we saw in Chapter 7, is whether the law in question is one that the people could give to itself. Certainly any official could fail to apply the appropriate legal rule, or misapply it. Nonetheless, the legal system as a whole must make the official answer the only possible answer, and so the only answer that can authorize the use of force. Closure with respect to the use of force generates the limit of legal acts to official acts, and legal powers are limited to those conferred by law. Thus the law cannot confer on any person or group of persons the power to use force outside the law.

This first, "legalistic" argument turns on connection between closure and legality. That requirement, as we saw in Chapter 7, does not require that the law be entirely determinate with respect to every particular, but instead that, with respect to any legal question, the legal system contains an answer about who is authorized to answer that question, and on what grounds. Rights are only conclusive if disputes about them are to be resolved in accordance with law. Kant provides a systematic exposition of the concept of closure at two places in Private Right. The first is in his discussion of possession through long use. The basic point is that if peo-

---

basic rights of the individual. In this way the courts of the United Kingdom, though acknowledging the sovereignty of Parliament, apply principles of constitutionality little different from those which exist in countries where the power of the legislature is expressly limited by a constitutional document." *R v. Secretary of State for the Home Department, Ex parte Simms* [2000] 2 AC 115 at 131.

ple are to have property as their own, then there must be a procedure through which property can be acquired without making an exhaustive historical determination about prior title. Conclusive rights are only possible provided that a person can establish that he or she has performed the requisite act establishing a right. That in turn requires that after a sufficient period of time, continuous possession establishes a right. Otherwise any use of land would be merely provisional, and could never be made conclusive, in case some other person came along and was able to claim earlier title. Kant's point here is not about the lack of information, but rather about the structure of rights: a conclusive right requires closure. This structure has the surprising implication that a long-term trespasser can acquire a right provided that his or her possession is adverse and hostile to the interests of the original owner.[16]

Kant makes an even stronger point about closure in his subsequent discussion of the traditional legal problem of recovery of a stolen object. The traditional legal rule says that a "bona fide purchaser for value" can acquire a stolen object provided that the purchase takes place without notice that the object is stolen and satisfies the legal formalities in effect in the jurisdiction. The bona fide purchaser for value is sometimes described as "a favorite of the law" because he or she is able to extinguish another innocent person's rightful title. Suppose somebody steals my horse, and you, in good faith and in a public market "regulated by police ordinances," purchase it from the thief.[17] I then see you with the horse, and accuse you of theft. You show me all the paperwork. We have both been cheated by a single rogue, who has dropped out of sight. Who gets to keep the horse? Kant notes that as a matter of natural right, it seems clear that I do, because a right in property is not extinguished just because the owner is no longer in physical possession of the thing. The same point might be made by saying that the thief cannot transfer better title than he has. Nonetheless, Kant argues that a court can make no such decision and must instead allow the purchaser to keep it. The bona fide purchaser is not a favorite of the law because he or she is innocent; so is the disappointed previous owner. Instead, the reason is systematic: any

16. 6:291–293.
17. 6:303.

owner's title is only as good as the procedures of the rightful condition that initially secured it. It is impossible to trace the history back to ensure that no wrong had occurred in all of the transactions relevant to my title in the horse (including the transactions through various people who acquired things they used in those transactions). Going back to my earlier acquisition faces exactly the same problem as your more recent one: the most I could ever show that matters to ownership is that I acquired it in a legitimate and publicly rightful way. Had I branded the horse, I would have made it much harder for the thief to sell it in a regulated market. Procedures for regulating transfers make the brand relevant; without them, the marking does not. Again, if we are in a system that has mandatory registration of titles, you might have realized something was amiss before you bought the horse. But if the formalities are somehow satisfied, then the problem comes up in just the same way. My claim to the horse is on all fours with yours, but you have a more recent, and so superior, public ratification of your title.[18]

Kant's point about the impossibility of judging the sovereign has the same structure: the only thing that *qualifies* the sovereign to rule is the constitution, with its procedures that *empower* the sovereign to rule. The examples of acquisition through long use and bona fide purchase for value show that there can be no rightful claim to property outside of a rightful condition, only a series of potentially competing provisional claims, none of which generates a coercive right in relation to any other. The same point applies to the right to rule: there is also no rightful claim to rule outside of a rightful condition, only potentially competing provisional claims. Those provisional claims may be better or worse on the basis of moral argument, but nobody has standing to adjudicate between them or enforce any of them, because they are merely unilateral.

Although Kant's argument focuses on the possibility of a *legal* right to revolution, it has broader implications, because on Kant's conception legality is the general precondition of the moral authorization to use force. The entire point of the argument is to show that there can be no moral authorization to use force except a legal one. There is a significant exception: outside of a rightful condition, there is a moral authorization to use

18. 6:303.

force to bring others into a rightful condition. Within a rightful condition, however, only legality can confirm the authorization to use force, because any other use of force is merely unilateral.

II. The Irrelevance of History

Kant's second argument focuses on the irrelevance of a state's historical origin to its status as a rightful condition that must be obeyed. Kant writes that "a people should not *inquire* with any practical aim in view into the origin of the supreme authority to which it is subject, that is, subject *ought not to reason* for the sake of action about the origin of this authority, as a right that can still be called into question *(ius controversum)* with regard to the obedience he owes it."[19] This argument does not focus on particular acts of the state, but rather on the state's historical origin. In one sense, it is simply a restatement of Kant's claim that the contractual basis of the state is an idea of reason: the original contract provides the only terms in which we can think of the legitimacy of the state, as an instance of a rightful condition, whatever its empirical limitations and imperfections,[20] in the same way that the moral concept of a person provides the terms in which we can think of ourselves as responsible for our actions, even when we give in to temptation. If the original contract is an idea of reason, though, there is no point in asking about when the contract was formed, any more than there would be a point to trying to ground the moral concept of a person in a series of empirical tests. An idea of reason never describes a datable historical event.

Examining history with practical aims faces a further difficulty: such a search is guaranteed to disappoint. We saw in Chapter 7 that until the state is in place, private transactions do not create enforceable powers. There could be no coherent description of the rightful process by which a people enters into a binding original contract, because a process can only justify its product if it is set up within a rightful condition. It follows that no process of creating a rightful condition could ever be sufficient to

19. 6:318.
20. 6:316.

justify it. We saw further that any set of private transactions in the distant past could not, on their own, that is, without a rightful condition, bind future generations. Thus showing that the state had its historical origins in force and war rather than in some set of peaceable and voluntary arrangements is not relevant to its legitimacy. Private transactions only bind people who are already in a rightful condition, so the peaceable terms on which a state was set up would not even be binding on those who participated in them. Setting up the state cannot be understood as just another private transaction.

Kant also makes the further claim that to search for a founding moment with a practical aim is inconsistent with right.[21] If the legitimacy of the state depends on its past, then the rights of those now living depend upon the deeds of past generations. Particular persons have rights that do depend on what happened in the past—who owns what depends on what was acquired by whom, and what subsequent transactions took place—but Kant's argument operates at a different level: the fact that a state was founded on violence cannot deprive you of your right to enjoy your freedom in a rightful condition. No act to which you were not party could deprive you of the entitlement to join others in a rightful condition.

The argument from the irrelevance of history does not simply deprive the revolutionary of one possible ground for overthrowing the government. It also has the more general implication that a rightful condition does not lose its claim to be rightful simply because it passes unjust or even oppressive laws. The existence of a rightful condition can no more be conditional on the prudence of its current rulers than it can on the justice of its founders. Unjust tax burdens do not render private rights merely provisional. More generally, no official act is sufficient to dissolve a rightful condition; the state must regard itself as existing in perpetuity. It follows, then, that no lesser act of injustice can dissolve a rightful condition. Thus the point about the origin of the state applies to its continuation: its right to rule depends on its satisfying the postulate of public right, and so does not depend on how well or badly it carries out its specific functions.

21. Ibid.

III. Peoples and Mobs

Kant's third argument turns on the more general idea that a system of rights is only possible through an omnilateral will, and the further claim that an omnilateral will is only possible through institutions. In the "General Remark" to Public Right, Kant summarizes the point by saying "a rightful condition is possible only by submission to its general legislative will,"[22] reiterating the claim we saw in Chapter 7 that a people differs from a multitude only by being united under laws. Any claim to act outside of the constitution cannot be a claim to act on the part of the people, and must instead be merely a unilateral claim, and so not a claim of right. The "legalistic" argument said that there was no juridical mechanism through which the people could reserve to itself the right of sedition or rebellion; this further argument says that there is no *people* except as represented by law. The first argument suggested that revolution could not be made legal (and, because of Kant's account of legality, could not be made moral); this argument aims to show that the right to revolution is impossible. The only way to understand the revolutionary's claim is as the right to plunge everyone into a state of nature for his or her own private purpose, because the revolutionary cannot coherently talk about acting for the people.

The juridical nature of Kant's argument leads to an exceptionless formulation: there can be no right to revolution. The same juridical nature leads to an inherent limitation on its scope. It applies only to a rightful condition. Anything satisfying the postulate of public right's requirement to "enter a condition in which each may be rendered what is his" counts as a rightful condition, and so in one sense there can never be a right of revolution against a state. Thus the fact that the state commits some injustice is something that citizens must simply "put up with."

IV. Barbarism

The cases in which Kant's denial of a right to revolution seems morally troubling are not cases involving particular unjust laws. Indeed, even Locke, the chief champion of the idea of a right to revolution, concedes

---

22. 6:320.

that an individual lacks the right to rebel on the grounds that his or her own personal rights have been violated. Lockean individuals preserve a right of private redress against the state, so that a private person may reclaim his property from the state even if his suit to reclaim it has been rejected by a public court of justice.[23] This Lockean right of recourse, however, is only a right to reclaim property from the state, not a right to overthrow the state itself.[24]

Instead, cases in which the political powers conduct themselves so egregiously are thought to give rise to a right to revolution. Nazi Germany is the clearest example.[25] These are cases of human rights violation so fundamental that they undermine the organization that commits them. Their wrongfulness, however, not only violates the individual rights of each of the human beings they target. It also violates what Kant calls "the right of human beings as such,"[26] that is, the right to live in conformity with the Universal Principle of Right, something that can only be done by uniting with others in a rightful condition.[27]

Kant does not consider such regimes explicitly, but his account of the nature of public right makes it clear that holding a near monopoly of force in a geographic area does not satisfy the postulate of public right. A powerful organization in violation of the postulate of public right is not entitled to allegiance from the residents of that area, so it opens up the possibility that those residents, as private persons, do no wrong by opposing it. The earlier analogy with reclaiming stolen goods makes this clear. The

---

23. Locke, *Second Treatise of Government*, §§11, 161, 168.

24. Katrin Flikschuh has shown that restricting the right of revolution to the people makes Locke's account less extreme, and more Kantian, than it is usually taken to be. Once the individual loses the right to revolt, Locke needs some analogue of the idea that the people can act only as it is represented, and so loses the right to revolution he sought to establish. See "Reason, Right and Revolution."

25. Arguably the same kind of analysis of complete failures by a regime to respect the basic rights of its citizens underwrites arguments in favor of external powers intervening to bring new regimes to failed states. In a parallel fashion, the fifth preliminary article for perpetual peace, prohibiting one state from intervening in the internal affairs of another, does not apply in cases of civil war (*Toward a Perpetual Peace*, 8:346).

26. 6:240; 6:308.

27. Kant treats these as equivalent at 6:349, when he says that for a foreign power to destroy a state would be a wrong against its people "which cannot lose its original right to unite itself into a commonwealth."

purchaser only gets to keep the horse if the purchase takes place in a public market with police ordinances. The purchaser gets to keep it even if those ordinances are imperfect in any number of ways. It does not follow from this that every transfer of stolen property, or even every transfer under the supervision of the local warlord, gives the new possessor good title. Your title to your property is only as good as the procedures that affirm it. If such procedures are in place, your title is also superior to that of the person who receives stolen goods in secret, or is aware that they are stolen. If no procedures are in place, or the ones that are in place are violated, you retain your coercive right against the purchaser.

In the same way, a constitutional system of government takes priority over the claims of natural right, even if the constitution and the positive law passed under it are flawed in any number of ways. It does not follow from this that every organized use of power and violence is a legitimately constituted state. Nor does it follow that those who find themselves oppressed by a powerful oppressor have no right to use force, either to protect themselves, or, if possible, to bring that person into a rightful condition with them. The defining feature of a state of nature is that all action in it is merely unilateral. Its fundamental flaw lies in its inconsistency with right because "a unilateral will cannot serve as a coercive law for everyone ... since that would infringe upon freedom in accordance with universal laws."[28] Nothing in the concept of unilateral action precludes it from displaying a significant degree of organization. Kant's argument thus leaves conceptual space for the claim that the world's most horrible regimes are in a state of nature, so that those to whom they do violence are not only *entitled* but *required* to use force if they can to bring them into a rightful condition in that way. To create a state out of a condition of barbaric violence is not a revolution; it is just the creation of a state where there was none before.

Institutions are central to Kant's view because they are the only way in which the use of force can have an omnilateral authorization. Institutions can only do this by being orderly and differentiated, but it does not follow that any organization that oversees the orderly use of force is a legal institution in Kant's sense. A criminal syndicate may be very well organized

---

28. 6:256.

without being a state. The warlord who pillages in an orderly fashion does not thereby make himself a legitimate ruler. Whether some particular situation fits this description cannot be determined *a priori*, nor can it be determined by the existence of partial apparatus of government.

In the final section of *Anthropology from a Pragmatic Point of View*, Kant distinguishes between four combinations of force with freedom and law.

1. Law and freedom without force, which is anarchy (this is a state of nature understood as an idea of reason).
2. Law and force without freedom, which is despotism.
3. Force without freedom and law, which is barbarism.
4. Force with freedom and law, which is a republic (this is a civil condition understood as an idea of reason).[29]

Despotism is a defective form of a republic, and Kant's remarks in the *Doctrine of Right* about "putting up with" oppressive legislation apply to despotic regimes. Despotism could be a possible form of the general will, because the arrangements made for the members of a despotic state are legal, and secure them in what is theirs.[30] Freedom is absent in a despotic condition, because although people know where they stand, and so can plan their affairs with some level of certainty, the rules that afford them that certainty are imposed from without. In such a situation, which every existing state exemplifies to at least some degree—only an imperfect state could be under a duty to improve itself, so imperfect states must indeed be states—the most citizens can do is "petition" against its excesses. Such excesses may be extreme, but even a state that is gravely deficient in the "effects with regard to rights that follow from the idea of the civil union" does not thereby fail to be a rightful condition.

The distinctive feature of barbarism is its violation of the postulate of

---

29. *Anthropology from a Pragmatic Point of View*, trans. Robert Louden (Cambridge: Cambridge University Press, 2006), 7:330. See also Jan Joerden, "From Anarchy to Republic: Kant's History of State Constitutions," *Proceedings of the Eighth International Kant Congress* (Milwaukee: Marquette University Press, 1995), 139–156.

30. Kant makes this point in the middle of the first paragraph of §52, when he notes that the people could want autocracy. See 6:340.

public right, not only of the idea of the original contract. Any condition that violates the postulate of public right thereby (by default) violates the idea of the original contract, but its failure to satisfy the postulate makes it a state of nature, rather than a defective rightful condition. The postulate requires that human beings "enter a condition in which what belongs to each can be secured to him against everyone else."[31] A condition of despotism satisfies the postulate of public right; a condition of barbarism does not. People do not make defective arrangements for others; some people just force others to do things. Such uses of force cannot give rise to any claims of right.

In the *Anthropology*, Kant offers several illustrations of barbarism, including polygamy and the barbarous condition in which women are kept "as domestic animals."[32] In the concluding passage of the "Right of Nations," Kant says that war is the "barbaric way of deciding disputes."[33] Such examples can be developed in two directions, corresponding to the two conditions of human beings with duties but no rights, slavery and serfdom.[34] First, if some persons are treated as (though they were) the property of others, or attacked or killed with impunity, they are in the opposite of a condition in which their rights can be secured to them against everyone else. They are slaves, and do not share a rightful condition with their masters. Second, even if their innate right of humanity is minimally secure, if members of a class of persons are forcibly prevented from having anything external as their own—excluded from the system of property, or permitted to use it only on terms set by another—through a social rule backed by armed thugs, they have the status of serfs. The members of a class of serfs are not in a rightful condition with those others. Indeed, even the postulate of private right does not apply to them, since they are forbidden from using usable things to set and pursue their purposes. The fact that one side regularly wins in deciding disputes by force does nothing to improve the situation. Those who are subject to the violence of others lack any public authorization to exercise their purposiveness, since

---

31. 6:237.
32. Kant, *Anthropology*, 7:304.
33. 6:351.
34. 6:241.

those others dictate whether they can use anything. In a state of nature persons can have things as their own, albeit only provisionally; in a defective state of nature some cannot even have things as their own provisionally, since organized force enables others to dispossess them.

As a defective form of a state of nature, a condition of barbarism can have no united will. All force is merely unilateral; when force is organized in a condition of barbarism, it takes the form of rule by prerogative, even if members of the more powerful group have elaborate procedures for decision-making. Unlike despotism, in which law is sometimes used for the private purposes of the rulers, in barbarism all exercises of power are *necessarily* for private purposes, even if they are highly organized, because there are no public purposes, only (at most) common ones. As such, the use of private force may be resisted with right. In a condition of barbarism, there is no freedom, because each person is subject to the unilateral choice of others. Moreover, unlike the ideal case of anarchy (freedom without force or law), in which everyone acts unilaterally, but none infringes on the right of any other, freedom is absent in barbarism because force is present but law still absent. Since that force cannot be characterized as an expression of a united will, it must be understood as merely unilateral. Those who resist barbarism with the aim of entering a rightful condition do right; those who uphold barbarism "do wrong in the highest degree." Barbarism is not a possible form of the general will, so no argument for preserving a united will has any application. Only an argument for creating one does.

Kant's conception of barbarism is important for understanding his opposition to revolution, because many of the examples that are often brought out to embarrass him—most notably Nazi Germany—are conditions of barbarism in Kant's sense. A regime that denies the innate right of people, and forbids them acquired rights, neither secures rights nor creates a condition in which "what belongs to each can be secured to him against everyone else."[35]

The normative significance of the concept of barbarism parallels the normative significance of the concept of a mob. The citizens as a collective body can only be distinguished from a mob on the basis of institu-

---

35. 6:237.

tions that represent them as giving themselves laws together. The significance of institutions does not, however, rest on the fact that they are complex, but on the contrast between right and violence that is the basis for public right.[36] A highly organized mob is still a mob, because it acts unilaterally.

The introduction of the concept of barbarism might be thought to reproduce the initial difficulty: who is to stand in judgment of the regime? The critics claim that the state is behaving barbarously; the rulers claim that they represent the general will. Since there is no purely empirical way of resolving the dispute, it might appear that the rulers are the only ones capable of giving judgment in their own case. That conclusion, however, presupposes the very point that is at issue in the characterization of a condition of barbarism, that is, whether the organized use of force in question satisfies the postulate of public right by "rendering to each." A condition in which some are not allowed to have anything as their own, or in which they are enslaved or murdered by others, is not a difficult case either about what belongs to whom or about how to secure the rights of everyone. The entitlement to judge particulars under concepts of right follows from the duty of those in power to create a rightful condition for all; those who do not even purport to do so are not entitled to judge in their own case. In *Theory and Practice*, Kant characterizes freedom of the pen as "the sole palladium of the people's rights" on the grounds that a citizen must assume that the ruler does not intend to wrong him, and so would want to know of any inadvertent wrongdoing.[37] In a condition of barbarism that assumption is impossible, because the only way a state can intend to do no wrong is if it at least attempts to act omnilaterally, which a barbaric regime cannot do. In such a situation, each person can only do "what seems right and good to it."[38] Although barbaric regimes sometimes might represent themselves as morally justified, and their particular barbaric acts as required by circumstances, justified by the greater goods they will bring, or inflicted on a lesser class of humans, they cannot claim to represent the people.

36. 6:307.
37. Kant, *Theory and Practice*, 8:304.
38. 6:312.

In the condition of barbarism, what is a person to do? Kant can give only one answer: unite with others to leave the state of nature. If an organized group is exercising barbaric power, however, they may not be available as people with whom to unite. Instead, they can be resisted with right. Human beings in such a situation are not required to engage in futile self-sacrifice to create a rightful condition, but they are permitted to use force to create one. This remains so even if barbarians have taken over aspects of the prior legal system, and even if they pass themselves off as a legal authority. Organized barbarism is still barbarism, not right.

V. The Right of Human Beings as Such

Focusing on the distinction between despotism and barbarism also explains why the "official" acts of a barbaric condition are without legal force. This issue is particularly pressing when a successor regime must decide what to do with crimes committed or sanctioned by the officials of the barbaric one that preceded it. Such cases arise both at the level of legislation and at the level of individual actors. At the level of legislation, a successor regime must determine what to do about edicts depriving persons of property or citizenship; at the level of individual actions, questions arise about crimes against persons committed on the basis of official orders, permitted by general rules, or carried out by officials.[39] In these cases, a crime, usually murder, is committed. Although the facts are not in dispute, the perpetrator argues that under the positive law in effect at the time of the event in question, the act was permitted (or required) by law.

---

39. Another response to cases of wrongdoing by officials is the setting up of a South African-type Truth and Reconciliation Commission, which cancels civil damages and criminal punishment for those who committed political crimes on the condition that they address their victims in a highly structured public procedure. Because those who refuse the process are liable to public punishment and civil damages, its application cannot be taken to be a founding moment of a state in response to a legal void. Had there been a legal void, there could be no wrongs committed by human beings among themselves, only wrongdoing in the highest degree. So there would be neither punishment nor civil damages from which to exempt people. Instead, for Kant, such a commission would have to be understood as presupposing the continuity of the new legal regime with the old, and so as the exercise of the sovereign's right to prevent dissolution of a state and passing into the state of nature, which is itself an instance of the sovereign's right to grant clemency. See 6:335, 6:337.

The overall morality of the situation is not controversial: obviously the act was a grievous wrong. The appropriate legal response to it is controversial: there is both a first-order question about how to dispose of such cases and whether, in particular, the appeal to the rules that were in effect in conditions of barbarism is legally sound, and further, a more abstract question about how to characterize such cases.

Much of the discussion of these cases has been framed by the debate between H. L. A. Hart and Gustav Radbruch. Hart and Radbruch agreed about the appropriate outcome in the cases that form their main point of contention. In one, a woman seeking to carry on an extramarital relationship with another man testified that her husband had spoken out against the Nazi regime. He was sentenced to death, but the sentence was not carried out; instead he was sent to near certain death at the eastern front. When prosecuted after the war, she argued that her act was legally permissible at the time, and so she violated no law. Radbruch argued that the laws in question were so morally odious as to be no law at all. On his analysis, positive law must pass a minimum moral standard in order to be legally valid:

> Where there is not even an attempt at justice, where equality, the core of justice, is deliberately betrayed in the issuance of positive law, then the statute is not merely 'flawed law', it lacks completely the very nature of law. For law, including positive law, cannot be otherwise defined than as a system and an institution whose very meaning is to serve justice. Measured by this standard, whole portions of National Socialist law never attained the dignity of valid law.[40]

Hart characterized Radbruch's formula as follows:

> His considered reflections led him to the doctrine that the fundamental principles of humanitarian morality were part of the very concept of *Recht* or Legality and that no positive enactment or statute, however clearly it was expressed and however clearly it conformed with

---

40. Radbruch, "Statutory Lawlessness and Supra-Statutory Law," *Oxford Journal of Legal Studies*, 26 (2006): 7.

the formal criteria of validity of a given legal system, could be valid if it contravened basic principles of morality.... [E]very lawyer and judge should denounce statutes that transgressed the fundamental principles not as merely immoral or wrong but as having no legal character, and enactments which on this ground lack the quality of law should not be taken into account in working out the legal position of any given individual in particular circumstances.[41]

Hart's objection to the argument so characterized combines moral and legal arguments:

> Many of us might applaud the objective—that of punishing a woman for an outrageously immoral act—but this was secured only by declaring a statute established since 1934 not to have the force of law, and at least the wisdom of this course must be doubted. There were, of course, two other choices. One was to let the woman go unpunished; one can sympathize with and endorse the view that this might have been a bad thing to do. The other was to face the fact that if the woman were to be punished it must be pursuant to the introduction of a frankly retrospective law and with a full consciousness of what was sacrificed in securing her punishment in this way. Odious as retrospective criminal legislation and punishment may be, to have pursued it openly in this case would at least have had the merits of candour. It would have made plain that in punishing the woman a choice had to be made between two evils, that of leaving her unpunished and that of sacrificing a very precious principle of morality endorsed by most legal systems. Surely if we have learned anything from the history of morals it is that the thing to do with a moral quandary is not to hide it.[42]

---

41. Hart, "Positivism and the Separation of Law and Morals," *Harvard Law Review* 71 (1958): 617.

42. Ibid., 619. Hart later conceded that he had misdescribed the facts of the case; see *The Concept of Law*, 2d ed. (Oxford: Clarendon, 1994), 304. Hart suggested that the example as he described it could be treated as a hypothetical, since it raises the issue of the ability of a barbaric regime to confer legal powers. I will discuss the example as Hart frames it. The actual

Two things are striking about Hart's approach here. The first is that Hart assumes that Radbruch is offering a criterion for the assessment of individual statutes, rather than the "whole portions" he explicitly mentions. As a result, he passes over Radbruch's entire discussion of cases in which Jewish property seized by the Nazis was returned because the directives under which it was seized were held to be void, his reference to a "system," and his comments about the possibility, raised later in the same article, that "it is at least questionable whether the so-called Führer and Chancellor of the Reich should ever have been regarded as the legal head of state at all."[43] Radbruch's concern in those discussions is not with the moral merits of a particular law, but with the regime's power to make law. Hart makes it look as though Radbruch is trying to introduce a legal norm—"humanitarian morality"—that has no basis in any official act, as a way of passing off retroactive punishment as ordinary punishment for an act illegal at the time it was committed.[44] Such an argument would conflict with the idea that legality requires positive law. But it is not Radbruch's argument. His actual argument focuses on the limits of the ability of an institution or official to make law. He argues that seemingly valid acts changing the law are void, and so leave the prior legal norms in place. That is why property owners are legally entitled to get their property back when it is taken from them under a permission granted by a barbaric regime. That is also why a barbaric regime cannot confer permission to murder on citizens. In both cases, the statutes that supposedly provided a new authorization for such acts are void. Murder and theft were prohibited by validly enacted laws, and a barbaric regime cannot change that.

The second striking feature of Hart's formulation is that the choice "between two evils" treats the principle that a person not be punished except for violation of a prior law as "a very precious principle of morality," one that shines like a jewel regardless of the moral character of the

---

issue before the court concerned the relations between the woman's guilt and the role of the court that sentenced the husband. The officials of the court acted under a legal duty; the woman did not. See Thomas Mertens, "Radbruch and Hart on the Grudge Informer: A Reconsideration," *Ratio Juris* 15, no. 2 (2002): 186–205, and David Dyzenhaus, "The Grudge Informer Case Revisited," *N.Y.U. Law Review* 83, no. 4 (2008): 1000–1034.

43. Radbruch, "Statutory Lawlessness and Supra-Statutory Law," 3.

44. H. L. A Hart, *The Concept of Law* (Oxford: Clarendon, 1961), 207.

processes that validates (or in this case suspends) decrees. Hart's other writings suggest that the moral principle he thought the postwar court should hold dear is in fact nothing more than the creation of stable expectations. In *The Concept of Law*, uncertainty is identified as the first respect in which Hart says a "pre-legal" condition is defective;[45] in *Punishment and Responsibility*, he argues that the criminal law should be a system in which the individual can "weigh the cost to him of obeying the law" and "the pains of punishment will for each individual represent the price of some satisfaction obtained from the breach of law." Something like this thought may lie behind his remark that the badness of the criminal law of repressive regimes (among which he explicitly includes Nazi Germany) is "mitigated by the fact that they fall only on those who have obtained a satisfaction from knowingly doing what they forbid."[46]

Hart's attempt to find a precious moral principle in certainty, regardless of what it is that one can be certain of, reflects his instrumentalist conception of the rule of law as focused on bringing about results. A noninstrumentalist account can say instead that the "precious principle" inherits its morality from the fact that the formal processes that validate positive law create a rightful condition, and that punishment without prior law goes wrong because punishment presupposes that the criminal has asserted "wild, lawless freedom" in opposition to a rightful condition.[47] Although a rightful condition ensures that citizens know where they stand in relation to those with power over them, the mere fact that human beings know where they stand with respect to violence does not, without more, make any moral principle apply. It may be better to know that some neighborhoods are more dangerous than others, and so be able to decide when to take a calculated risk by entering one. Yet the "benefit"

---

45. Ibid., p. 90.
46. Hart, "Legal Responsibility and the Excuses," in his *Punishment and Responsibility* (Oxford: Oxford University Press, 1968), 47.
47. Earlier formulations of the principle construe it narrowly, to cases in which "it is impossible that the party could foresee that an action, innocent when it was done, should be afterwards converted to guilt by a subsequent law: he had therefore no cause to abstain from it" (Blackstone, *Commentaries on the Laws of England*, ed. Stanley N. Katz [Chicago: University of Chicago Press, 1979], vol. 1, p. 46). That murder should be "converted" to a wrong by subsequent law is hardly unforeseeable.

conferred by the gang of criminals that makes its plans known does nothing to "mitigate" its use of force. Such force is wrongful because inconsistent with each person's right to independence, even if it is predictable. Again, the fact that a criminal organization or corrupt official had undertaken to protect someone in the commission of a crime does not give that person the protection of the precious moral principle.

Still, Kant would have to agree with Hart that something is wrong with imposing a moralized test of legality, and so with saying that a particular law is invalidated simply because of its odious nature, all the more so if the test is the one that Hart purports to find in Radbruch: if all of "humanitarian morality" is a precondition of legality in each particular case, a law that is *in any way* defective from a moral standpoint is not a law at all. In such a situation, the value of legality is lost, as it is fully subordinated to morality, without any authorization for a particular official to apply it to particulars.[48] Each would have no option but to do what seemed "right and good to it," even if it often seemed right or good to do as officials said. All action would be merely unilateral, with officials providing nothing more than a salient coordination point.

Kant's general approach generates a fundamentally different way of thinking about statutes enacted in a period of barbarism that follows the destruction of a rightful condition. The problem with the condition of barbarism is not only that terrible laws are passed that fail the tests of critical morality. A despotic but rightful condition has that flaw, and a republican system of government will sometimes exhibit it. Instead, the problem with barbarism is that it is a condition of force with neither freedom nor law. As such, a condition of barbarism cannot be represented as the expression of any kind of a united will, and so cannot be represented as a defective version of a rightful condition. It is not a rightful condition at all.

Kant's approach has significant implications for the legal (as well as moral) status of any such acts. As we have seen, in Kant's discussion of each of private law damages and criminal punishment, the basic structure

---

48. Hart thus reads Radbruch as developing a position similar to the one subsequently developed (in relation to Hart's own work) by Ronald Dworkin, according to which each citizen must consult morality to determine what the law requires in a particular situation.

of his account is that wrongdoing never changes rights. If I injure you wrongfully, your entitlement to compensation is not an entitlement to anything more than your entitlement that I not injure you. Instead, it is the form in which the entitlement is once more made effective in space and time. In the same way, the punishment of the criminal is just the supremacy of the law in space and time.

The same analysis can be applied to a period of barbarism that follows the destruction of the institutions of civil society. If the transition from the Weimar Republic to Nazism is a transition from legality to barbarism, then what happened during the condition of barbarism, no matter how well organized, is just unilateral force, and so not law. Moreover, it is just unilateral force, and not law, apart from its other moral qualities. In a footnote to *Theory and Practice*, Kant argues that if a "previous existing constitution has been torn up" by a mob and a new commonwealth has not been created, a condition of anarchy arises "with all of the horrors that are at least possible by means of it."[49] The classification in the *Anthropology* shows that barbarism provides a better characterization of the situation in which law is absent and force prevails.

The only law through which transactions and actions taking place during the Nazi period can be assessed is the antecedent law of Weimar Germany. If a rightful condition is restored after a condition of barbarism, then it is continuous or even identical with the rightful condition prior to the barbaric period, and does not require an affirmative act to identify its laws. If wrongs do not change rights, then, the laws of the Weimar Republic, whatever their moral ambiguities or defects, are not changed by anything that happened in the condition of barbarism. The survival of the old constitution through the period of barbarism is particularly clear in the case of a failed revolution. Kant remarks that considering only successful revolutions is an obstacle to clear thinking.[50] Not only does it lead to undue optimism; it also masks the juridical issues raised by failed revolutions. If a mob briefly overthrows a government but it is subsequently restored, the regime's temporary loss of power does not deprive its laws of their rightful force. Unlike the French Revolution as Kant characterizes

---

49. *Theory and Practice*, 8:302.
50. Ibid., 8:301.

it, this is not a situation in which a new rightful condition is set up, capable of passing laws that bind its citizens. Instead, the effectiveness of the old regime was temporarily compromised, but its right to rule was not. That is why the exiled governments of Denmark or the Netherlands could return after the Allied victory and regard their prewar laws as still valid. During their exile they were merely provisional, that is, lacking in coercive force, but their right to rule remained.

The downward spiral into barbarism differs from a successful revolution precisely because the successful revolutionary *ends up* speaking for the people, even though his or her pre-revolutionary claim to carry out the revolution *in the name of* the people is incoherent. The barbarian who destroys a rightful condition has no power to bind anyone, and so the people remain provisionally bound by the antecedent legal system.

Kant characterizes revolution as not merely the violation but rather the "annihilation" of the constitution, and he might be expected to say the same about the collapse into barbarism.[51] Yet the sense in which the constitution is annihilated depends in part on what happens afterward. If the revolution breaks out and has been defeated, it never did manage to change the constitution, even if the government was ineffective for a period during which only force ruled. On the other hand, if the revolution is successful and consolidates its power, then the old constitution gave way at the moment of its destruction. In this, the situation is analogous to Kant's discussion of acquisition by long possession: if I occupy your property for long enough, then it has been mine since I took possession of it; if you depose me just before the relevant limitation period expires, then I was a trespasser the whole time. The examples differ because there is no public statutory limitation period for interruptions of a rightful condition, precisely because there is no public legal order. That only means that an extended period of barbarism still has no lawmaking powers; only the setting up of a rightful condition does. Order might have been set up and vigorously maintained, but it is neither republican nor legal. Once a legal order is restored, the legal order can regard itself as continuous with the one that was suspended by the period of barbarism. In the same way, it can recognize as legitimate private transactions that took place during the period of barbarism in the way that a new civil condition would rec-

---

51. Ibid., 8:299.

ognize the provisional rights established in a state of nature that precedes it. That recognition does not require it to give legal effect to acts of barbarism, any more than such recognition would require it to give legal effect to documented theft that took place during the period.

The upshot of this is that the woman discussed by Radbruch and Hart does not have a defense available to her, because her claim can only be analyzed as an appeal to the authority of a unilateral though powerful will. The fact that what the law must regard as some private person purported to confer on her an exemption from a legal prohibition, and even to provide her with institutional means to get rid of her husband, could not possibly serve to exempt her from punishment.[52] On Kant's analysis, though, there can be no other way of understanding her claim.[53]

Kant's analysis leads to the same result when applied to the Nazi race decrees, including those stripping people of their property and citizenship. Those laws can only be understood as orders given by a unilateral will. Thus they must lack the force of law. If a gang of criminals broke into government offices and, using the right stationery, wrote out a series of decrees, it would immediately be recognized that their acts had no legal force, any more than one person shredding another's citizenship documents could deprive the latter of citizenship. Conceptually, barbarism is no different from this, however much more powerful and thus difficult to defeat it may be.[54]

Kant's rejection of the right of revolution has the surprising implica-

---

52. The statute which she appealed to did not order her to testify against her husband, so no issues of duress arise.

53. Not every case of barbarism follows the destruction of a rightful condition, and so in certain cases there might be no antecedent law to follow. In such a situation, individual human beings can still take up arms against barbarism, but there can be no legal basis for enforcing judgments with respect to what took place in the condition of barbarism. Perhaps if barbarism that destroys a rightful condition lasts long enough, the rightful condition that follows would regard itself as beginning *de novo* in this way.

54. The Kantian analysis of decrees being void because unilateral is of more than academic interest, since it has enabled people to reclaim what they lost through the terrible political nightmares of the twentieth century. I am among those who have benefited from the descendents of the Kantian idea that wrong never changes rights, and was able to regain my German citizenship because my mother was stripped of hers by the Nazi race laws. When I received my citizenship certificate, the consular officer, Herr Schmidt, characterized the proceedings in quintessentially Kantian terms: "And now you have what you would have had if certain terrible things had not happened."

tion, then, that the cases in which it is supposed that revolution is easiest to justify are actually conditions of barbarism in which private persons are entitled to use force to create a rightful condition. It is no small irony that the problem with barbarism is exactly the problem that Kant identifies with the revolutionary. Whatever the barbarian may think, and whatever complex procedures may be set up to consolidate its power, barbarism may be resisted with right by those seeking to enter a rightful condition. To resist barbarism is to use force to enter into a rightful condition, and so to resist wrongdoing in the highest degree.

VI. Conclusion: From the Innate Right of Humanity to the Right of Human Beings as Such

The starting point for Kant's theory of right is each person's innate right of humanity, and so the entitlement of each human being to be independent of every other person's choice, to be treated as his or her own master, a person, not a thing. The extension of those fundamental ideas to the situation in which purposes could be pursued with things other than each person's own body generated private right. Private right in turn required public right: the only way that a plurality of persons can enjoy their freedom consistently with the freedom of others is to unite with those others and enter a rightful condition. As the systematic realization of everyone's freedom consistent with that of the others under universal law, a rightful condition is not merely the right of each human being considered severally, but of all of them considered together. Freedom under public law is the right of human beings as such.

Appendix

Index

APPENDIX

"A Postulate Incapable of Further Proof"

The Categorical Imperative is the centerpiece of Kant's practical philosophy and, indeed, of the critical philosophy as a whole, for it is the principle that reason must answer only to itself, rather than to anything outside of it. Kant represents it as the supreme principle of morality, and uses it to connect morality to his account of human freedom. Kant's legal and political thought appears to go in a very different direction. The central principle of the *Doctrine of Right* is the Universal Principle of Right, which is introduced as a "postulate incapable of further proof." Unlike the Categorical Imperative, the Universal Principle of Right is not supposed to be the incentive to action; instead, it is identified with "the authorization to use coercion." It is said to be "constructed" from "*a priori* intuitions." The emphasis on coercion seems to distance the Universal Principle of Right from the Categorical Imperative; talk of *a priori* intuitions seems to invite comparison with the *Critique of Pure Reason* rather than the *Critique of Practical Reason*. My aim in this appendix is to use the first *Critique* to explain both the coercive aspect of the Universal Principle of Right and its relation to the Categorical Imperative. I will argue that the differences between the Universal Principle of Right and the Categorical Imperative reflect the differences between the comparison of concepts and the comparison of objects.

One of the aims of this book has been to explain Kant's normative arguments about right without taking on the full commitments of his broader project in practical philosophy. Still, the relation between the Categorical Imperative and the Universal Principle of Right raises textual, philosophical, and even political questions. The textual question arises because, whatever advice we might want to give him,[1] Kant included the *Doctrine of Right* in *The Metaphysics of Morals*. He didn't just include it, however; he put it *first*. The phrase "Categorical Imperative" periodically appears in the *Doctrine of Right*, but it does not appear to play a systematic role in the argument, and neither deeds nor maxims are directly measured against it.[2] Yet the vocabulary that typically surrounds the Categorical Imperative in Kant's other works can be found at various pivotal points in the argument: right is only possible "under universal law"; rightful honor requires that you never allow yourself to be "treated as a mere means," and the people must "give laws to themselves." The central contrasts of the *Doctrine of Right* also parallel those of the rest of the moral philosophy. The right to be your own master, independent of the choice of any other person, parallels the contrast drawn in the *Groundwork* between autonomy and heteronomy.

Philosophically, large questions of practical philosophy are at stake: can the Kantian distinction between right and ethics be sustained in a way

---

1. Marcus Willaschek, "Why the *Doctrine of Right* Does Not Belong in the *Metaphysics of Morals*: On Some Basic Distinctions in Kant's Moral Philosophy," *Jahrbuch für Recht und Ethik* 5 (1997): 205–227.

2. The Categorical Imperative appears in the Introduction to *The Metaphysics of Morals* at 6:221, 6:222, 6:223, 6:225, 6:227. It appears three times in Private Right: 6:252 (the postulate of practical reason with regard to rights), 6:273 (on why one must perform a contract), 6:280n (on the creation of free beings as a possibility for morally practical purposes). All of these are cases in which the Categorical Imperative licenses an inference from empirical deeds to conclusions about freedom. I discuss the first of these below. The Categorical Imperative also occurs twice in Public Right: 6:318 (on the duty to strive for the conformity of the constitution with right) and 6:331 (punishment as a Categorical Imperative). In both of these examples, it figures *contrastively* in rejecting any appeal to empirical consequences as the basis for legal duties or powers. It also occurs once in the Appendix, in which Kant replies to Bouterwek's review in the *Gottingen Journal*, at 6:371 (the duty to obey the authority who has power over you in what does not conflict with inner morality). This final reference parallels the references in Private Right, because the Categorical Imperative licenses the inference from the existence of a powerful authority to a legitimate ruler. Strikingly, it does not occur in the introduction to the *Doctrine of Right*, where the Universal Principle of Right is introduced.

that right is a moral concept but not just an application of some broader "comprehensive" theory of morality to the issue of force? Since the Categorical Imperative is, for Kant, the manner in which practical reason is more than a tool, it must have *some* bearing on the way in which right is something other than a tool for achieving something else—not even a tool for giving effect to the Categorical Imperative. Kant's practical philosophy always focuses on the form of moral principles, rather than regarding form as a useful tool for approximating something that can be specified without reference to form. If the *Doctrine of Right* is not to be an awkward exception to this orientation, then the Universal Principle of Right must be something more than an adaptation of the Categorical Imperative to typical human circumstances.[3] Yet it must be related somehow if it is to cohere with Kant's remark in the Preface to the *Groundwork:* "I think it useful to issue separately this preparatory work on its foundations so that later I need not insert the subtleties inevitable in these matters into doctrines more easy to understand."[4]

Politically, the stakes are also high. Thomas Pogge has argued that the *Doctrine of Right* is not a "comprehensive" form of liberalism, because it does not depend upon accepting Kant's moral philosophy in its entirety.[5] My sympathy with this view should be apparent from the argument of the past eleven chapters. But the independence of right from the full package of Kantian morality must not be purchased at too high a price. If the Universal Principle of Right cannot be connected in *any* way to the larger project of Kantian morality, there is a danger that the principle will be comprehensive in a different way, because it will be inconsistent with Kantian morality, which, whatever its difficulties, controversies, and even obscurities, is certainly to all appearances a *reasonable* comprehensive view about morality. This brings me to a further textual problem: in both

---

3. In his essay "Themes from Kant's Moral Philosophy," in *Collected Papers*, ed. Samuel Freeman (Cambridge, Mass.: Harvard University Press, 1999), 497–528, John Rawls interprets the Categorical Imperative as requiring factual premises about typical human circumstances. Rawls's approach is interesting, but differs from Kant's own, as it blurs the distinction between the *metaphysics* of morals that he provides and a possible *anthropology* of morals that looks to the particularity of the human situation.

4. Kant, *Groundwork of the Metaphysics of Morals*, 4:391–392.

5. Thomas Pogge, "Is Kant's *Rechtslehre* a 'Comprehensive Liberalism'?" in *Kant's Metaphysics of Morals*, ed. Mark Timmons (Oxford: Oxford University Press, 2002), 153–158.

the introduction to *The Metaphysics of Morals* and the *Doctrine of Virtue*, Kant says that all duties of right are indirectly duties of virtue, that is, that there is an obligation of virtue to act on the principles of right, to make them your own principles of action. If that is correct, however, there must be some way of bringing them within the reach of the *Doctrine of Virtue* that is not at the same time a way of making right depend on virtue.

I believe that Kant has a way of solving each of these problems, so that the Universal Principle of Right really does follow from the Categorical Imperative, but is not equivalent to it. It also provides the structure through which the *Doctrine of Virtue*, the second part of *The Metaphysics of Morals*, addresses relations between human beings. The key to his solution is to be found in his remarks about the nature of "external" freedom, and his claim that "reason has taken care to furnish the understanding as far as possible with a priori intuitions for constructing the concept of right."[6] Right is concerned with external freedom, and intuitions are required to construct it precisely because right governs the relations between free and rational beings who occupy space.[7] Just as the *a priori* features that every object of possible experience must have cannot be derived from the pure forms of judgment (or anything else purely conceptual), so, too, the *a priori* features of rightful relations between rational beings who occupy space cannot be derived from the Categorical Imperative. The difference between inner willing and outer freedom is, as Kant notes of the parallel distinction between the intellectual and the sensible, transcendental rather than merely logical.[8]

---

6. 6:233.

7. In the *Critique of Practical Reason*, Kant denies that we have a special intuition of freedom: "The possibility of such a supersensible nature, the concept of which can also be the ground of its reality through our free will, requires no a priori intuition (of an intelligible world), which in this case, as supersensible, would also have to be impossible for us" (5:45). "Instead of intuition, however, it takes as its basis those laws, the concept of their existence in the intelligible world, namely the concept of freedom" (5:46). The potential role of intuition is dismissed at 5:49: "If reason sought to do this, it would have to show how the logical relation of principle and consequence can be used synthetically in a different sort of intuition from the sensible; that is how a *causa noumenon* is possible; this it cannot do; and, as practical reason, it does not even concern itself with it."

8. *Critique of Pure Reason*, trans. Paul Guyer and Allan Wood (Cambridge: Cambridge University Press, 1996), A44/B61.

In order to make this point, I want to take up Kant's claim that the principle of right enters as "a postulate that is incapable of further proof." The characterization of it as a postulate appears immediately following the claim that it is *not* equivalent to the Categorical Imperative—"but it does not at all expect, far less demand, that I myself *should* limit my freedom to those conditions just for the sake of this obligation; instead, reason says only that freedom *is* limited to those conditions in conformity with the idea of it and that it may also be actively limited by others."[9] The Universal Principle of Right is not a principle for self-legislation. Instead, others may enforce it. A postulate is required to establish such a principle.

I. The Other Postulates in the Doctrine of Right

Kant uses the term "postulate" throughout his critical writings. Although its meaning is controversial, certain features are clear. The postulates from the *Critiques* of Pure and Practical Reason—God, freedom, and immortality—are shown to be warranted on practical grounds, and Kant sometimes characterizes them as theoretical beliefs that are so warranted. Yet they are not theoretical beliefs in any simple or straightforward sense: Kant characterizes the conviction that there is a God as a "not **logical** but **moral** certainty" because it is "so interwoven with my moral disposition."[10] The same point applies even more clearly to freedom. It is not a theoretical hypothesis that can be integrated with the rest of theoretical cognition; it can neither explain anything nor add anything to our cognition. Instead, each of us is warranted by the *factum* of reason[11] to think of his or her own deliberations as expressions of our freedom. Kant argues in the Transcendental Aesthetic and again in the Transcendental Deduction of the categories in the *Critique of Pure Reason* that we are aware of ourselves only as "appearances" in time, not as we are in ourselves; in his discussion of the Paralogisms he argues that the logical form of first-

---

9. 6:231.
10. *Critique of Pure Reason*, A829/B857.
11. It is not a fact, but a *factum*, that is a deed. See Paul Franks, *All or Nothing* (Cambridge, Mass.: Harvard University Press, 2005), chap. 5; Marcus Willaschek, *Praktische Vernunft: Handlungstheorie und Moralbegrundung bei Kant* (Stuttgart: J. B. Metzler, 1992).

personal descriptions shows nothing about a self as it is in itself. The postulate of freedom provides moral grounds for supposing that our thoughts and deliberations, which are themselves in time, and so individuated through theoretical cognition rather than aspects of things in themselves, are nonetheless expressions of freedom. It requires you to think of yourself and act "under the idea of freedom," even though epistemic grounds for doing so are not only absent but necessarily impossible. The only way I can represent my self is by representing it as in time; to do so, however, is to represent myself as empirically real, and so subject to causal necessitation. I must nonetheless regard myself as free, because I have a moral obligation to suppose that my deliberations are the empirical manifestations of a free person.[12] I can have no theoretical license for (or against) this conclusion, because I have no theoretical grounds for any views whatsoever about the individuation of things in themselves. Instead, I am obligated—morally—to think of myself as free, and so to think of my deliberations and choices as manifestations of that freedom. Moral concepts thus ground the entitlement both to regard the in-itself as including persons and to regard your deliberating self as a free person. They thereby both construct the moral concept of a person and demand of each of us that we apply to ourselves in the first-person case.[13]

---

12. *Critique of Practical Reason*, 5:49.

13. The same line of argument is introduced in the Introduction to the *Critique of Practical Reason*, at 5:5, and developed in detail beginning at 5:55. Like the postulates of empirical thought in the *Critique of Pure Reason*, they do not "augment the concepts to which they apply" (A219/B266). In the first *Critique*, postulates are said to "express the relation of a concept to the faculty of knowledge." By contrast, practical postulates express the relation of empirical concepts to freedom. Because freedom and obligation reciprocally imply each other (*Critique of Practical Reason*, 5:29), the postulate of freedom is also the postulate of the moral law.

Kant never explicitly relates the postulates of empirical thought to the practical postulates of God, freedom, and immortality, but if those postulates are understood as practical, then they, too, add no content to the concept of their objects, but instead bring other objects under new sets of modal categories of obligation and prohibition. In the case of the categorical imperative, the modal concepts correspond to those in the logical table of judgments. In the logical case, the middle term is only a placeholder: everything is logically possible or logically necessary, but nothing is logically actual, so, too, inner morality says only that certain maxims are permissible (or not) and others obligatory (or not); any analogue of the category of existence has no determinate application. In the logical table of judgments, the middle term is "assertoric," that is, asserting a proposition. In the case of inner morality, the middle term

The Universal Principle of Right is a postulate in the same sense: it provides a license to consider things in space and time under laws of freedom, to apply moral concepts to empirical objects, and so establishes an entitlement that could not be established on theoretical grounds. The *factum* of reason requires us to understand our thoughts in terms of moral concepts of freedom, even though they are in time. The Universal Principle of Right requires us to understand embodied human beings—both ourselves and others—as instances of the moral concept of a person. In that sense, it requires a postulate, rather than either an inference or a discovery.[14] At the same time, the postulates in the *Doctrine of Right* also introduce new laws of freedom. The manner in which they do so is somewhat easier to grasp in relation to the second postulate that Kant introduces. At the beginning of Private Right, the postulate of practical reason with regard to rights *also* enters as a "postulate incapable of further proof," which enables reason to "extend itself a priori."[15]

---

would be willing a maxim. In the case of the postulate of right, the modal categories have correlates, yielding Kant's deontic hexagon of permissible/forbidden, merely permissible/not imputable, and obligatory/nonobligatory. The middle pair, corresponding to existence/nonexistence in the first *Critique,* reflect the role of permissive laws, which underwrite imputation on the basis of merely permissible actions, such as acquisition of property, the making of contracts, and entering into status relations; its correlate involves merely permissible actions on the basis of which no rightful consequences can be imputed, such as using an object you have not acquired (6:269), or saying or doing something to others that does not interfere with what is already theirs (6:238). For the significance of the deontic hexagon in Achenwall, from whose textbook Kant taught natural right, see Joachim Hruschka, *Das deontologische Sechseck bei Gottfried Achenwall im Jahre 1767* (Hamburg: Vandenhoek und Ruprecht, 1986).

14. Contrary to Robert B. Pippin, "Mine and Thine? The Kantian State," in Paul Guyer, ed., *Cambridge Companion to Kant and Modern Philosophy* (Cambridge: Cambridge University Press, 2006), 416-446, the introduction of additional postulates does not require a separate *factum* of reason for each. Instead, the *factum* of reason—that there are obligations—licenses each of the postulates, which apply laws of freedom to additional domains of objects.

15. 6:247. The *Doctrine of Right* also includes a third postulate, concerning "Public Right." Since my expository strategy focuses on the structure of the second postulate rather than the details of Kant's argument, I will limit myself to only a brief remark about it. First, like the other two postulates, it serves to extend concepts of freedom to a new class of objects in space and time, namely public legal institutions and the officials who serve within them. Kant says that this possibility can be "explicated analytically from the concept of right in external relations, in contrast with violence *(violentia)*" (6:307). The possibility of analytical explication follows from the role, discussed in Chapter 7, of legal institutions in bringing individual

My strategy will be to show that this second postulate provides the appropriate model for thinking through the first. In order to do so, I will show why the Universal Principle of Right is sufficient to ground the innate right of humanity in one's own person, but requires a further postulate to generate rights to property, contract, and relations of status. After examining the structure through which such a postulate interacts with the Universal Principle of Right, I will propose a parallel structure to explain the introduction of the Universal Principle of Right itself.

The Universal Principle of Right states that

> any action is *right* if it can coexist with everyone's freedom in accordance with a universal law, or if on its maxim the freedom of choice of each can coexist with everyone's freedom in accordance with a universal law.[16]

In the "Introduction to the *Metaphysics of Morals* as a Whole," Kant characterizes choice in terms of "consciousness of the ability to bring about its object by one's action" and contrasts it with mere wish, which is "not joined with this consciousness."[17] Freedom of choice *(Willkur)*, then, must be understood in terms of the ability to choose which ends to pursue, which, on Kant's analysis, can only be done in light of the powers one has available. The coexistence of freedom of choice in accordance with universal law is thus the ability of each of a plurality of persons to use the powers he or she has to set and pursue his or her own purposes, consistent with the ability of others to do the same.

The conception of equal freedom articulated by the Universal Principle of Right governs interacting persons. It also entails a definition of

---

exercises of freedom under universal law. Thus the postulate of public right does not introduce novel incompatibility relations between private persons, but subjects private persons to public law. This new form of potential incompatibility requires bringing legal institutions under laws of freedom. It thus applies to actual institutions, and requires people to understand them as defective instances of the idea of the original contract, "in terms of which alone," as we saw in Chapter 7, "we can think of the legitimacy of the state." The pure case provides the only possible standard through which the actual case can be thought of as rightful.

16. 6:230.
17. 6:213.

wrong as that which is incompatible with right: uses of a person's powers to set and pursue ends in ways that are *not* consistent with the ability of others to use their powers. Kant treats the concept of equal freedom under right as sufficient for the innate right of humanity in your own person, your right to be free from the choice of others under universal laws.

As a principle limiting the actions of separate persons, the Universal Principle of Right is not sufficient to generate any further rights that extend beyond your innate right of humanity in your own person. As we saw in Chapter 3, your innate right of humanity in your own person does not contain the idea of rights with regard to external objects of choice, that is, those things *other* than your own person that you can use in setting and pursuing your own purposes. Nothing in the Universal Principle of Right precludes the possibility of a type of persons capable of setting and pursuing their own purposes but unable to subject any external object to their choice. As we saw, a striking feature of all acquired rights is that they have a "mine or yours" structure, and because of that require an affirmative act to establish them. We also saw that the normative argument for acquired rights focuses on the ways in which things could be usable, consistent with the formal structure of each person's purposiveness. They are not available only for specific uses, such as Lockean self-preservation, but must be available to be used *simpliciter*.

The introduction of external objects of choice creates new ways in which my choice and yours with respect to some object can be incompatible. Precisely because it could be "mine or yours"—it could belong to someone else—any object of choice that is yours must be subject to your choice even when it is not, factually, subject to your control. So long as you are in physical possession of the object—you have your hand wrapped around an apple—I wrong you by interfering with your physical possession of it, simply because in so doing I interfere with your person.[18] The postulate extends the principle of right to the case in which I can wrong you with respect to an object even if I am *not* interfering with your person, thus setting up a potential *further* incompatibility between my deeds and your rights. In the same way, the postulate extends the principle of right to the case in which I have transferred my future conduct to you

18. 6:250.

through a contract. Without the postulate, I would owe you no affirmative obligations of right. Those obligations are requirements that I make my deeds compatible with your acquired rights. Novel incompatibilities generate novel obligations.

For each of the three titles of private right, the second postulate both establishes the relevant laws of freedom and underwrites the application of laws of freedom to objects in space and time. The postulate removes "all conditions of intuition which establish empirical possession," "in order to extend the concept of possession beyond empirical possession." Kant marks this other form of possession as "nonphysical,"[19] "intelligible," or "noumenal."[20]

As Wilfrid Sellars has pointed out, the intuitive idea here is simple and familiar: we have obligations to others that take objects in space and time as their objects, such as the obligation to pay a debt of a dollar. Since obligations are governed by laws of freedom, which must be noumenal rather than phenomenal, it follows that there must be some sense in which it is possible to have noumenal possession of empirical dollars.[21] We can have no theoretical grounds for supposing that noumenal possession of dollars is possible, because we can have no theoretical grounds for *any* suppositions about the noumenal realm, and have no basis in theoretical reason either for individuating objects in it or for supposing that it has parts that are in any way isomorphic with empirical objects. We can, however, have *practical*, i.e. moral, grounds for accepting the possibility of noumenal possession of dollars: if I owe you a dollar, then you have noumenal possession of my transfer of a dollar to you. If I wrongfully take it from you, then you have noumenal possession of a dollar of which I have physical possession.[22] More generally, the postulate licenses an abstraction from

---

19. 6:252.
20. 6:255.
21. Sellars's choice of example is potentially misleading, insofar as dollars might be thought to be nonempirical because abstract. The same point could be made about an obligation to return another person's property: the owner has noumenal possession of an empirical object.
22. Sellars, *Kant and Pre-Kantian Themes*, ed. Pedro Amaral (Atascadero: Ridgeview, 2002), 61. This book is an edited version of lectures that Sellars gave in his Kant course at the University of Pittsburgh in 1975 and 1976. He gave the same examples in a course I attended in the fall term of 1982.

empirical possession to rightful possession by licensing the extensions of laws of freedom to objects in space and time.[23]

The postulate of practical reason with regard to rights articulates the structure of noumenal possession. It shows that I can be entitled to think of external objects of choice in abstraction from conditions of space and time. The license for the abstraction does not come from theoretical reason—that is why Kant denies that the postulate represents an extension of cognition—but from practical reason. A system of equal freedom requires that it be morally permissible for usable things to be used, in accordance with Kant's formal conception of what it is to use something: to have it subject to your choice, so that you may set and pursue purposes with it. Thus the possibility of having something usable as your own requires that you be able to have it generally, that is, that it be subject to your choice, as opposed to that of another, even when you are not in possession of it. The structure of property is just the power to have some physical object in space subject to your choice even when you are not holding it; the structure of contract is the entitlement to have another person's action subject to your choice, even before the action has been performed. You can release your contracting partner from the contract, but your partner cannot release himself. The structure of status requires that one person act for the purposes of another and so, when acting within the status, that she surrender independent purposiveness. In each of these cases, your entitlement applies to something apart from you; it can only so apply if physical objects and human actions can be thought of as expressions of a noumenal order in the same way that, in deciding what to do, I can regard my deliberations as reflections of noumenal choice.[24]

---

23. Kant remarks that the entitlement in the postulate of practical reason with regard to rights is just the fact of reason. "No one need be surprised that *theoretical* principles about external objects that are mine or yours get lost in the intelligible and represent no extension of cognition, since no theoretical deduction can be given for the possibility of the concept of freedom on which they are based. It can only be inferred from the practical law of reason (the categorical imperative), as a fact of reason" (6:252). Kant's claim here parallels the arguments of the *Critique of Pure Reason* and *Critique of Practical Reason* about the entitlement to regard ourselves as free.

24. In the *Doctrine of Right*, Kant uses both "Fact of Reason" and Categorical Imperative" to characterize this warrant. See 6:252.

II. The Universal Principle of Right

Focusing on the second postulate gives us a way of understanding what leads Kant to introduce the first one, which he elsewhere calls the "axiom of outer freedom."[25] The postulate of private right extends the Universal Principle of Right to take account of a type of incompatibility relation that it does not already presuppose. The Universal Principle of Right extends the Categorical Imperative to take account of a type of incompatibility relation that is not presupposed by it. The novel nature of that incompatibility is the source of the familiar *difficulty* of deriving the Universal Principle of Right from the Categorical Imperative. The possibility of coercion is not contained in the Categorical Imperative as it is formulated in either the *Groundwork* or the *Critique of Practical Reason*. In order for the Categorical Imperative, in any of its formulations, to be an internal constraint *on the will,* there must be the potential for certain forms of incompatibility: a maxim must be internally incapable of being willed as a universal law. Putting to one side various details about the relevant type of contradiction, the relations between the formulations of the Categorical Imperative, and the ways in which types of contradiction can be classified, the uncontroversial aspect of the Categorical Imperative is that it is supposed to show that certain maxims could not be universal laws because of defects in their internal form. Either the use of inappropriate means for given ends or the failure to adopt ends that are mandatory for any finite rational being is a defect of will, which arises entirely at the level of what *could* be willed, quite apart from what anyone else does, or even whether there is anyone else.

The incompatibility relations that are the concern of the Categorical Imperative are internal to the willing of the maxim at issue. Kant classifies the presupposition of a free will as synthetic; if his argument is accepted, the contradictions at issue are conceptual but not analytic. The conceptual nature of the incompatibility is apparent in the case of what Kant calls "perfect" duties, because the maxims he considers cannot even be *conceived* to be universal laws—they contradict *themselves,* quite apart from the way the world turns out to be. Even in the case of what Kant calls "im-

---

25. 6:268.

perfect" duties to adopt the ends of one's own perfection or the happiness of others, for which the contradiction is "in the will," rather than "in conception," the incompatibility is still conceptual: a will could not repudiate its own freedom by choosing a world in which it had no developed powers, or in which cooperation and mutual aid were impossible.[26] Its own concern for its own purposiveness requires that it leave these possibilities open. A universal law that precluded the development of your powers and aiding others as possible ends would impose an arbitrary limit on freedom. Thus they must be among your ends, simply because you are a rational being capable of setting your own purposes, for their possibility is contained in the concept of a rational will.[27]

For both perfect and imperfect duties, then, the Categorical Imperative identifies maxims that are internally defective. Its conceptual structure is fundamental to Kant's argument that the Categorical Imperative is a principle of pure practical reason. If there were only one person, the Categorical Imperative would still be his or her autonomous principle of reason.[28]

---

26. Kant's arguments in each case receive much more detailed treatment in the *Doctrine of Virtue*, the second part of *The Metaphysics of Morals*, than they do in the *Groundwork*. For discussion of this, see Barbara Herman, "The Scope of Moral Requirement" and "The Will and Its Objects," both in *Moral Literacy* (Cambridge, Mass.: Harvard University Press, 2007).

27. I am assuming here that the Categorical Imperative is to be understood in terms of either of what Christine Korsgaard describes as the "logical contradiction" or "practical contradiction" interpretations, rather than the "teleological" interpretation. Korsgaard rejects both the logical and teleological conceptions, but nothing in the argument of the text depends upon the differences between the logical and practical conceptions. It does, however, depend on rejecting the teleological interpretation, according to which the Categorical Imperative is an empty formula requiring consequentialist considerations to apply to anything. That is plainly not the way that Kant conceived of it. See Korsgaard, "Kant's Formula of Universal Law," in her *Creating the Kingdom of Ends* (Cambridge: Cambridge University Press, 1996), 77–105.

28. Although I cannot defend this claim in detail here, I believe that the Categorical Imperative underlies the entire critical system. As reason's own law, that is, it expresses the requirement that reason can be answerable only to itself, and never to anything outside of it. On the strongest reading, the idea that reason has a law of its own provides the philosophical inspiration for transcendental idealism: the transcendental realist, whether represented as the dogmatist or the skeptic, is the philosopher who insists that reason is answerable to something other than itself. The tower-building dogmatist of the Preface of the first *Critique* seeks to use reason as a tool to pierce the heavens, so as to finally grasp what is really real. The tower-smashing skeptic humbles the dogmatist by humbling reason, showing that it is not

If your maxim makes reference to other persons, directly or indirectly, the Categorical Imperative requires you to take account of them, but the requirement that you do so is a rational requirement of your own freedom; the Categorical Imperative grounds the demand for consistency with others in the requirement of consistency in your own maxim.

If we understand the Categorical Imperative in this way, then it locates the requirement of consistency in the will of the particular agent. The *subject matter* of this incompatibility often concerns the deeds and ends of others, but the *test* of its compatibility is purely internal. As reason's law, the Categorical Imperative treats all agents as in precisely the same situation: their task is to give laws for all rational beings. At the same time, that task is in each case *mine,* that is, the question is always one of what principle the agent in particular should act on. Each of us is supposed to select maxims as if we were legislating for the kingdom of ends; there is no question of reconciling separate exercises of our outer freedom by the use of force.

I take these observations about the Categorical Imperative to be neutral between competing interpretations and assessments of it. Without more, none of these can generate the Universal Principle of Right, which authorizes coercion.[29] They can, however, do so by means of a postulate, that is, something that introduces a new set of incompatibility relations by applying moral concepts to things that are incompatible in a different way. The postulate of right does exactly that.

Kant makes conspicuous use of spatial images throughout the *Doctrine of Right*. Innate right is modeled on the incompatibility of different people occupying the same place. In Private Right, the basic case of property is land,[30] understood as a specific region of the Earth's surface; noumenal

---

properly suited to the dogmatist's ambition. What they share is not merely, as is so often noted, the idea that we can have cognition of things as they are in themselves. That claim is a reflection of their deeper shared agreement that reason itself is tool for investigating something that has a fully determinate nature apart from that investigation. For further development of this line of argument, see Onora O'Neill, "Reason and Politics in the Kantian Enterprise," in her *Constructions of Reason* (Cambridge: Cambridge University Press, 1989), 3–27.

29. Marcus Willaschek, "Right and Coercion: Can Kant's Conception of Right Be Derived from his Moral Theory?," *International Journal of Philosophical Studies* 17, no. 1 (2009): 49–70.

30. 6:261.

possession abstracts from space and time because physical possession is the simple case of possession; the initial example of a contract is a present transfer of a physical object.[31] In Public Right, territory marks the limits of the state, and is even represented as the state's body; the state is the "supreme proprietor of the land" because only it is competent to divide it into parts.[32] The choice of models comes as no surprise, since space is, for Kant, the form of outer sense, and the Universal Principle of Right is the law of outer (external) freedom. In the Transcendental Aesthetic of the *Critique of Pure Reason,* Kant argues that space is the form in which objects appear as outer; in the *Doctrine of Right* he says that "reason has taken care to furnish the understanding with a priori intuitions for constructing the concept of right."[33] The *Critique* teaches that intuitions can only be *a priori* if they are formal, so the intuitions with which the concept of right is constructed must be formal. The principle of right governs outer freedom, so a priori intuitions for it must conform to the form of outer intuition—space.[34]

---

31. 6:272.

32. Although the state is the proprietor in accordance with any antecedent "provisional" rights to things, such provisional rights become conclusive only when the state's territory is considered as the manifestation of its general will; this territory is then divided in accordance with the "formal principle of division, instead of with principles of *aggregation* (which proceeds from parts to the whole)." Kant's characterization of the spatiality of land here parallels his claim in the *Critique of Pure Reason* that the parts of space "cannot as it were precede the single all-encompassing space as its components (from which its composition would be possible) but rather are only thought **in it**" (see 6:323 and *Critique of Pure Reason,* A25/B39).

33. 6:233.

34. How can an intuition be "provided" for constructing the concept of right if "no corresponding intuition can be given" for a rational concept? Kant makes the latter claim in the context of a discussion of the postulate of practical reason with regard to rights, which concerns the synthetic principle arrived at by removing all "conditions of intuition which establish empirical possession" (6:252). The concept of nonempirical possession takes the already constructed concept of right, including interfering with a person by interfering with something that she is holding, and disregards its particular conditions of intuition. This removal, or disregard, of empirical conditions removes all conditions of intuition, and depends on the entitlement to individuate the noumenal realm on practical grounds. Such individuation is nonempirical, so no intuition can be given for it. Instead, the incompatibility between different persons occupying the same space is "extended" to cover objects by abstracting away from the particular location of the object in relation to its owner. The extension is synthetic because it introduces something new.

Kant's central claim is that we are rational beings who occupy space. This postulate is "incapable of further proof," because nothing would qualify as a successful proof of it. It cannot be given a proof from concepts, because, as Kant argues in the Transcendental Aesthetic, space is nonconceptual and cannot be reduced to any concept or relations between them. The details of that argument are complex and contested, but its basic gist is simple and familiar: space is nonconceptual because it has a different kind of generality than any concept does. A concept is general in the sense that (possible) instances fall under it. Space, in contrast, has parts rather than instances. Instances of a concept are more specific than it, and have more determinate content, so that the concept of a horse is more determinate than that of a mammal; parts of space are all the same, and differ only in their external relations, that is, their location. Moreover, Kant argues that space as a whole is prior to its parts: it is not built up of discrete parts, but rather its parts are demarcated by dividing it. The parts of space thus stand in a nonconceptual form of incompatibility relations. Nor could the postulate be given a proof from either experience or *a priori* intuition of space, as neither of these contains the concept of a rational being.[35]

If no proof is available, then a postulate is required to introduce the norms governing the concept of an embodied rational being, that is, one that both occupies space and falls under laws of freedom. Embodied persons have both duties and entitlements because they are rational beings; the form of the duties and entitlements reflects the distinctive incompatibility relations between beings that occupy space. The synthetic *a priori* truth that two bodies cannot occupy the same space at the same time[36] is

---

35. Although the principle of virtue is synthetic, because it "goes beyond the concept of outer freedom and connects with it, in accordance with universal laws, an *end* that it makes a *duty*." See *Doctrine of Virtue*, 6:396.

36. Strictly speaking, the incompatibility is not generated by the concept of space, but rather by the concept of a solid in space. In the *Metaphysical Foundations of Natural Science*, ed. Michael Friedman (Cambridge: Cambridge University Press, 2004), 4:496ff., Kant argues that the concept of a solid is empirical. See also *Critique of Pure Reason*, B5, where he includes "even" impenetrability among the empirical aspects of the concept of body; B35, where he characterizes impenetrability among the things that "belong to sensation"; and A41/B58, where the existence of objects in space is found only through experience. Nothing in this appendix turns on the resolution of the nature of impenetrability. Whether a particular object is

incorporated into the law of freedom that no person may invade the space occupied by another; if the postulate requires us to individuate persons spatially, then any potential incompatibility between the occupation of space by different persons becomes a moral incompatibility.

Kant never explicitly argues that the Universal Principle of Right is the unique moral principle for rational beings who occupy space, but an argument can be provided by analogy with the argument for the postulate of practical reason with regard to rights. That argument showed that the terms on which persons are entitled to use things other than their bodies must be formal rather than material, because otherwise the usability of usable objects would depend on the matter of other persons' choices. The same point applies here: if you were prohibited from using your body in any way, or, what comes to the same thing, you were conditionally prohibited, so that your entitlement to do anything with your own body was subject to the choice of others, as a material principle would demand (perhaps everyone, or even someone, had to approve any action you chose to perform), your capacity to set and pursue your own purposes would be subject to their choice. No material principle of that sort could be a universal law under the criteria set out in the *Groundwork*, because as a rational being you could not will a universal law under which you could never set a purpose for yourself, or one under which you could only do so with the leave of another. So once spatial forms of incompatibility are introduced, only the formal principle of outer freedom—the

---

impenetrable is empirical, but the concept of impenetrability, understood as incompatible occupations of space, is not; it is, as Longuenesse points out, a purely relational feature of things in relation to other things in space (Beatrice Longuenesse, *Kant and the Capacity to Judge* [Princeton: Princeton University Press, 1998], 144). In the "Observation" on the paralogisms, Kant says that the "doctrine of body can be cognized *a priori* from the mere concept of an extended impenetrable being" (A381). Kant makes a similar claim in the *Opus Postumum*, trans. Eckart Forster and Michael Rosen (Cambridge: Cambridge University Press, 1993), at 21:475. Even if penetrable objects could be individuated in space and time (ghosts, for example), the role of the postulate is to apply moral concepts to persons already individuated in space and time, and so to generate incompatibility relations characteristic of things so individuated. For a more skeptical account of the role of impenetrability in the *Doctrine of Right*, see Douglas Moggach, "The Construction of Juridical Space: Kant's Analogy of Relation in the *Metaphysics of Morals*," in *Proceedings of the Twentieth World Congress of Philosophy*, vol. 7, ed. Mark Gedney, Philosophy Documentation Center, Bowling Green, Ohio, 2000, pp. 201–209.

Universal Principle of Right—could govern the exercise of free but spatially individuated persons. Such an argument is not a derivation of the Universal Principle of Right from the Categorical Imperative; it only shows the former to be the legitimate extension of the latter.[37]

If moral persons are individuated spatially, then the only way to have freedom under universal law is for each embodied rational being to have, in virtue of its humanity, a right to its own person—that is, to its own body. Such a right must be innate, because nothing could count as an affirmative act establishing it—the right applies to any rational being that occupies space, because its right is nothing more than the right that it has to the space that it happens to occupy.

As we saw in Chapter 2, what legal systems identify as "wrongs against the person" are, unsurprisingly, wrongs against the body, because your body just is your person. You do not occupy your body; your person occupies space. Your body enables you to set and pursue purposes in space and time, but you must do so in a way that is consistent with the ability of other embodied rational beings to set and pursue their purposes in space and time. As Kant notes, this compatibility can only be achieved in abstraction from the "*matter* of choice, that is, of the end each has in mind with the object he wants." Instead, "all that is in question is the *form* of the relation of choice on the part of both, insofar as choice is regarded merely as *free*."[38] That is, the rational purposiveness of each is only consistent with the rational purposiveness of others if each person's body is subject to his or her exclusive choice. Each person is prohibited from injuring or using the body of another. Injury and use in turn can be identified without reference to the maxim on which the wrongdoer acts. Personal injury is just injury to another's person, that is, bodily damage; the familiar legal wrong of battery—an unauthorized touching of another's person—is the simplest case of using a person for a purpose he or she has not authorized. Injuring a person interferes with his purposiveness, either by depriving him of some of the powers he has to set purposes, or by using his powers—his person—for purposes he has not set.

If space is governed by the part/whole relation rather than the concept/ instance relation, then embodied rational beings can stand in a novel type

---

37. I am grateful to Calvin Normore for pressing me to address this issue.
38. 6:230.

of incompatibility relation *to each other,* in addition to the conceptual incompatibility of potential maxims that are the object of the Categorical Imperative. In particular, because they occupy space, the only way their activity can be rendered consistent under universal law is if they neither occupy nor interfere with the space occupied by others. As Kant puts it, each of us has a right to be "wherever nature or chance" might have placed us—to occupy the space that we happen to occupy.[39] Conversely, each is constrained by the spatial occupation of the other. That is why Kant says that, prior to any acquisition, the surface of the Earth is held "disjunctively," that is, in terms of mutual exclusion. The "innate possession in common"[40] that precedes any acquisition is neither a Lockean idea of God having given the Earth to men nor a Grotian idea of a primitive community. Instead, each person is entitled to occupy whatever space is not currently occupied by any other.[41]

III. The Universal Principle of Right and the Critique of Pure Reason

The general structure that distinguishes the Universal Principle of Right from the Categorical Imperative has its roots in the *Critique of Pure Reason.* The details and cogency of Kant's argument there are disputed, but once again, its broad outlines are clear. The Transcendental Analytic provides an account of objects of possible experience in terms of the combined roles of both sensibility and understanding. Together, sensibility and understanding make objects of experience possible. Without sensibility—and in particular, without the distinctive types of incompatibility characteristic of space—reason alone lacks the resources to individuate objects, and can operate only on concepts. The Logical Forms of Judgment govern conceptual thought; the Categories govern thinking about objects. In the same way, the Categorical Imperative governs the willing of

---

39. 6:262.
40. 6:246.
41. In both the "Metaphysical Deduction" in the *Critique of Pure Reason* and the *Lectures on Logic,* Kant treats disjunction as a logical category of mutual exclusion. The category of the understanding corresponding to the logical form of disjunction—the form it takes when applied to objects in space and time—is community, that is, reciprocal limitation of bodies in space.

maxims; the Universal Principle of Right governs the choice of deeds. The additional relational content introduced through space does not merely add something new. It also makes the purely conceptual case insufficient for judgments about objects in space and time. In the Transcendental Aesthetic, Kant argues that objects of experience *could not be* things in themselves, because our only access to them comes by way of their relational features, that is, their location in space.[42] The argument takes it for granted that things as they are in themselves must be characterized solely in terms of their inner determinations rather than their outer ones. The argument does not seek to show that objects of experience have no inner determinations; only that such determinations have no bearing on our cognition of those objects; they are necessarily beyond experience.

In the same way, the Universal Principle of Right abstracts from the maxim on which a person acts, focusing instead on the purely external relation between agents. As a principle of inner determination, a person's maxim is fundamental. But it has no bearing on the outer obligations that one embodied person owes another. I wrong you if I interfere with your rights, regardless of what maxim I act on, but I do not wrong you by acting on an immoral maxim unless I interfere with your person or property.[43]

Kant provides a more complete elucidation of the differences between concepts and objects in the appendix to the chapter Noumena and Phenomena, called the "Amphiboly of Concepts of Reflection." Leibniz is the explicit target of Kant's criticisms, but the points that he makes are of much broader import. He articulates his critique of Leibniz through an examination of what he identifies as the four ways in which *objects* can be compared. In each case, he distinguishes these comparisons from the ways in which *concepts* can be compared. Each of these has a parallel in the contrast between the Universal Principle of Right and the Categorical Imperative. In this section I use the contrasts considered in the Amphiboly discussion to explain the role of forms of sensibility in generating the other marks of the difference between the Universal Principle of Right

---

42. *Critique of Pure Reason*, A26/B42.

43. If I attempt to wrong you but fail, I may commit a crime, but (unless your apprehension of a battery makes my act an assault) I do not commit a private wrong against you.

and the Categorical Imperative: (i) "identity/difference," which yields two distinct ways of individuating actions; (ii) "agreement/opposition," which explains why wrong under the Categorical Imperative is internal contradiction, but wrong under the Universal Principle of Right merits external coercion; (iii) "inner/outer," which generates the concept of rights against, and duties owed to, particular persons; and (iv) "form/matter," which explains why principles of right do not take account of ends. In each case, the metaphysical distinctions between concepts and objects generate differences in the laws of freedom appropriate to concepts and appropriate to beings that stand in external relations.[44]

(i) Identity/difference (individuating actions)

Kant's discussion of Leibniz begins with the distinction between qualitative[45] and numerical identity and difference: two drops of water can be

---

44. In a letter to Heinrich Jung-Stilling, Kant explains how the categories apply to "how laws should be given in a civil society that is already presupposed;

1. As regards quantity, the laws must be of such a nature that one [citizen] might have decreed them for all, and all for one;
2. As regards quality, it is not the citizen's purpose that the laws must decide, for all citizens may be allowed to pursue their own happiness in conformity with their own inclination and power; but laws concern only the freedom of every person and the forcible limitation on that freedom imposed by the condition that each person's freedom must be compatible with that of every other person;
3. As regards the category of relation, it is not those of the citizen's actions that relate to that person or to God that are to be condemned but only those external actions that restrict the freedom of a person's fellow citizens;
4. As for modality, the laws (qua coercive) must not be given as arbitrary and accidental commandments required for the sake of some purposes that happen to be desired; they must be given only insofar as they are necessary for the achievement of universal freedom" (Kant, *Correspondence*, trans. Arnulf Zweig [Cambridge: Cambridge University Press, 1999], 23:494.

This division brings practical concepts to bear on objects in a way that corresponds to division in the text: quantity to identity/difference (which, in public right, individuates the rights of each through the rights of all); quality to agreement/opposition (which is external, not internal); relation to inner/outer; modality to form/matter (and thus the priority of freedom over particular purposes.) On the relation between the amphiboly and the categories, see Longuenesse, *Kant and the Capacity to Judge*.

45. Kant includes *"qualitas et quantitas"* in his characterization of objects of the pure understanding. The inclusion of quantity, and its contrast with number, follow his

qualitatively and quantitatively identical but numerically distinct because they occupy different locations. The parallel contrast marks the difference between the Categorical Imperative as a conceptual test and the Universal Principle of Right as a spatial one. The incompatibility between our embodied persons—the fact that we cannot both be in the same place at the same time—introduces a way in which our deeds can come into conflict regardless of the maxims on which we act. That is why the Universal Principle of Right can be articulated without reference to "everyone's consciousness of obligation in accordance with a law."[46] Consciousness of obligation—presumably in the form of the Categorical Imperative—is the basis of right, but it "may not and cannot be appealed to as an incentive to determine his choice in accordance with this law."[47] No consciousness of obligation is required in order to identify those acts that are prohibited by the Universal Principle of Right. Instead, acts are individuated in terms of their potential incompatibility with other people's occupation of space.

(ii) Agreement/opposition (enforcement)

The second concept of reflection considered in the *Critique* is agreement and opposition. Kant criticizes Leibniz for failing to grasp the difference between a logical opposition and real opposition. Kant concedes Leibniz's claim that reality, as represented by the pure understanding, admits of no oppositions, because it represents only concepts, for which the only form of opposition is negation. Logical opposition is just negation. "Realities in appearance *(realitas phaenomenon)*, on the contrary, can certainly be in opposition with each other and, united in the same subject, one can partly or wholly destroy the **consequence of the other,** like two moving forces in the same straight line that either push or pull a point in opposed directions."[48] He later glosses the same argument with the re-

---

characterization of quantity in the table of "Logical function of the Understanding in Judgments" (*Critique of Pure Reason*, A70/B95). Two concepts can differ in the understanding if they are qualitatively the same but one is universal and the other singular.
46. 6:232.
47. Ibid.
48. *Critique of Pure Reason*, A265/B321.

mark "where $A - B = 0$, where one reality, if combined in one subject with another, cancels out the effect of the latter, which is unceasingly placed before our eyes by all hindrances and countereffects in nature, which, since they rest on forces, must be called *realitates phaenomena*."[49] Kant goes on to contend that general mechanics can provide the condition of this opposition *a priori*.[50]

A parallel argument appears in the Introduction to the *Doctrine of Right*. Kant's emphasis on the authorization to use coercion is stated first in the vocabulary of hindrances and then in that of action and reaction. This is more than a linguistic parallel: the violation of the Categorical Imperative is a kind of self-contradiction for which the agent must reproach him- or herself in conscience. Your own obligation to perfect yourself animates the possibility of this reproach. Since you have no duty to perfect others (or they to perfect you), other persons do not have (juridical) standing to reproach you. If you act on a maxim that contradicts the Categorical Imperative, your principle of action contradicts itself. The bad effects of such wrongs can be imputed to you, by your own conscience.[51] From the standpoint of the Categorical Imperative, the wrong itself does not need to be canceled; a maxim that contradicts itself simply cancels itself.[52] As with concepts represented by the understanding, the only opposition is logical.

If you violate a duty of right, however, *others* are entitled to hinder your hindrance to freedom. This hindrance is not a strategic attempt to reduce

---

49. Ibid., A273/B329.

50. On Kant's conception of forces, see *Metaphysical Foundations of Natural Science*, chap. 2: "Metaphysical Foundations of Dynamics," 4:496ff. For detailed discussion of Kant's conception of dynamics and impenetrability, see Daniel Warren, *Reality and Impenetrability in Kant's Philosophy of Nature* (New York: Routledge, 2001). Alexander Aichele has pointed out to me that Kant is less explicit than he might be in this passage, since he moves from a general discussion of comparison of *objects*, each of which is potentially the subject term of a judgment, to comparisons of *forces*, which act on objects. This shift suggests that the analogous principle in the case of right governs opposing choices.

51. 6:431.

52. *Critique of Pure Reason*, A274/B330. The self-contradictory nature of an inconsistent maxim does not entail that the person who acts on one may not have a further duty to repair moral relationships damaged by it. As soon as the concept of a relationship (or repair of it) is introduced, persons have been individuated spatially. The present point concerns only the nature of the inconsistency that makes the maxim, and so the act on it, wrongful.

the number of violations; it is simply the underlying right reasserting itself in a system in which choices reciprocally limit each other in accordance with universal law. If I invade the space you occupy, you can push me away. If I take what is yours, I must give it back, for no other reason than that it is yours. As Kant observes, if another person "has wronged me and I have a right to demand compensation from him, by this I will still only preserve what is mine undiminished."[53] Compelling someone to give me something so as to "preserve what is mine undiminished" cancels the wrong, leaving my external person and means intact. The initial wrong hinders my freedom by depriving me of powers with which I was able to set and pursue my purposes. The remedial force that is exercised in exacting payment cancels the initial, wrongful force, thus "hindering a hindrance" to freedom. The *form* of the hindering of the hindrance—the matching of the remedy to the wrong, to make it as if the wrong had not occurred—can be shown *a priori*. Its *matter* in any particular case—the value of the thing I deprived you of, for example—requires a judgment about empirical particulars, which must be made in accordance with rational concepts, but is not exhausted by them.

The contrast between the conceptual incompatibility and opposition in space and time thus explains why right may be enforced by others: the enforcement of a right is not the institutional expression of blame, or an attempt to guide conduct prospectively. Either of those would treat legality as a tool. Instead, as we saw in Chapter 10, it is simply the upholding of the underlying right. At the same time, the *prospect* of coercion provides an alternative incentive to rightful conduct. The rightfulness of conduct does not depend on its incentive, but the prospect of coercion provides an additional incentive to rightful conduct. The incentive operates because just as one force hinders another, so too one choice can hinder another. Kant's claim that "strict right can also be represented as the possibility of a fully reciprocal use of coercion"[54] generalizes this idea of mutual limitation through mutual opposition. Like interacting bodies in space,

---

53. 6:271. See also 6:232.
54. 6:232.

rational beings who occupy space can limit each other; because they are rational, they can do so under a universal law of freedom.

(iii) Inner/outer (duties to other persons)

Recent philosophical writing has drawn attention to the relational nature of concepts of right, focusing on the formal difference between a morality that emphasizes duties and one that emphasizes relational duties flowing from one person to another.[55] The latter are said to be irreducible, raising a question, analogous to the central question about the Universal Principle of Right, of their relation to nonrelational types of duty. Kant's analysis of the difference between the inner and outer shows how rights are both irreducibly relational and also expressions of the Categorical Imperative.

In the Amphiboly, Kant criticizes Leibniz for ignoring the nature of outer relations:

> In an object of the pure understanding only that is internal that has no relation (as far as the existence is concerned) to anything that is different from it. The inner determinations of the *substantia phaenomenon* in space, on the contrary, are nothing but relations, and it is itself entirely a sum total of mere relations. We know substance in space only through the forces that are efficacious in it, whether in drawing others to it (attraction) or in preventing penetration of it (repulsion and impenetrability).[56]

A parallel structure (without its taking the form of a criticism) applies to the Categorical Imperative: in the first instance, it identifies an inner wrong, that is, the inconsistency of a free will with itself. As such, it en-

---

55. Michael Thompson, "What Is It to Wrong Someone? A Puzzle about Justice," in R. Jay Wallace, Philip Pettit, Samuel Scheffler, and Michael Smith, eds., *Reason and Value* (Oxford: Oxford University Press, 2004), 333–384, and Stephen Darwall, *The Second Person Standpoint: Morality, Respect, and Accountability* (Cambrdige, Mass.: Harvard University Press, 2006).

56. *Critique of Pure Reason*, A265/B321.

gages with the question of what it is for one person to wrong another only indirectly. The "Formula of Humanity"[57] and that of the "Kingdom of Ends" both make reference to others, but do so by incorporating other free beings into the ends of action and the maxims on which an agent acts, respectively. By attending to ends in maxims, these formulations preserve their equivalence to the Formula of Universal Law. As Kant remarks in the *Groundwork,* "The essence of things is not changed by their external relations; that which, not taking account of those relations, alone constitutes the worth of a human being."[58]

Under any of the three formulations, the Categorical Imperative prohibits some deeds permitted by the Universal Principle of Right, and may recommend ones that the Universal Principle of Right regards as merely permissible, that is, entirely optional. The Categorical Imperative has the resources to reproach the honest shopkeeper who acts from a concern for his own reputation, either because of the maxim on which he acts or because of the ends for which he acts.[59] The Universal Principle of Right, by contrast, focuses exclusively on the purely external question of whether one person has wronged another.

Things that are internally alike can differ externally, just as two drops of water can be internally (qualitatively) indistinguishable but externally (numerically) distinct. Numerically distinct but qualitatively identical objects can be incompatible because they cannot occupy the same location (at the same time.) The *Groundwork*'s examples of acts that are not wrong but have no moral worth conform to the Universal Principle of Right, because they are all alike in their external relations to others. You do have an obligation of ethics to make right your principle of action, so all duties of right are "indirectly" duties of virtue.[60] Examples of innocent trespasses

---

57. The question of whether another could consent to the maxim on which a deceiving promisor acts complicates this picture somewhat, since it would appear that the possibility of consent does not depend on the deceiver's will, but on his deed. This complication is particularly visible in the examples of wrongs against persons and property in *Groundwork*, 4:430. Even these examples, however, are introduced as showing that it is "obvious that he who transgresses the rights of human beings intends to make use of the person of others merely as a means."

58. Ibid., 4:439.

59. Ibid., 4:387.

60. 6:221.

show that making right your maxim does not guarantee that you will not wrong another. A trespass against land involves using the land of another person without the owner's authorization. Use requires intention in the sense that you use the land in order to do something else, but does not require intention with respect to title. You are not a trespasser if the wind blows you onto your neighbor's land, but you are if you are mistaken about where the boundary is, because you are still using another person's land. So even if you make it your maxim to respect the property of others, you might interfere with what properly belongs to them.

The "Formula of Humanity" might at first appear closer to the Universal Principle of Right, as each focuses on the means available for choice. They are distinct, however, because each can be violated without the other's being violated. I can treat you as a mere means externally while acting on an acceptable maxim: I might innocently, or mistakenly, use your person or property for a purpose you have not authorized. If I mistakenly remove coal from your land because I become disoriented while following the underground seam, there is nothing wrong with my maxim, yet I wrong you from the standpoint of right. Again, if I make a contract with you in good faith but am unable to perform at the appointed time, I wrong you, even if the maxim on which I acted could have been a universal law.[61] If you seek damages from me, you are not seeking them because you find my maxim objectionable; you are seeking them because of what I did to you.

The ways in which an action can violate the Categorical Imperative, but still be rightful, or, conversely, have its maxim conform to the Categorical Imperative, yet still be inconsistent with right, reflect the distinction between what I did, and what I did to you. What I *do* is individuated by the maxim on which I act, and is assessed entirely in terms of the possiblility of all rational beings using such means for such ends. What I *do to you* is individuated by whether I interfere with some thing to which you have a right. What I do is non-relational; what I do to you is relational.

---

61. Assuming that the relevant maxim is something along the lines of "advance your purposes by making agreements only if you are in a position to keep them," rather than the excessively stringent and freedom-defeating "advance your purposes by making agreements only if it is impossible for circumstances to prevent you from honoring them."

The relational aspect of right reflects the fact that a wrong is always a wrong against some other person in particular.[62] If I wrong you, whether innocently or culpably, I wrong you in particular, and you in particular have a complaint against me. If I violate the Categorical Imperative without infringing anyone's rights, by contrast, any complaint others might have against me for violating a duty of virtue that affects them—lying about a matter not related to rights, for example—must ultimately be rooted in my own violation of my own rational principle.

The irreducibility of categories of relation also explains why right does not require an internal incentive in the way that the Categorical Imperative does. An external incentive would deprive the Categorical Imperative of its rational purity, because the agent would be responding to the matter of the incentive, rather than to the form of his maxim alone. Indeed, that is the point of the *Groundwork*'s examples of acts lacking in moral worth, both of which turn on the nature of the incentive. The Universal Principle of Right, in contrast, identifies the acceptable limits on external freedom relationally. Since outer relations are always external, whether someone is in conformity with a specific norm of outer relation does not depend upon that person's inner determinations, that is, on the principle on which he or she acts.

The contrasts that Kant elaborates between the comparison of concepts (or maxims) and the comparison of objects (or actions) in his discussion of the amphiboly of concepts of reflection thus explain why right is coercively enforceable in each of two respects: right does not need to be the incentive to an action, and force may be used to uphold a right, either reactively, as in the case when I need to pay you compensation for having wronged you, or prospectively, as when the prospect of needing to pay you compensation itself provides an incentive for me to act in conformity with rights. If I respect your rights because of fear of legal sanction, my maxim (e.g., avoid taking the property of others in order to stay out of jail) has no moral worth, but it is in conformity with right, because it forbears to use prohibited means. The incentive of enforcement is available

---

62. From the standpoint of right, wrongs against other persons are what Kant calls "material" wrongs. He notes that there are also "formal wrongs," which are "wrong in the highest degree" because "contrary to the right of human beings as such." Formal wrongs are inconsistent with the possibility of persons living together in a rightful condition, and can be committed even without committing a material wrong, that is a wrong against anyone in particular.

because the consequence that I fear is itself nothing more than the upholding of your entitlement in a system of equal freedom under universal law. Right does not permit threats to be issued based solely on their efficacy in guiding conduct, but it permits them to be issued if the threatened consequence is itself simply the upholding of a right. If I know I will have to pay you damages, I may be more careful about your safety; if I know I will be punished should I choose to commit a wrong against you, I will think twice about doing so. In both cases, the prospect that, should I injure your freedom, my freedom will itself be hindered operates both as an expression of the system of freedom under universal law and, at the same time, as an incentive to conformity with it.

(iv) Form/Matter (means without ends)

In the *Critique of Practical Reason,* Kant argues that the Categorical Imperative is a purely formal principle.[63] The form/matter distinction thus accords priority to form over matter within the Categorical Imperative. However, there is a further distinction between form and matter that applies to the *Doctrine of Right.* If the arguments of the *Groundwork,* the *Critique of Practical Reason,* and the *Doctrine of Virtue* are successful, then the Categorical Imperative itself imposes mandatory ends. Indeed, the idea that humanity is an end is the idea that the representation of the form of a maxim can itself be the incentive to act on that maxim: to act out of respect for the moral law, you must take up means *in order to* give effect to the Categorical Imperative. Thus form can generate its own matter, at least in the limiting case of the requirement that the will take its own characteristic form of activity as its object.

The Universal Principle of Right is formal in a further sense.[64] In a passage already mentioned, Kant insists that the "reciprocal relation of choice" takes no account "of the matter of choice, that is, the end each has in mind with the object he wants."[65] Even when Kant formulates the Universal Principle of Right in terms of maxims, they enter without reference

---

63. *Critique of Practical Reason,* 5:31.

64. The idea that Kant works with different levels of the form/matter distinction in the *Logic* and the *Critique of Pure Reason* is developed by Longuenesse, *Kant and the Capacity to Judge,* 149.

65. 6:213.

to their matter: "Any action is *right* if it can coexist with everyone's freedom in accordance with a universal law, or if on its maxim the freedom of choice of each can coexist with everyone's freedom in accordance with a universal law."[66] If a maxim is taken to be a subjective principle of volition,[67] the second of these paired formulations seems surprising, even more so when treated as equivalent to the first. When Kant characterizes the Universal Principle of Right as a "principle of maxims," he immediately cautions that "it cannot be required that this principle of all maxims be itself in turn my maxim, that is, it cannot be required that *I make it the maxim* of my action; for anyone can be free so long as I do not impair his freedom by *my external action,* even though I am quite indifferent to his freedom or would like in my heart to infringe upon it."[68]

This further formality of the Universal Principle of Right entails that maxims play a different role in right than in ethics. For purposes of ethics, the Formula of Universal Law tests maxims in terms of the fit between the end set and the means used to achieve it. In the famous suicide example in the *Groundwork,* the difficulty with the suicide's maxim is not the means chosen, but the incoherence of those means with their end. In the same way, the example of the lying promise is ruled out on the grounds that the use of lying promises could not advance the liar's purposes if they were a universal law. In the *Critique of Practical Reason,* the false promise to return a deposit is repudiated on the grounds that it could never achieve its purpose if made a universal law. In each of these examples, the Categorical Imperative is supposed to show that the means could not be used to achieve the end. In other examples, such as the failure to aid others or develop your talents, the will's own rational structure requires it to adopt specific ends.

The Universal Principle of Right introduces the further formalism of focusing exclusively on the means a person uses, quite apart from any question about their suitability to a given end. By abstracting from the "matter" of choice, the Universal Principle of Right focuses only on whether a particular action uses external means—objects in space and time—in ways consistent with the freedom of others to use their means.

---

66. 6:230.
67. *Groundwork,* 4:401.
68. 6:231.

The development of the Universal Principle of Right in Kant's discussions of the Innate Right of Humanity, and again in Private Right, follows this pattern. The Innate Right of Humanity includes each person's right to use his or her own body in setting and pursuing purposes, consistent with the entitlement of other persons to use their own bodies. That is, it prohibits using another person's body, or using your own in a way that interferes with the ability of others to use theirs. The tripartite division of Private Right focuses on the ways in which a person can have an "external object of choice" available for setting and pursuing ends, and in each case the right in question constrains the conduct of others: each must use his or her external means in ways consistent with the ability of others to use theirs.

Although the Categorical Imperative as the basic form of laws of freedom may seem more fundamental than the Universal Principle of Right as their spatial form, the spatial form of right enjoys priority over the representation of humanity within a maxim because the two mandatory ends specified in the *Doctrine of Virtue* could only be objects of a universal law if a plurality of free beings could pursue them consistently. For beings who occupy space, the promotion of other people's happiness or their own self-perfection could come into conflict unless there were some way of limiting the external means that are acceptable in pursuit of either.[69] For free rational beings who occupy space, limiting the means that can be used is just the problem of right.

The applicability of the differences outlined in the Amphiboly to the Categorical Imperative does not show that it is defective or that it is "Leibnizian" in an objectionable way. To the contrary, it shows its strength by

---

69. On this point Kant's remark about Leibniz might well be applied to the position often ascribed to Kant according to which the *Doctrine of Right* must be subordinated to the good will. See, for example, "The intellectualist philosopher could not bear it that form should precede things and determine their possibility; a quite appropriate criticism if he assumed that we intuit things as they are (though with confused representation)" (*Critique of Pure Reason*, A267/B323). The same charge might be leveled against putatively "Kantian" positions that saddle Kant with the claim that the primary focus of morality is the goodness of your own will. Such views would find the priority of external freedom too much to bear. They bear a striking similarity to the utilitarian view that moral rules are simply a confused representation to the principle of utility; utilitarians (and their descendents in the legal academy, including legal realists, economic analysts, and critical legal scholars) "could not bear it" that legal rules should precede the consideration of their effects.

showing what it is, and reveals the genuine though limited sense in which Kant conceives of things in themselves in a broadly Leibnizian way. The argument for transcendental idealism in the Aesthetic turns on characterizing the objects of experience as exhausted by their relational properties, and things in themselves as constituted solely by their nonrelational, i.e. monadic, ones.[70] The same point applies to the will considered as pure self-legislation. The will could only have a law of its own freedom if that law is independent of everything other than itself, including the form of its own sensibility.[71] Stripped of the particularities of a form of sensibility, the Categorical Imperative must be nonrelational, and limited to inner determinations; anything external to it could only be made relevant by making it an internal feature of the will's own representation of it. That is why the Categorical Imperative can only focus on the inner consistency of maxims. As a principle for maxims, the Categorical Imperative is just a system of pure inner determination. Anything relational is unavailable to it. That is why its only question concerns whether a maxim *could* be willed as a universal law for rational beings, entirely apart from any question of what other rational beings are actually doing. But that is just to say, as Kant does, that when reason grasps its own freedom under the Categorical Imperative, it is unconditioned: it is the thing in itself.

The Categorical Imperative *would* be objectionably Leibnizian if it took the further step of supposing that external relations are merely confused representations of internal ones, that is, if the obligations owed to other persons under the Universal Principle of Right were treated as confused representations or approximations to the inner autonomy promised by the Categorical Imperative. Some of Kant's interpreters have sought to portray the Universal Principle of Right in exactly this way, and as a result have seen coercion as either irrelevant or, alternatively, standing in a merely causal relation to the Categorical Imperative,[72] and others have

---

70. On the significance of this point for Kant's account of things in themselves, see Warren, *Reality and Impenetrability in Kant's Philosophy of Nature*, 45ff.

71. This is the form of Problems I and II in the *Critique of Practical Reason*, 5:28.

72. Hermann Cohen, *Kant's Begründung der Ethik*, 2d ed. (Berlin: Bruno Cassirer, 1910); Jeffrie G. Murphy, "Hume and Kant on the Social Contract," *Philosophical Studies* 33 (1978): 76; Patrick Riley, *Kant's Political Philosophy* (Totowa: Rowman & Littlefield, 1983), 98–99; Paul Guyer, "Kant's Deductions of the Principles of Right," in *Kant's Metaphysics of Morals*, 25–26.

thought Kant should have taken such an approach.[73] Kant's distinction between the comparison of concepts and the comparison of objects, and thus between relations among concepts and relations between objects, provides the resources to understand why the Categorical Imperative is fundamental to his practical philosophy but, nonetheless, the Universal Principle of Right is irreducible.

The contrasts underscore the relationships and differences between the standards to which you must hold yourself as you exercise your freedom and the standards to which others, acting through the state, may rightly hold you. At the level of the Categorical Imperative, you must act from maxims that could be willed to be a universal law. The obligation to act on the maxims that you could choose as a universal law applies to *you* as *you* decide what to do. If morality is freedom, it is *your* freedom, a demand for consistency in your own actions.

The postulate of outer freedom *demands* that external aspects of each person's conduct be consistent with that of others. It is a postulate because the embodiment of a plurality of rational beings—that is, the fact that they occupy space—is not contained in the Categorical Imperative. So the Categorical Imperative must be brought to bear on embodied rational beings. The only way to extend it is to impose universal laws of freedom on the occupation of space. Considered externally, you are entitled to protect your freedom by protecting your space, and so you have standing to compel others to limit their freedom to make it consistent with yours under universal law.

IV. Conclusion

If I am right about the role of the postulate, then the textual, philosophical, and political problems have a solution. Textually, the *Doctrine of Right* belongs in *The Metaphysics of Morals*. It belongs at the beginning, and the principles of right, including public and private right, constrain the means available for agents to use, and *thereby* constrain the maxims on which they may act. The *Doctrine of Virtue*'s discussions of duties owed to others presupposes the individuation of persons as embodied rational

---

73. Stuart M. Brown, Jr., "Has Kant a Philosophy of Law?" *Philosophical Review* 71 (1962): 36.

beings.[74] Philosophically, Kant has a distinctive conception of right, one that enables us to avoid the reactive and reductive themes that continue to cast their shadow over political philosophy. Attempts to derive the Principle of Right from the Categorical Imperative on its own fail, and end up rejecting the Principle of Right, or both the Categorical Imperative and the Principle of Right. Focusing exclusively on the Categorical Imperative, of course, coercion must seem accidental, in something broadly like the way in which external relations and even physical objects must, from a Leibnizian perspective, seem to be confused representations of something inner. Finally, we solve the political problems by solving the first textual problem. Kant's *Doctrine of Right* has a great deal to recommend it even to those who are unable to accept the full argument of the *Groundwork* and *Critique of Practical Reason*. It has been my aim in this appendix to suggest that it also has a great deal to recommend it to those who are prepared to accept Kant's more ambitious claim that morality is freedom.

---

74. Kant's surprising claim that human beings owe duties of virtue only to other human beings, but not to animals or God, rests on exactly this point (6:442).

Index

Acquired right, 49, 51, 56, 81, 93, 143n43, 146, 160–161, 165, 168, 270, 297, 341, 363–364, 385; types of, 17–18, 20, 57–59, 62, 65–66, 76–80, 110, 162, 362, 365; acquisition of, 22–24, 57–60, 62, 65–66, 69, 75, 85–87, 90, 93–94, 96–106, 275, 363; role in argument for public right, 23, 146, 152, 162, 168, 176, 180–183, 190–191, 201, 335; remedies for violation of, 27, 69, 81–85, 132n24, 165–167, 173, 180, 304–305, 314, 319, 343n39, 348–349, 378; absent in right of nations, 29, 228–229; distinguished from innate right, 35, 47, 57–61, 67–68, 138, 160, 162, 176–177, 180–181, 241, 363; and coercion, 56, 81–85; change in the context of choice, 56, 61, 64–65, 90–91, 99, 107–112, 115, 118, 122, 132, 134–135, 144, 153, 208, 241–242, 272, 276–277, 281, 288, 364; mine-or-yours structure, 59–60, 66, 68, 93, 138, 142, 228, 241, 363, 365n23; and wrongdoing, 60–85, 269, 310, 312n31; formality condition in, 62–65, 85, 91, 275, 312–313n31; relation of, to categories of the understanding, 79–80n28; and permissive law, 103–104n19, 154, 361n13; objective standards in, 146, 171, 181, 191, 227; and equity, 257; and protection across national borders, 297. *See also* Coercion; Contract; Freedom; Postulate, of practical reason with regard to right; Property; Property acquisition; State of nature; Status

Aichele, Alexander, 377n50

Allison, Henry, 7n13

Antinomy, 9; of public right, 9, 224–225; and instrumentalism, 10, 197n24, 218, 221n64, 255, 268, 301, 318n41, 325–326, 357, 367n28, 378; of property, 95

Aquinas, Thomas, 23, 199n31

Arendt, Hannah, 10n18

Aristotle, 14, 40, 174n38

Assurance, conditional nature of, 23, 159–160, 162–164; and enforcement, 23–24, 26, 29, 49, 146–148, 158–167, 180, 190–192, 277–279, 302–303, 306, 311–312, 319–320, 322, 325, 328–329, 334, 376–378, 382–383; public law nature of, 23–24, 87, 146, 148n6, 159–161, 165–168, 172–174, 190–192, 225, 272, 278–279, 306, 312, 319–320, 326, 334; requires an executive branch, 24, 146, 159, 174–175, 182, 192, 194, 214, 272, 314; inapposite in right of nations, 29, 227–230; reconciles Ulpian's precepts, 160–162; contrasted with radical evil, 163–164; and punishment, 306–308, 319–320, 322, 324. *See also* Acquired right; Coercion; Institutions; Separation of powers; State of nature

Austin, John L., 56, 200n33

Authority, parental, 21, 28, 48n26, 71–73, 138n35, 177n44, 193–194, 223, 246, 288, 290, 295

Authority, public, 4–6, 9, 23–24, 77, 90, 97, 106, 145, 147–150, 152–159, 167–168, 170, 172–176, 179, 181, 183–185, 188n7–191, 194–198, 206–208, 213–214, 219–234, 237–238, 243, 249–250, 255, 259, 262, 266, 272–273, 279, 282–285, 290, 295, 301, 306, 309, 311, 314, 316, 323n51, 326–331, 333–

Authority, public *(continued)*
334, 338, 340, 343, 346, 348, 351, 356n2; relation to representation, 146, 195–199, 202–203, 205n38, 208, 243, 258, 266, 271–272, 294, 312, 325, 328, 331, 336–337n24, 342–343, 348; Raz's theory of, 197n24. *See also* Authority, parental; Coercion; Institutions; Original contract, idea of; Representation; Status

Barak, President Aharon, 220
Barbarism: and distinction between a rightful condition and organized violence, 323n51, 338–339, 341–343, 347–351; National Socialism as, 337, 341, 346, 349, 351; right and duty to use force to leave a condition of, 338, 343, 351n53; definition of, 339, 348–349; as a violation of the postulate of public right, 339–340; distinguished from despotism, 339–341, 348; and absence of united and omnilateral will, 341–342, 348, 350–351; and provisional authority of antecedent legal system, 343n39, 346, 349–350; and case of grudge informer, 343–348, 351. *See also* Despotism; Hart, H. L. A.; Postulate, of public right; Radbruch, Gustav; Revolution; Slavery; State of nature
Barbeyrac, Jean, 100n18
Baumgarten, Alexander Gottlieb, 37n14
Beauvoir, Simone de, 74n22
Begging, 133, 261–263, 280. *See also* Poverty; Property
Bentham, Jeremy, 3, 7–8, 54–56, 200n33, 251n23, 255
Berlin, Isaiah, 160n18; negative freedom, 33, 42–43; positive freedom, 42–43. *See also* Freedom
Bird, Colin, 46n22
Blackstone, William, 237, 347n47
Bouterwerk, Friedrich, 356n2
Brett, Nathan, 119n11
Brighouse, Harry, 288n29
Brown, Stuart M., 1, 2–3, 6, 11, 13, 387n73
Brudner, Alan, 124n18
Byrd, Sharon, 113n4, 163–164n23, 226n70, 300–303, 307–308n16, 321n48, 327n5

Cardozo, Judge Benjamin N., 44n20
Cavallar, George, 229n79
Coercion, 3; relation to freedom, 4–6, 9–10, 17, 27–35, 52–56, 69, 71, 81–82, 110, 112, 117, 136, 146, 153, 157, 159–160, 162–166, 168, 170, 180, 186–190, 194, 213, 218, 220, 222, 228, 236, 238–239, 242–243, 250, 256, 260–261, 266–267, 269, 272, 274, 295, 301, 305–306, 320, 329, 331, 333–334, 355, 377–378, 383, 387; and distinction between right and virtue, 12, 269, 319–320, 355, 359, 366, 368, 375, 377–378, 386–388; remedies for, 27, 54, 69, 82–85, 132nn24,25, 149, 165–167, 173, 180–181, 304–305, 314, 319, 329, 378, 382; sanction theory of, 31, 52–55, 84; as protective justice, 81, 161, 177, 181, 306, 319; punishment of, 6, 8, 25, 27, 145, 196, 205, 220, 232–233, 251n23, 300–303, 306–308, 314–316, 319–320, 324, 351. *See also* Acquired right; Crime; Freedom; Punishment; Virtue
Cohen, G. A., 8n14, 10n16, 32, 119, 137n32, 288n28, 289n31
Cohen, Hermann, 11, 386n72
Coleridge, Samuel Taylor, 32, 63
Consent: relation to freedom, 18, 45, 47, 70–71, 74n22, 107–118, 120, 122, 127–129, 134–135, 144, 192–193; and contract, 20, 66, 71, 76–77, 80, 107–111, 115, 118, 130–131, 133–135; bilateral nature of, 20–21, 69–70, 97, 107–110, 113–114, 118–127, 131–133; assumption of responsibility, 21, 116–117, 121n15, 124, 127–128, 130, 133, 135, 143n41, 184; wounding, 47, 127, 129, 133, 141–142; murder and gladiatorial contests, 108, 129, 133, 140–143, 193; choice/wish distinction, 108–109, 124–126; waiver of, 117–118, 128, 132; attitudinal and expressive theories of, 118–119, 130; mistakes about, 124–126, 130–131; *volenti non fit injuria*, 126–127; tension with Mill's harm principle, 126–127, 129; contrasted with forfeiture, 128; to murder contrasted with *Groundwork* argument against suicide, 142–143; to assisted suicide, 142–143n41; unsuitable as a basis for public order, 184–185. *See also* Contract; Original contract, idea of; Status

Constant, Benjamin, 51n
Contract, 49, 59, 62–63, 74–76; transfer, 12, 20–21, 61, 64, 69, 71, 82, 88, 94, 112–126, 132, 135–137, 139n36, 147; promising, 20, 111–112, 115n7, 136, 189; reliance on, 22, 121n15, 130; offer-and-acceptance structure of, 50n27, 113, 115–116, 120–123, 125–126, 131–132, 257; and fraud, 51, 80, 108, 128–132, 135, 205n38, 210, 310n23; use but not possession of another's choice, 58, 66, 69, 76, 80n28, 112, 118, 135, 138n35, 139, 365; formality condition in, 64, 108, 116, 129, 133; and remedy, 69, 82, 110, 121n15, 132nn24,25, 166, 304; limited by rightful honor, 76, 115n7, 131n22, 135–136; wrongs against, 69, 76–77, 80, 108–110, 111n3, 112, 117, 119n12, 122, 132n25, 135, 166–167; grounded in a united will, 109–118, 120, 122–123, 125–127, 131–133, 135, 138n35, 140–142, 205; present transfer contrasted with abandonment/acquisition, 112–124, 116n7, 128, 369; and force, 108, 110–112, 117, 121, 128–132, 135, 138n35, 140–142, 148–149, 305; analytical status of united will, 113, 116; Kant's analysis of in *Feyerabend*, 113n4; preparatory and constitutive moments of, 114n5, 131n23, 132n25; and contrast between united will and collective agency, 115; doctrine of consideration in, 115–116n7; and wills, 116–117n8, 152; and incontrovertible benefit, 117n8, 121; and distinction between *in personam* and *in rem*, 120n14; and firm offer, 122n17; and fraud contrasted with mistake, 130; unconscionability in, 131n22; relation to public policy, 133, 137–138; in Lockean political philosophy, 184. *See also* Acquired right; Consent; Original contract, idea of; Slavery contract; United will
Cooper, John, 174n38
Cosmopolitan right, 28–29, 229n77, 295; distinguished from public right, 296; limited to universal hospitality, 296–298n48; and analogy to public duty to support the poor, 297–298; and right to exclude limited by innate right, 297, 299. *See also* International law; Right of nations

Crime, 18, 43, 108, 124–126, 130, 133, 142, 196, 207, 212n51, 216–217, 219–220, 250–251, 300–304, 338, 343, 345, 347–349, 351, 374; as self-exemption from public law, 302, 306–308, 311–317, 320–321; definition, 309; and criminal's maxim, 309–311, 313, 315–316, 322; employment of wrongful means, 310–311, 315, 321n48; akin to remaining in state of nature, 311, 313; international, 323n51; *mala prohibita*, 251; *mala in se*, 251. *See also* Assurance; Barbarism; Coercion; Consent; Formal wrongdoing (wrong in the highest degree); Hart, H. L. A.; Incentives; Punishment

Dan-Cohen, Meir, 307n16
Darwall, Stephen, 109n1, 115n6, 379n55
Dean v. Peel, 72n19
de Marneffe, Peter, 251n24
Dershowitz, Alan M., 219n62
Despotism, 43, 45, 47, 49, 50, 195–196n20, 213, 226, 339; as defective form of rightful condition, 175, 284n25, 339–340; definition, 339; distinguished from barbarism, 339–341, 343, 348. *See also* Original contract, idea of; Postulate, of public right
Devlin, Lord Patrick, 129
Director of Public Prosecutions v. Morgan, 124n18
Doyle, Michael, 229n78
Drassinower, Abraham, 95n13
Dubber, Markus D., 237n9, 251n23, 261n34
Duplessis, Maurice, 210–211n49
Dworkin, Ronald, 10n15, 348n48; traffic rules, 32, 234–237, 239–240, 249, 254; Hercules as ideal judge, 191n12, 235n3; distinction between rights and interests, 235–236, 239–240, 254; equality of resources, 236n6; associative obligations, 238n12; on formal equality of opportunity, 286n26, 287; choices and circumstances, 287–288
Dyzenhaus, David, 346n22

Ebbinghaus, Julius, 161n16
Edmundson, William, 250n21

Edwards v. Lee's Administrator, 83n31
Existence, 360n13

Fair play, principle of, 184–190, 238–239; relation to Locke's theory of property, 186n3, 188; Simmons's revision, 187–189; relation to unjust enrichment, 188–189. *See also* Hart, H. L. A.; Nozick, Robert; Rawls, John
Feinberg, Joel, 46n23, 119n11, 129, 268
Ferguson v. Miller, 100n18
Feuerbach, Paul Johann Anselm, 11n20, 251n23, 261n34
Fichte, J. G., 278–279
Finnis, John, 199n31
Fishkin, James, 288n29
Flikschuh, Katrin, 104n19, 147n6, 327n5, 337n24
Forfeiture: contrast with consent, 128; and public right, 221n64
Formal equality of opportunity, 205, 232, 267, 287–295; as mandatory means of sustaining a rightful condition, 268, 270, 272, 295–296, 299; arguments rejecting hereditary nobility and entailed estates, 289–291, 309; private discrimination inconsistent with rightful honor, 292; and education, 292–295. *See also* Original contract, idea of; United will
Formal wrongdoing (wrong in the highest degree), 51–52n29, 87, 164, 168, 204–205n38, 226–227, 310–316, 318, 320–321, 323n51, 326, 341, 343n39, 352, 382n62. *See also* Barbarism; Crime; Postulate, of public right; Revolution; State of nature
Fountainbleau Hotel Corp v. Forty-Five Twenty-Five, Inc., 78n25
Fox-Decent, Evan, 194n15
Franks, Paul, 359n11
Frederick the Great, 195n20
Freedom: equal, 4, 6, 10, 13–19, 29–37, 39, 52n29, 54–56, 62–63, 77, 81–85, 91, 107, 133–134, 140, 146–147, 159, 170–171, 174, 180, 183, 214, 221n66, 224, 237–243, 255–256, 258–259, 266, 270n4, 272, 283, 285, 301, 306, 308, 310, 313–314, 322, 325, 331, 344, 362–363, 365, 383; as nondomination, 4–6, 13–19, 21–22, 24, 26–27, 29–30, 33–50, 68, 70, 81, 102, 109–110, 117–118, 120, 124, 134, 137, 145, 162, 165, 203, 210, 217, 222, 241–243, 246–249, 266, 273–275, 279, 283, 286, 291, 330, 348, 352, 356, 363, 372, 385; external, 11–12, 15, 18, 37, 40–41, 58, 60, 62, 68–70, 73, 77–82, 85, 95–96, 151, 154, 167, 172, 179, 199, 246–247, 251, 280–281, 297–298, 302, 304–306, 310, 314–315, 318–319, 324, 349, 358, 361, 364–366, 368–376, 378–379, 382, 384–385, 387; as subject of innate right, 13, 30, 35, 240; formal, 13–16, 19, 25, 33–34, 45, 62–65, 85, 91–92, 94, 98, 104, 108, 116, 129, 133, 163–164, 168, 170, 192, 196, 205n38, 207, 209, 213, 222–223, 245–247, 251–252, 274–276, 281, 283–284, 299, 306, 310, 312–313n31, 315–318, 362–363, 365, 369–372, 375, 379, 382n62, 383–384. *See also* Berlin, Isaiah; Coercion; Formal equality of opportunity; Innate right; Right
Fried, Charles, 111n2
Friedman, Michael, 370n36
Frost, Robert, 299
Fuller, Lon L., 240n15

Gardner, John, 46n22, 198n25
Gregor, Mary, 2n3, 3, 3n4, 59n3, 163n23
Grotius, Hugo, 89, 98n15, 100n18, 155–156, 158
Guyer, Paul, 148n6, 176n43, 279n19, 386n72

Habermas, Jürgen, 10n15, 226n73
Hale, Robert L., 240n15
Hart, H. L. A., 31–32, 34n9, 53, 56, 216, 235n3, 236n5; on overlap of law and morality, 67–68, 303–304; power conferring rules, 156–159; principle of fair play, 185–187, 189; account of excuses, 216; theory of punishment, 300n2, 307, 347; response to Radbruch, 344–348, 351; legal certainty, 347. *See also* Barbarism; Crime; Positive law; Punishment
Hegel, Georg Wilhelm Friedrich, 13, 57n2, 63n8, 97, 104, 149

Herman, Barbara, 10, 74n22, 204n35, 367n26
Herzog, Werner, 251n23
Hill, Thomas, 137n34, 300–301n2, 301n3, 327n6
Hobbes, Thomas, 23, 40, 145–146, 164, 184, 195, 240, 242
Höffe, Otfried, 10n18, 148n6, 226n70
Hoffman, Lord Leonard, 330n15
Hohfeld, Wesley Newcomb, 88n4, 118n10, 119n12, 120n14
Honoré, Tony, 88n4, 244n18, 269n2
Hruschka, Joachim, 103–104n19, 113n4, 163n23, 163–164n24, 226n70, 327n5, 361n13
Hume, David, 200n33, 248
Hunter v. Canary Wharf Ltd., 247n19
Hurd, Heidi M., 119n11

Iacobucci, Justice Frank, 211n50
Incentives, 49–50, 252, 260n31, 263; and distinction between right and virtue, 11–12, 56, 85, 355, 358–359, 376, 382, 384, 387; and conformity with law, 27, 56, 84–85, 193–194, 209, 319–320, 322, 382–383; coercion, 27–28, 82, 84–85, 132, 302, 306–307, 318–319, 322, 378; and assurance, 165–168, 180, 191, 302, 306–307, 314, 318–320, 322, 324
Indeterminacy, 23–24, 146, 168; and determinative judgment, 10–11, 147, 169–170, 172–176, 179–181, 183, 191–192, 198, 202, 214–215, 224, 229, 231–232, 271, 284, 306, 312, 326, 328; and the judiciary, 17, 24, 146, 159, 172–175, 177, 182, 191–192, 194, 214, 228, 255; and self-defense, 162, 177–179, 227, 229; and settling function of law, 169; contrasted with empirical disagreement, 169–170; and objective standards, 171, 181, 191, 227; and judicial review, 219, 330–331
Innate right, 4–7, 9, 11, 13, 15, 17, 27, 30, 35–37, 45, 50, 64, 98n15, 108, 140, 194, 206, 210–212, 218, 231, 236, 240–241, 247–248, 257, 273, 352, 356; distinguishes persons from things, 4n10, 12, 14–15, 18, 20, 36–37, 48, 74–75n22, 76, 131n22, 134–135, 137, 139–141, 161–163, 173, 179, 193, 206, 208, 256–257, 282, 284, 320, 352, 356, 380n57, 381; as right to be beyond reproach, 7, 18, 39, 51–52, 210–211, 215, 217–218, 220, 251, 291, 297; as freedom of expression, 7, 39, 50–51, 204, 209–211, 213–215, 218, 221n66; relation to body, 12, 14–17, 19, 22, 35, 39–47, 57–62, 68, 85–86, 88, 91, 93–96, 101, 105, 109, 127, 132, 137–139, 142, 149, 162, 176–177, 179–182, 240–241, 243, 257, 273, 277, 279–281, 297–298, 304–305, 317, 326, 352, 362–363, 368–376, 385; basis of acquired rights, 13, 19, 35, 37–38, 56, 63–65, 85, 135, 137–140, 149, 241, 278, 352; rightful honor, 18, 26, 37–38, 76, 115n7, 131n22, 135–136, 161–162, 163n21, 165, 167–168, 177n45, 179, 203, 204n35, 206, 208, 212–213, 222, 256, 272, 277–279, 282, 292; and reputation, 19, 51–52, 210; implications for burden of proof, 51, 210, 291; and self-defense, 55–56, 81, 161–162, 177–179, 319; in state of nature, 176–181; as freedom of association, 210; distinction between core and peripheral instances of, 214; as dignity, 221–222, 274, 330. *See also* Barbarism; Coercion; Freedom; Postulate; Right
Institutions, 1–2, 5, 89n7, 187n4, 209, 217, 233, 236, 344, 346, 349, 351; Kant's account of, 7, 9–11, 14, 17, 22, 27–28, 49, 146–147, 173, 183, 191, 194–198, 201–204, 215, 224–225, 255, 266, 285, 295, 301, 306–307, 309, 318n41, 325–328, 330–331, 336, 338, 340–341, 361–362n15, 378; consequentialist account of, 7–9; deontological account of, 8–9; Lockean account of, 8–9, 169, 224–225; egalitarian account of, 8–9, 224–225, 287–289; person/office distinction, 17, 19, 26, 29, 38, 43–44, 73n21, 138n35, 144n43, 145, 152–153, 172–176, 182, 190–198, 202–203, 204n35, 205n38, 210–211, 230–231, 255–256, 271–273, 278, 282–285, 298, 312, 321n48, 323n51, 326, 351, 361–362n15; and omnilateral will, 172–174, 183, 190–192, 196, 202, 214, 218, 231, 272, 279, 282, 306, 336, 338; utilitarian account of, 224–225, 255–256. *See also* Assurance; Indeterminacy; Political philosophy; Positive law

International law, 157, 204n38, 226, 228; private, 297-298. *See also* Cosmopolitan right; Crime, international; Right of nations

Joerden, Jan, 339n29
Jung-Stilling, Heinrich, 375n44
Justinian, 37n14, 100n18, 160

Kersting, Wolfgang, 270n5, 327
Kleingeld, Pauline, 226n70
Klimchuk, Dennis, 322n50
Korsgaard, Christine, 7n13, 13n22, 75n22, 273n9, 327, 367n27
Kristol, Irving, 129, 141
Kymlicka, Will, 235, 287, 289

Ladd, John, 3
Legal positivism: minimal definition, 198n25; relation to authority, 345-348. *See also* Hart, H. L. A.
Leibniz, Gottfried, 113, 374-376, 379, 385-386, 388
Lipson, Morris, 288n29
Little Sisters Book and Art Emporium v. Canada (Minister of Justice), 211n50
Lochner v. New York, 237n8
Locke, John, 169; conception of the state of nature, 1, 8-9, 23, 145-146, 148, 165, 201, 224-225; theory of property, 22, 57n2, 65, 86, 89n7, 90, 93n11, 97-100, 102, 104, 148-149, 165, 186n3, 188, 224-225, 337, 363, 373; proviso in theory of property, 98, 149, 249; conception of public law, 169, 184, 186n3, 224-225, 270-271, 336-337, *See also* Contract; Fair play, principle of; Indeterminacy; Institutions; Property; State of nature
Longuenesse, Beatrice, 371n36, 375n44, 383n64
Ludwig, Bernd, 147n6, 175n42, 203n35, 205n40, 270n5

Maitland, Frederick W., 32, 63
Mandle, Jon, 187n4

Mayor, etc. of Bradford v. Pickles, 78n25
McCleskey v. Kemp, 212n51
McDowell, John, 10
McGregor, Joan L., 119n11
Merle, Jean-Christophe, 303n5
Mertens, Thomas, 346n42
Mill, John Stuart, 3, 98; view of relation between legal and political philosophy, 1; harm principle, 42, 45-47, 50, 92n9, 126-127, 129; sanction theory of coercion, 52-53, 55; conception of property, 98n15
Miller, Paul, 76n23
Moggach, Douglas, 371n36
Money, 121-122, 305, 310-311, 317
Morris, Herbert, 312n29
Mulholland, Leslie, 148n6
Murphy, Jeffrie G., 11n21, 386n72
Murphy, Liam, 10, 89n7, 270n4
Muthu, Sankar, 297n46

Nagel, Thomas, 89n7, 270n4
Necessity, 131, 209, 274-275, 278, 321-322
Nicholas, Barry, 54n35
Normore, Calvin, 372n37
Noumenal: realm as standpoint, 7n13, 314; possession, 67, 72, 95-96, 166-167, 175n42, 311, 314, 332, 358n7, 364-365, 368-369, 374; nonrelational nature, 386
Nozick, Robert: role of welfare in his theory of rights, 4n10; criticism of principle of fair play, 187, 189; economic redistribution, 270-271

O'Neill, Onora, 7n13, 10n17, 11n21, 33n8, 206, 268, 271n5, 368n28
Original contract, idea of: imposes a duty on the state to perfect itself, 26, 194, 198-204, 207-208, 223, 226, 264, 273, 284-285, 292-295, 325, 328-329, 339; relation to innate right, 26-27, 31, 56, 193n13, 215, 266, 279n19, 293, 299; limits discretion, 26-27, 155, 202, 204n35, 210-212, 223-225, 294, 314, 320-321; and republican government, 28, 203, 227, 229, 292, 294, 327, 339, 348, 350; governs the means through which perfection is pursued, 56, 203-204, 208, 212, 219-220, 229, 264-266, 268,

284–285, 293–295, 322, 330; as an idea of reason, 74n22, 183, 198–202, 325, 334, 339; relation to postulate of public right, 198, 202, 328–329, 335, 340, 361–362n15; contrasted with considerations of advantage, 206–209, 211–213, 215, 222, 280, 286, 290–291, 296; active and passive citizens, 208, 212–213, 284, 298; role in theory of property, 224–225. *See also* Despotism; Formal equality of opportunity; Innate right; Postulate; Poverty; Separation of powers; United will

Paley, William, 200n33
Patterson, Orlando, 140n37
Penner, James, 93
People, 261, 321, 326–329, 334, 339–340, 342; self-legislation of, 5, 12, 24–29, 146, 175–176, 183–184, 196, 199, 202–214, 218, 220, 222, 225, 229, 231, 241, 243, 256, 258, 273, 278–279, 285, 289, 291–294, 309, 312–315, 325, 328, 330–331, 350, 356; created by representation through institutions, 5, 28, 146, 195–196, 199, 203, 231, 255, 266, 273, 306, 309, 327, 331, 336, 337nn24,27, 342, 350, 352, 362n15; possible consent of, 25–26, 76, 110, 155, 206–209, 213, 215, 221–222, 231, 277, 279, 286, 289, 291–292, 328, 330–331; contrasted with mob, 229n77, 328, 336, 341–342, 349. *See also* Barbarism; Despotism; Innate right; Original contract, idea of; Postulate; Revolution; United will
Peterson, Jonathan, 95n13, 207n42, 264n39
Pettit, Philip, 43n18, 175
Pierson v. Post, 100n18
Pippin, Robert B., 38n15, 148n6, 361n14
Plato, 88n5
Pogge, Thomas, 215–216, 270n5, 357
Police power, 18–19, 25, 194, 205, 218, 233, 237–239, 251n23, 261, 263–266, 268, 271; and provision of roads as public rights of way, 237, 239, 243, 248–250, 253n27, 254, 259, 261–263, 280; relevance of efficiency and convenience in public provision of roads, 233–239, 241–243, 249, 254–256, 262; relation between roads and rules, 233, 249–251; and limited government, 237, 254, 265–266; aim of equal freedom, 237–239, 254–256, 265–266; traditional exercises of, 239–240, 261–263; provisions of public markets analogous to roads, 239, 252; and public health, 145, 194, 239–240, 259–261, 267, 285; and national defense, 194, 239–240, 259–261
Political philosophy, 22–23, 86, 197n24, 233, 237, 268, 271; and moral philosophy, 1–2, 6–7, 11, 53, 388; and institutions, 2, 7; not a response to circumstances or defects of human nature, 2, 4, 323, 357; Kant's influence on, 3, 31, 267; normative character of Kant's, 3–4, 10–11, 29, 42, 52–53, 90, 165, 256, 267–278, 323, 388; and judgment, 10, 265; and contractarianism, 26. *See also* Antinomy; Institutions
Pollock, Baron Charles, 188
Positive law, 2, 11, 13, 23, 87, 145, 148, 157, 174–175, 178–179, 191n12, 198, 203, 209, 211–214, 218–219, 240, 251n24, 258–259, 276, 286, 290–291, 306, 312, 329, 330–331, 338–339, 343–347; and the legislature, 17, 24, 29, 146–148, 157, 173–175, 182, 192, 194, 198, 203, 211n49, 214, 218, 221n6, 228–230, 255, 266, 272–273, 295, 298, 306, 321, 328, 330–331, 336; overlap with morality, 67–68, 303–304; and relation to authority, 173–174, 176, 179, 181, 191, 198, 273, 286; and significance of official acts, 198; minimal definition of, 198n25. *See also* Representation; United will
Postulate, 359–360; universal principle of right as, 12, 355, 359, 361–362, 366, 368–379, 383, 387; of practical reason with regard to right, 19, 49, 57n2, 58–62, 86, 88, 95–96, 146, 150, 154, 196, 352, 356n2, 361–366, 368, 369n34, 371; of public right, 38, 52n29, 182–183, 196–198, 202, 328–329, 335–337, 339–340, 342, 352, 361n15, 382n62; of empirical thought, 360n13. *See also* Right
Poverty, 25–27, 193n13, 204n35, 232, 263, 267–274, 278, 280, 282–284, 292, 295, 297, 309; as dependency on a private will, 263, 274, 276, 279–281, 292, 298–299; and public support as mandatory means of sustaining a rightful condition, 268, 270, 276, 282–283, 285, 295–296, 298; and

Poverty *(continued)*
  charity as a duty of virtue, 271n5, 274–276, 278, 281–284; as incompatible with united will, 274, 278–280, 282–284, 286, 296; distinguished from factual dependency in private right, 276–277, 281. *See also* Original contract, idea of; Slavery contract; United will
Property, 14, 20, 49, 57–58, 63, 70–71, 86, 149, 224, 292, 382; and right to exclude, 12, 24, 25–26, 59, 64, 67–68, 70, 79n26, 88, 90, 93n10, 94–95, 98, 100–102, 104, 127, 150, 154, 159, 164–165, 168, 186, 190, 242–245, 250, 253, 271, 277, 280–283, 284n25, 316, 318, 365; land as basic case of, 12, 78, 79n26, 95–96, 158, 244–245, 251; distinguished from *usufruct,* 19, 104; as external means, 19–20, 23, 57–63, 66–69, 80n28, 84–85, 86, 88–91, 93–94, 96, 154–155, 159–160, 162, 164–165, 168, 173, 176, 179–180, 228–229, 277, 279, 315–316, 319, 340, 363, 365, 384–385; right to possession and use, 20, 67–68, 76, 79–80, 87–88, 94–95, 99, 105, 151, 153–154, 166, 244, 246–247, 277, 311, 346, 365; guardian spirit account of, 22, 92–93; systematic requirements of, 23, 90–91, 96–97, 103–104n19, 253; inheritance of, 23, 139, 290, 309; requirement of public spaces, 25, 249, 252, 259, 265, 271; Hegel's theory of, 57n2, 63n8, 97, 104, 149; title to, 67, 96, 165, 172, 176, 180, 184, 290, 332–333, 338, 381; as parallel with innate right, 68, 88, 91, 105–107, 149; Lockean theories of, 86, 89n7, 90, 93n11, 98–100, 104, 148–149, 165, 188, 224–225, 249, 270–271, 373; public law theories of, 86–90, 148; bundle theory of, 88; Grotius's account of, 89, 98n15, 100n18, 155–156, 158, 373; collective, 89, 155, 158; Kant's precritical view of, 93; intellectual, 95n13, 151–152, 210, 281n20; and permissive law, 103–104n19, 154, 361n13; control as limit of, 251n25; social production versions of, 270n4; adverse possession, 284, 331–332, 350. *See also* Acquired right; Locke, John; Mill, John Stuart; Noumenal, possession; Nozick, Robert; Postulate, of practical reason with regard to right; Poverty; Property acquisition; Property wrongs; State of nature

Property acquisition, 22–23, 57n3, 60, 62, 85–86, 90, 94, 96–99, 103, 106, 150, 155–158, 172–173, 333; unilateral nature of, 23–24, 65n12, 90, 97–98, 103, 105–106, 110, 148, 150–154, 157–158, 172–174, 176, 181, 272, 283; and authority structure of an omnilateral will, 24, 90, 98, 106, 150, 152, 154–160, 172–174, 181, 272, 277, 283; and things that cannot be acquired, 62; and apprehension, 90, 100, 103–104, 150, 154, 158; contrasted with labor theory, 96–102; and capture, 99–100, 102; irrelevance of effort in, 101–103; and giving a sign, 104–105, 150, 154, 158. *See also* Acquired right; Postulate, of practical reason with regard to right; Property

Property wrongs, 303–304, 374, 380n57; damage, 16, 67, 77, 82, 151, 153, 166, 304; trespass, 67–68, 77, 92, 95, 98, 100, 106, 151, 153, 166–167, 331–332, 350, 381. *See also* Acquired right; Crime; Property; Property acquisition

The Public Committee against Torture in Israel v. The State of Israel, 220n63

Pufendorf, Samuel von, 100n18, 155–156

Punishment, 1, 6, 8, 25, 52, 54, 205, 209, 212, 216–217, 220, 232, 233, 251n23, 278, 300–302, 308, 343n39; clemency and discretion in, 25, 319–321, 343n39; relation to equal freedom under law, 27, 301, 306, 308, 310, 312n29, 314, 317–318, 322; as jointly requiring retribution and deterrence, 27, 302–303, 307–308, 319, 323; as supremacy of law against criminal's unilateral will, 27–28, 196, 302–309, 311, 314–316, 318, 322–323, 347, 349, 351; and retribution, 27–28, 300–302, 306–308, 312n29, 315, 317–319, 323–324; and deterrence, 27–28, 300–302, 306–308, 318–319, 322–324; content of, 308, 315–318. *See also* Assurance; Coercion; Crime; Hart, H. L. A., theory of punishment; Mill, John Stuart, sanction theory of coercion; Rawls, John, presumption of innocence

R v. Secretary of State for the Home Department, 331n15
Radbruch, Gustav, 344, 346, 348, 351
Rand, Justice Ivan, 211n49
Rawls, John, 10–11, 38n16, 40, 52n31, 140n37, 215–216, 270; benefits of social cooperation, 3; circumstances and psychology in normative theory, 3n8, 248, 357n3; contrast with Kant, 3–4, 11, 217–219, 248, 293n39, 357n3; maximum equal liberty, 31–32; moral powers, 40; fair play, 187n4; strains of commitment, 208–209; presumption of innocence, 216–219
Raz, Joseph, 34n9, 53n33, 197n24
Reason, idea of, 87, 277, 325, 334, 339; definition, 74n22; and natural teleology, 74n22, 200–201. *See also* Original contract, idea of; State of nature; United will
Representation: as acting for purposes of another, 194–198, 206, 271; as omnilateral, 196–199, 203, 214–215, 218–219, 228, 231–232, 238, 243, 255, 258, 272, 279, 294, 298, 306, 311–312, 319, 321–322, 325–326, 328, 330, 336, 338, 341–343, 375n44; relation to status, 192–194. *See also* Authority; Institutions; Original contract, idea of; People
Revolution, 205–206, 309, 311, 325, 337–338, 341, 349, 351–352; and distinction between unilateral and omnilateral will, 28, 309, 328, 336, 350, 352; impossibility of a right to, 28, 327, 329–334, 336; and irrelevance of state's historical origin, 326–327, 334–335; and distinction between postulate of public right and idea of the original contract, 329, 335. *See also* Barbarism; Despotism; Postulate, of public right
Right, 14–16, 22, 385; relation to anthropology, 2, 4–5, 7, 202, 290, 293, 321, 357n3; politics must conform to, 5, 27, 158, 255–256, 285, 292, 321; Universal Principle of, 7, 10, 12–13, 18, 30, 35, 37, 56–58, 60–62, 77, 85, 136, 204, 285, 292, 337, 355–359, 361–363, 366, 368–369, 371–376, 379–388. *See also* Acquired right; Coercion; Cosmopolitan right; Freedom; Innate right; Postulate, of public right; Right of nations
Right of nations, 28, 157, 177, 180, 204, 225; and rejection of world government, 28–29, 225–227; and ideal of perpetual peace, 28–29, 229–230; and distinctions between states and private persons, 29, 227–229; and right to withdraw from alliances, 157, 230; analogy to state of nature, 177n46, 226, 229; and right to employ defensive force, 226–230; and ideal of a permanent congress of states, 227–231. *See also* Cosmopolitan right; International law; State of nature
Riley, Patrick, 11, 386n72
Roman law, 36, 54, 65n12, 139
Roncarelli v. Duplessis, 210n49
Rosen, Allen, 268n1, 271n5
Rousseau, Jean-Jacques, 237, 278, 310n24

Sartre, Jean-Paul, 74n22
Satz, Debra, 193n13
Scanlon, T. M., 214n56
Schloendorff v. Society of New York Hospital, 44n20
Sellars, Wilfrid, 364
Separation of powers: and republican government, 14, 43, 146–147, 174–176, 182, 194, 203, 219n61, 328; and defects in state of nature, 23–24, 146–147, 159, 173, 328; contrast with Montesquieu, 174–175
Shapiro, Scott, 194n14
Shiffrin, Seana, 111n2, 122n16, 131n22
Shute, Stephen, 46n22
Sidgwick, Henry, 10, 13, 32, 63, 236n7
Simmons, John, 98n15, 151–153, 187–189, 298n47
Skinner, Quentin, 43n18
Slavery, 18, 134, 223; and dependence, 15, 18, 36, 280–282, 286; barbarism, 28, 340; and charity, 281. *See also* Barbarism; Innate right, rightful honor; Slavery contract
Slavery contract, 113n4; impossibility of being bound, 18, 135–140, 193, 209, 211, 280, 286; rightful honor and, 38, 135–137; united will and, 133, 135–136, 139–140, 209, 211, 274, 280, 286; self-ownership, 133, 139n36; analogy with murder, 133, 140; person/thing distinction, 134–140, 193, 281–282, 340; contrast with vice of

Slavery contract *(continued)*
  servility, 137, 142, 163n21; incomplete versions of, 139. *See also* Contract; Innate right, rightful honor; Slavery; United will
Smith, M. B. E., 250n21
State of nature: provisional nature of acquired rights in, 22, 26, 87, 90, 146, 148, 160, 165, 173, 176–177, 179–182, 184, 190, 194, 224, 271, 276–277, 279, 332–335, 341, 350–351, 369n32; innate right in, 26, 38, 165, 171, 176–182, 276, 279, 312; barbarism as defective form of, 28, 338, 341, 343; as idea of reason, 87, 339; duty to exit from, 145–147, 156, 161, 164n24, 165, 168, 182, 197, 201, 226, 257–258, 286, 312, 326, 328, 333–338, 340, 343, 352; defects in, 145–149, 151–152, 173, 176, 180–183, 185, 196–198, 201, 227, 230–231, 232, 272, 276, 298, 338; doing what seems good and right in, 146–147, 164, 171, 178–181, 198, 226–227, 230, 342, 348; violence in, 164–165, 168, 177–181, 198, 227, 229, 313, 319, 342, 361n15; between nations, 177n46, 226–227; and cosmopolitan right, 296. *See also* Acquired right; Locke, John; Postulate, of public right
Status, 20–21, 59, 62, 65, 69–77, 162, 361n13, 365; and servants, 17, 75–76; relationship between parents and children, 21, 48, 65, 71–72, 77, 138n35, 177, 192–194, 223, 246; nonconsensual nature of, 21, 66, 70–73, 76, 79, 110, 192; as right to possession but not use, 21, 66, 72, 76, 79–80, 138n35, 140n38, 365; wrongs against, 22, 72–73, 76–77; and fiduciary obligations, 57, 73, 76n23, 138n35; and marriage, 59–60, 74–75n22, 79n27; and representation, 72, 76, 110, 192, 194, 202; and public officials, 76, 192–193, 202. *See also* Acquired right; Innate right
Stewart, Justice Potter, 212n51
Swift, Adam, 288n29

Taxation, 1, 6, 25, 89n7, 145, 187, 194, 197, 203–204, 214, 232–233, 238n12, 253–254, 258–259, 261, 268–270, 282–283, 294–295, 298, 326, 335

Taylor, Charles, 32, 233–240, 249, 254, 260n31
Taylor v. Laird, 188n8
Taylor v. Whitehead, 253n26
Thomasius, 164n24
Thompson, Michael, 109n1, 201n34, 379n55
Tierney, Brian, 103n19

Ulpian precepts, 18, 37n14, 160–161, 179. *See also* Acquired right; Innate right; Postulate, of public right
Unberath, Hannes, 204n35
United will: in public right, 25, 28, 38, 156, 182, 190, 195, 205n38, 212, 230–231, 272–274, 277–279, 283, 286, 296, 298, 325, 336, 328, 337, 341, 343, 348, 352; restricted by rightful honor, 25–26, 31, 56, 76, 115n7, 131n22, 135–136, 140–142, 205n38, 206, 208–214, 218, 220–223, 272–274, 277–279, 283, 291–292, 328, 341; as idea of reason, 74n22, 183, 199, 277, 325, 334, 339; rational structure of, 123. *See also* Consent; Contract; Innate right; Original contract, idea of

Valcke, Catherine, 171n35
Vallentyne, Peter, 288n29
Varden, Helga, 3
Virtue, 10, 137, 201, 370; and the Categorical Imperative, 1–2, 6, 11–13, 355–360, 365–368, 372–377, 379–388; relation to right, 6–7, 11–12, 14, 25, 38, 136, 143, 160, 162–164, 167, 177, 203–204n35, 268–269, 271n5, 274, 283, 301, 319–321, 355–359, 368, 374–375, 380–388; benevolence, 15, 36, 43, 248, 271, 281, 283; and inner duties, 18, 37, 136, 161, 203–204n35, 256, 329; and adopting ends, 36, 143, 162, 204n35, 269, 274n12, 284, 367–368, 370n35, 375, 380–385; ideal case of, 201

Waldron, Jeremy, 169n34
Walzer, Michael, 237–238
Warren, Daniel, 377n50, 386n70
Weinrib, Ernest, 66n13, 277n16

Weinrib, Jacob, 52n29, 205n38, 213n54, 312n30
Wertheimer, Alan, 119n11
Westen, Peter, 119n11
Westphal, Kenneth, 327n5

Willaschek, Marcus, 356n1, 359n11, 368n29
Williams, Bernard, 160n18
Williams, Glanville, 124n18
Williams, Howard L., 148n6, 271n5
Wood, Allen, 75n22, 272n7